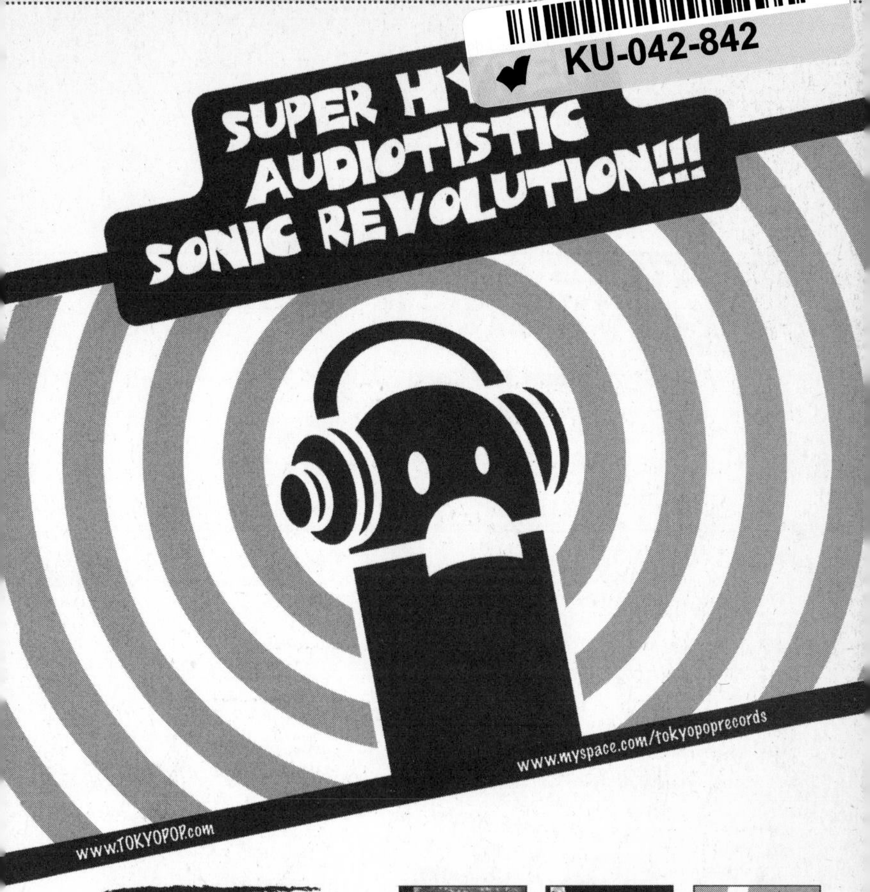
SUPER HY
AUDIOTISTIC
SONIC REVOLUTION!!!
www.myspace.com/tokyopoprecords
www.TOKYOPOP.com

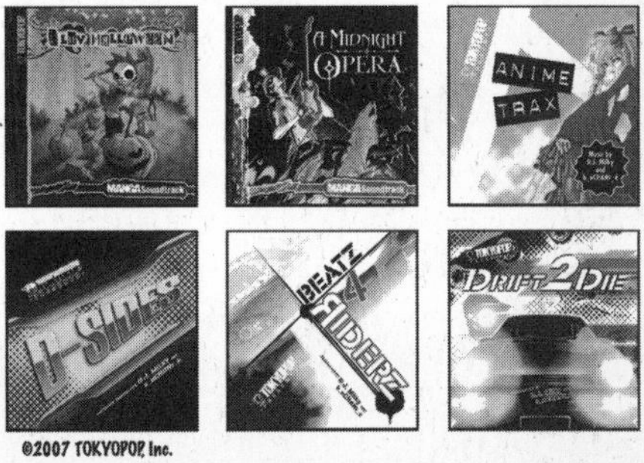
A MIDNIGHT OPERA
ANIME TRAX
BEATZ 4 RIDERZ
DRIFT 2 DIE

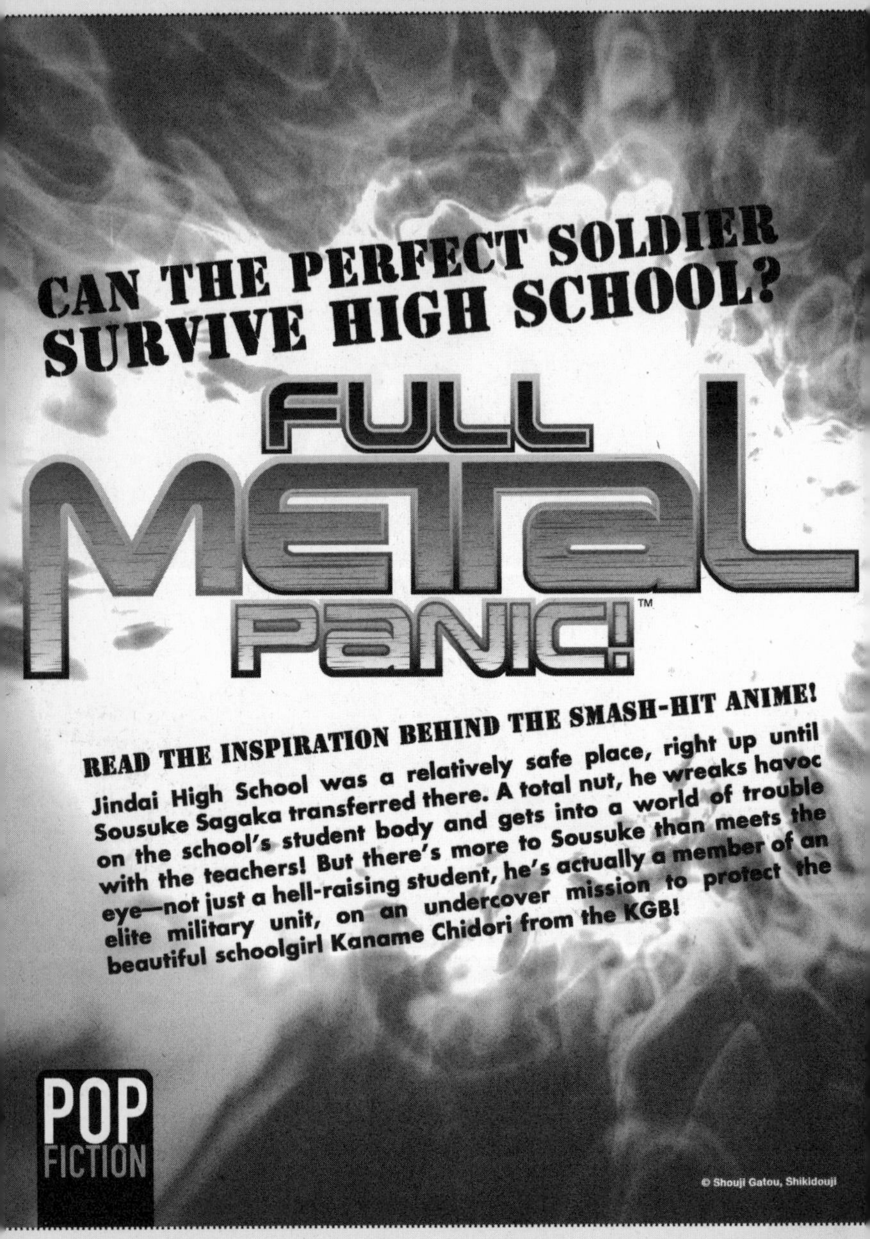
CAN THE PERFECT SOLDIER
SURVIVE HIGH SCHOOL?
FULL METAL PANIC!™
READ THE INSPIRATION BEHIND THE SMASH-HIT ANIME!
Jindai High School was a relatively safe place, right up until Sousuke Sagaka transferred there. A total nut, he wreaks havoc on the school's student body and gets into a world of trouble with the teachers! But there's more to Sousuke than meets the eye—not just a hell-raising student, he's actually a member of an elite military unit, on an undercover mission to protect the beautiful schoolgirl Kaname Chidori from the KGB!
POP FICTION
© Shouji Gatou, Shikidouji

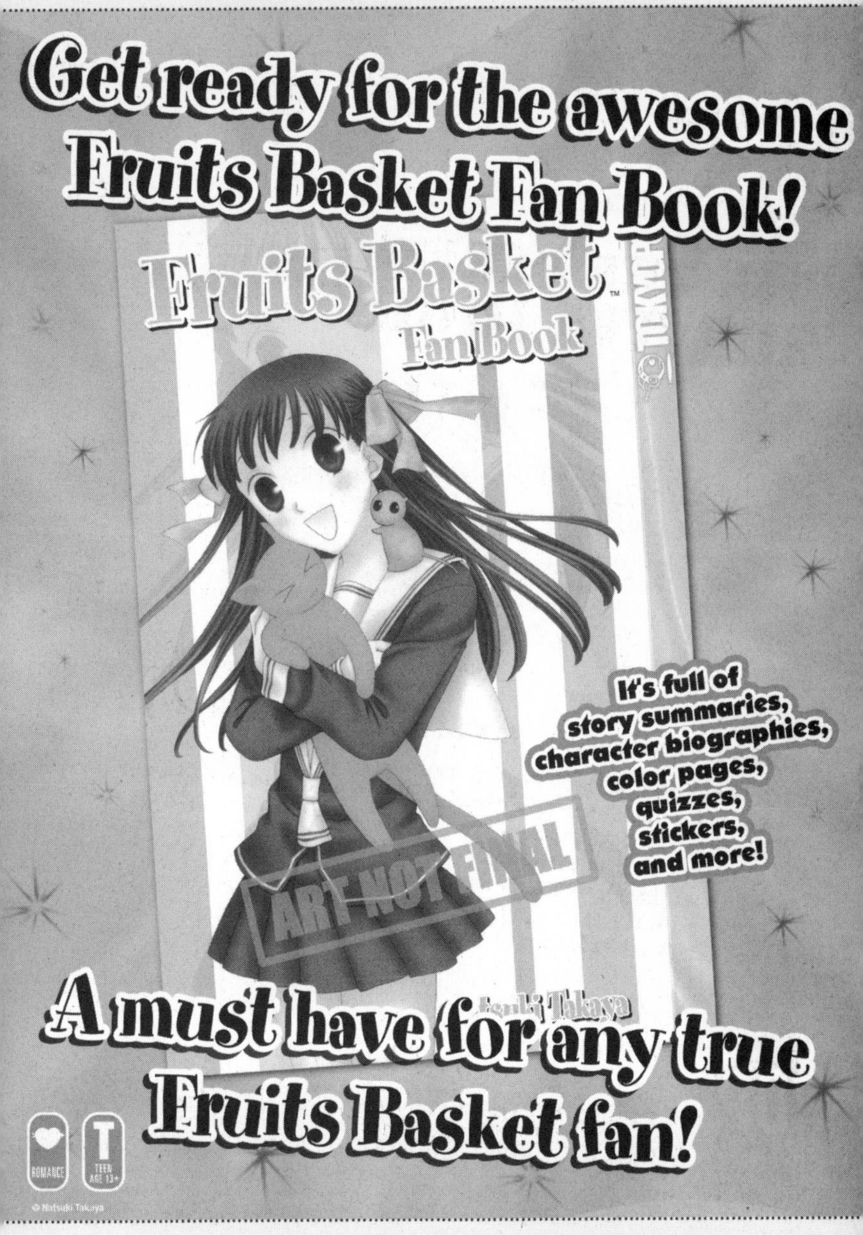

Get ready for the awesome Fruits Basket Fan Book!
Fruits Basket™ Fan Book
TOKYOPOP
It's full of story summaries, character biographies, color pages, quizzes, stickers, and more!
ART NOT FINAL
A must have for any true Fruits Basket fan!
ROMANCE
T TEEN AGE 13+
© Natsuki Takaya

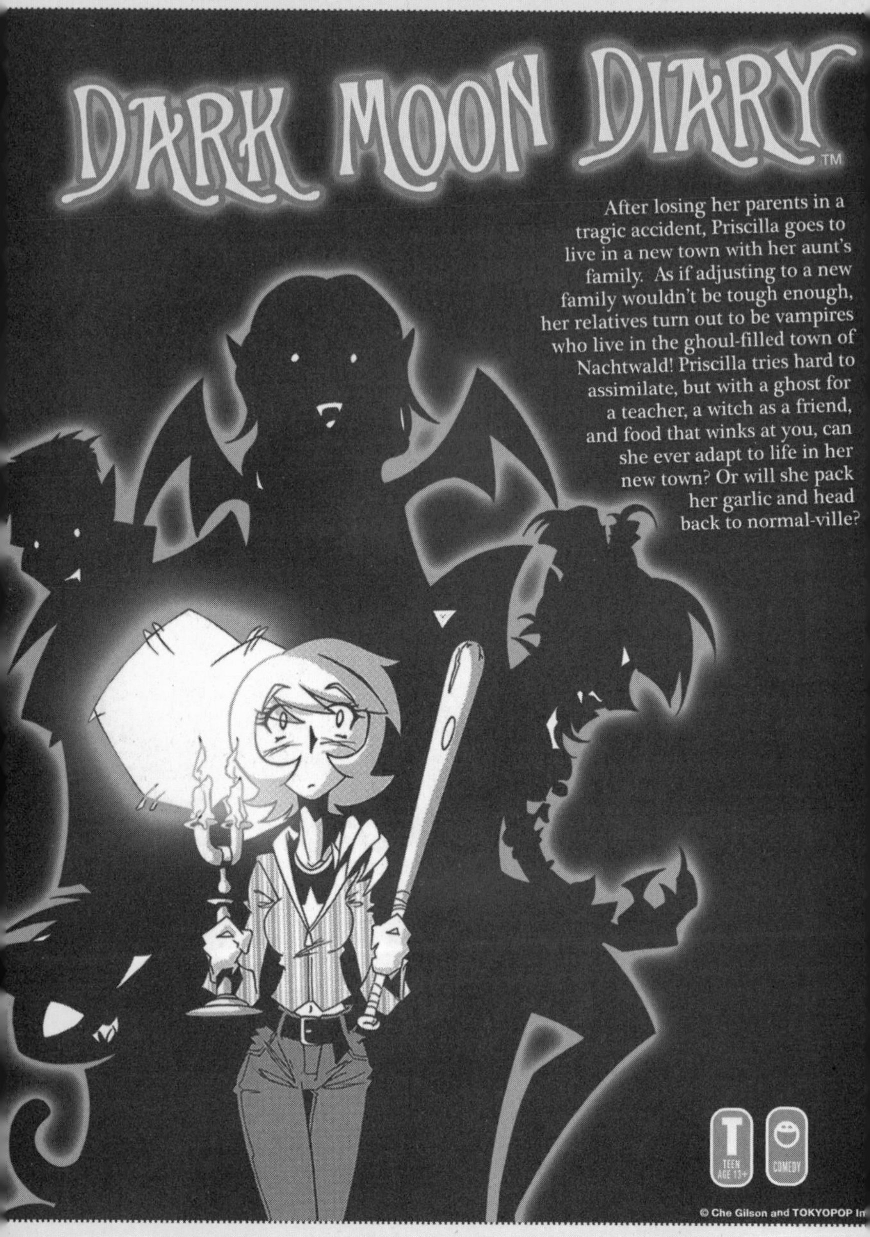
DARK MOON DIARY™
After losing her parents in a tragic accident, Priscilla goes to live in a new town with her aunt's family. As if adjusting to a new family wouldn't be tough enough, her relatives turn out to be vampires who live in the ghoul-filled town of Nachtwald! Priscilla tries hard to assimilate, but with a ghost for a teacher, a witch as a friend, and food that winks at you, can she ever adapt to life in her new town? Or will she pack her garlic and head back to normal-ville?
T
TEEN AGE 13+
COMEDY
© Che Gilson and TOKYOPOP In

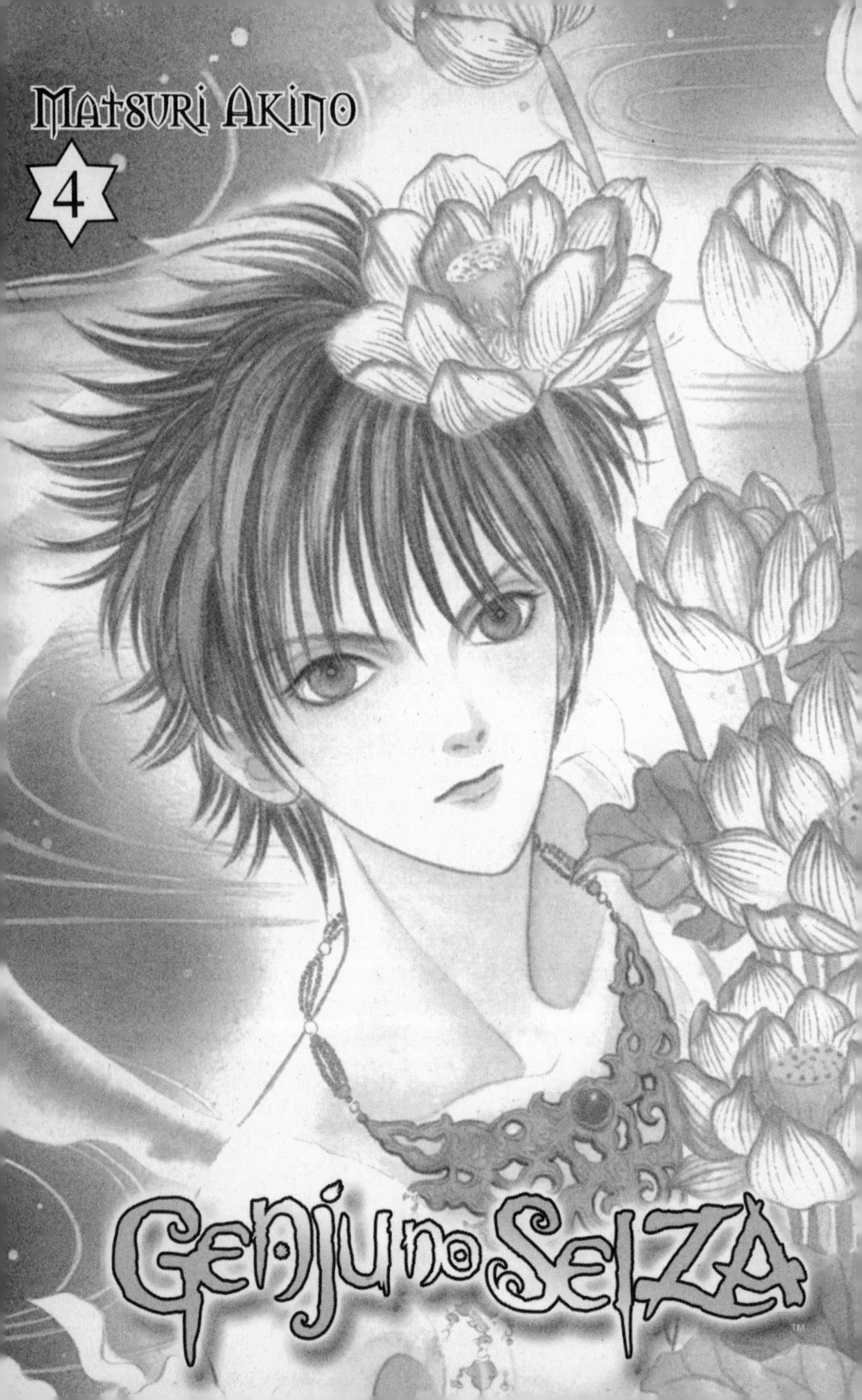
Matsuri Akino
4
Genju no Seiza
™

Genju no Seiza Volume 4
Created by Matsuri Akino

Translation - Mike Kiefl
English Adaptation - Christine Boylan
Retouch and Lettering - Star Print Brokers
Production Artist - Vicente Rivera, Jr.
Graphic Designer - John Lo

Editor - Tim Beedle
Digital Imaging Manager - Chris Buford
Pre-Production Supervisor - Erika Terriquez
Art Director - Anne Marie Horne
Production Manager - Elisabeth Brizzi
Managing Editor - Vy Nguyen
VP of Production - Ron Klamert
Editor-in-Chief - Rob Tokar
Publisher - Mike Kiley
President and C.O.O. - John Parker
C.E.O. and Chief Creative Officer - Stuart Levy

A  Manga

TOKYOPOP and  are trademarks or registered trademarks of TOKYOPOP Inc.

TOKYOPOP Inc.
5900 Wilshire Blvd. Suite 2000
Los Angeles, CA 90036

E-mail: info@TOKYOPOP.com
Come visit us online at www.TOKYOPOP.com

ISBN: 978-1-59816-610-1

First TOKYOPOP printing: August 2007
10 9 8 7 6 5 4 3 2 1
Printed in the USA

Genju no Seiza™

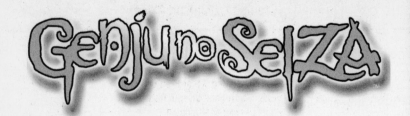

Volume 4

Created by
Matsuri Akino

TOKYOPOP®

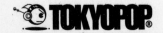

HAMBURG // LONDON // LOS ANGELES // TOKYO

Genju no Seiza

Table of Contents

Story So Far

An empty throne...

Not in the literal sense (but I'll get to that in a moment), but for the past forty years, that is in truth what Dhalashar has had. For forty years, we've been without a king. But that has all changed now. We have found our heir to the throne. He is the half-Sherpa son of a world-famous photographer, and his name is Fuuto Kamishina. Currently living in Japan with his mother, young Fuuto has already begun to exhibit some of the powers of our king, and although he is unaware of this, his use of them has affirmed to me that he will be a good king. However, he is also a tad stubborn, and to this day he refuses to accept his role as our new sovereign and religious leader.

There are further complications as well. While the people of Dhalashar have been without their TRUE king for quite some time, they have not been without a king. The Snake-God, Naga, a treacherous and deceitful deity, recently sensed opportunity upon our vacant throne. He has instilled an impostor king—little more than a puppet to Naga's ambitions—to rule Dhalashar. And much to my chagrin, many people of my nation have accepted this false sovereign as our next heir to the throne. However, Naga knows his king is false and that the emergence of the true sovereign will prove that to the people of Dhalashar. He fears young Fuuto Kamishina, and will do what he can to ensure he never ascends to the throne. He has already dispatched several assassins, and I fear more may be on the way.

—Garuda, Guardian Beast of the true King of Dhalashar

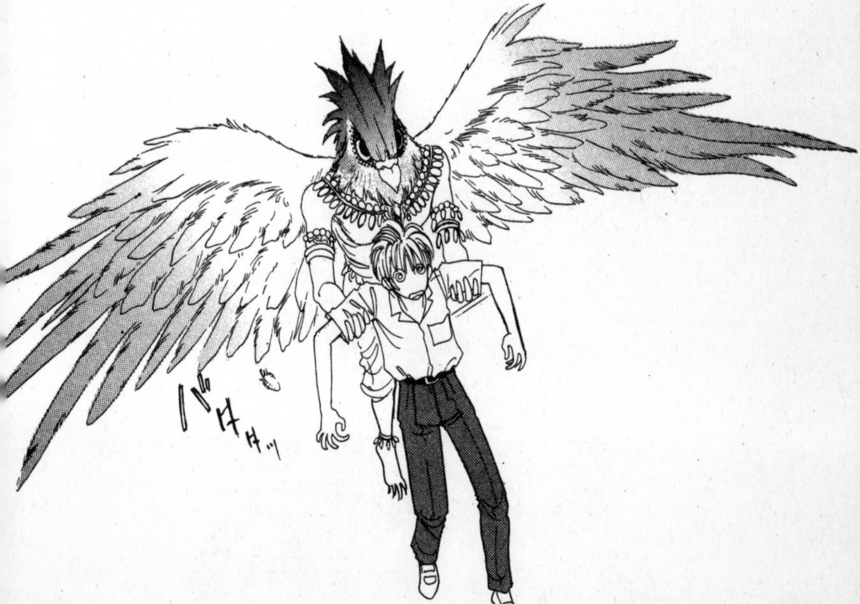
バササッ

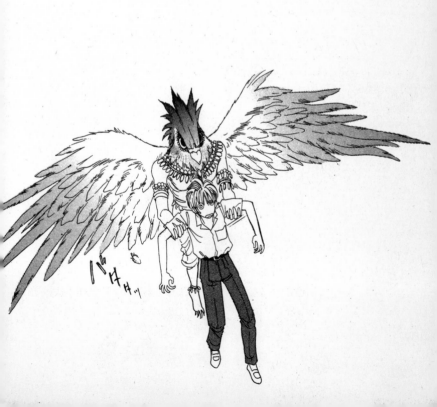

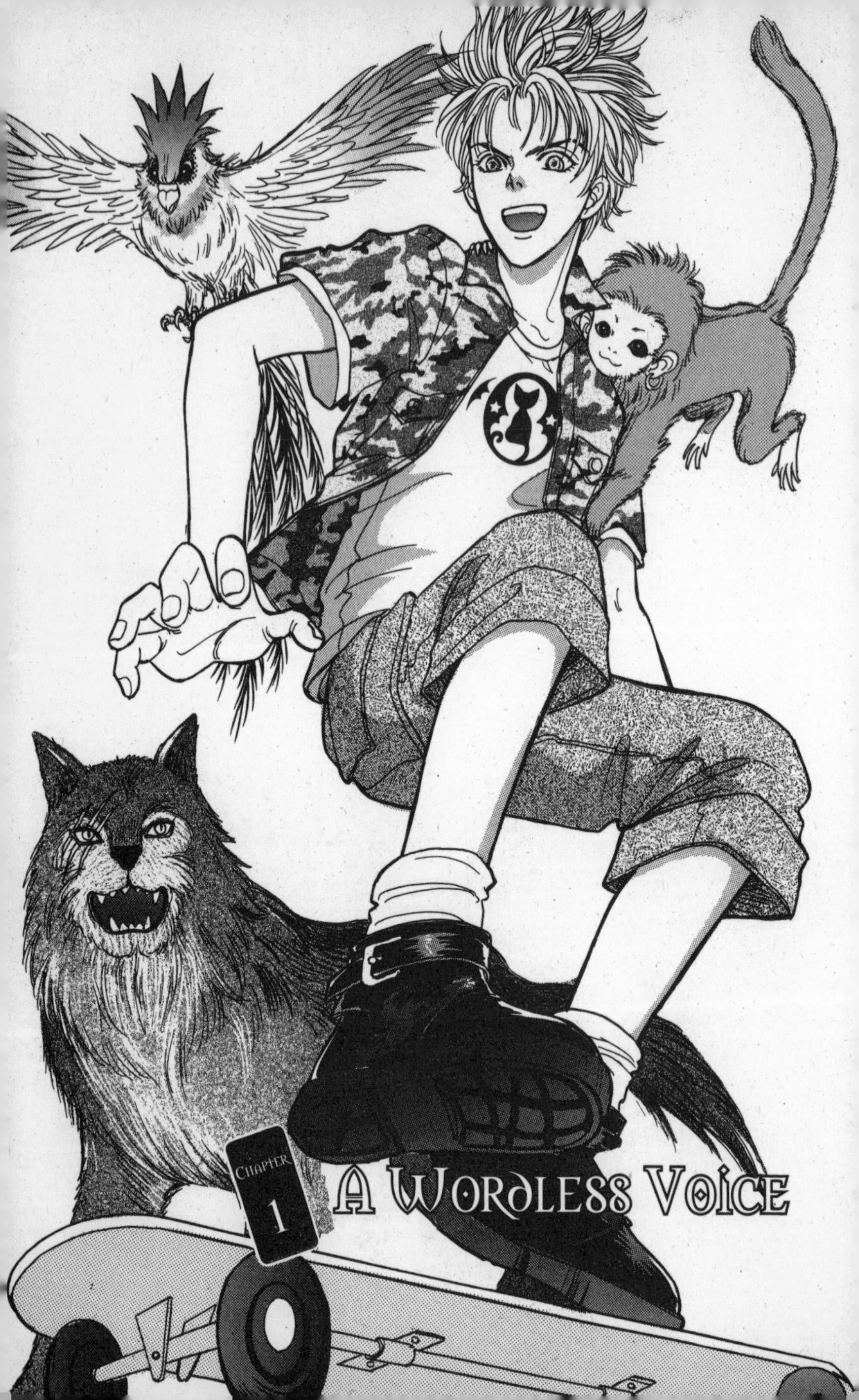
CHAPTER
1
A WORDLESS VOICE

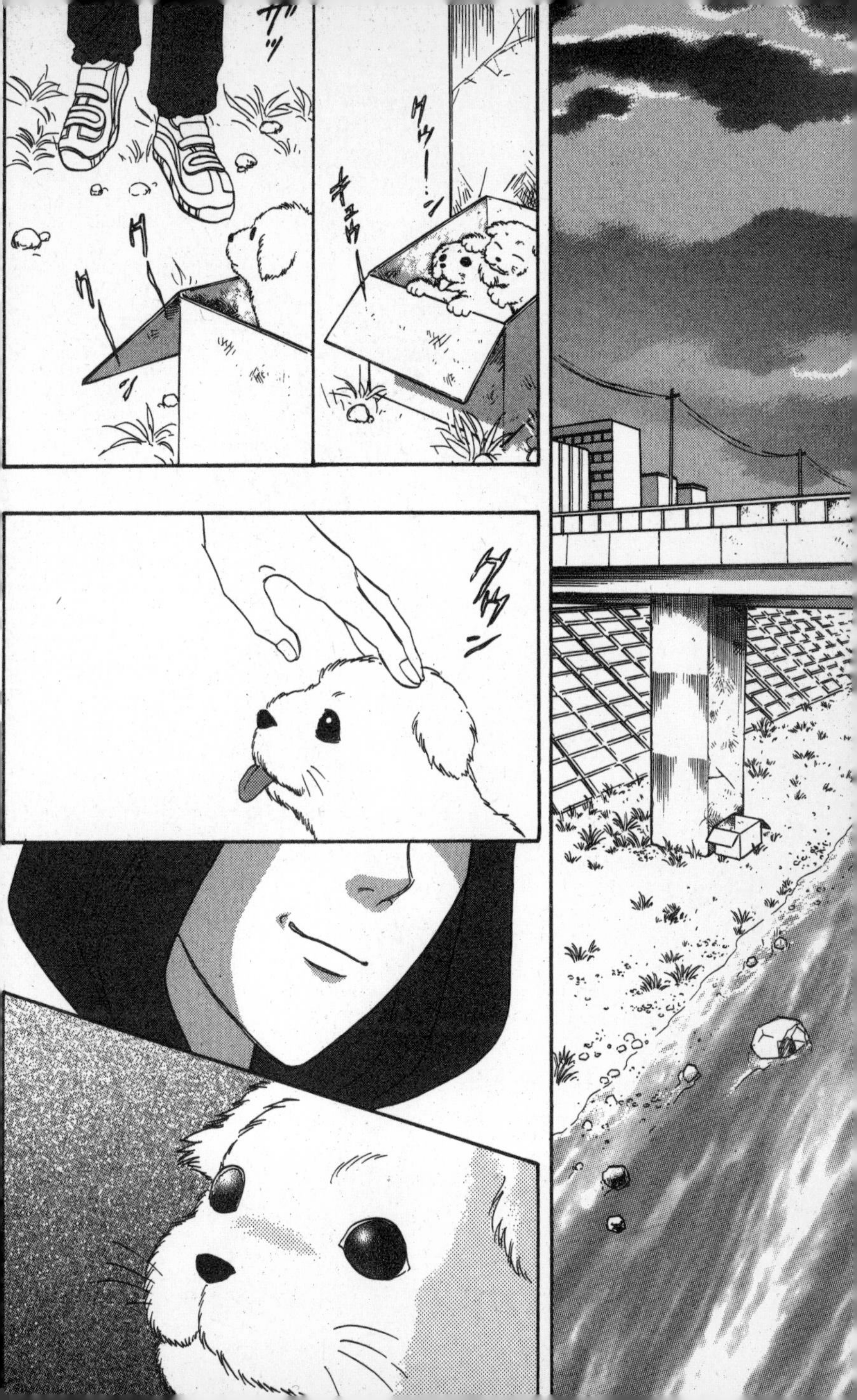
ザッ
クーン
クゥー…ン
キュウ…
クゥン

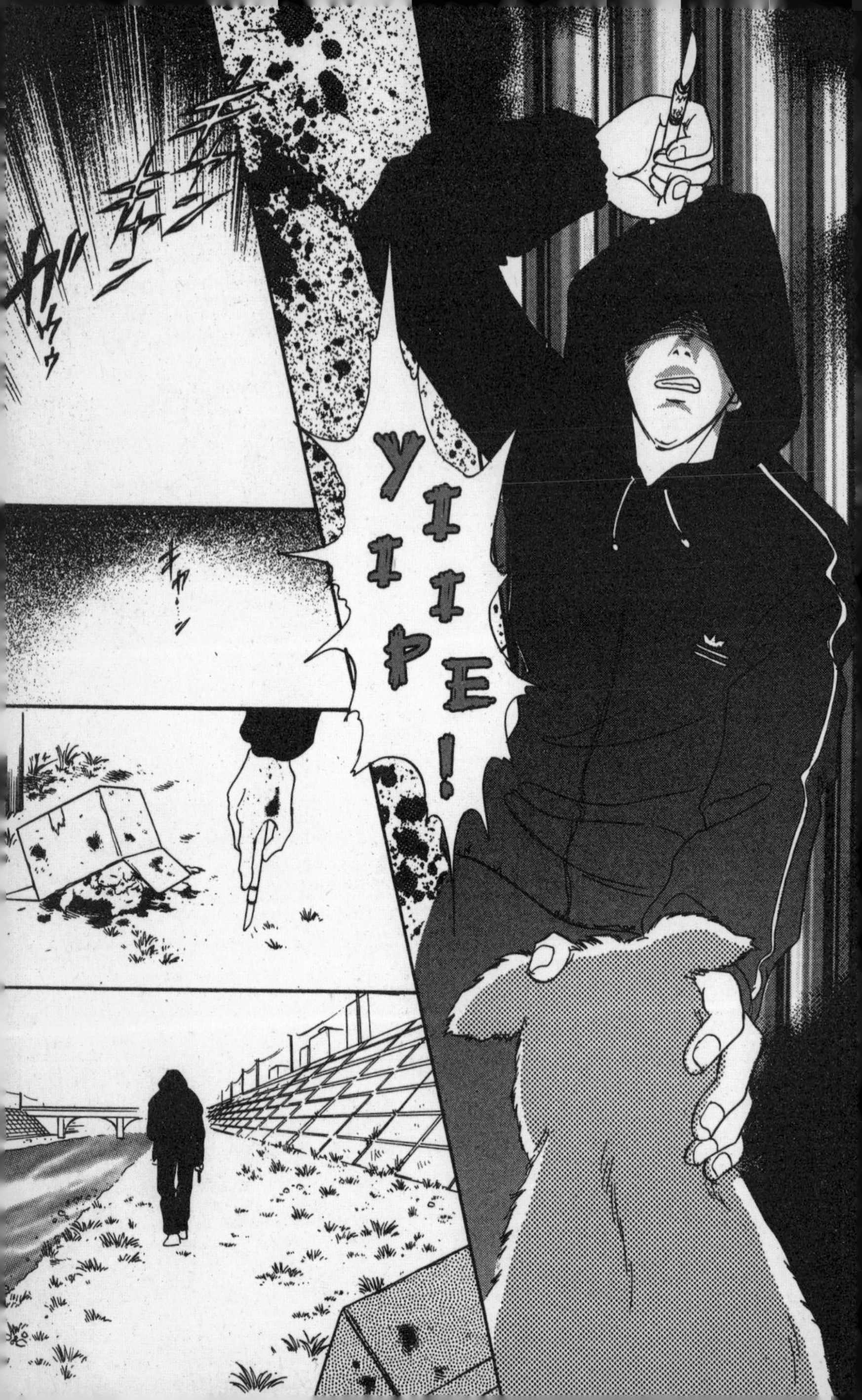
YIIIIPE!

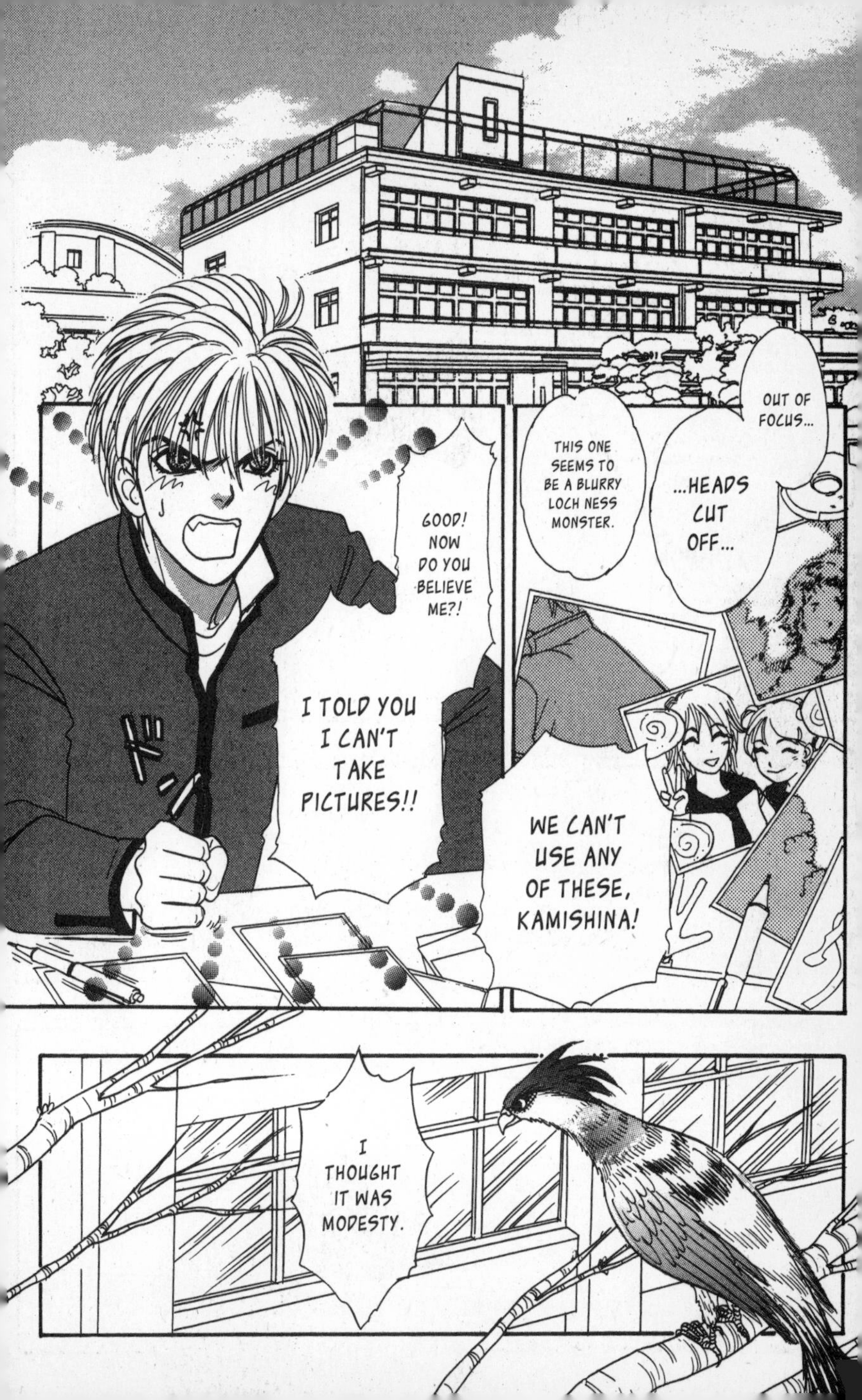
OUT OF FOCUS...
...HEADS CUT OFF...
THIS ONE SEEMS TO BE A BLURRY LOCH NESS MONSTER.
WE CAN'T USE ANY OF THESE, KAMISHINA!
GOOD! NOW DO YOU BELIEVE ME?!
I TOLD YOU I CAN'T TAKE PICTURES!!
I THOUGHT IT WAS MODESTY.

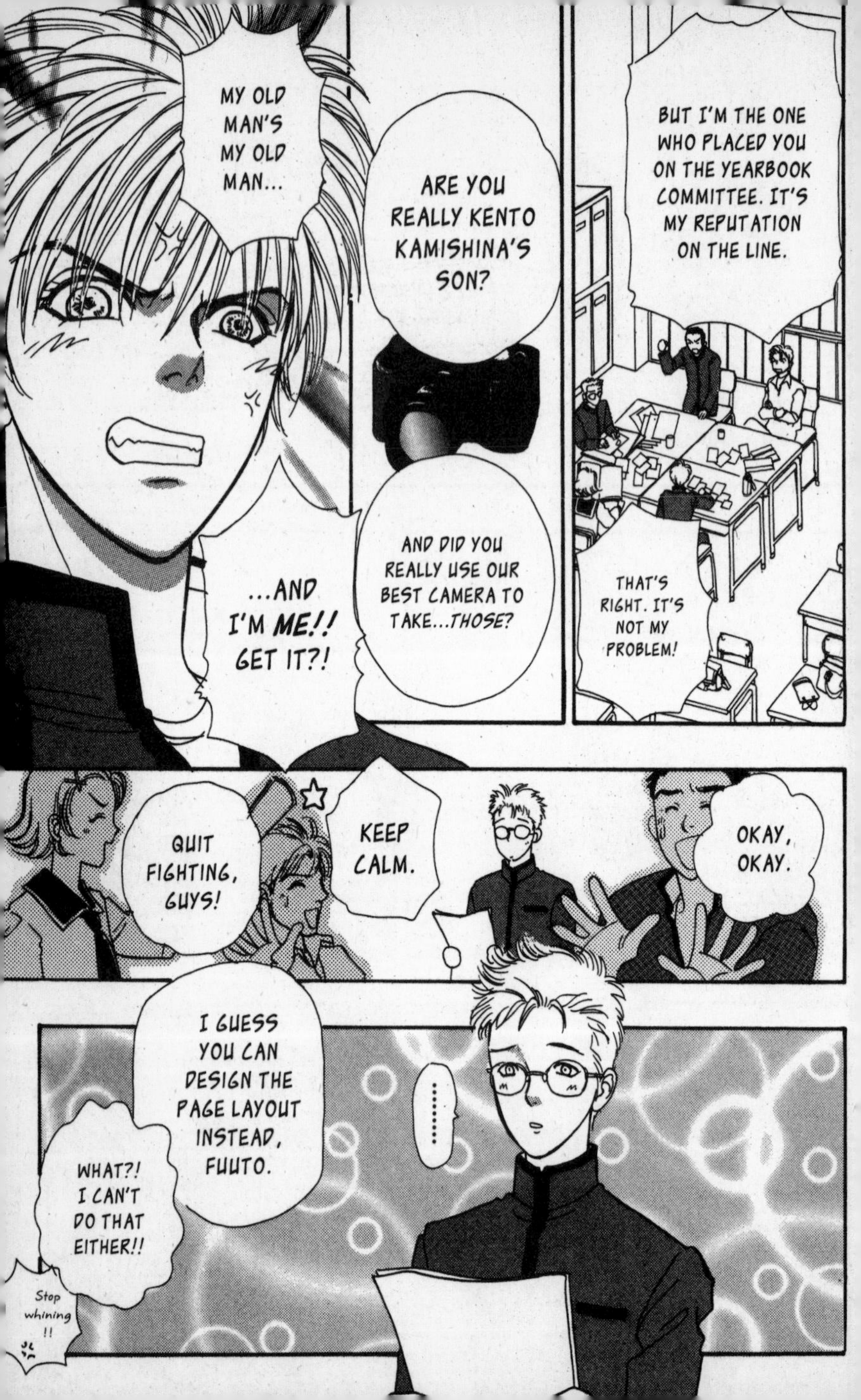
BUT I'M THE ONE WHO PLACED YOU ON THE YEARBOOK COMMITTEE. IT'S MY REPUTATION ON THE LINE.
THAT'S RIGHT. IT'S NOT MY PROBLEM!
ARE YOU REALLY KENTO KAMISHINA'S SON?
AND DID YOU REALLY USE OUR BEST CAMERA TO TAKE...*THOSE?*
MY OLD MAN'S MY OLD MAN...
...AND I'M ***ME!!*** GET IT?!
OKAY, OKAY.
KEEP CALM.
QUIT FIGHTING, GUYS!
....
I GUESS YOU CAN DESIGN THE PAGE LAYOUT INSTEAD, FUUTO.
WHAT?! I CAN'T DO THAT EITHER!!
Stop whining!!

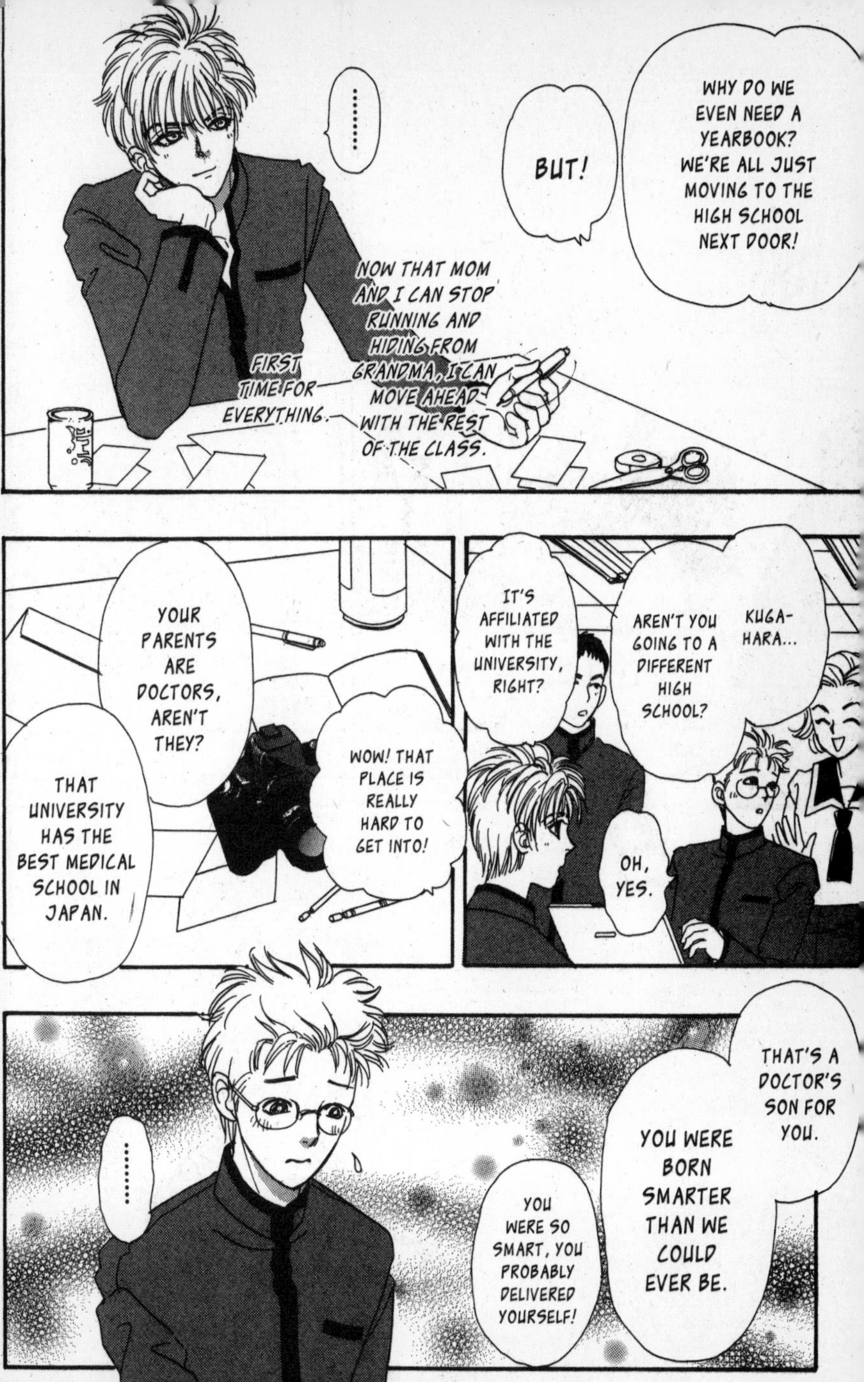
WHY DO WE EVEN NEED A YEARBOOK? WE'RE ALL JUST MOVING TO THE HIGH SCHOOL NEXT DOOR!
BUT!
……
NOW THAT MOM AND I CAN STOP RUNNING AND HIDING FROM GRANDMA, I CAN MOVE AHEAD WITH THE REST OF THE CLASS.
FIRST TIME FOR EVERYTHING.
KUGA-HARA...
AREN'T YOU GOING TO A DIFFERENT HIGH SCHOOL?
IT'S AFFILIATED WITH THE UNIVERSITY, RIGHT?
OH, YES.
YOUR PARENTS ARE DOCTORS, AREN'T THEY?
WOW! THAT PLACE IS REALLY HARD TO GET INTO!
THAT UNIVERSITY HAS THE BEST MEDICAL SCHOOL IN JAPAN.
THAT'S A DOCTOR'S SON FOR YOU.
YOU WERE BORN SMARTER THAN WE COULD EVER BE.
YOU WERE SO SMART, YOU PROBABLY DELIVERED YOURSELF!
……

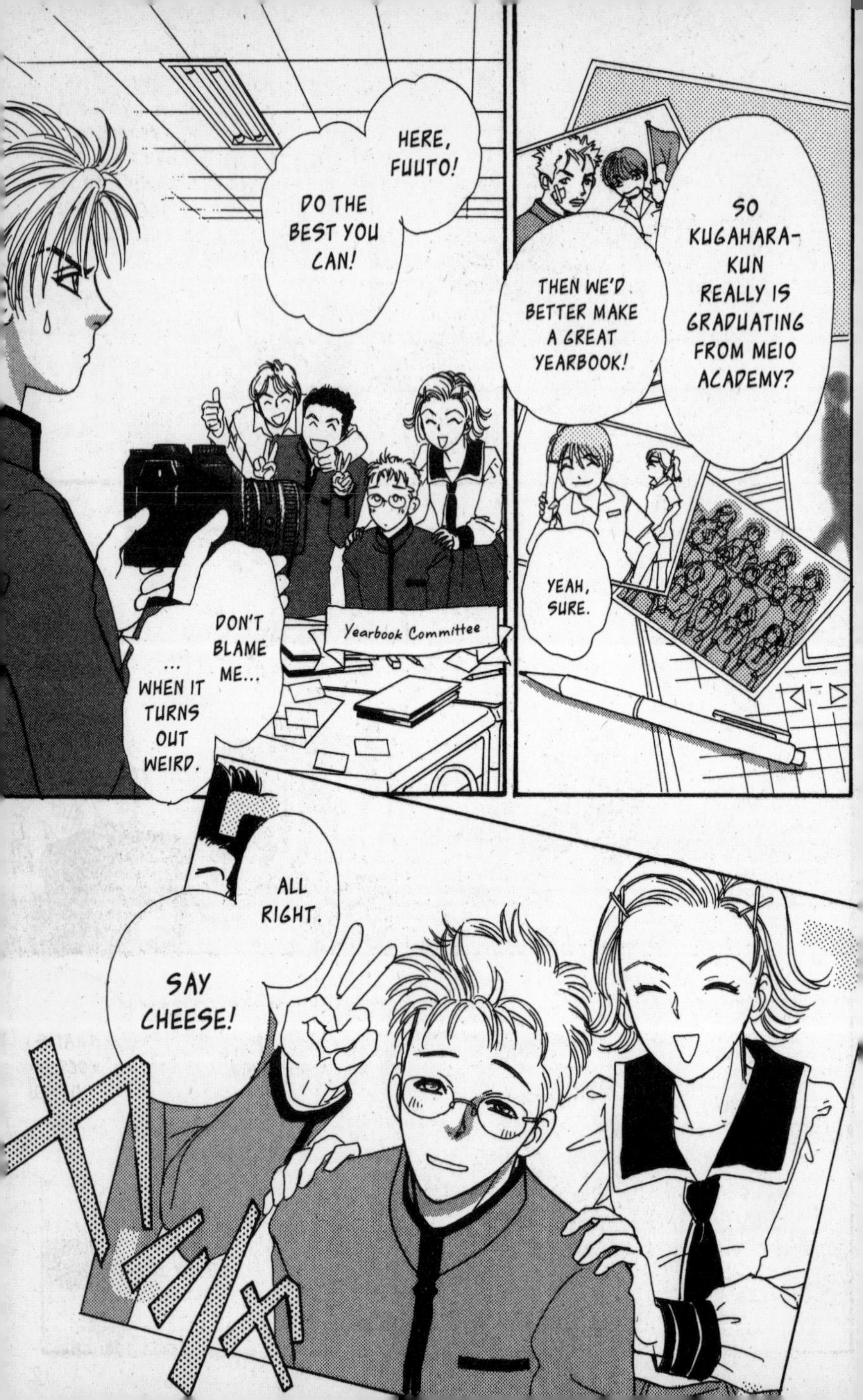
SO KUGAHARA-KUN REALLY IS GRADUATING FROM MEIO ACADEMY?
THEN WE'D BETTER MAKE A GREAT YEARBOOK!
YEAH, SURE.
HERE, FUUTO!
DO THE BEST YOU CAN!
Yearbook Committee
DON'T BLAME ME...
... WHEN IT TURNS OUT WEIRD.
ALL RIGHT.
SAY CHEESE!

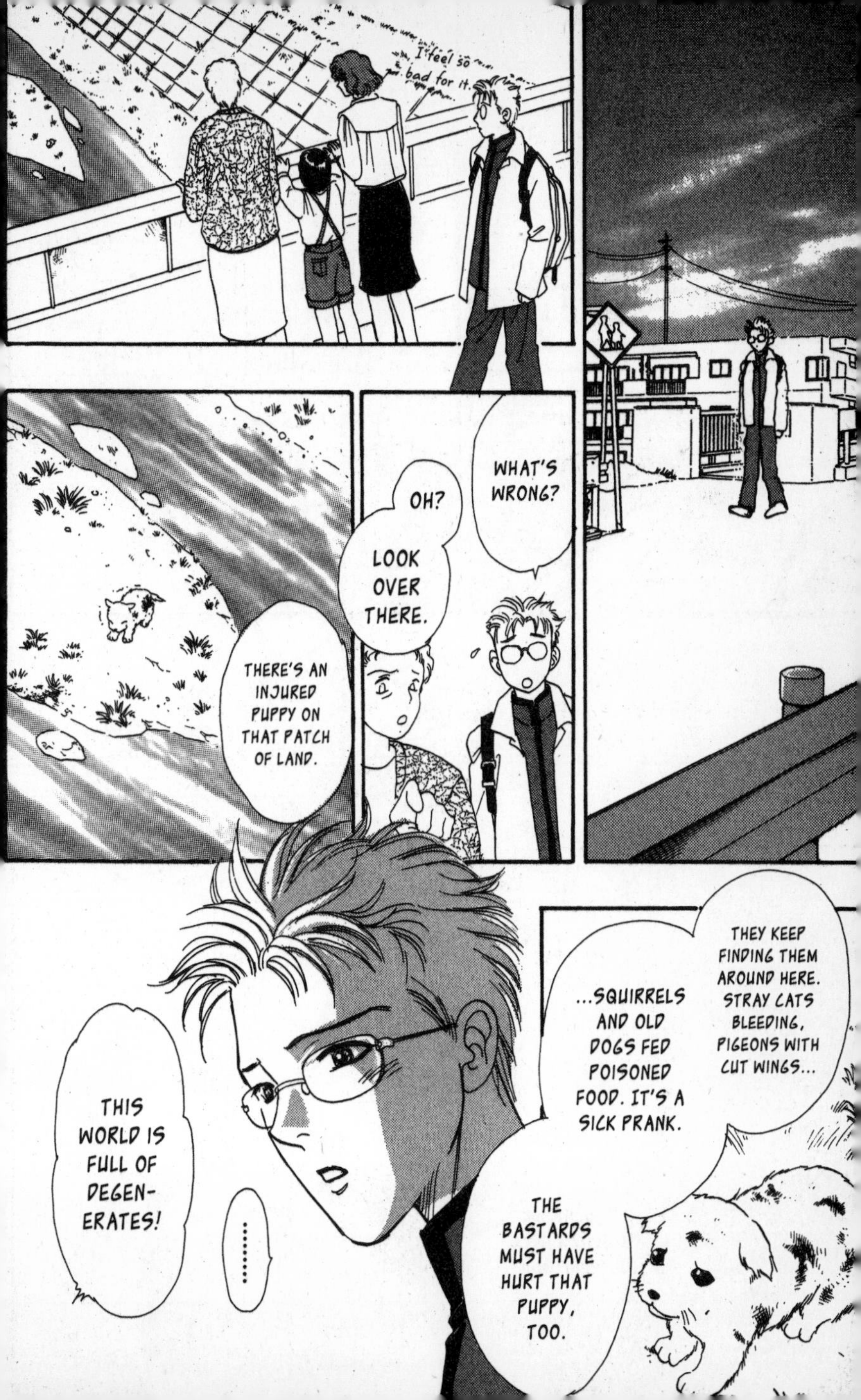
I feel so bad for it.
WHAT'S WRONG?
OH?
LOOK OVER THERE.
THERE'S AN INJURED PUPPY ON THAT PATCH OF LAND.
THEY KEEP FINDING THEM AROUND HERE. STRAY CATS BLEEDING, PIGEONS WITH CUT WINGS...
...SQUIRRELS AND OLD DOGS FED POISONED FOOD. IT'S A SICK PRANK.
THE BASTARDS MUST HAVE HURT THAT PUPPY, TOO.
THIS WORLD IS FULL OF DEGEN- ERATES!
....

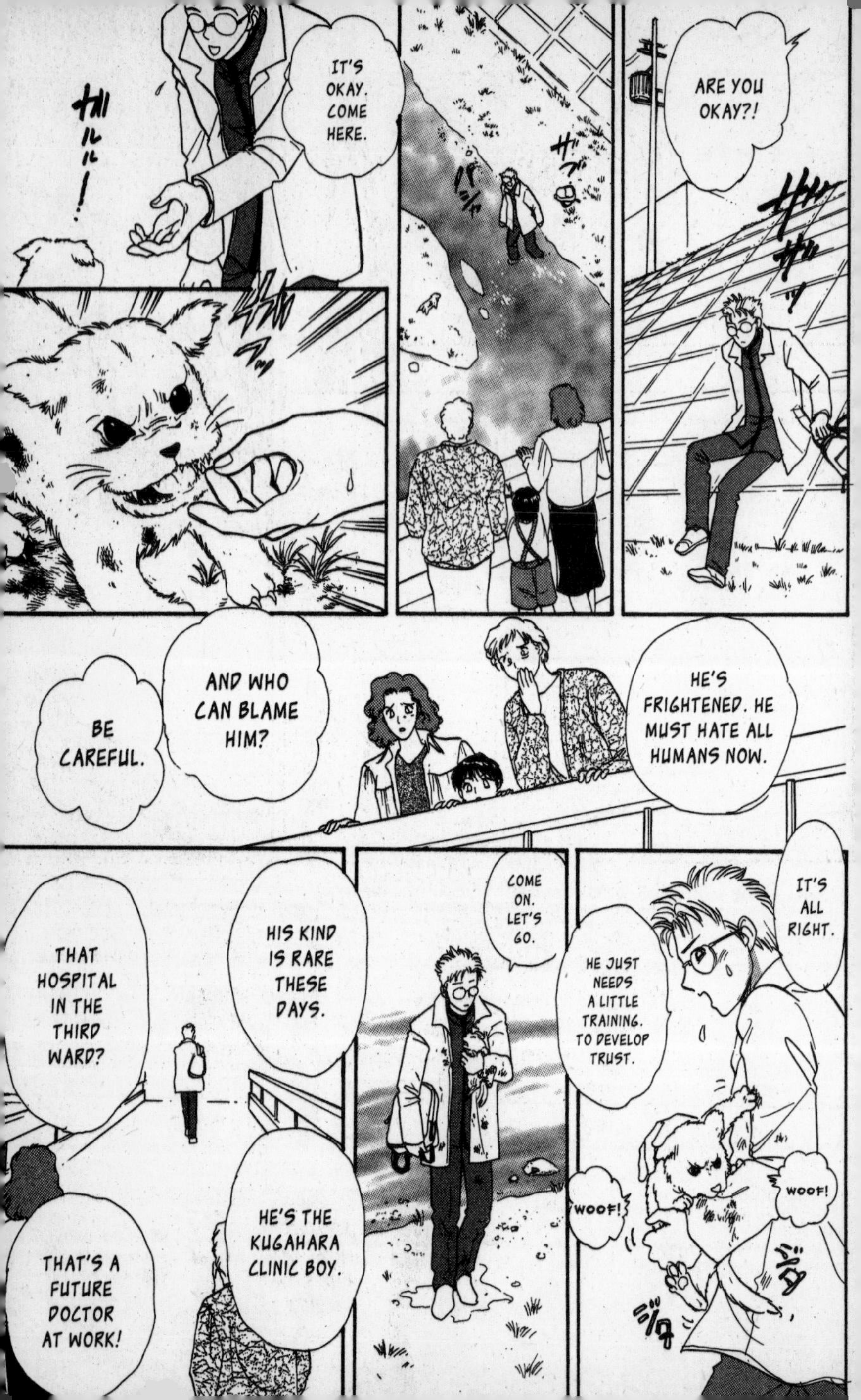

ARE YOU OKAY?!
IT'S OKAY. COME HERE.
HE'S FRIGHTENED. HE MUST HATE ALL HUMANS NOW.
AND WHO CAN BLAME HIM?
BE CAREFUL.
IT'S ALL RIGHT.
HE JUST NEEDS A LITTLE TRAINING. TO DEVELOP TRUST.
WOOF!
WOOF!
COME ON. LET'S GO.
HIS KIND IS RARE THESE DAYS.
THAT HOSPITAL IN THE THIRD WARD?
HE'S THE KUGAHARA CLINIC BOY.
THAT'S A FUTURE DOCTOR AT WORK!

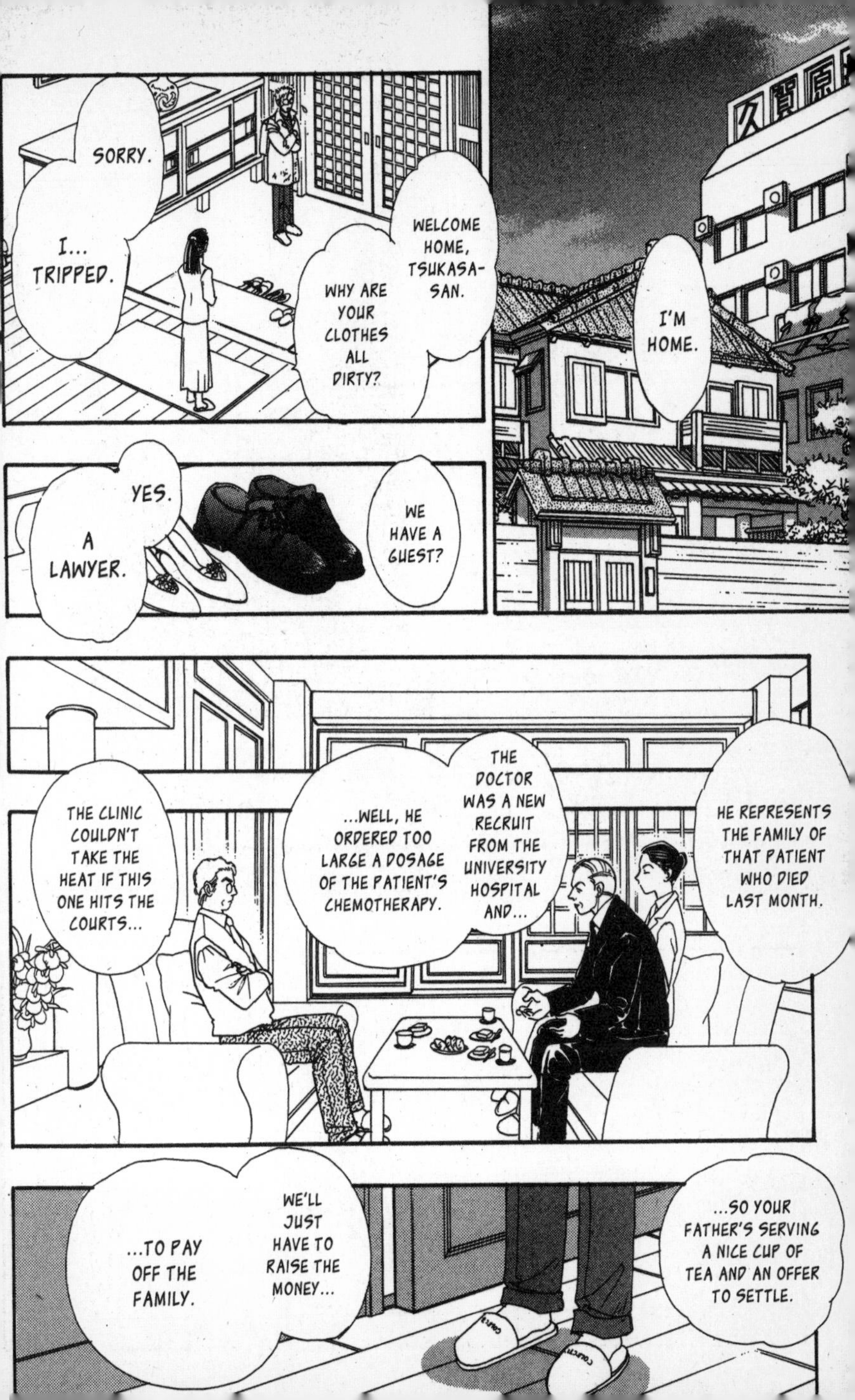

久賀原
I'M HOME.
WELCOME HOME, TSUKASA-SAN.
WHY ARE YOUR CLOTHES ALL DIRTY?
SORRY.
I... TRIPPED.
WE HAVE A GUEST?
YES.
A LAWYER.
HE REPRESENTS THE FAMILY OF THAT PATIENT WHO DIED LAST MONTH.
THE DOCTOR WAS A NEW RECRUIT FROM THE UNIVERSITY HOSPITAL AND...
...WELL, HE ORDERED TOO LARGE A DOSAGE OF THE PATIENT'S CHEMOTHERAPY.
THE CLINIC COULDN'T TAKE THE HEAT IF THIS ONE HITS THE COURTS...
...SO YOUR FATHER'S SERVING A NICE CUP OF TEA AND AN OFFER TO SETTLE.
WE'LL JUST HAVE TO RAISE THE MONEY...
...TO PAY OFF THE FAMILY.

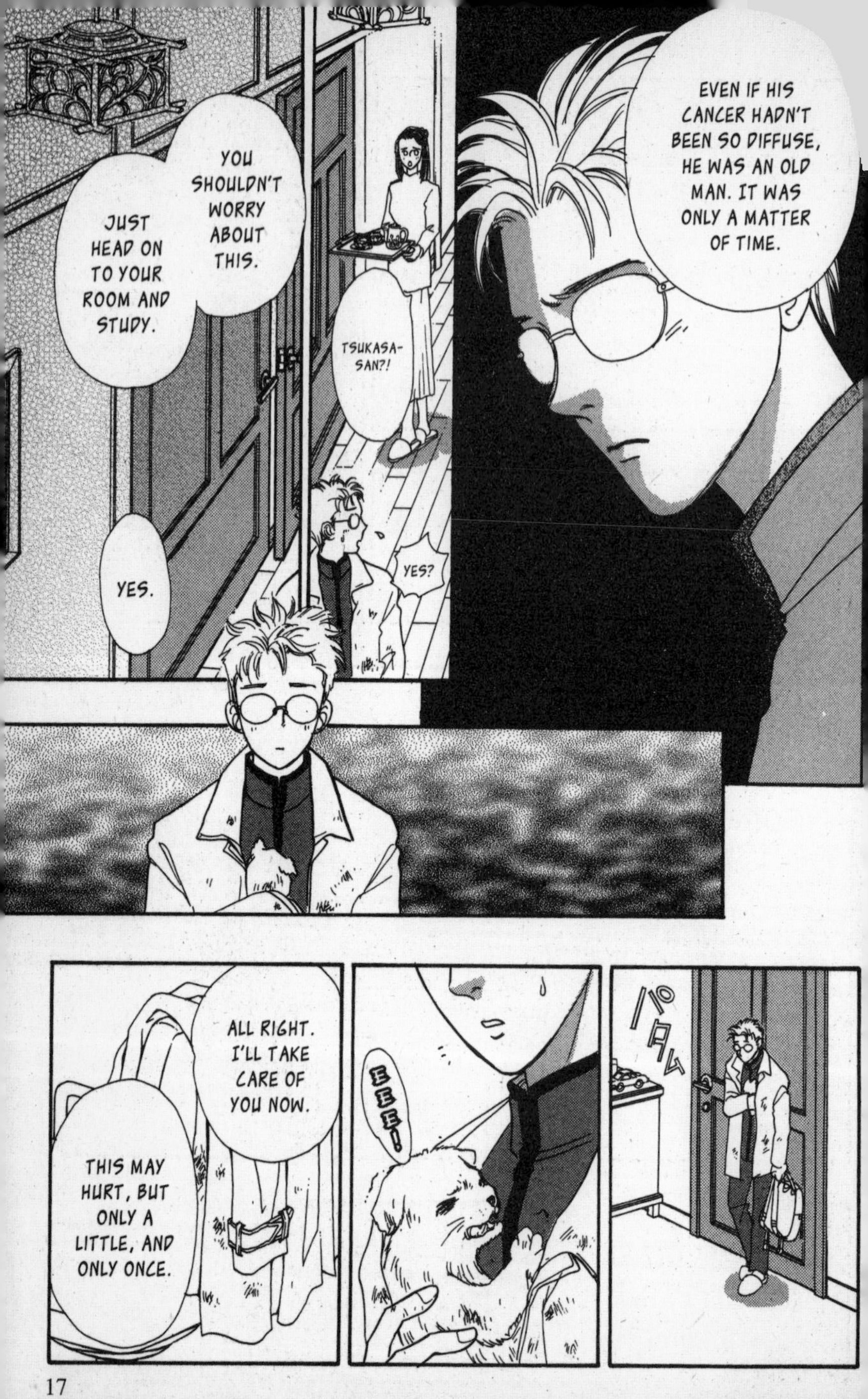
EVEN IF HIS CANCER HADN'T BEEN SO DIFFUSE, HE WAS AN OLD MAN. IT WAS ONLY A MATTER OF TIME.
TSUKASA-SAN?!
YES?
YOU SHOULDN'T WORRY ABOUT THIS.
JUST HEAD ON TO YOUR ROOM AND STUDY.
YES.
パタム
EEEE!
ALL RIGHT. I'LL TAKE CARE OF YOU NOW.
THIS MAY HURT, BUT ONLY A LITTLE, AND ONLY ONCE.

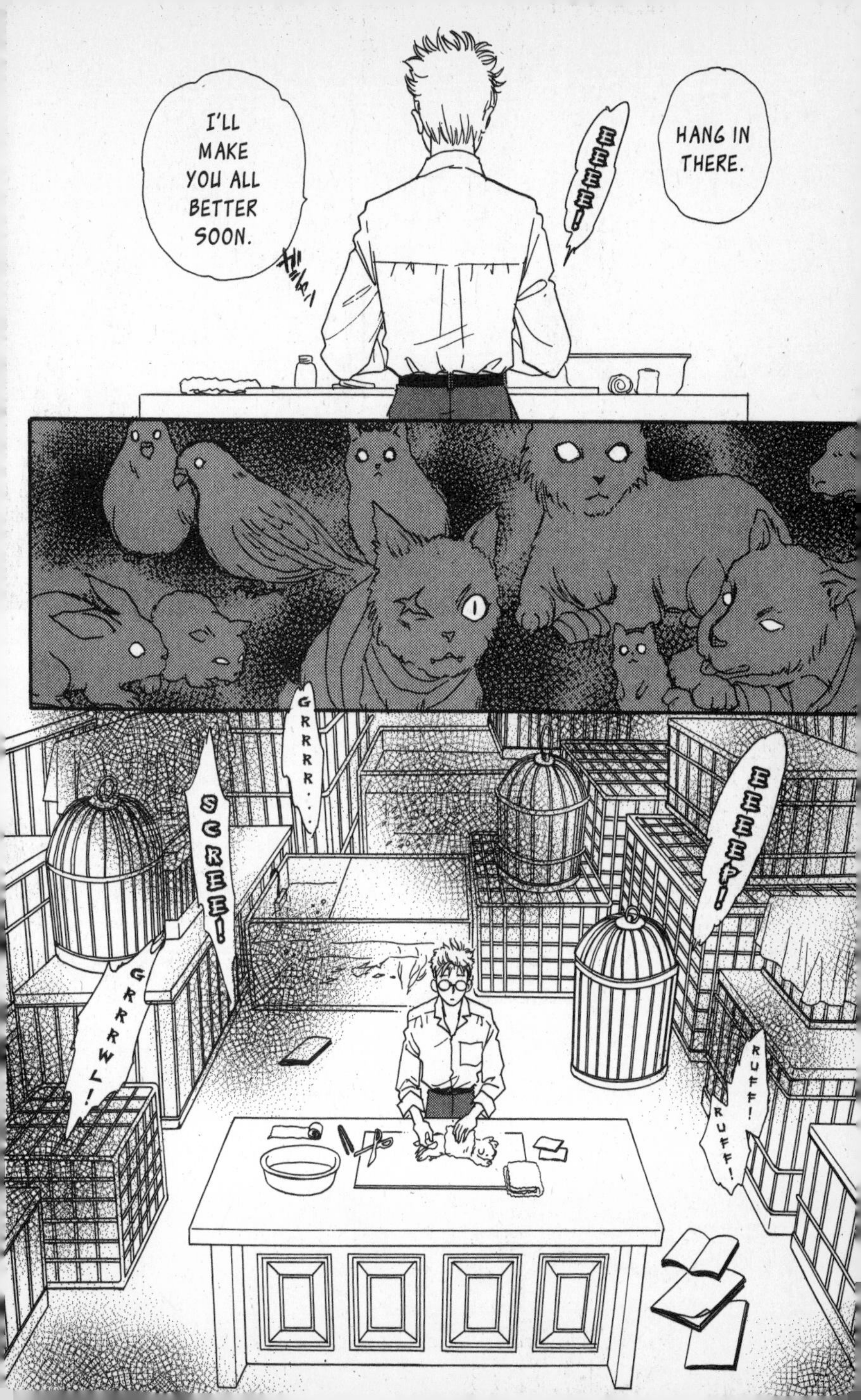
I'LL MAKE YOU ALL BETTER SOON.
EEEEEE!
HANG IN THERE.
GRRRR...
SCREEE!
EEEEEP!
GRRRWL!
RUFF! RUFF! RUFF!

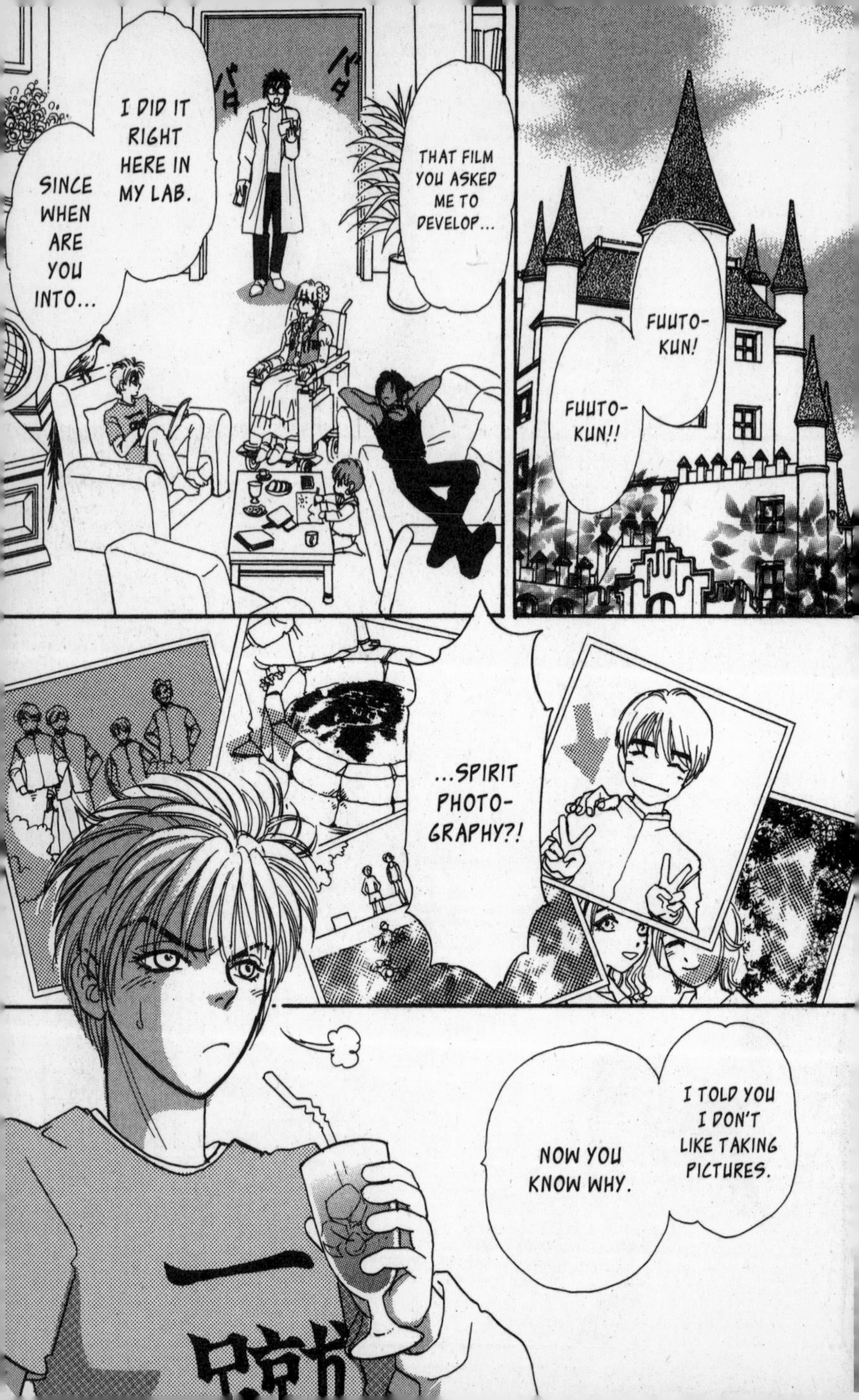
FUUTO-KUN!
FUUTO-KUN!!
THAT FILM YOU ASKED ME TO DEVELOP...
I DID IT RIGHT HERE IN MY LAB.
SINCE WHEN ARE YOU INTO...
...SPIRIT PHOTOGRAPHY?!
I TOLD YOU I DON'T LIKE TAKING PICTURES.
NOW YOU KNOW WHY.

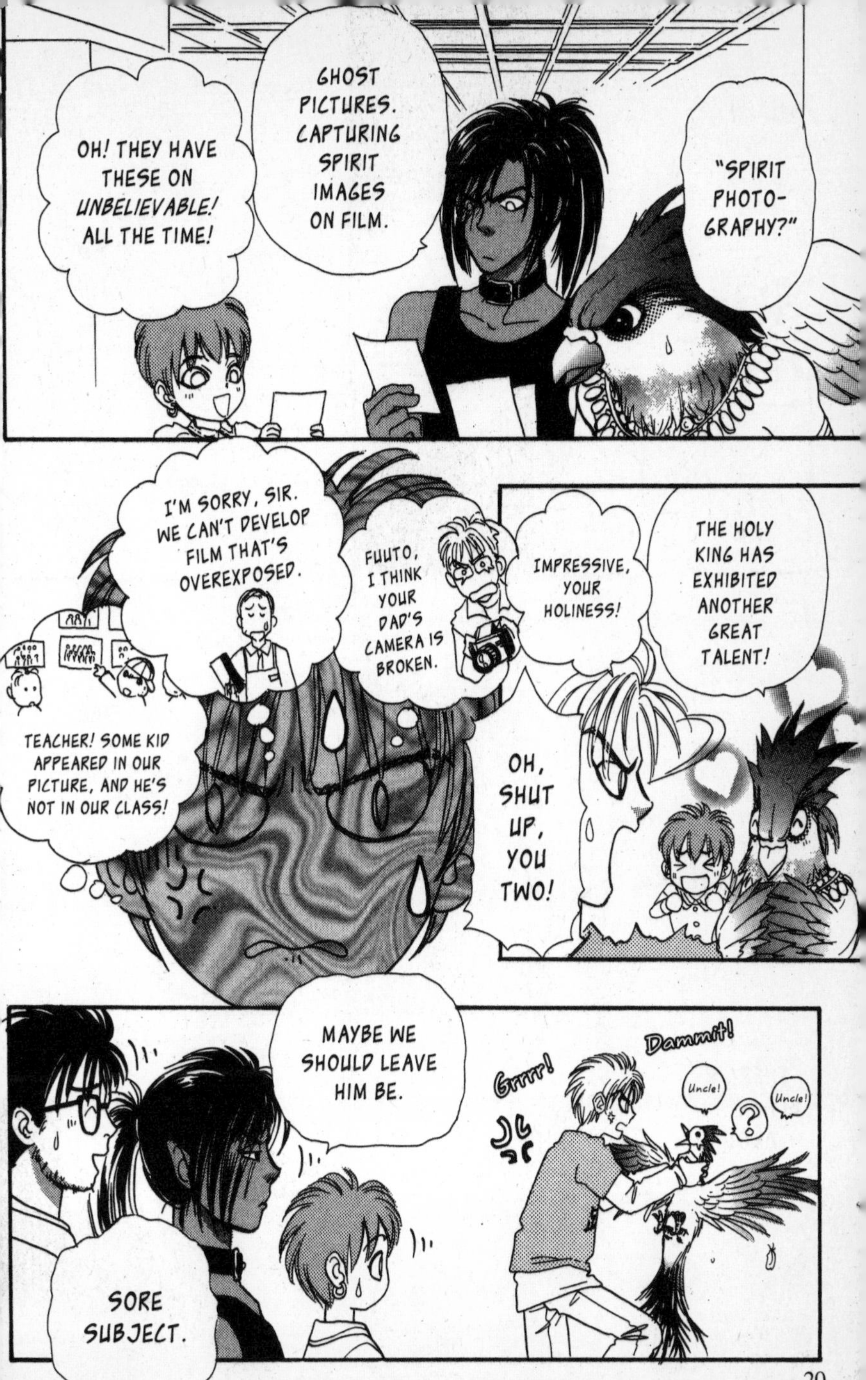
"SPIRIT PHOTOGRAPHY?"
GHOST PICTURES. CAPTURING SPIRIT IMAGES ON FILM.
OH! THEY HAVE THESE ON UNBELIEVABLE! ALL THE TIME!
THE HOLY KING HAS EXHIBITED ANOTHER GREAT TALENT!
IMPRESSIVE, YOUR HOLINESS!
OH, SHUT UP, YOU TWO!
FUUTO, I THINK YOUR DAD'S CAMERA IS BROKEN.
I'M SORRY, SIR. WE CAN'T DEVELOP FILM THAT'S OVEREXPOSED.
TEACHER! SOME KID APPEARED IN OUR PICTURE, AND HE'S NOT IN OUR CLASS!
Dammit!
Grrrr!
Uncle!
?
Uncle!
MAYBE WE SHOULD LEAVE HIM BE.
SORE SUBJECT.

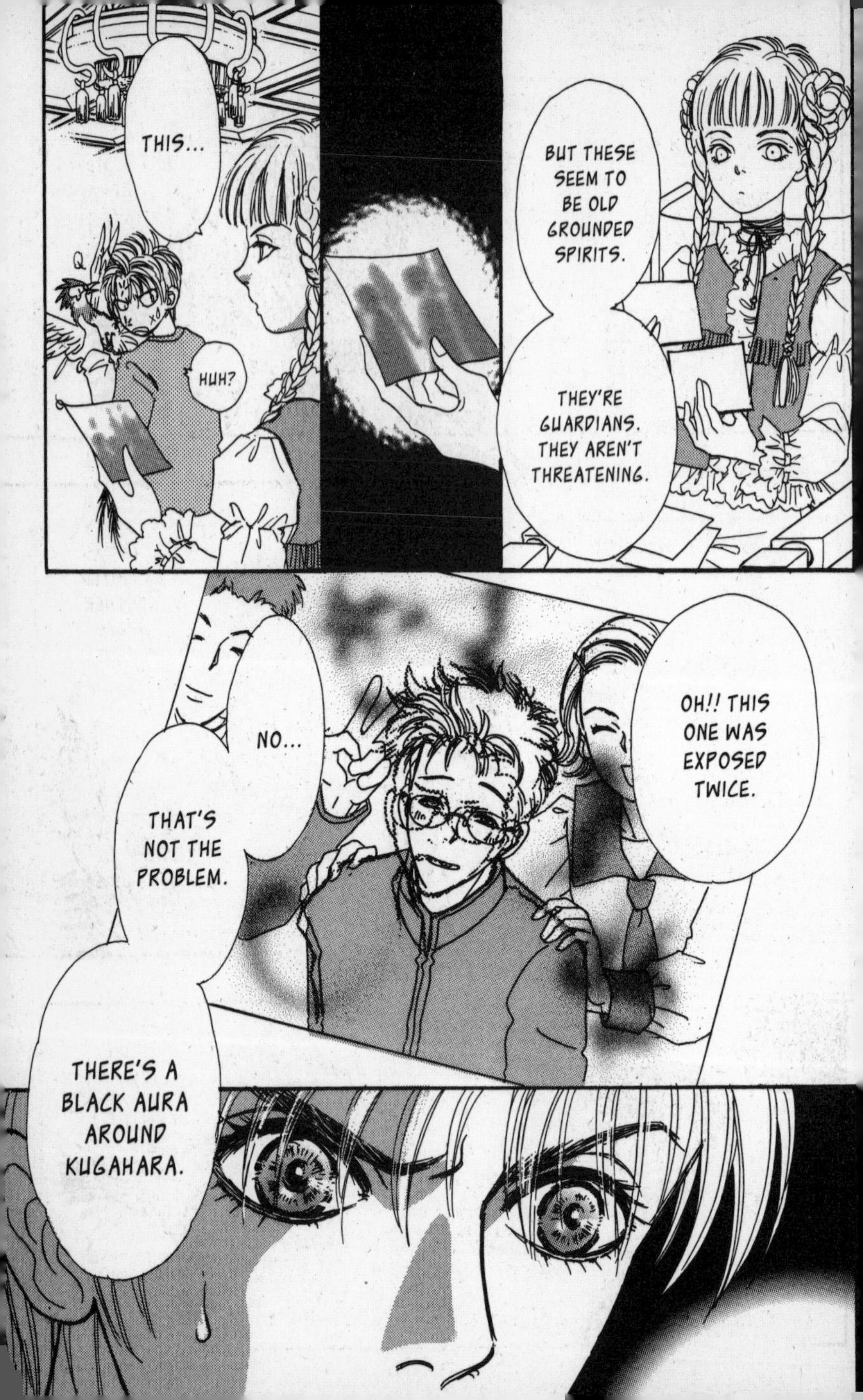

THIS...
HUH?
BUT THESE SEEM TO BE OLD GROUNDED SPIRITS.
THEY'RE GUARDIANS. THEY AREN'T THREATENING.
OH!! THIS ONE WAS EXPOSED TWICE.
NO...
THAT'S NOT THE PROBLEM.
THERE'S A BLACK AURA AROUND KUGAHARA.

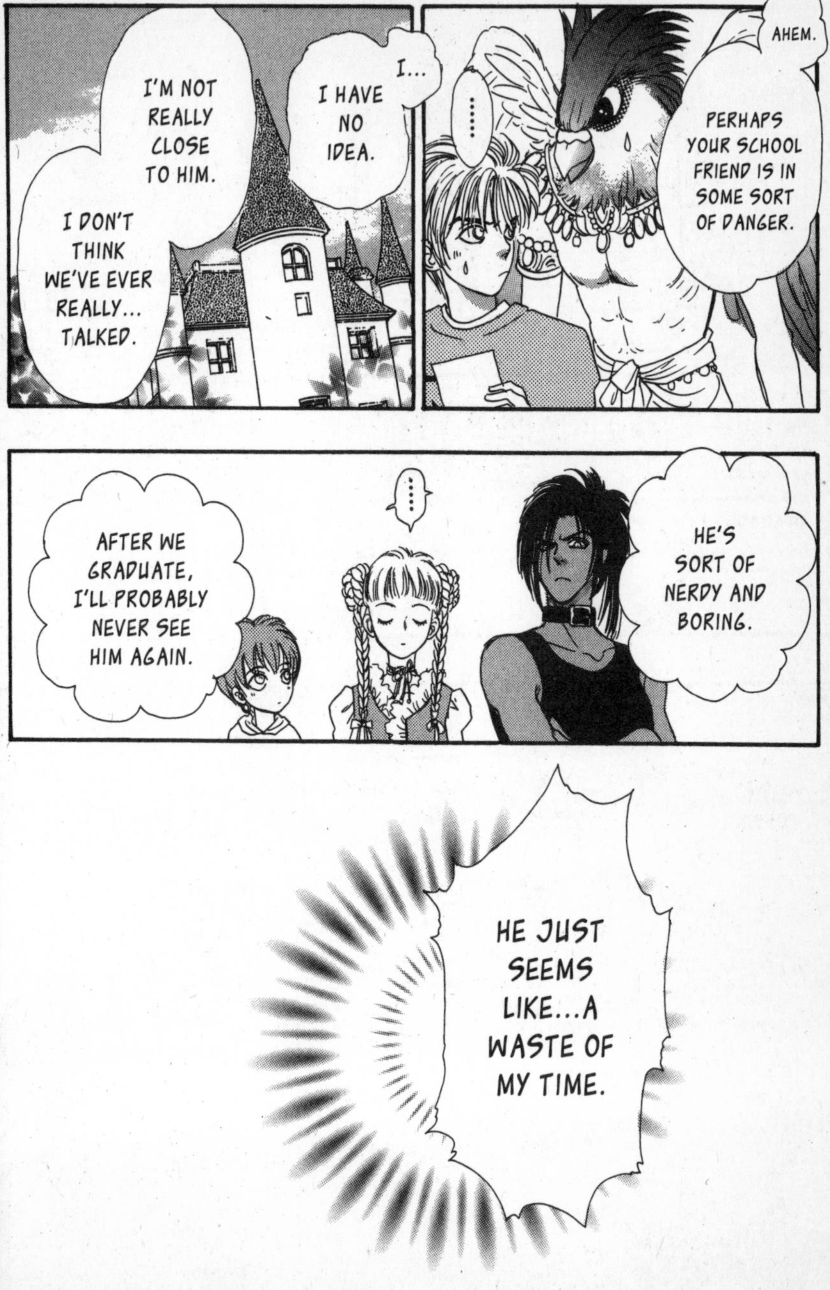
AHEM.
PERHAPS YOUR SCHOOL FRIEND IS IN SOME SORT OF DANGER.
......
I...
I HAVE NO IDEA.
I'M NOT REALLY CLOSE TO HIM.
I DON'T THINK WE'VE EVER REALLY... TALKED.
HE'S SORT OF NERDY AND BORING.
......
AFTER WE GRADUATE, I'LL PROBABLY NEVER SEE HIM AGAIN.
HE JUST SEEMS LIKE...A WASTE OF MY TIME.

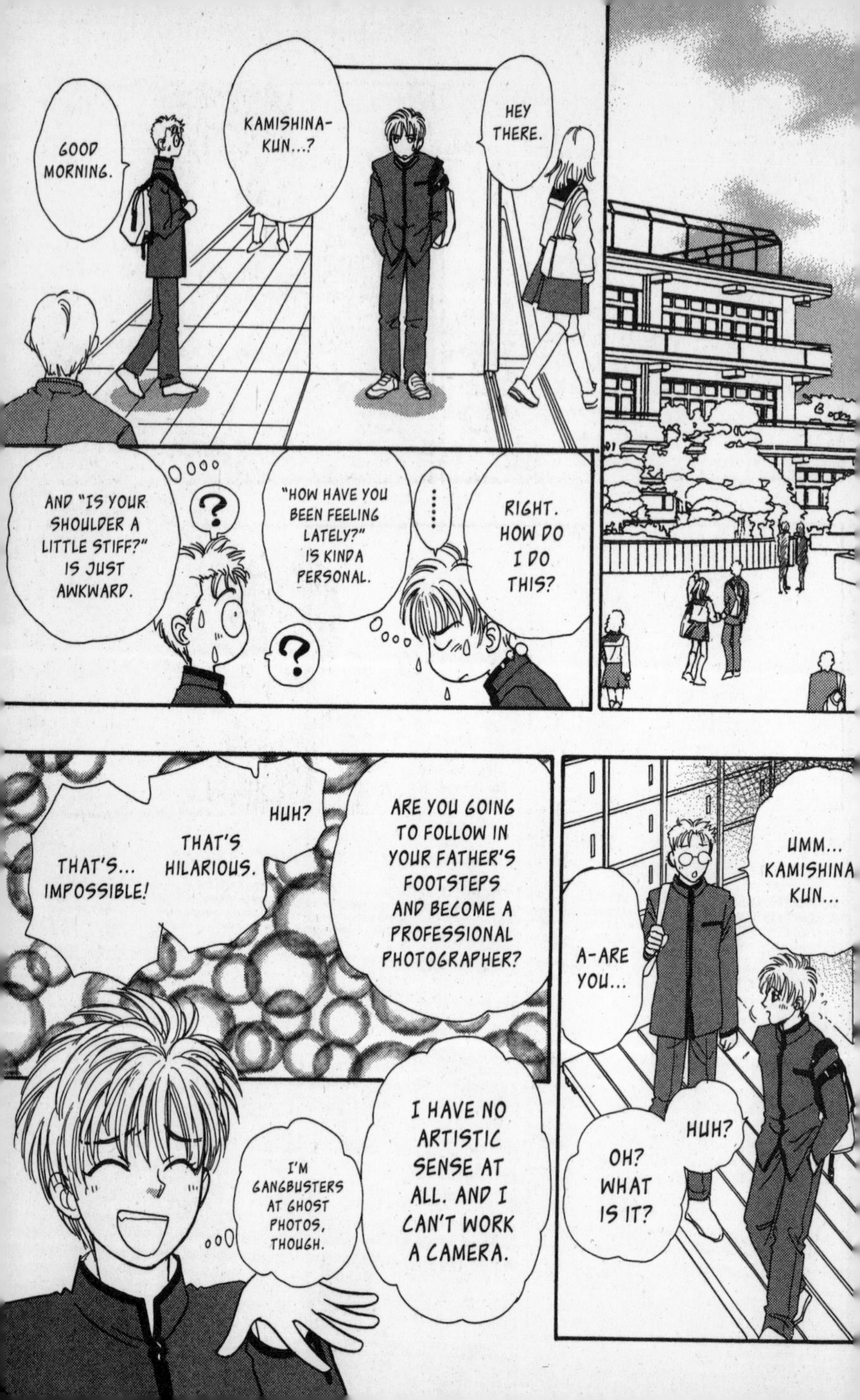
HEY THERE.
KAMISHINA-KUN...?
GOOD MORNING.
RIGHT. HOW DO I DO THIS?
......
"HOW HAVE YOU BEEN FEELING LATELY?" IS KINDA PERSONAL.
?
?
AND "IS YOUR SHOULDER A LITTLE STIFF?" IS JUST AWKWARD.
UMM... KAMISHINA KUN...
A-ARE YOU...
HUH?
OH? WHAT IS IT?
ARE YOU GOING TO FOLLOW IN YOUR FATHER'S FOOTSTEPS AND BECOME A PROFESSIONAL PHOTOGRAPHER?
HUH?
THAT'S HILARIOUS.
THAT'S... IMPOSSIBLE!
I HAVE NO ARTISTIC SENSE AT ALL. AND I CAN'T WORK A CAMERA.
I'M GANGBUSTERS AT GHOST PHOTOS, THOUGH.

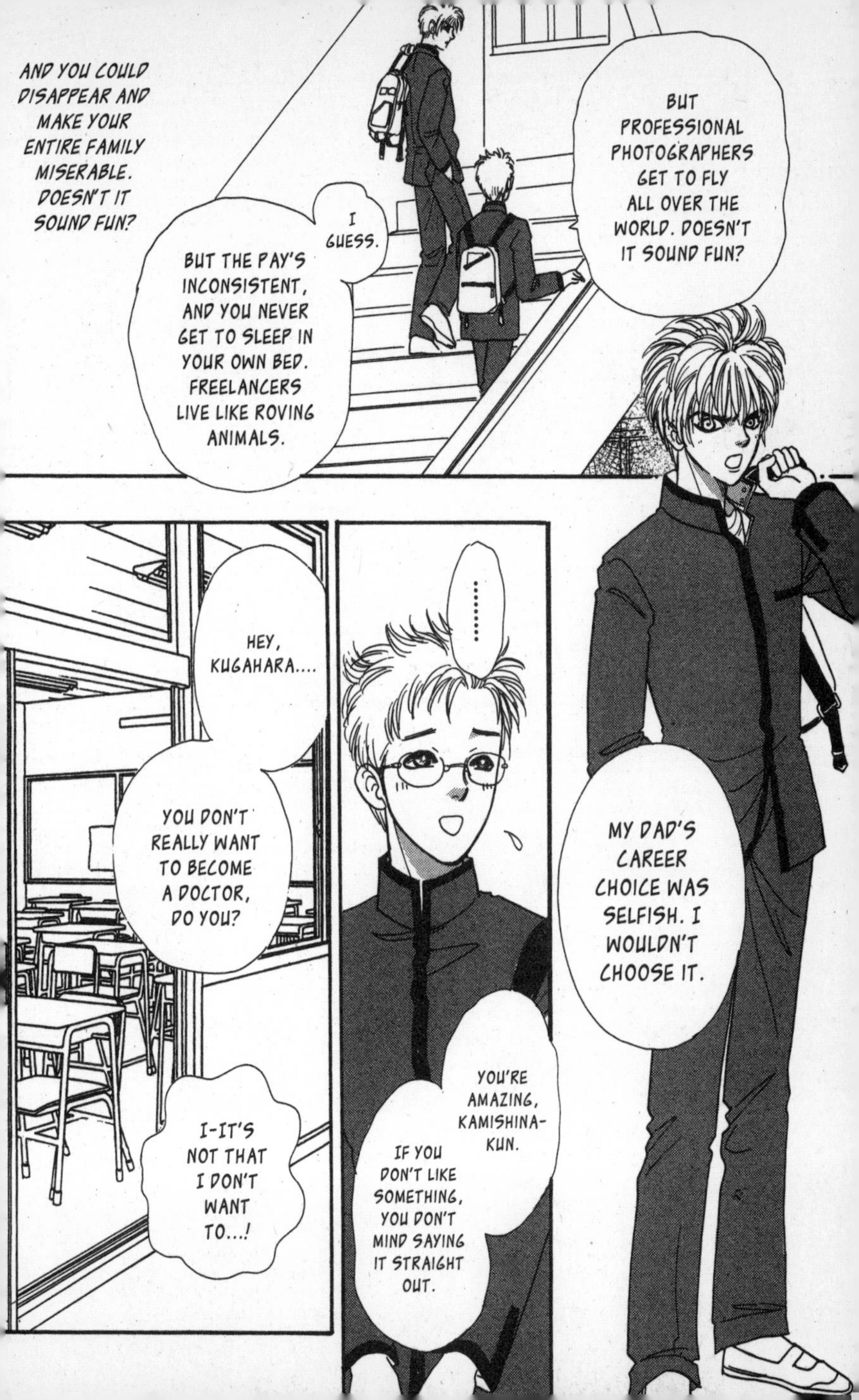
BUT PROFESSIONAL PHOTOGRAPHERS GET TO FLY ALL OVER THE WORLD. DOESN'T IT SOUND FUN?
I GUESS.
BUT THE PAY'S INCONSISTENT, AND YOU NEVER GET TO SLEEP IN YOUR OWN BED. FREELANCERS LIVE LIKE ROVING ANIMALS.
AND YOU COULD DISAPPEAR AND MAKE YOUR ENTIRE FAMILY MISERABLE. DOESN'T IT SOUND FUN?
MY DAD'S CAREER CHOICE WAS SELFISH. I WOULDN'T CHOOSE IT.
......
YOU'RE AMAZING, KAMISHINA-KUN.
IF YOU DON'T LIKE SOMETHING, YOU DON'T MIND SAYING IT STRAIGHT OUT.
HEY, KUGAHARA....
YOU DON'T REALLY WANT TO BECOME A DOCTOR, DO YOU?
I-IT'S NOT THAT I DON'T WANT TO...!

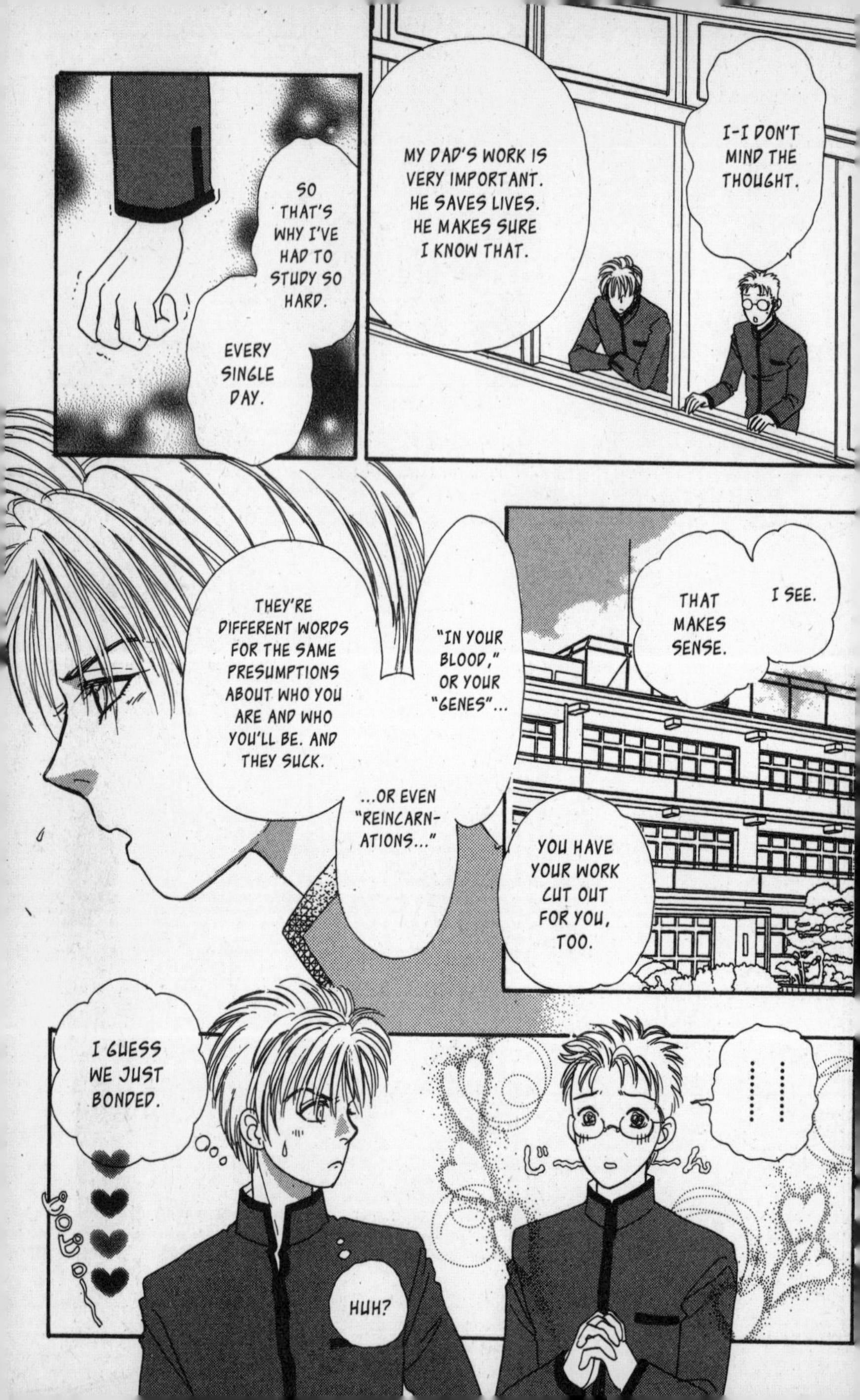
MY DAD'S WORK IS VERY IMPORTANT. HE SAVES LIVES. HE MAKES SURE I KNOW THAT.
SO THAT'S WHY I'VE HAD TO STUDY SO HARD.
EVERY SINGLE DAY.
I-I DON'T MIND THE THOUGHT.
"IN YOUR BLOOD," OR YOUR "GENES"...
...OR EVEN "REINCARNATIONS..."
THEY'RE DIFFERENT WORDS FOR THE SAME PRESUMPTIONS ABOUT WHO YOU ARE AND WHO YOU'LL BE. AND THEY SUCK.
I SEE.
THAT MAKES SENSE.
YOU HAVE YOUR WORK CUT OUT FOR YOU, TOO.
I GUESS WE JUST BONDED.
HUH?
……
じ〜ん

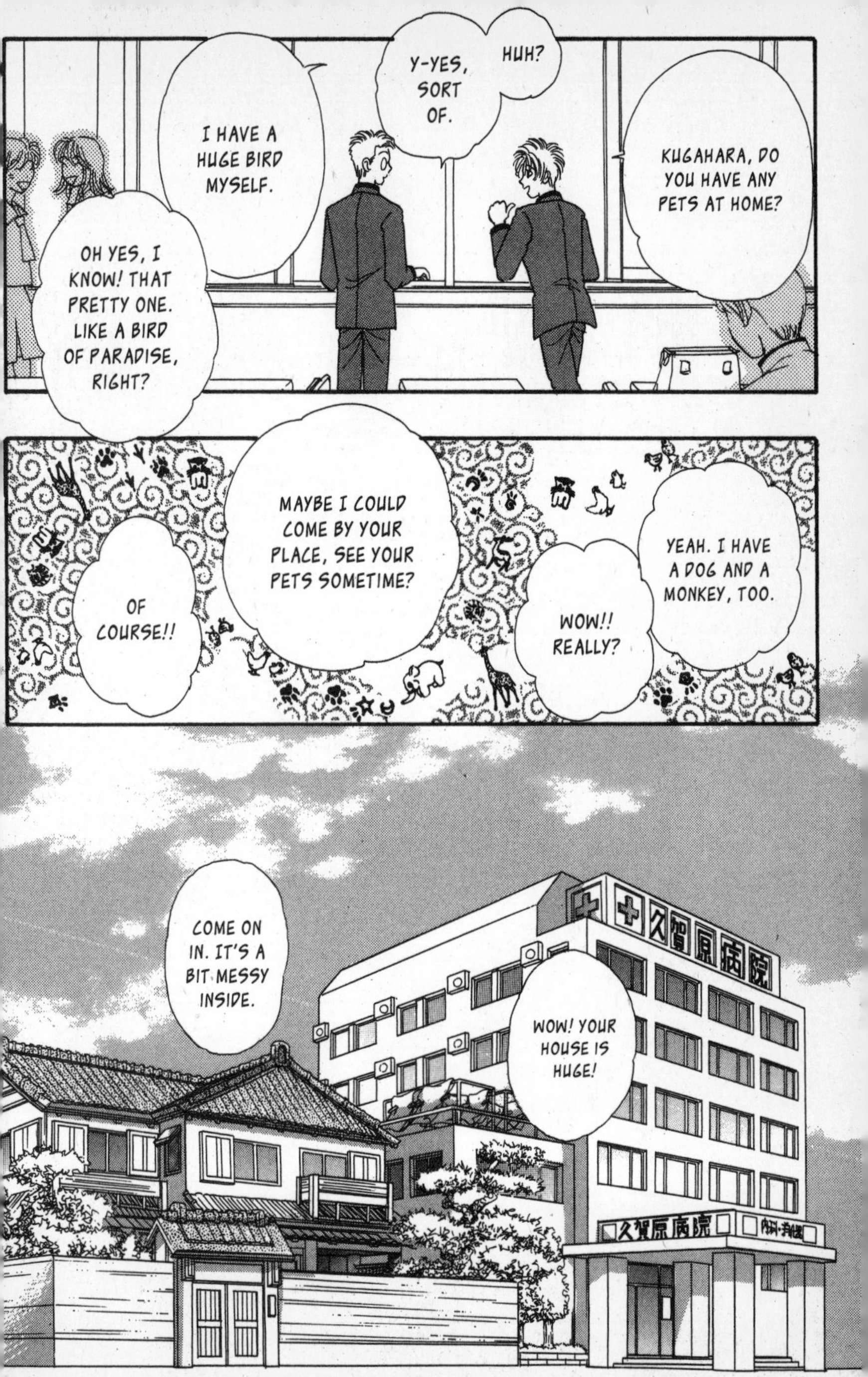
KUGAHARA, DO YOU HAVE ANY PETS AT HOME?
HUH?
Y-YES, SORT OF.
I HAVE A HUGE BIRD MYSELF.
OH YES, I KNOW! THAT PRETTY ONE. LIKE A BIRD OF PARADISE, RIGHT?
YEAH. I HAVE A DOG AND A MONKEY, TOO.
WOW!! REALLY?
MAYBE I COULD COME BY YOUR PLACE, SEE YOUR PETS SOMETIME?
OF COURSE!!
久賀原病院
久賀原病院
WOW! YOUR HOUSE IS HUGE!
COME ON IN. IT'S A BIT MESSY INSIDE.

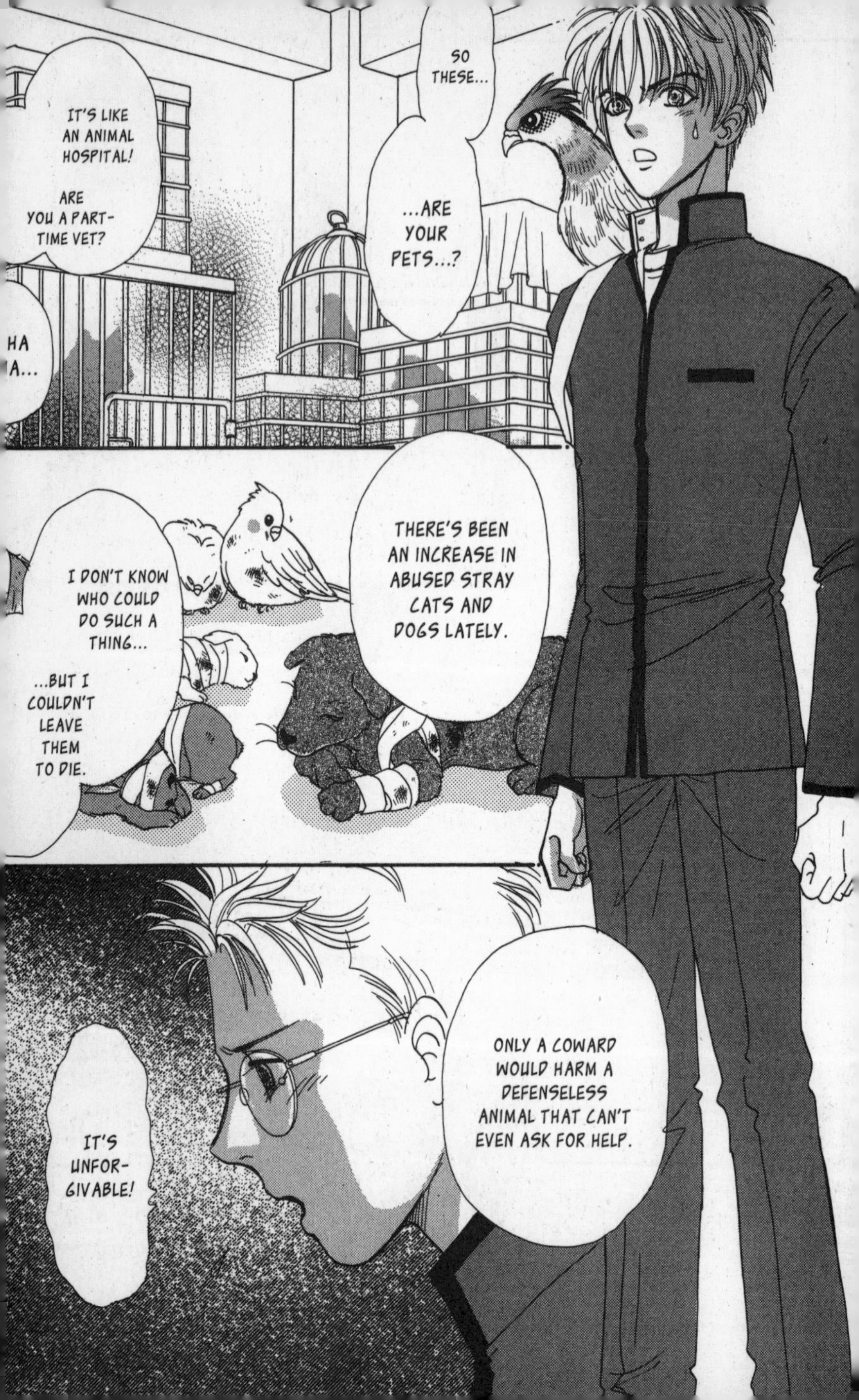
SO THESE...
...ARE YOUR PETS...?
IT'S LIKE AN ANIMAL HOSPITAL!
ARE YOU A PART-TIME VET?
HA A...
THERE'S BEEN AN INCREASE IN ABUSED STRAY CATS AND DOGS LATELY.
I DON'T KNOW WHO COULD DO SUCH A THING...
...BUT I COULDN'T LEAVE THEM TO DIE.
ONLY A COWARD WOULD HARM A DEFENSELESS ANIMAL THAT CAN'T EVEN ASK FOR HELP.
IT'S UNFORGIVABLE!

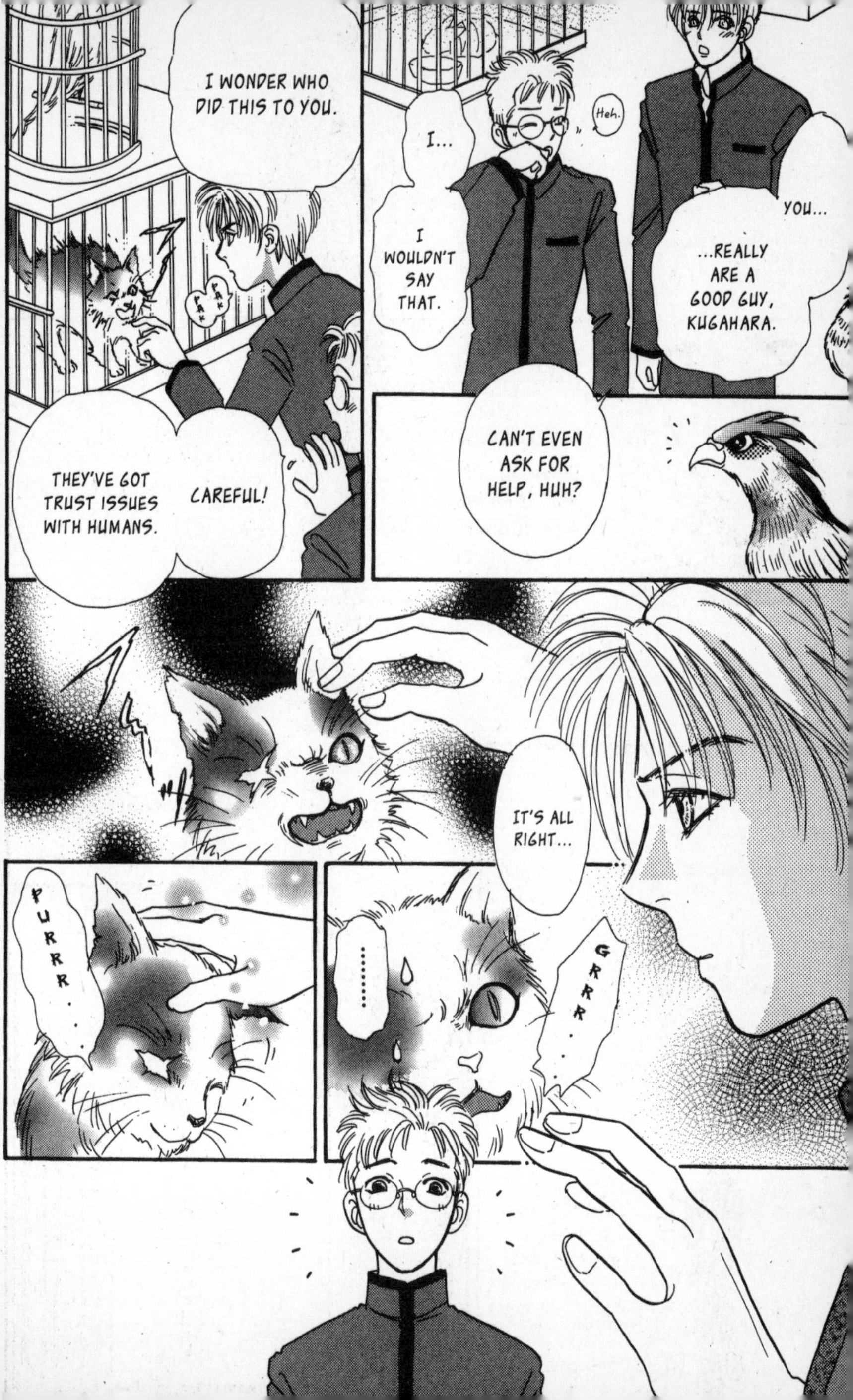

I WONDER WHO DID THIS TO YOU.
PAK PAK
THEY'VE GOT TRUST ISSUES WITH HUMANS.
CAREFUL!
I...
I WOULDN'T SAY THAT.
Heh.
YOU...
...REALLY ARE A GOOD GUY, KUGAHARA.
CAN'T EVEN ASK FOR HELP, HUH?
IT'S ALL RIGHT...
PURRR...
......
GRRR...

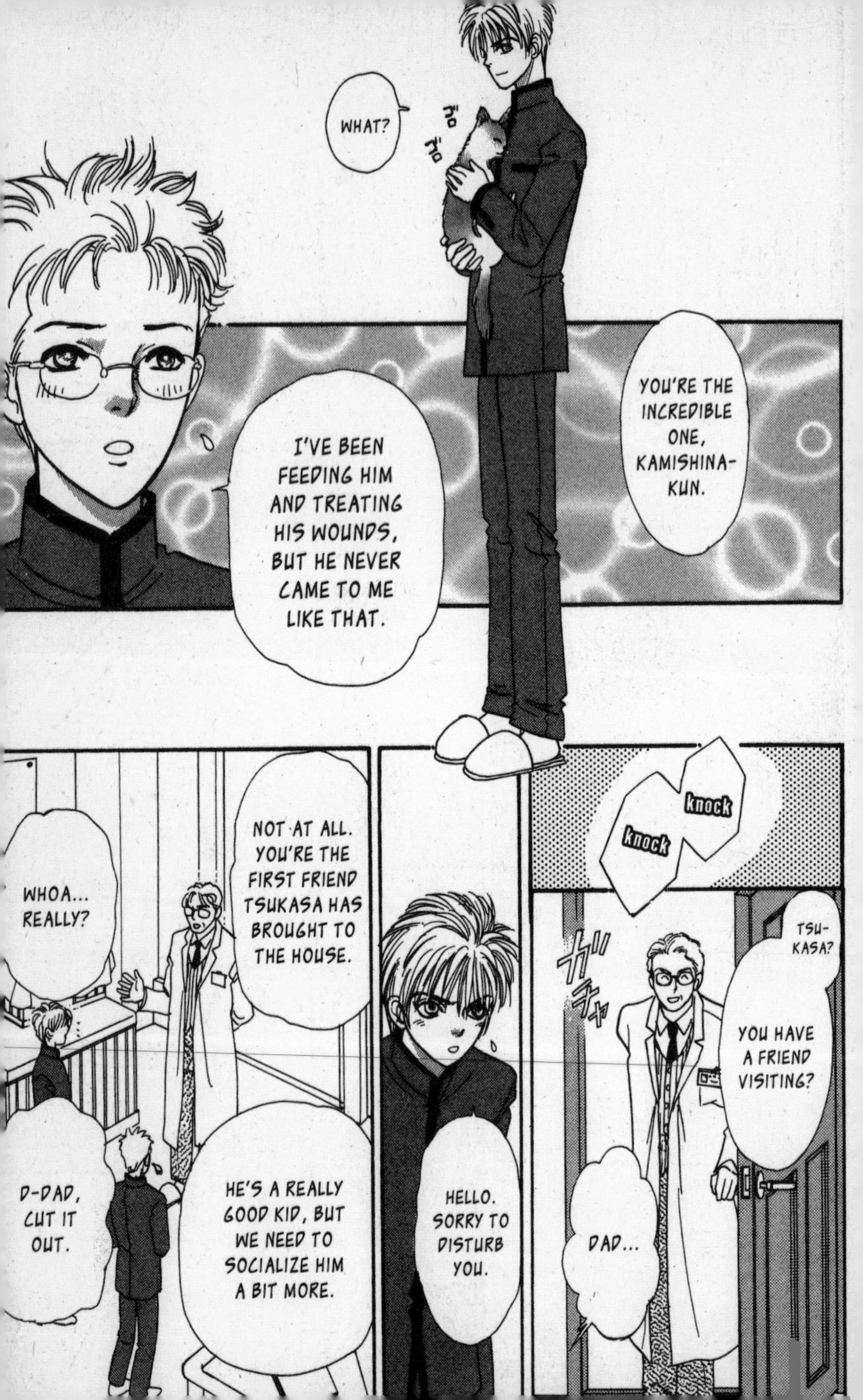
I'VE BEEN FEEDING HIM AND TREATING HIS WOUNDS, BUT HE NEVER CAME TO ME LIKE THAT.
YOU'RE THE INCREDIBLE ONE, KAMISHINA-KUN.
WHAT?
ゴロ ゴロ
knock
knock
ガチャ
TSU-KASA?
YOU HAVE A FRIEND VISITING?
DAD...
HELLO. SORRY TO DISTURB YOU.
NOT AT ALL. YOU'RE THE FIRST FRIEND TSUKASA HAS BROUGHT TO THE HOUSE.
WHOA... REALLY?
HE'S A REALLY GOOD KID, BUT WE NEED TO SOCIALIZE HIM A BIT MORE.
D-DAD, CUT IT OUT.

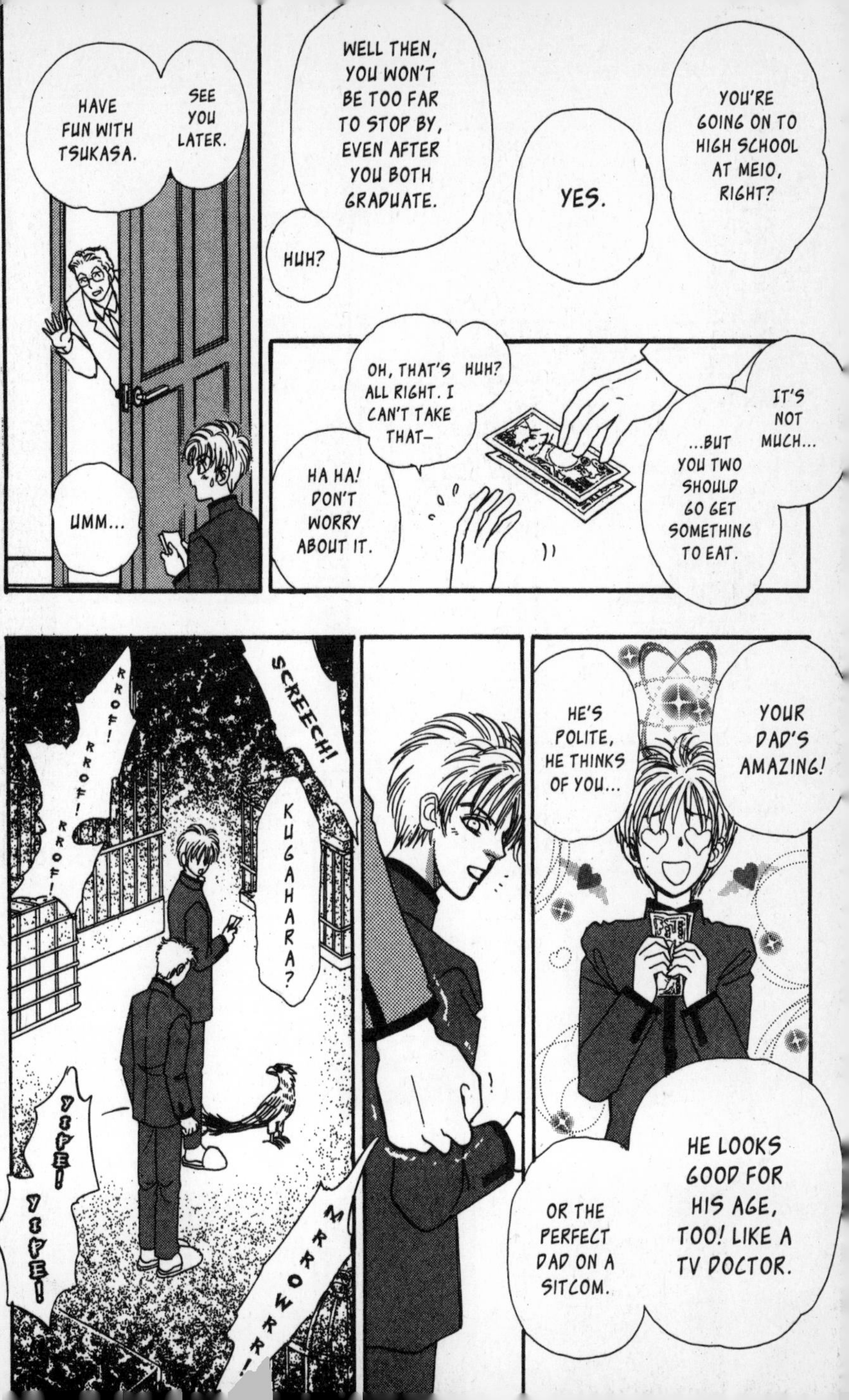

YOU'RE GOING ON TO HIGH SCHOOL AT MEIO, RIGHT?
YES.
WELL THEN, YOU WON'T BE TOO FAR TO STOP BY, EVEN AFTER YOU BOTH GRADUATE.
HUH?
IT'S NOT MUCH...
...BUT YOU TWO SHOULD GO GET SOMETHING TO EAT.
HUH?
OH, THAT'S ALL RIGHT. I CAN'T TAKE THAT—
HA HA! DON'T WORRY ABOUT IT.
SEE YOU LATER.
HAVE FUN WITH TSUKASA.
UMM...
YOUR DAD'S AMAZING!
HE'S POLITE, HE THINKS OF YOU...
HE LOOKS GOOD FOR HIS AGE, TOO! LIKE A TV DOCTOR.
OR THE PERFECT DAD ON A SITCOM.
SCREECH!
KUGAHARA?
RROF! RROF! RROF!
YIPE! YIPE!
MRROWRR!

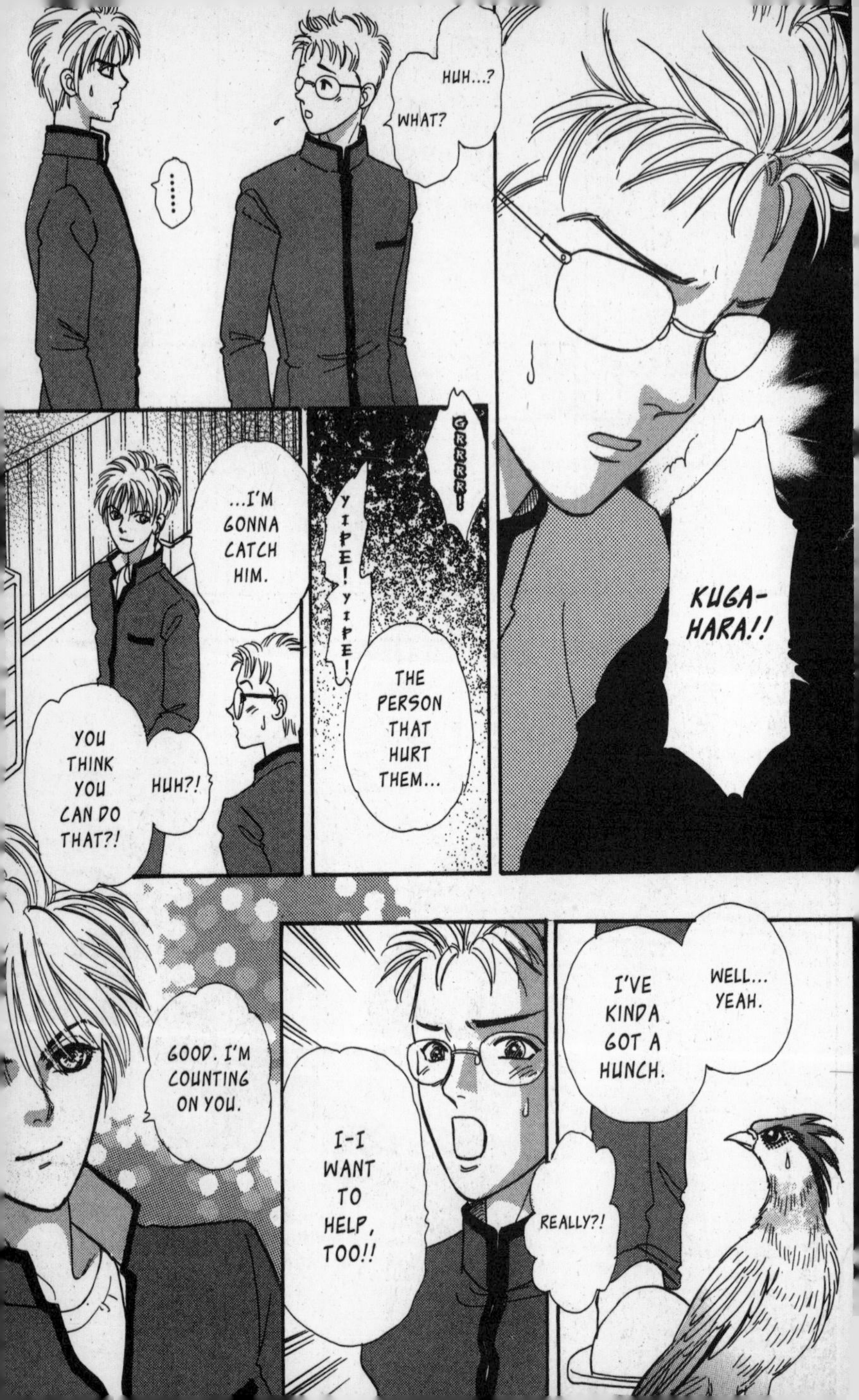
......
HUH...? WHAT?
KUGA-HARA!!
GRRRR!
YIPE! YIPE!
THE PERSON THAT HURT THEM...
...I'M GONNA CATCH HIM.
YOU THINK YOU CAN DO THAT?!
HUH?!
WELL... YEAH.
I'VE KINDA GOT A HUNCH.
REALLY?!
I-I WANT TO HELP, TOO!!
GOOD. I'M COUNTING ON YOU.

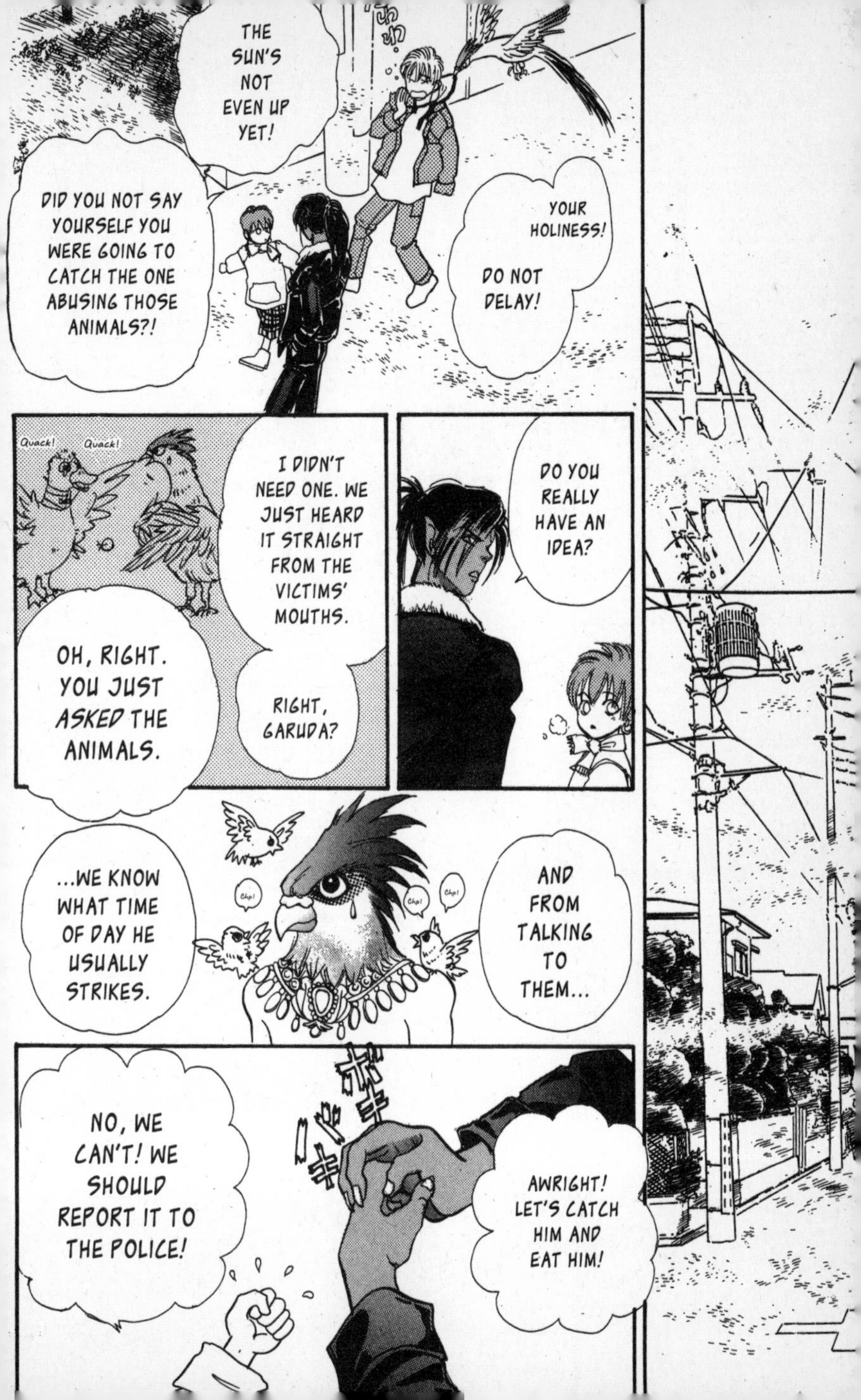
YOUR HOLINESS! DO NOT DELAY!
THE SUN'S NOT EVEN UP YET!
DID YOU NOT SAY YOURSELF YOU WERE GOING TO CATCH THE ONE ABUSING THOSE ANIMALS?!
DO YOU REALLY HAVE AN IDEA?
I DIDN'T NEED ONE. WE JUST HEARD IT STRAIGHT FROM THE VICTIMS' MOUTHS.
RIGHT, GARUDA?
Quack! Quack!
OH, RIGHT. YOU JUST *ASKED* THE ANIMALS.
AND FROM TALKING TO THEM...
Chp! Chp! Chp!
...WE KNOW WHAT TIME OF DAY HE USUALLY STRIKES.
AWRIGHT! LET'S CATCH HIM AND EAT HIM!
NO, WE CAN'T! WE SHOULD REPORT IT TO THE POLICE!

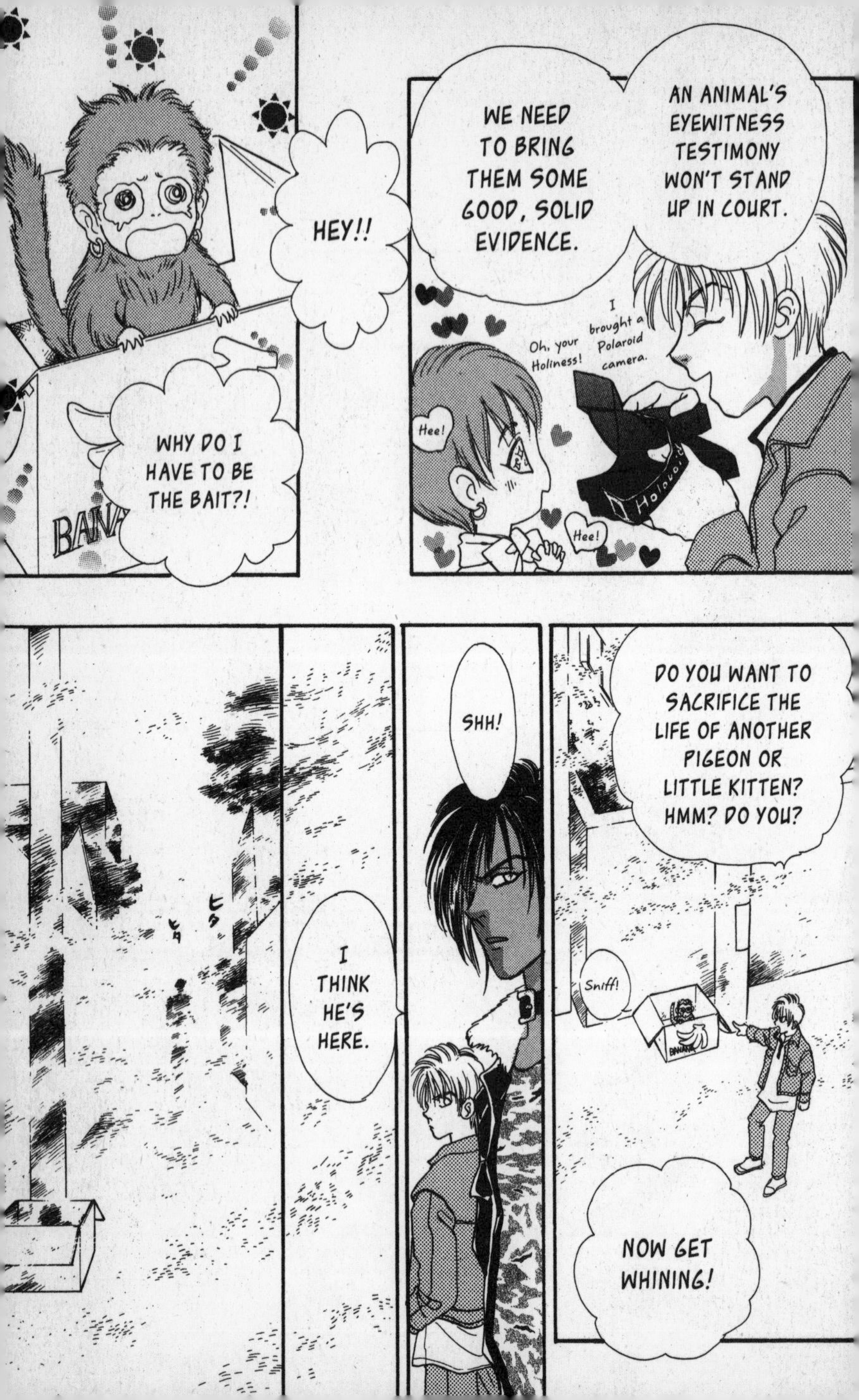
AN ANIMAL'S EYEWITNESS TESTIMONY WON'T STAND UP IN COURT.
WE NEED TO BRING THEM SOME GOOD, SOLID EVIDENCE.
I brought a Polaroid camera.
Oh, your Holiness!
Hee!
Holoroid
Hee!
HEY!!
WHY DO I HAVE TO BE THE BAIT?!
BANA
DO YOU WANT TO SACRIFICE THE LIFE OF ANOTHER PIGEON OR LITTLE KITTEN? HMM? DO YOU?
Sniff!
NOW GET WHINING!
SHH!
I THINK HE'S HERE.
ヒタ
ヒタ

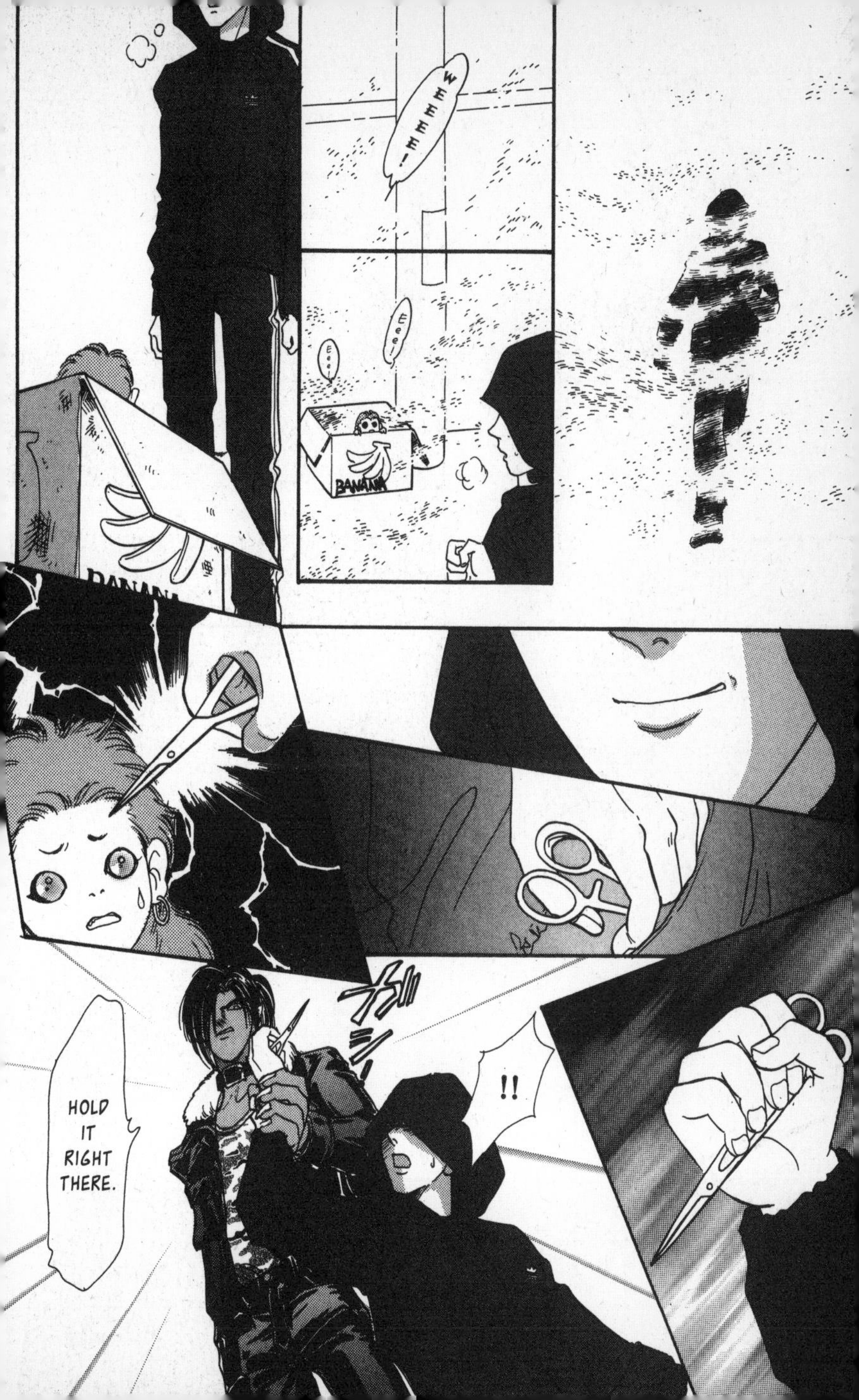
WEEEEE!
Eee!
Eee!
BANANA
BANANA
!!
HOLD IT RIGHT THERE.

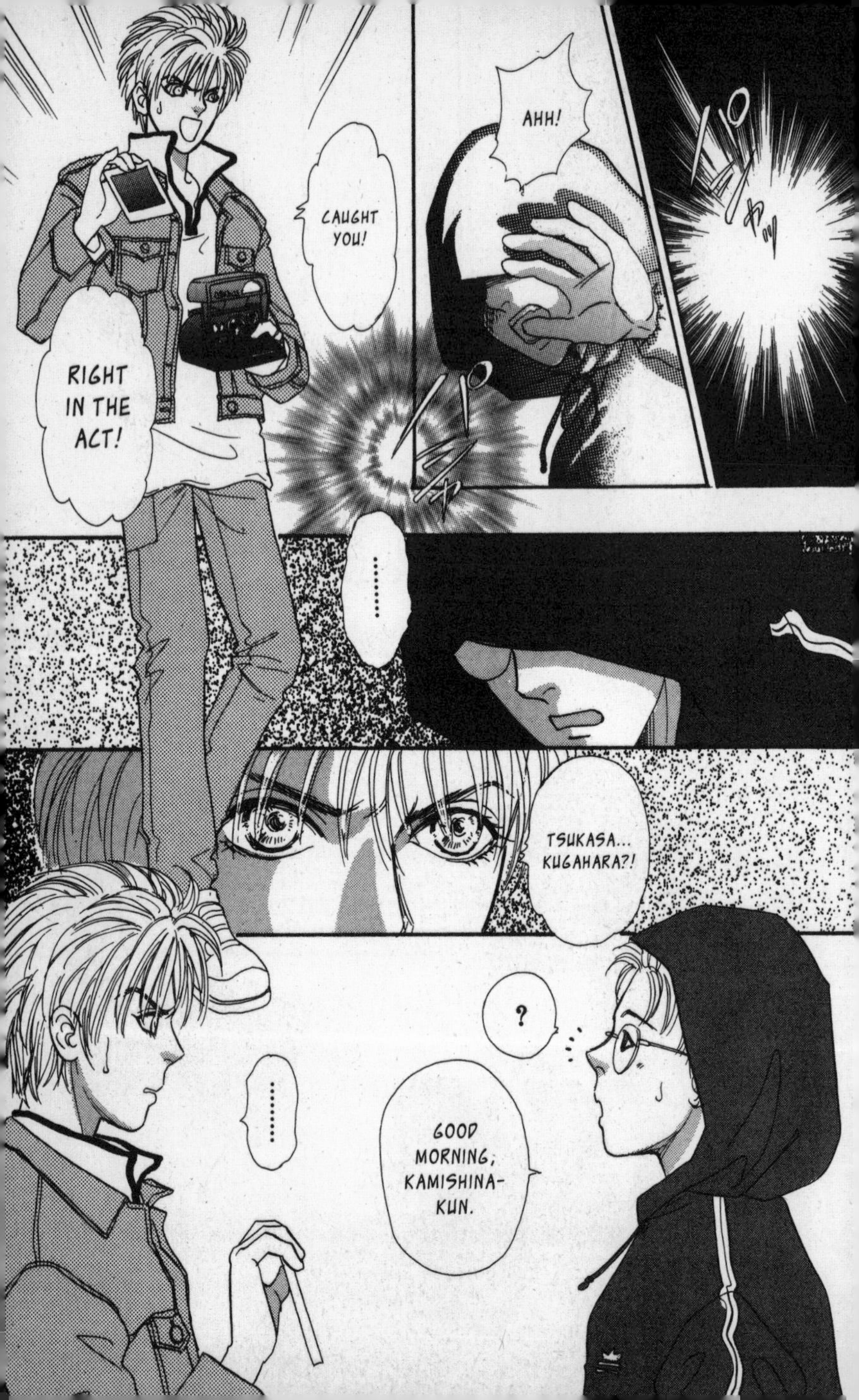
AHH!
CAUGHT YOU!
RIGHT IN THE ACT!
......
TSUKASA... KUGAHARA?!
?
GOOD MORNING, KAMISHINA-KUN.
......

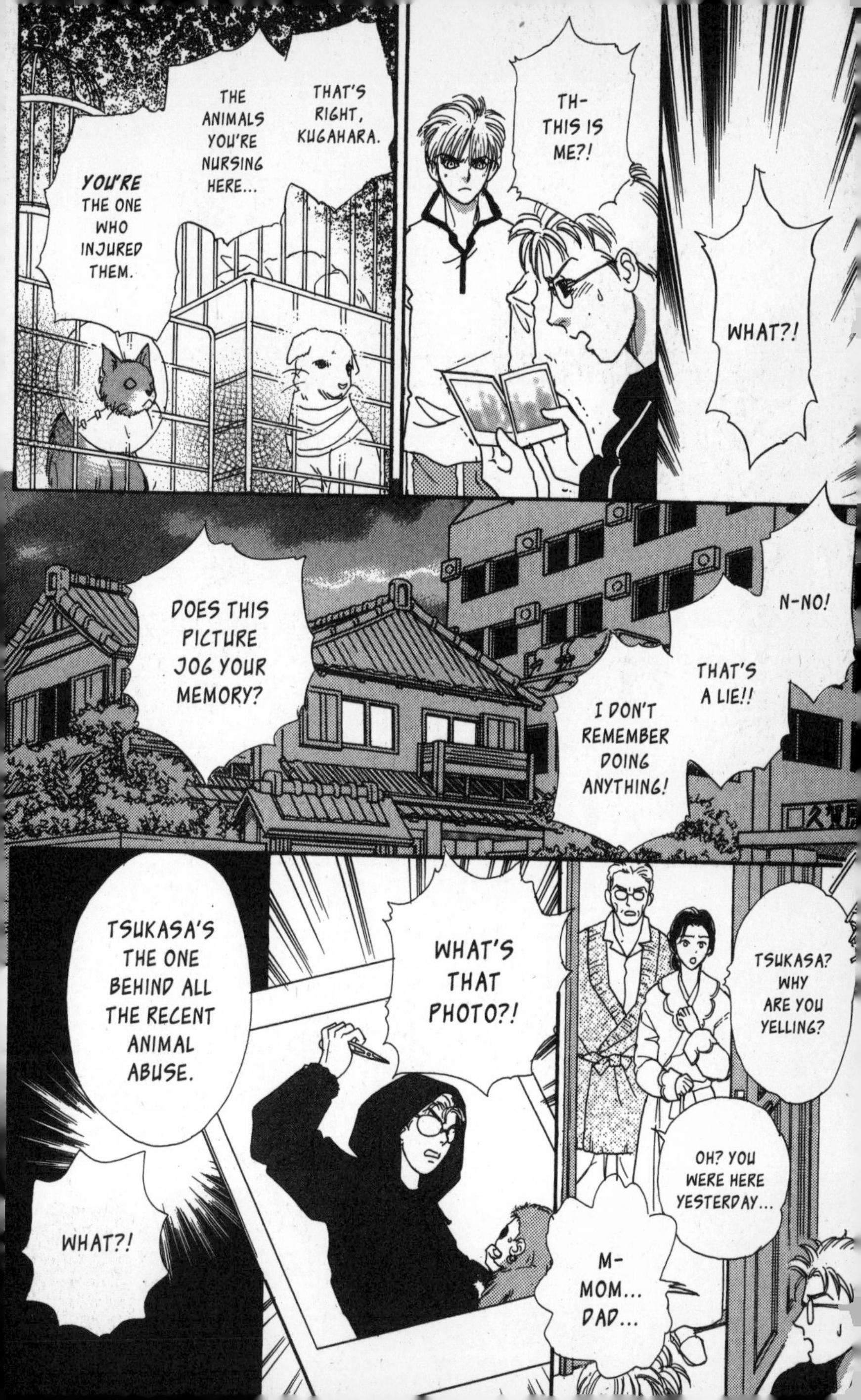
WHAT?!
TH- THIS IS ME?!
THAT'S RIGHT, KUGAHARA.
THE ANIMALS YOU'RE NURSING HERE...
YOU'RE THE ONE WHO INJURED THEM.
N-NO!
THAT'S A LIE!!
I DON'T REMEMBER DOING ANYTHING!
DOES THIS PICTURE JOG YOUR MEMORY?
TSUKASA? WHY ARE YOU YELLING?
OH? YOU WERE HERE YESTERDAY...
M- MOM... DAD...
WHAT'S THAT PHOTO?!
TSUKASA'S THE ONE BEHIND ALL THE RECENT ANIMAL ABUSE.
WHAT?!

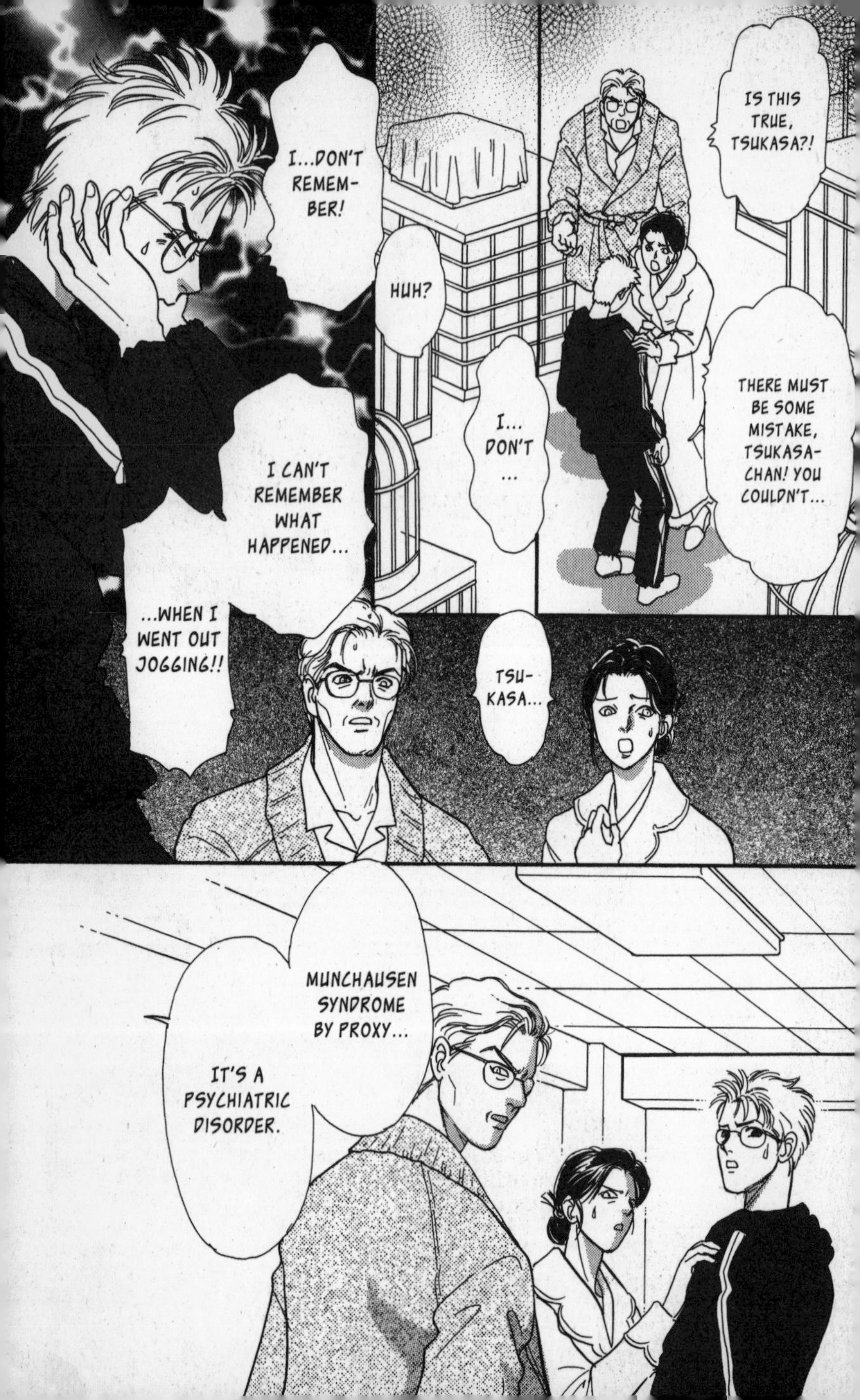

IS THIS TRUE, TSUKASA?!
THERE MUST BE SOME MISTAKE, TSUKASA-CHAN! YOU COULDN'T...
I... DON'T ...
HUH?
I...DON'T REMEMBER!
I CAN'T REMEMBER WHAT HAPPENED...
...WHEN I WENT OUT JOGGING!!
TSUKASA...
MUNCHAUSEN SYNDROME BY PROXY...
IT'S A PSYCHIATRIC DISORDER.

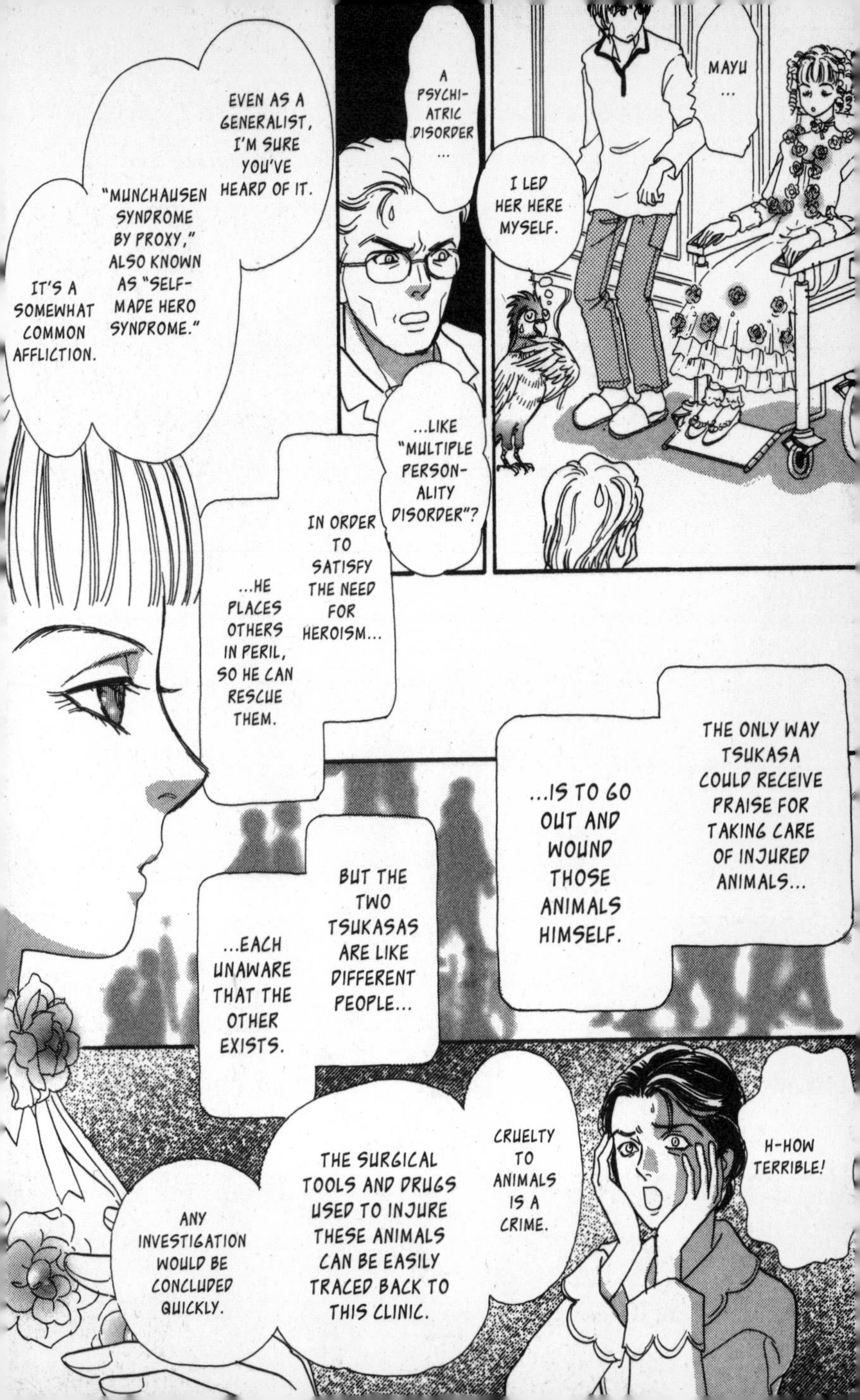
MAYU...
I LED HER HERE MYSELF.
A PSYCHIATRIC DISORDER...
...LIKE "MULTIPLE PERSONALITY DISORDER"?
EVEN AS A GENERALIST, I'M SURE YOU'VE HEARD OF IT.
"MUNCHAUSEN SYNDROME BY PROXY," ALSO KNOWN AS "SELF-MADE HERO SYNDROME."
IT'S A SOMEWHAT COMMON AFFLICTION.
IN ORDER TO SATISFY THE NEED FOR HEROISM...
...HE PLACES OTHERS IN PERIL, SO HE CAN RESCUE THEM.
THE ONLY WAY TSUKASA COULD RECEIVE PRAISE FOR TAKING CARE OF INJURED ANIMALS...
...IS TO GO OUT AND WOUND THOSE ANIMALS HIMSELF.
BUT THE TWO TSUKASAS ARE LIKE DIFFERENT PEOPLE...
...EACH UNAWARE THAT THE OTHER EXISTS.
H-HOW TERRIBLE!
CRUELTY TO ANIMALS IS A CRIME.
THE SURGICAL TOOLS AND DRUGS USED TO INJURE THESE ANIMALS CAN BE EASILY TRACED BACK TO THIS CLINIC.
ANY INVESTIGATION WOULD BE CONCLUDED QUICKLY.

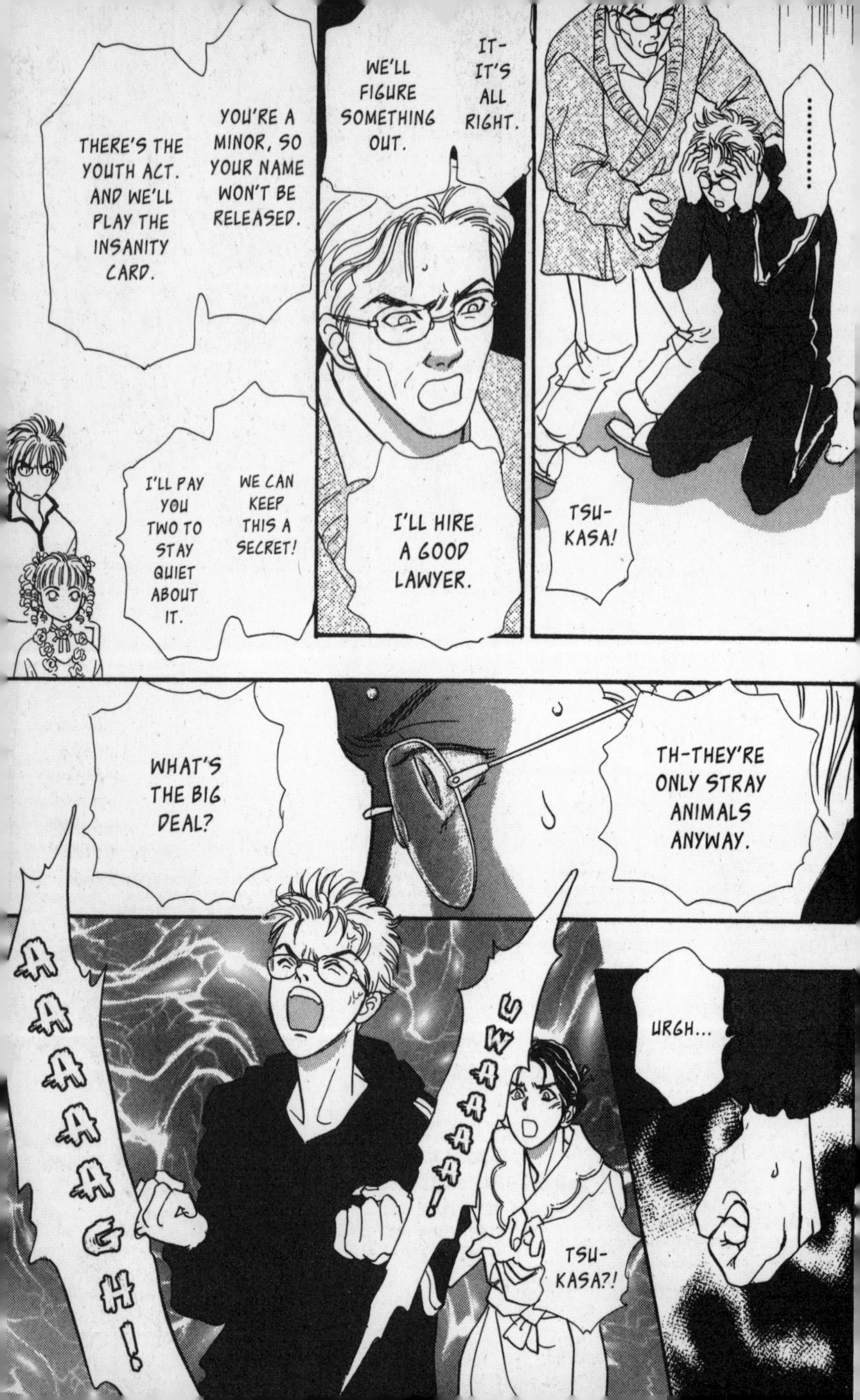
......
TSU-KASA!
IT- IT'S ALL RIGHT.
WE'LL FIGURE SOMETHING OUT.
I'LL HIRE A GOOD LAWYER.
YOU'RE A MINOR, SO YOUR NAME WON'T BE RELEASED.
THERE'S THE YOUTH ACT. AND WE'LL PLAY THE INSANITY CARD.
WE CAN KEEP THIS A SECRET!
I'LL PAY YOU TWO TO STAY QUIET ABOUT IT.
TH-THEY'RE ONLY STRAY ANIMALS ANYWAY.
WHAT'S THE BIG DEAL?
URGH...
TSU-KASA?!
UWAAAA!
AAAAAGH!

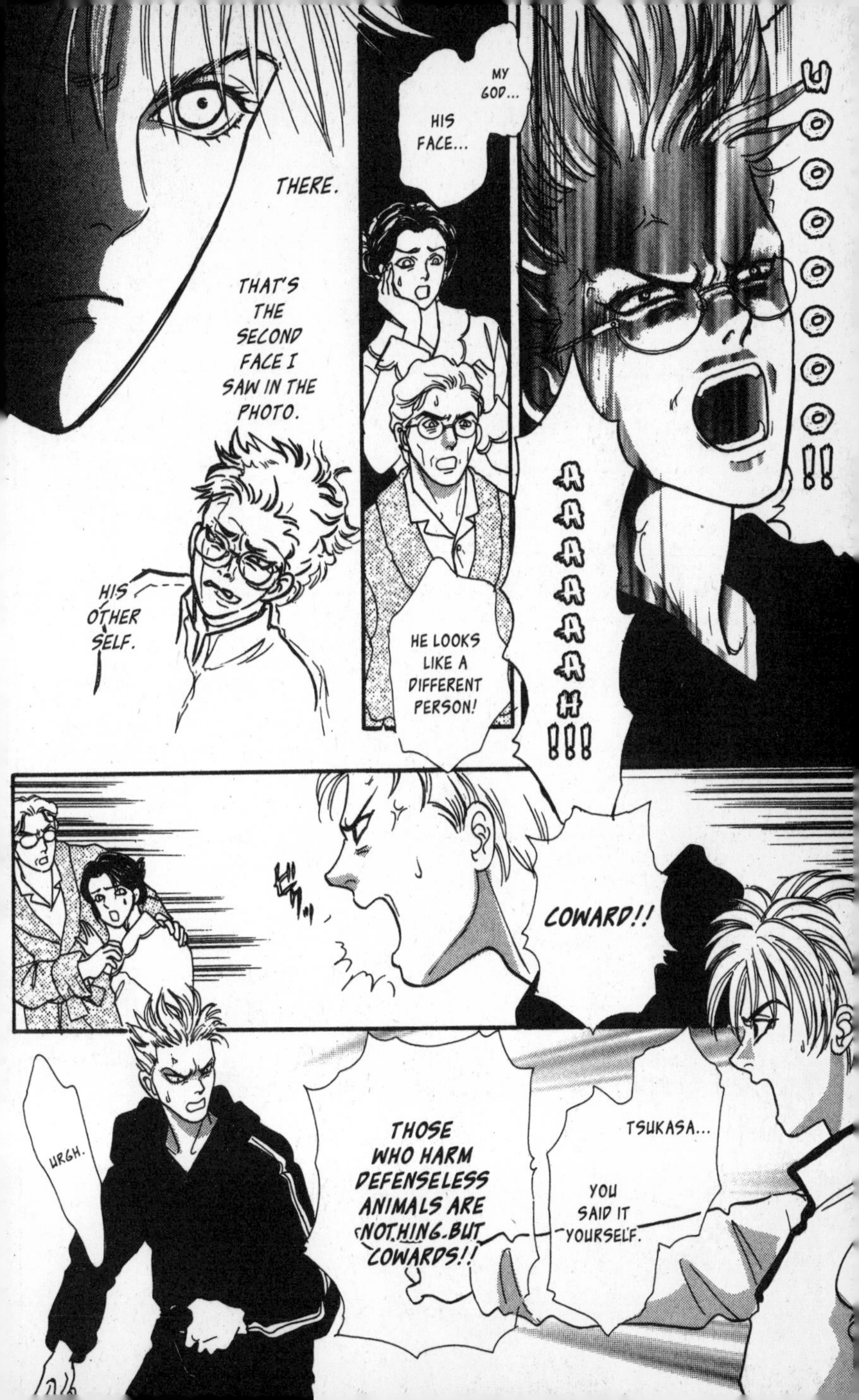
UOOOOOOOOOO!!
AAAAAAH!!!
MY GOD...
HIS FACE...
HE LOOKS LIKE A DIFFERENT PERSON!
THERE.
THAT'S THE SECOND FACE I SAW IN THE PHOTO.
HIS OTHER SELF.
COWARD!!
TSUKASA...
YOU SAID IT YOURSELF.
THOSE WHO HARM DEFENSELESS ANIMALS ARE NOTHING BUT COWARDS!!
URGH.

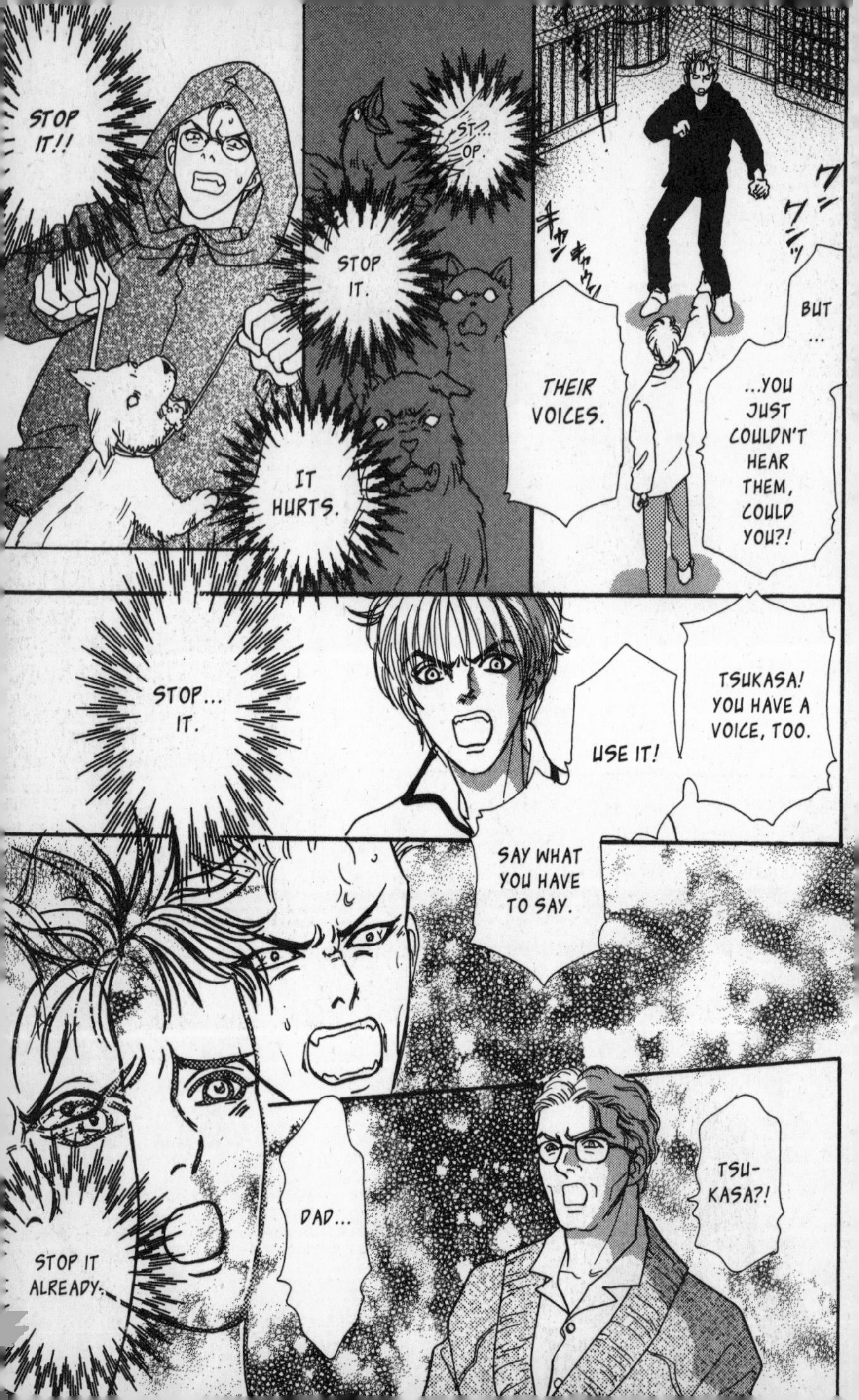
BUT ...
...YOU JUST COULDN'T HEAR THEM, COULD YOU?!
THEIR VOICES.
ST... OP.
STOP IT.
IT HURTS.
STOP IT!!
TSUKASA! YOU HAVE A VOICE, TOO.
USE IT!
STOP... IT.
SAY WHAT YOU HAVE TO SAY.
TSU-KASA?!
DAD...
STOP IT ALREADY.

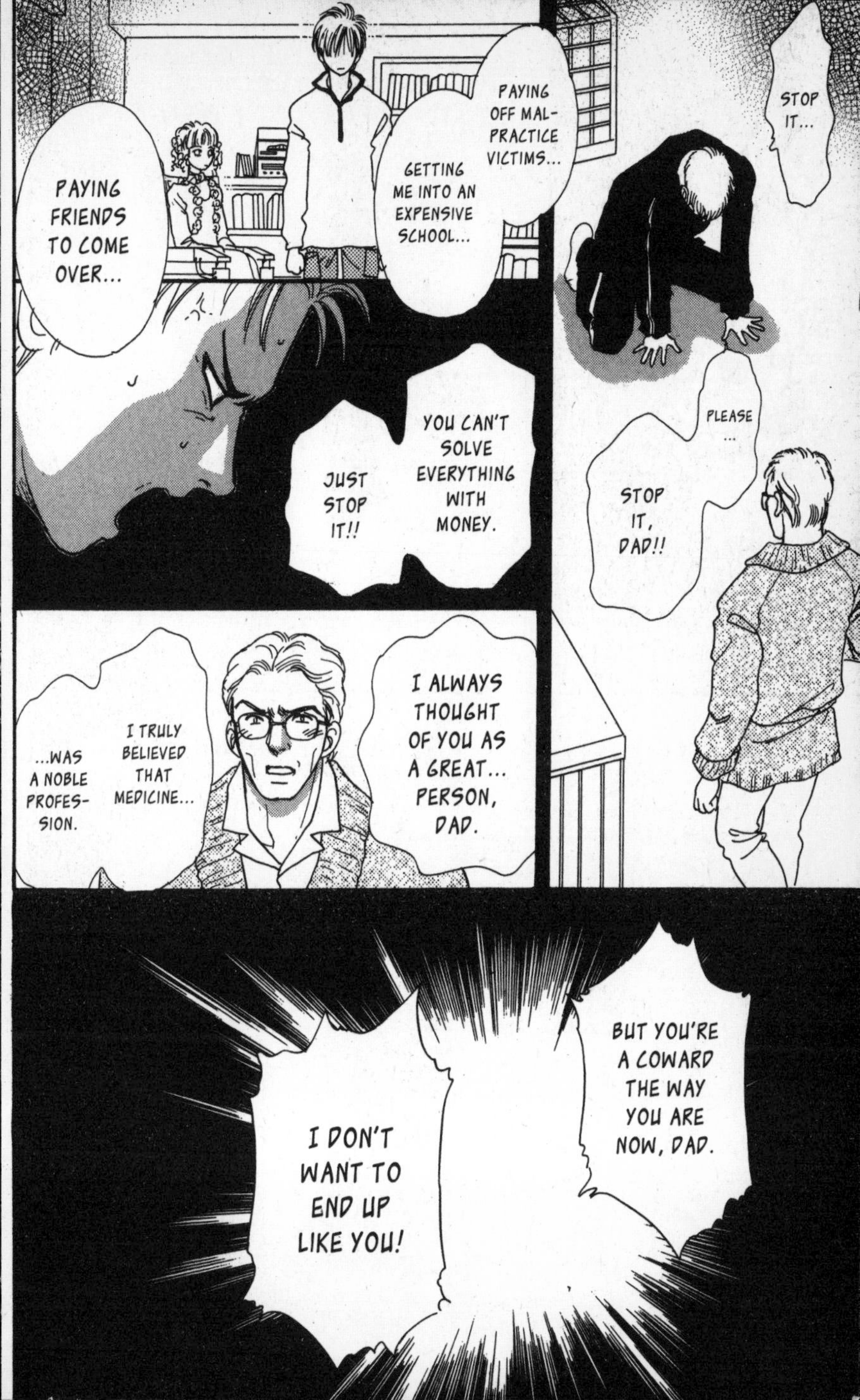
STOP IT...
PAYING OFF MAL-PRACTICE VICTIMS...
GETTING ME INTO AN EXPENSIVE SCHOOL...
PAYING FRIENDS TO COME OVER...
YOU CAN'T SOLVE EVERYTHING WITH MONEY.
JUST STOP IT!!
PLEASE ...
STOP IT, DAD!!
I ALWAYS THOUGHT OF YOU AS A GREAT... PERSON, DAD.
I TRULY BELIEVED THAT MEDICINE...
...WAS A NOBLE PROFES-SION.
BUT YOU'RE A COWARD THE WAY YOU ARE NOW, DAD.
I DON'T WANT TO END UP LIKE YOU!

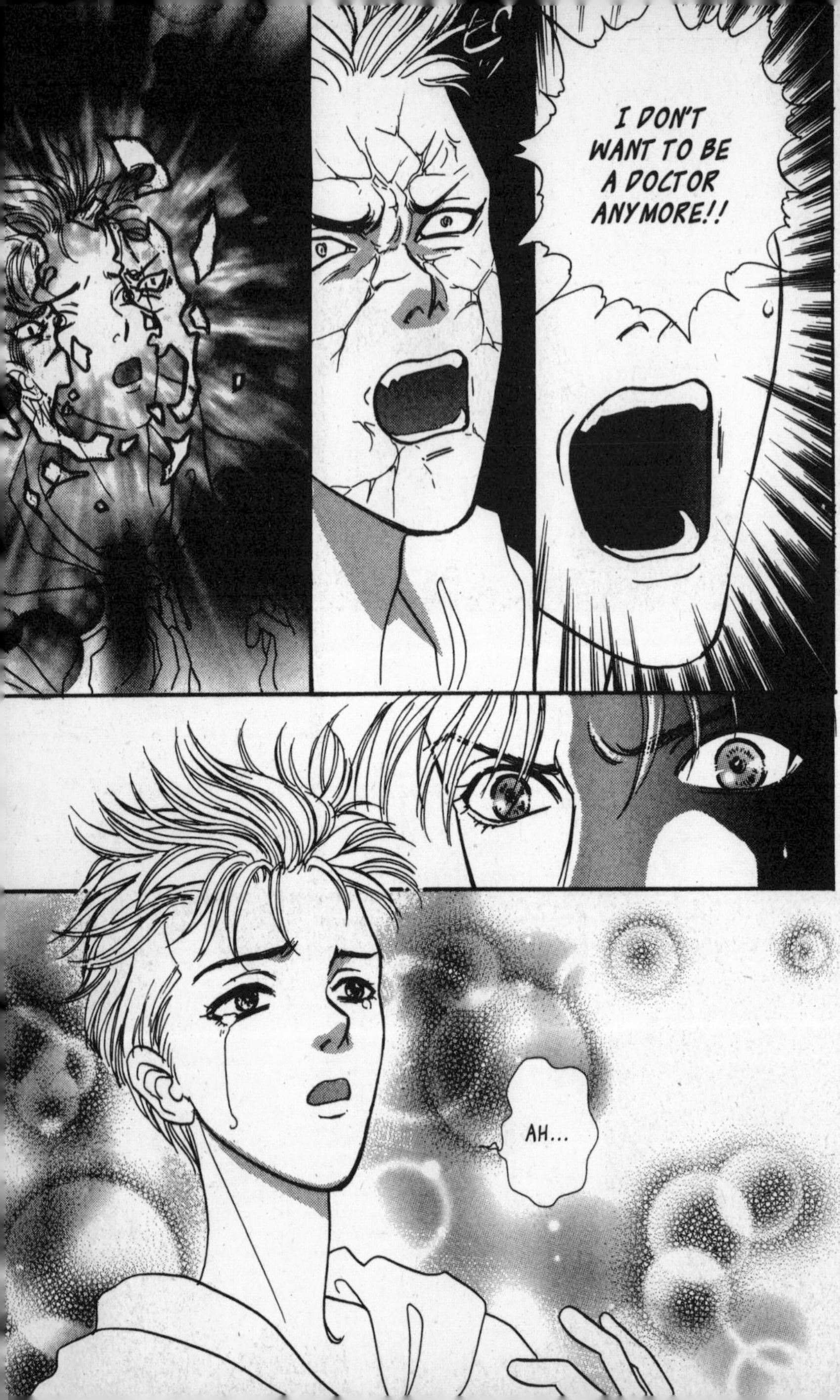
I DON'T WANT TO BE A DOCTOR ANYMORE!!
AH...

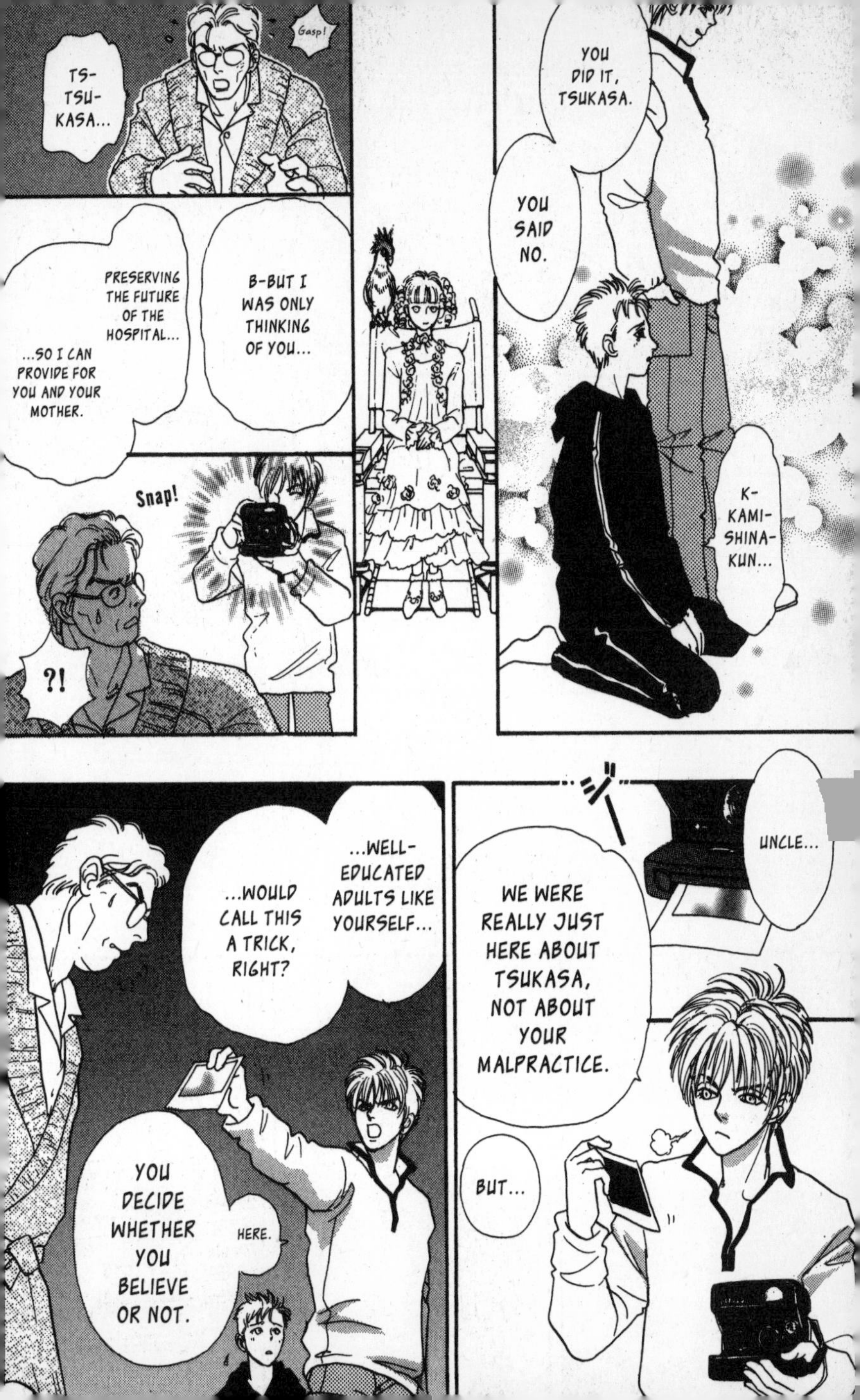
YOU DID IT, TSUKASA.
YOU SAID NO.
K-KAMI-SHINA-KUN...
Gasp!
TS-TSU-KASA...
B-BUT I WAS ONLY THINKING OF YOU...
PRESERVING THE FUTURE OF THE HOSPITAL...
...SO I CAN PROVIDE FOR YOU AND YOUR MOTHER.
Snap!
?!
UNCLE...
WE WERE REALLY JUST HERE ABOUT TSUKASA, NOT ABOUT YOUR MALPRACTICE.
BUT...
...WELL-EDUCATED ADULTS LIKE YOURSELF...
...WOULD CALL THIS A TRICK, RIGHT?
HERE.
YOU DECIDE WHETHER YOU BELIEVE OR NOT.

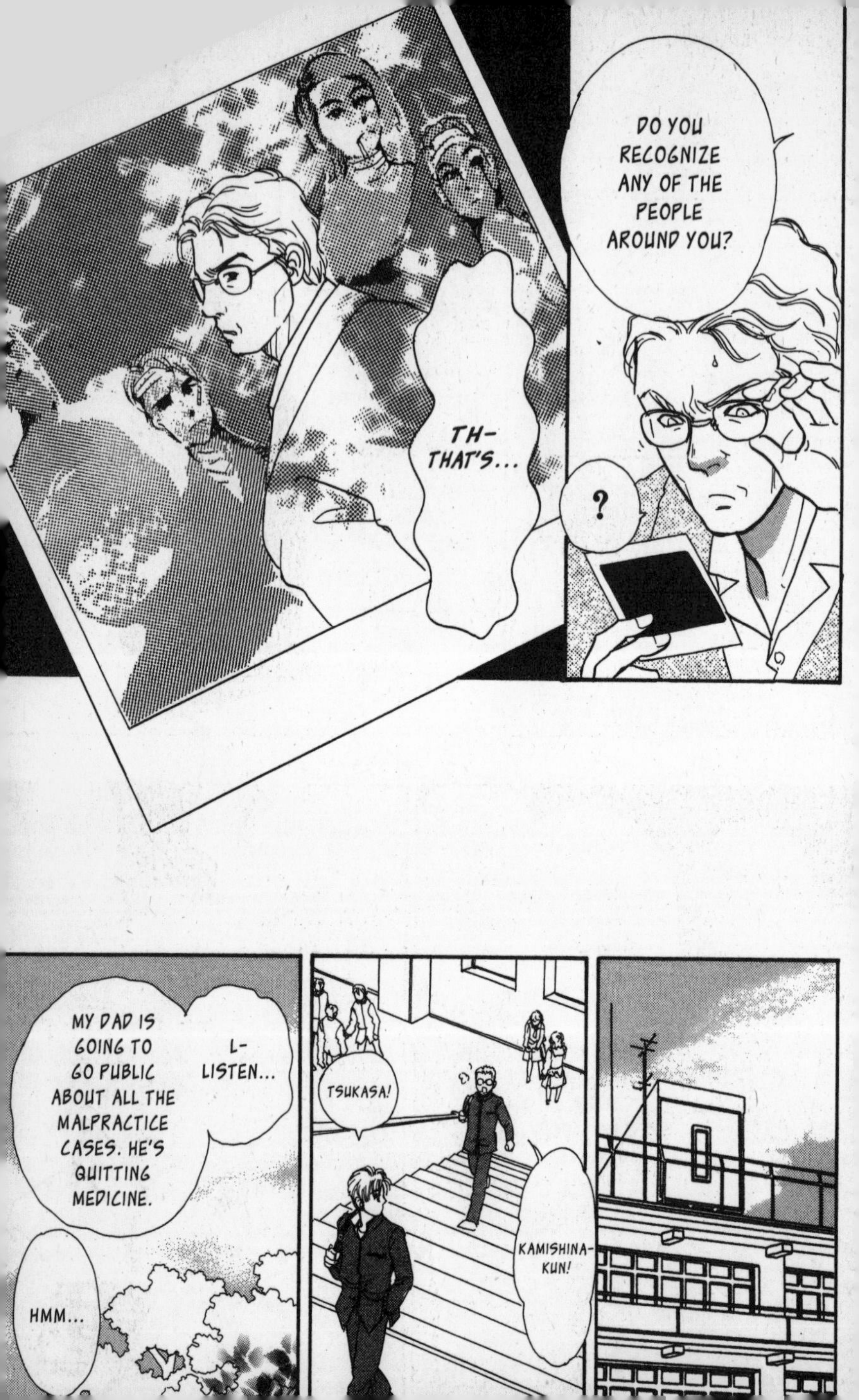
DO YOU RECOGNIZE ANY OF THE PEOPLE AROUND YOU?
?
TH-THAT'S...
KAMISHINA-KUN!
TSUKASA!
L-LISTEN...
MY DAD IS GOING TO GO PUBLIC ABOUT ALL THE MALPRACTICE CASES. HE'S QUITTING MEDICINE.
HMM...

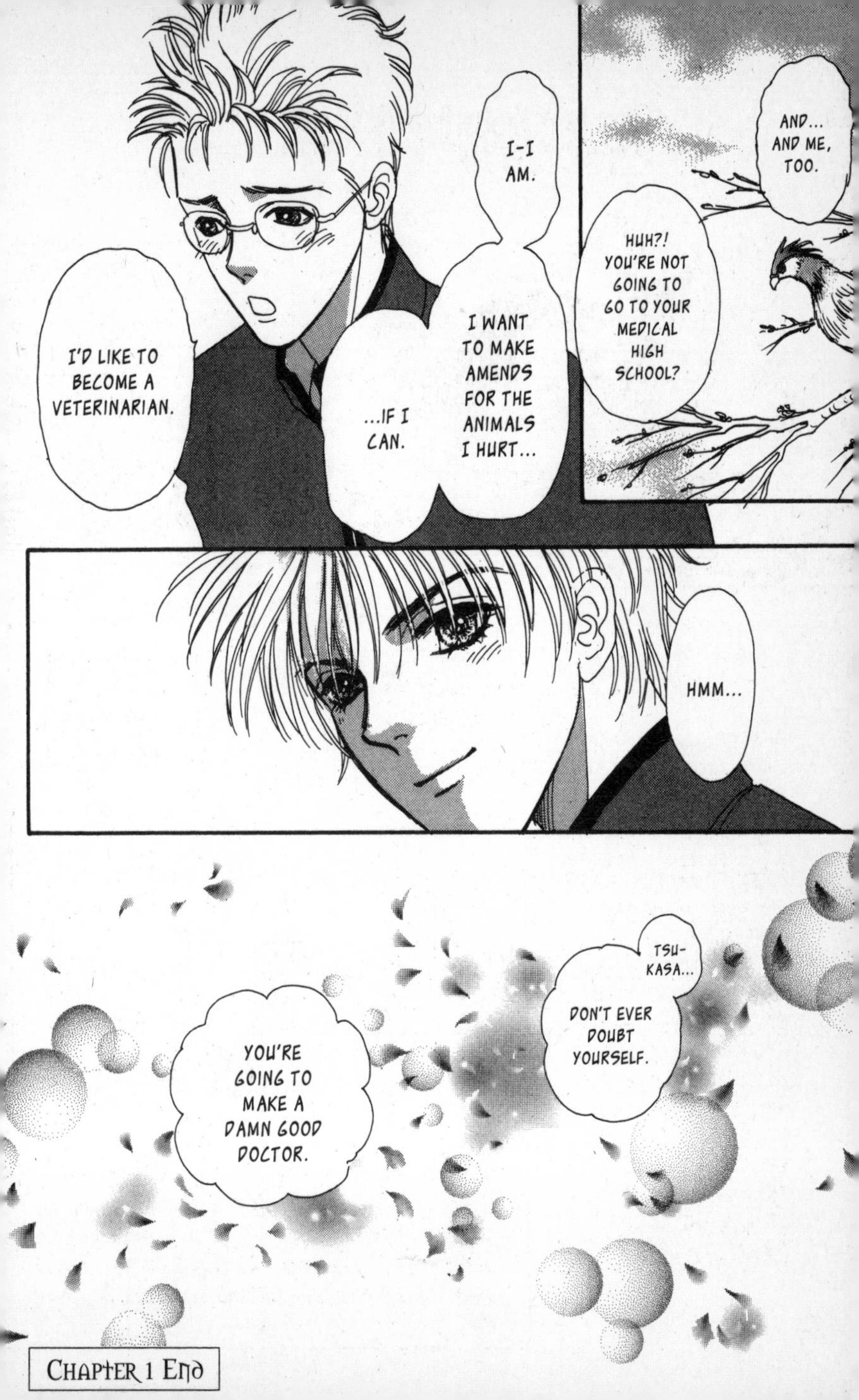
AND... AND ME, TOO.
HUH?! YOU'RE NOT GOING TO GO TO YOUR MEDICAL HIGH SCHOOL?
I-I AM.
I WANT TO MAKE AMENDS FOR THE ANIMALS I HURT...
...IF I CAN.
I'D LIKE TO BECOME A VETERINARIAN.
HMM...
TSU-KASA...
DON'T EVER DOUBT YOURSELF.
YOU'RE GOING TO MAKE A DAMN GOOD DOCTOR.
CHAPTER 1 END

THE GENJU FILES #2

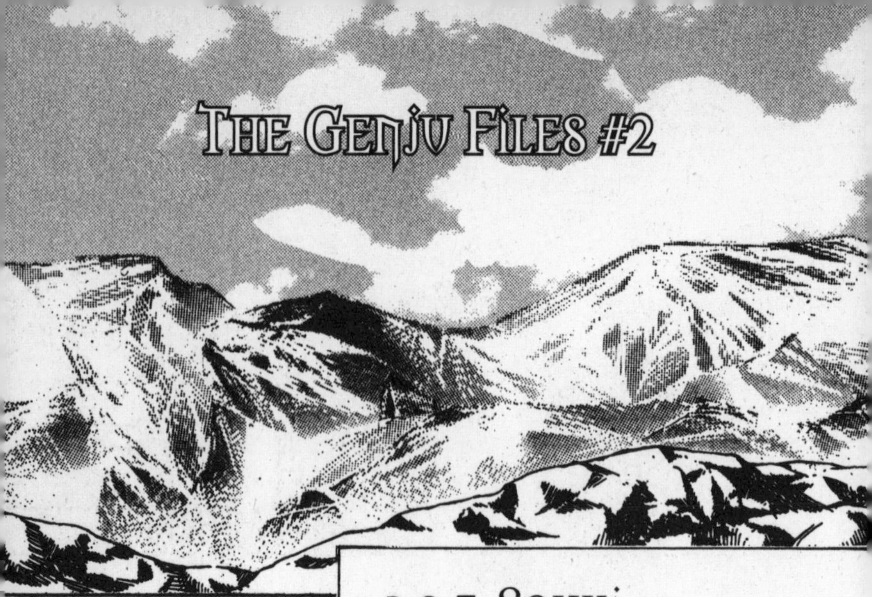

NO.7 SOHKI

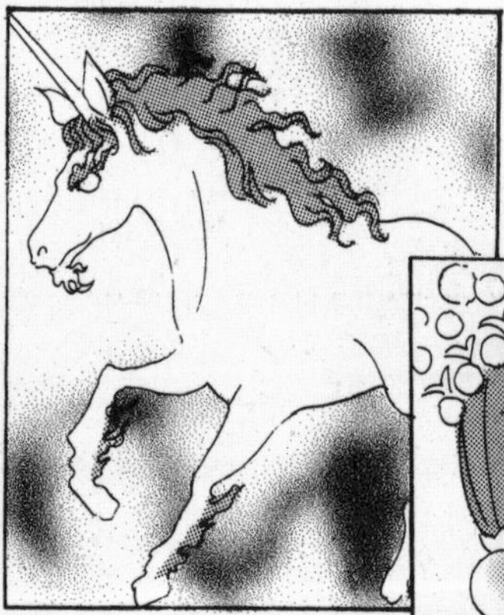

麒

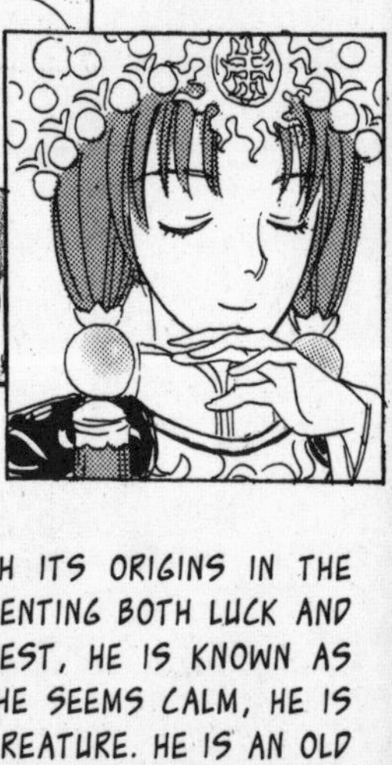

SOHKI (QI LIN) IS THE OLDEST OF THE PRESENT GUARDIAN BEASTS AND HOLDS THE HIGHEST STATURE. WIELDING THE POWER TO KNOW THE TRUE HOLY KING, HE STANDS IN THE MIDDLE OF THE QUARREL BETWEEN NAGA AND GARUDA. ABLE TO TRAVEL SWIFTLY, HE IS TODAY BY THE SEA AND TOMORROW IN THE KUNLUN RANGE. HE NEVER STAYS IN ONE PLACE FOR ERY LONG. HE LACKS RONG EYESIGHT, HAS THE ABILITY EAD THOUGHTS.

A MAGICAL BEAST WITH ITS ORIGINS IN THE BEIJING OPERA, REPRESENTING BOTH LUCK AND MISFORTUNE. IN THE WEST, HE IS KNOWN AS THE UNICORN. THOUGH HE SEEMS CALM, HE IS A CUNNING, SCHEMING CREATURE. HE IS AN OLD MAN, AFTER ALL. (ACCORDING TO GENRO.)

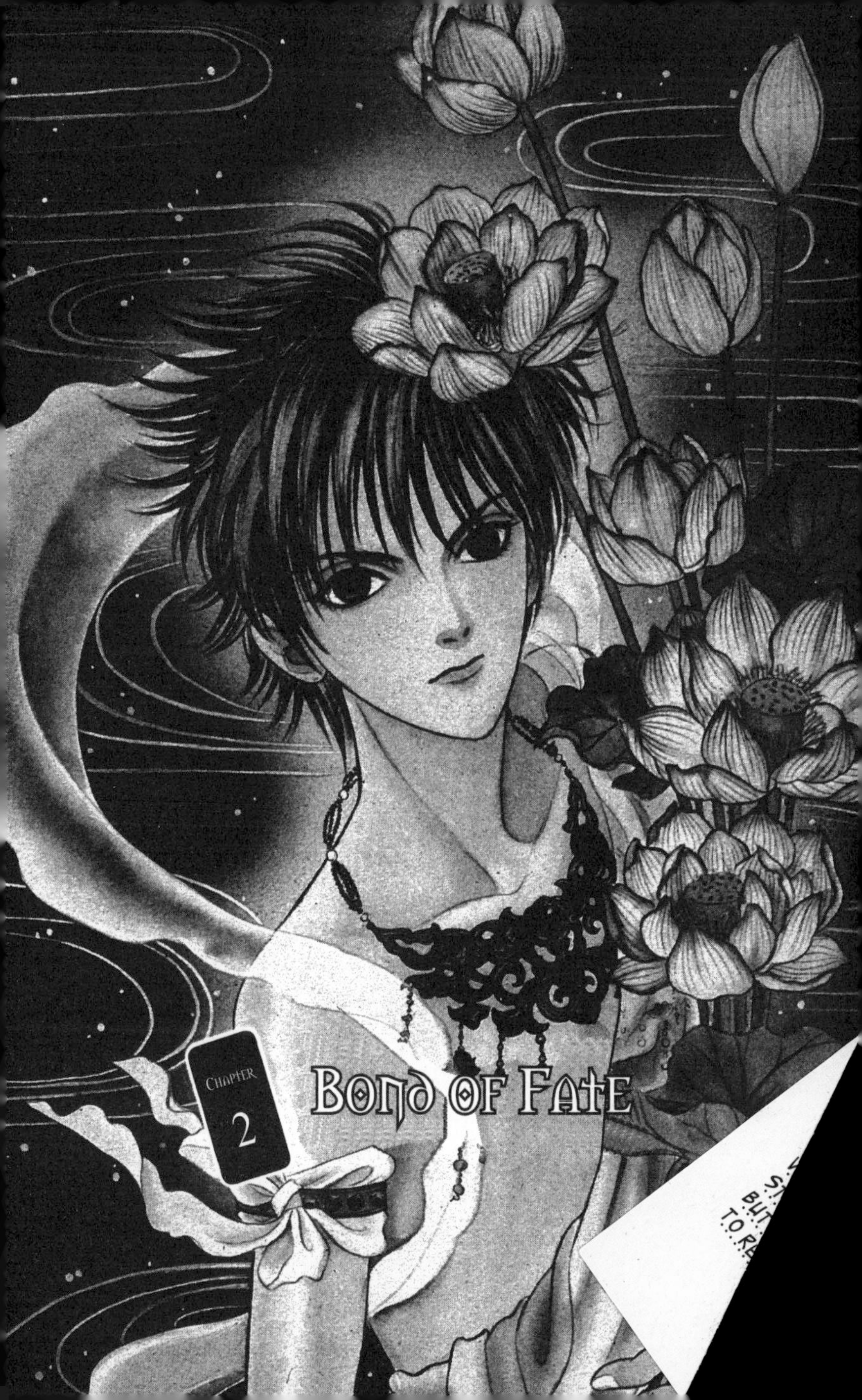
Chapter
2
Bond of Fate

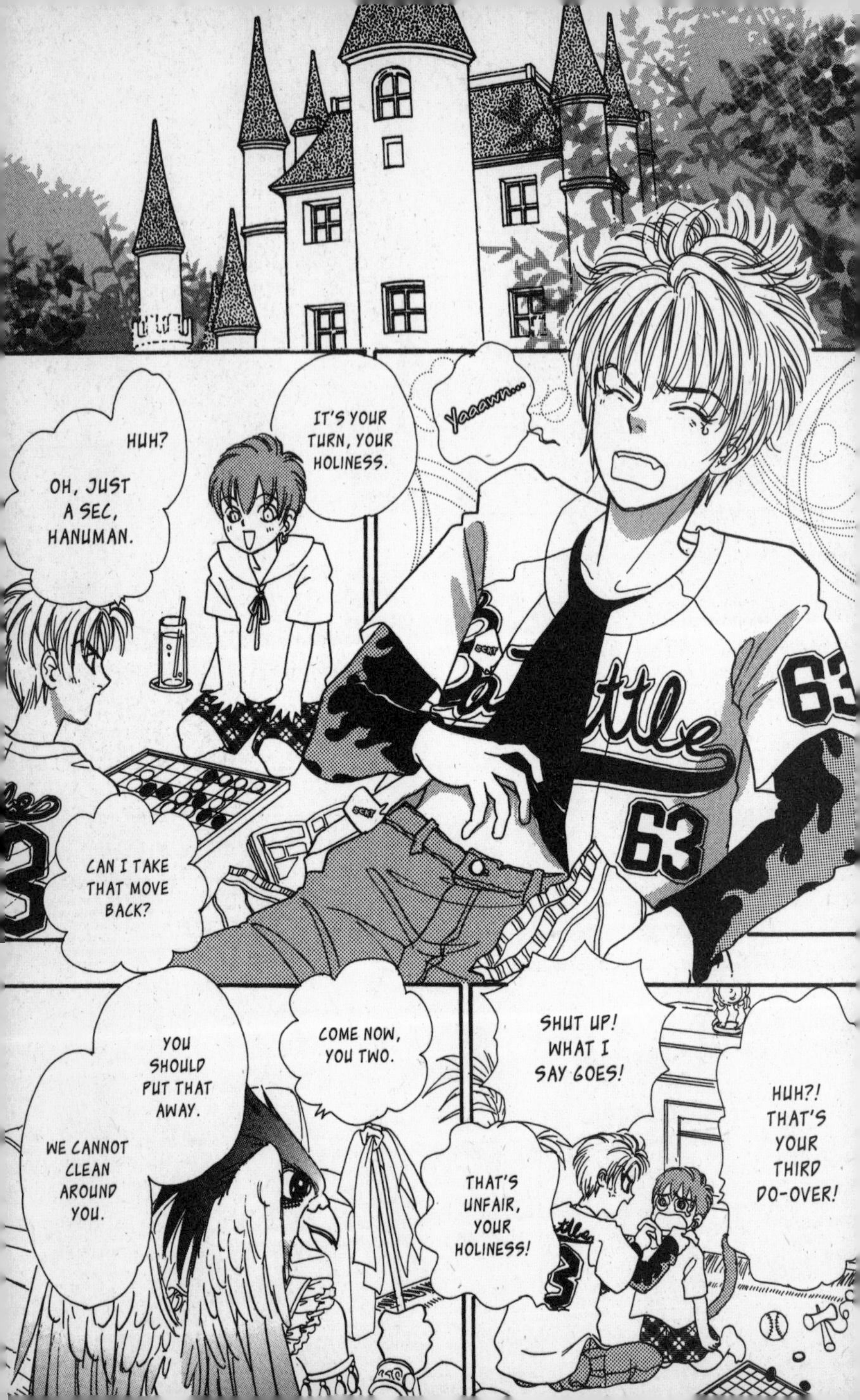
Yaaawn...
IT'S YOUR TURN, YOUR HOLINESS.
HUH?
OH, JUST A SEC, HANUMAN.
CAN I TAKE THAT MOVE BACK?
HUH?! THAT'S YOUR THIRD DO-OVER!
SHUT UP! WHAT I SAY GOES!
THAT'S UNFAIR, YOUR HOLINESS!
COME NOW, YOU TWO.
YOU SHOULD PUT THAT AWAY.
WE CANNOT CLEAN AROUND YOU.

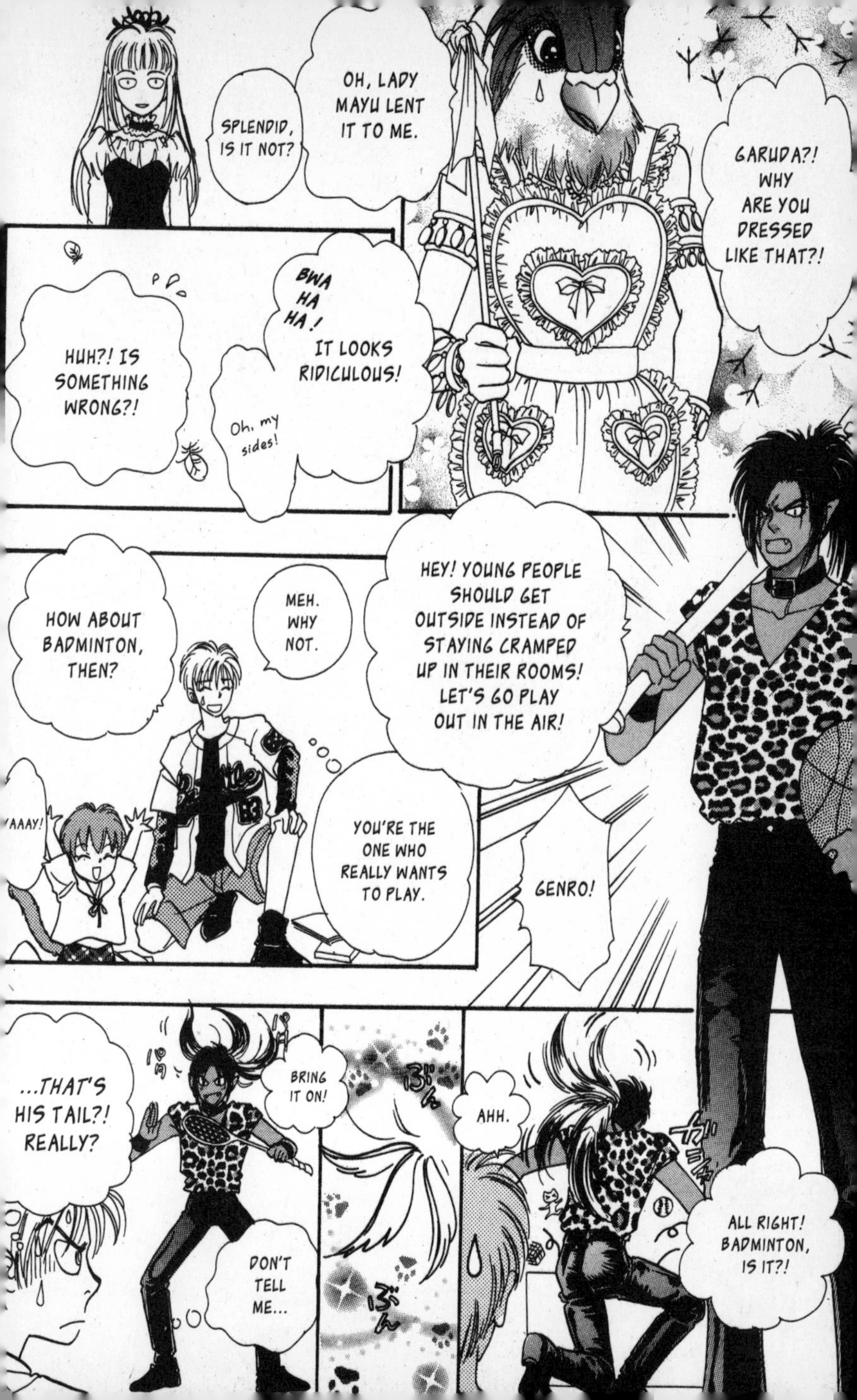
GARUDA?! WHY ARE YOU DRESSED LIKE THAT?!
OH, LADY MAYU LENT IT TO ME.
SPLENDID, IS IT NOT?
BWA HA HA! IT LOOKS RIDICULOUS!
Oh, my sides!
HUH?! IS SOMETHING WRONG?!
HEY! YOUNG PEOPLE SHOULD GET OUTSIDE INSTEAD OF STAYING CRAMPED UP IN THEIR ROOMS! LET'S GO PLAY OUT IN THE AIR!
GENRO!
MEH. WHY NOT.
HOW ABOUT BADMINTON, THEN?
YOU'RE THE ONE WHO REALLY WANTS TO PLAY.
AAAY!
ALL RIGHT! BADMINTON, IS IT?!
AHH.
ぶん
ぶん
BRING IT ON!
...THAT'S HIS TAIL?! REALLY?
DON'T TELL ME...

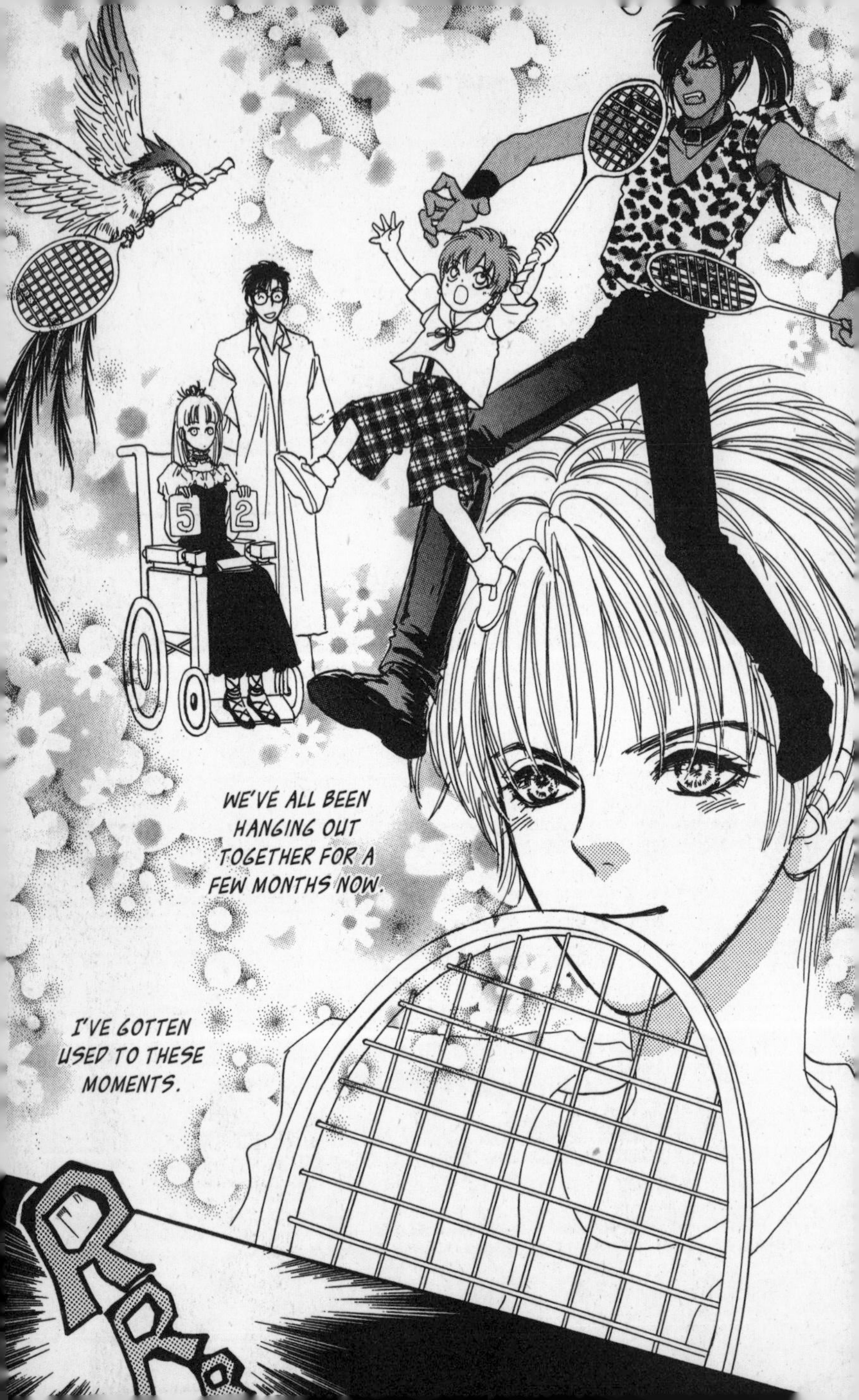

5
2
WE'VE ALL BEEN HANGING OUT TOGETHER FOR A FEW MONTHS NOW.
I'VE GOTTEN USED TO THESE MOMENTS.

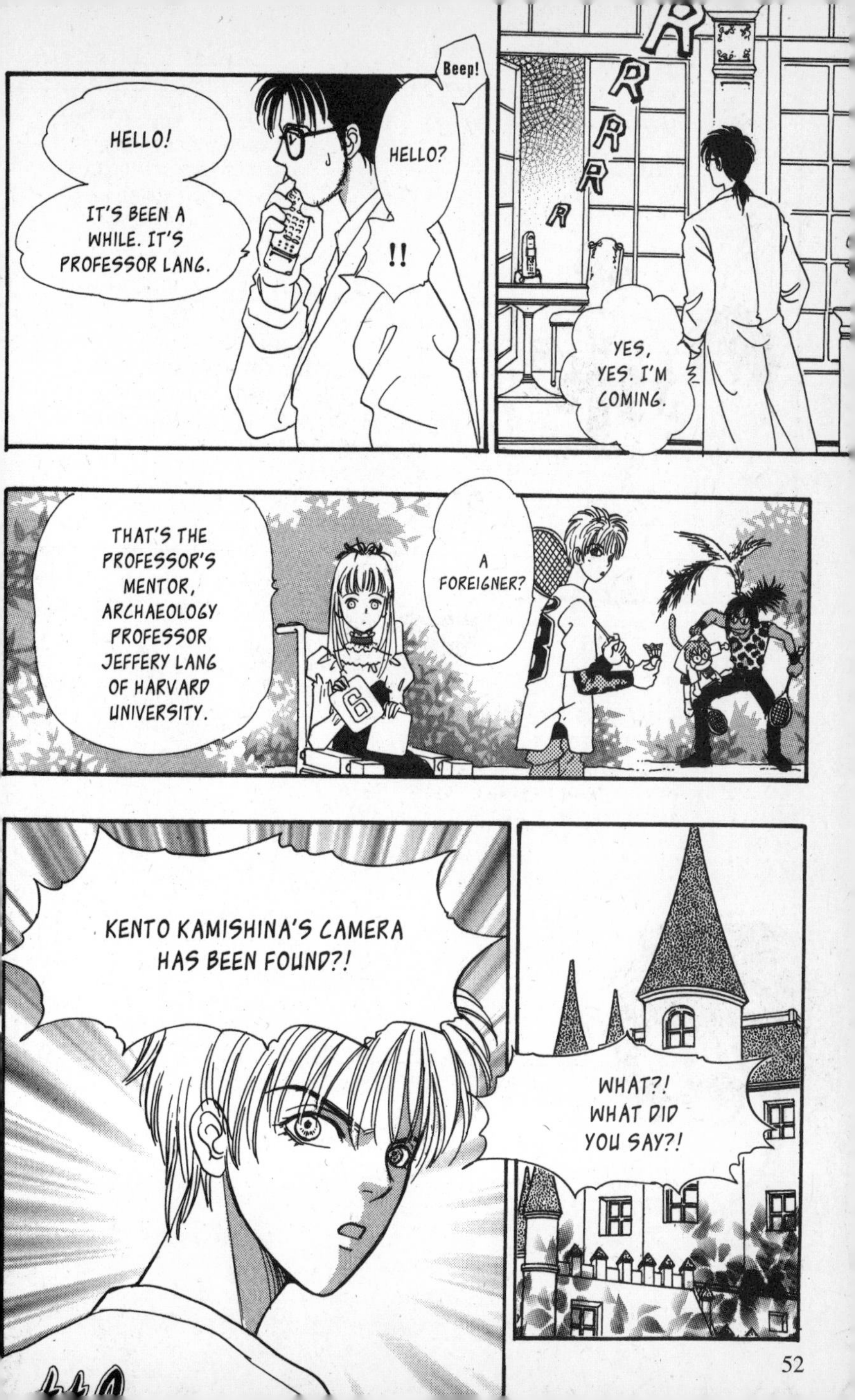

R R R R R
YES, YES. I'M COMING.
Beep!
HELLO?
HELLO!
IT'S BEEN A WHILE. IT'S PROFESSOR LANG.
!!
A FOREIGNER?
THAT'S THE PROFESSOR'S MENTOR, ARCHAEOLOGY PROFESSOR JEFFERY LANG OF HARVARD UNIVERSITY.
WHAT?! WHAT DID YOU SAY?!
KENTO KAMISHINA'S CAMERA HAS BEEN FOUND?!

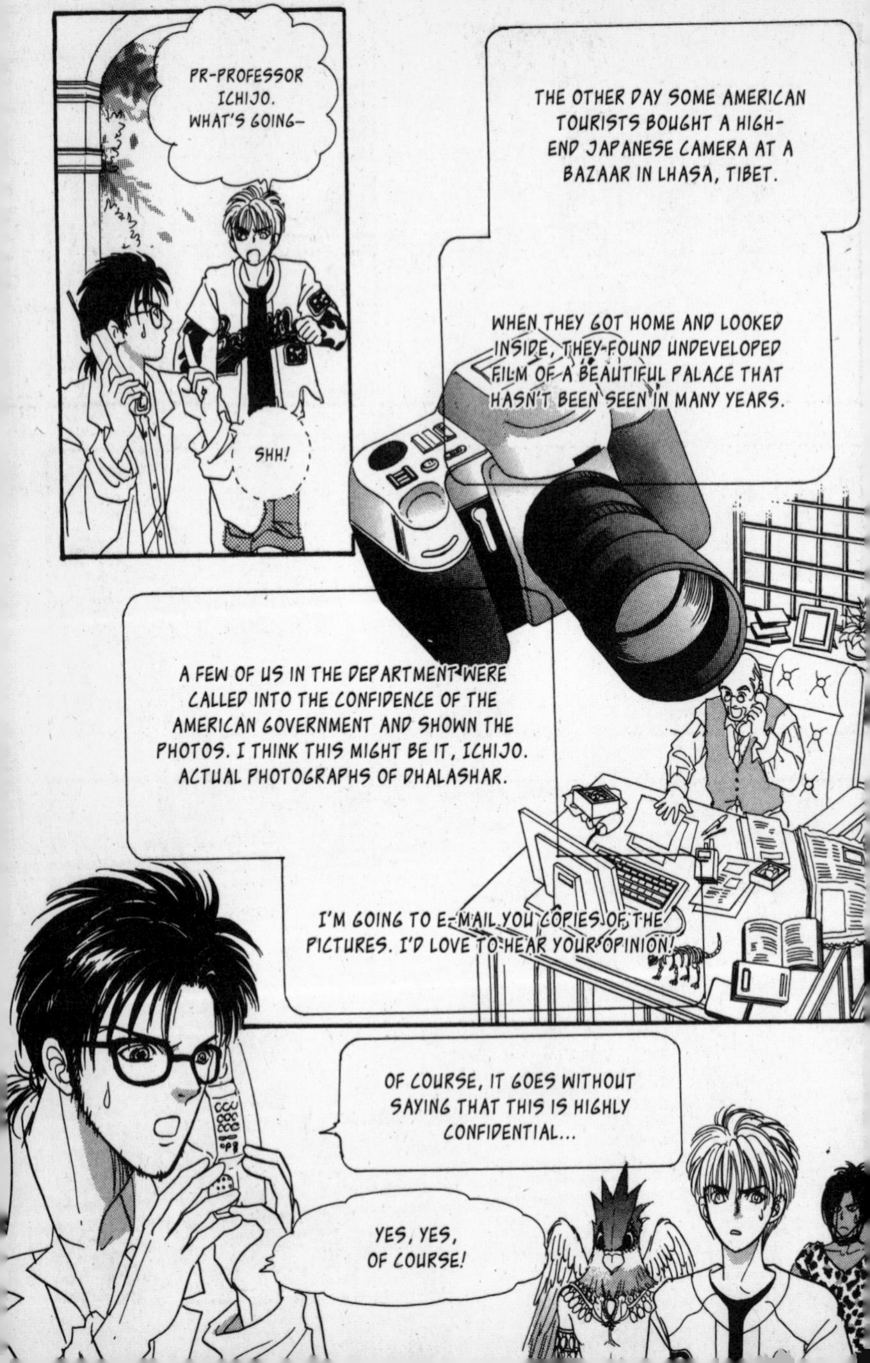
PR-PROFESSOR ICHIJO. WHAT'S GOING–
SHH!
THE OTHER DAY SOME AMERICAN TOURISTS BOUGHT A HIGH-END JAPANESE CAMERA AT A BAZAAR IN LHASA, TIBET.
WHEN THEY GOT HOME AND LOOKED INSIDE, THEY FOUND UNDEVELOPED FILM OF A BEAUTIFUL PALACE THAT HASN'T BEEN SEEN IN MANY YEARS.
A FEW OF US IN THE DEPARTMENT WERE CALLED INTO THE CONFIDENCE OF THE AMERICAN GOVERNMENT AND SHOWN THE PHOTOS. I THINK THIS MIGHT BE IT, ICHIJO. ACTUAL PHOTOGRAPHS OF DHALASHAR.
I'M GOING TO E-MAIL YOU COPIES OF THE PICTURES. I'D LOVE TO HEAR YOUR OPINION!
OF COURSE, IT GOES WITHOUT SAYING THAT THIS IS HIGHLY CONFIDENTIAL...
YES, YES, OF COURSE!

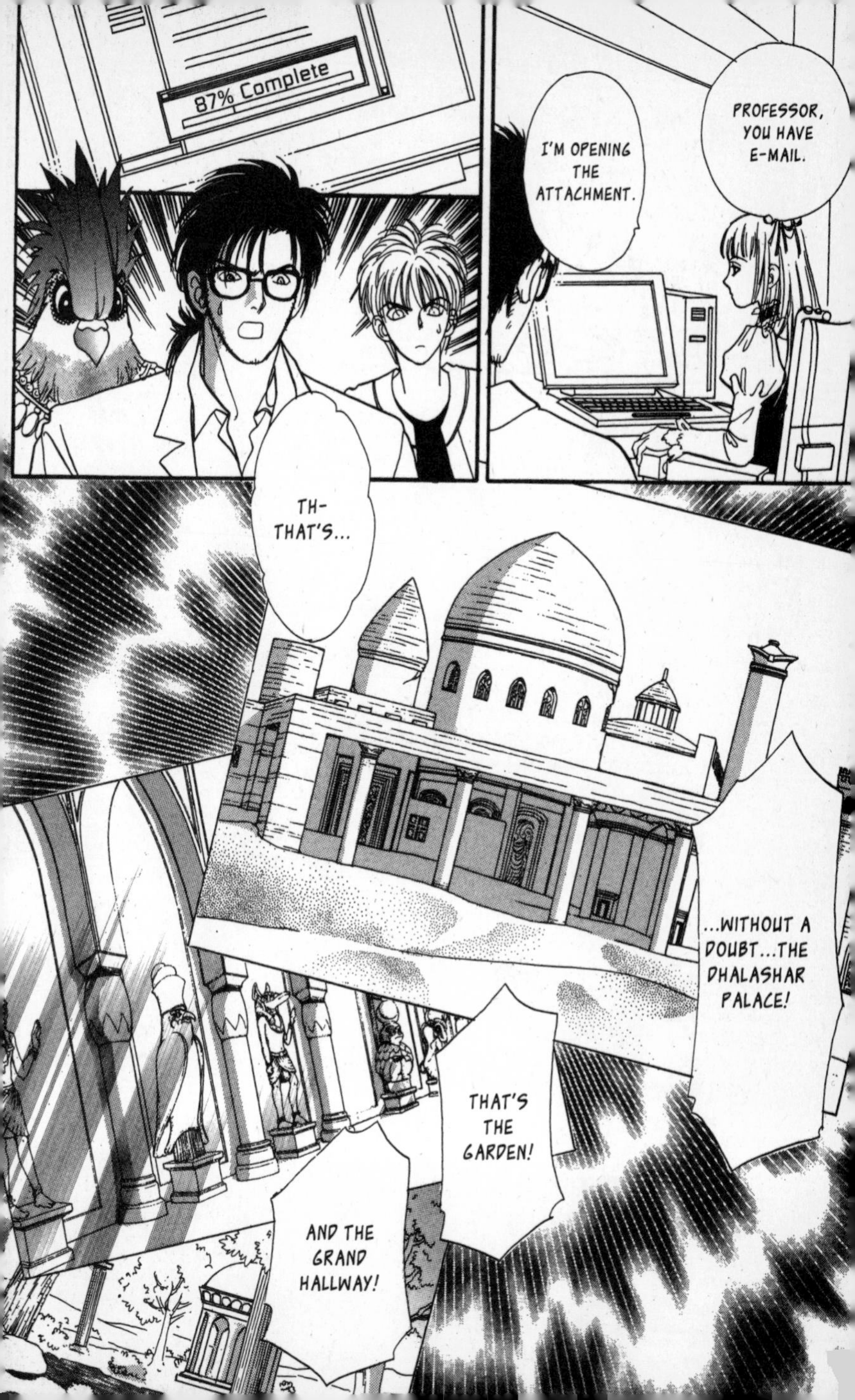
PROFESSOR, YOU HAVE E-MAIL.
I'M OPENING THE ATTACHMENT.
87% Complete
TH-THAT'S...
...WITHOUT A DOUBT...THE DHALASHAR PALACE!
THAT'S THE GARDEN!
AND THE GRAND HALLWAY!

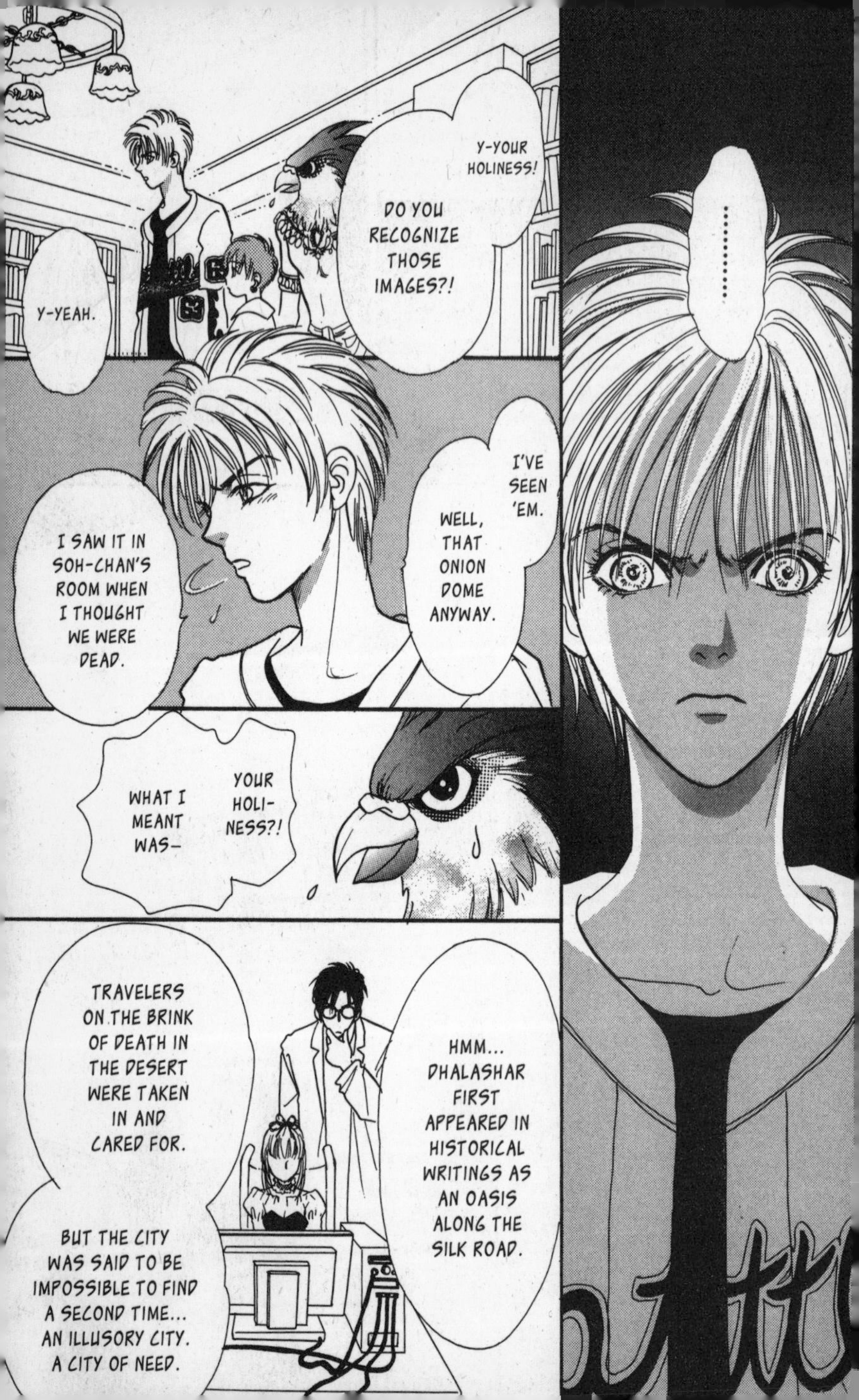

Y-YOUR HOLINESS!
DO YOU RECOGNIZE THOSE IMAGES?!
.....
Y-YEAH.
I'VE SEEN 'EM.
WELL, THAT ONION DOME ANYWAY.
I SAW IT IN SOH-CHAN'S ROOM WHEN I THOUGHT WE WERE DEAD.
YOUR HOLI-NESS?!
WHAT I MEANT WAS–
HMM... DHALASHAR FIRST APPEARED IN HISTORICAL WRITINGS AS AN OASIS ALONG THE SILK ROAD.
TRAVELERS ON THE BRINK OF DEATH IN THE DESERT WERE TAKEN IN AND CARED FOR.
BUT THE CITY WAS SAID TO BE IMPOSSIBLE TO FIND A SECOND TIME... AN ILLUSORY CITY. A CITY OF NEED.

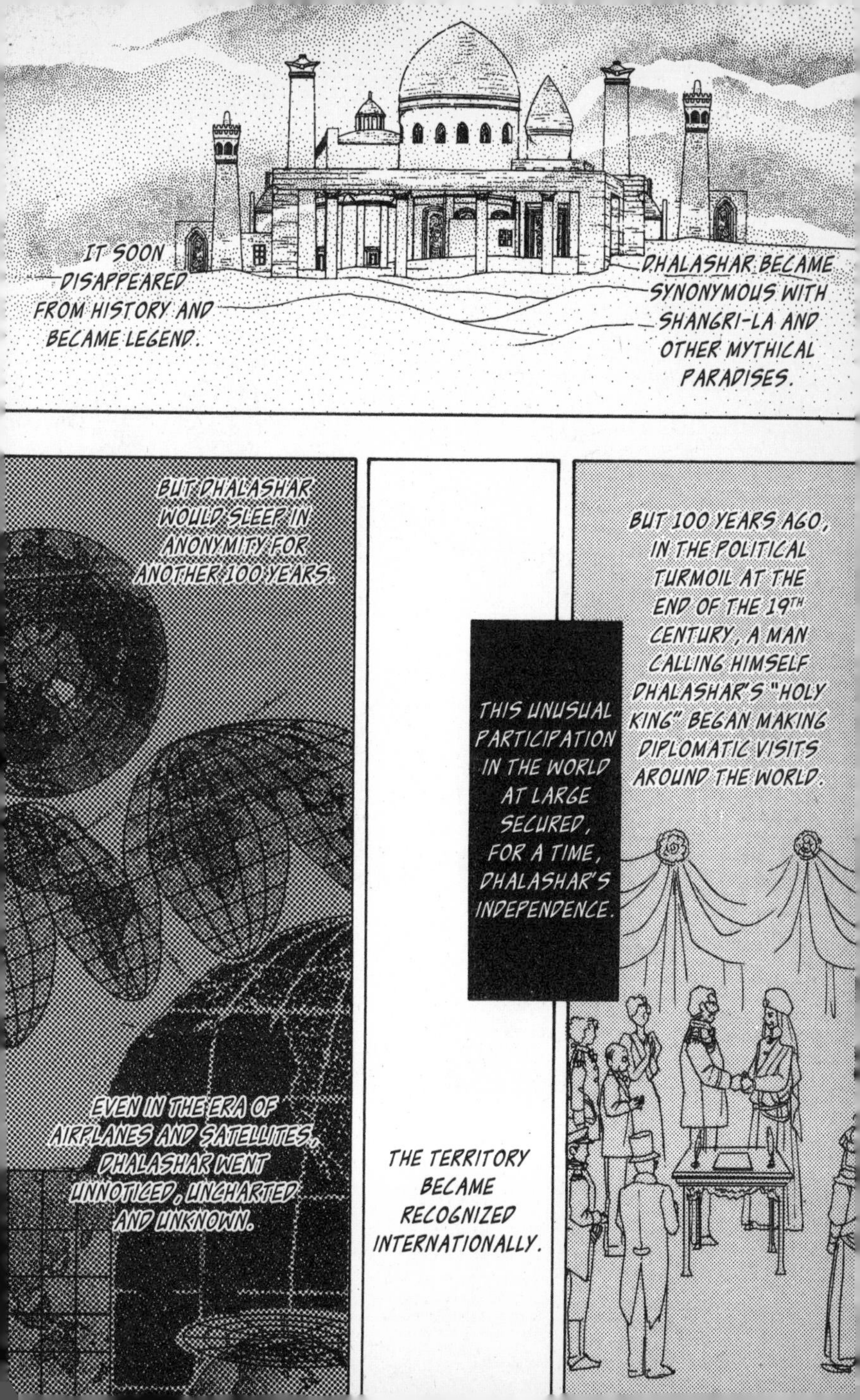
IT SOON DISAPPEARED FROM HISTORY AND BECAME LEGEND.
DHALASHAR BECAME SYNONYMOUS WITH SHANGRI-LA AND OTHER MYTHICAL PARADISES.
BUT DHALASHAR WOULD SLEEP IN ANONYMITY FOR ANOTHER 100 YEARS.
EVEN IN THE ERA OF AIRPLANES AND SATELLITES, DHALASHAR WENT UNNOTICED, UNCHARTED AND UNKNOWN.
BUT 100 YEARS AGO, IN THE POLITICAL TURMOIL AT THE END OF THE 19TH CENTURY, A MAN CALLING HIMSELF DHALASHAR'S "HOLY KING" BEGAN MAKING DIPLOMATIC VISITS AROUND THE WORLD.
THIS UNUSUAL PARTICIPATION IN THE WORLD AT LARGE SECURED, FOR A TIME, DHALASHAR'S INDEPENDENCE.
THE TERRITORY BECAME RECOGNIZED INTERNATIONALLY.

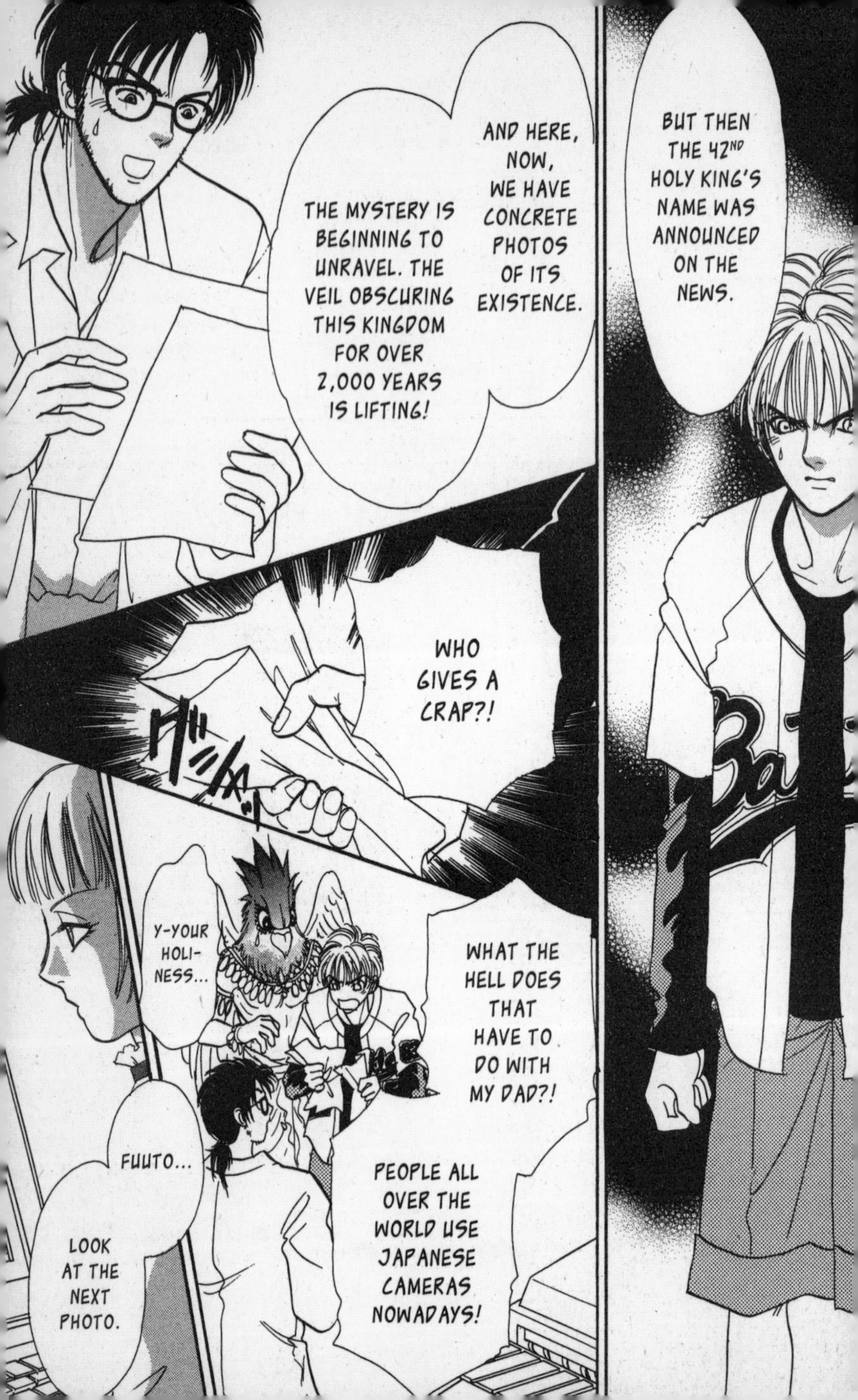
BUT THEN THE 42ND HOLY KING'S NAME WAS ANNOUNCED ON THE NEWS.
AND HERE, NOW, WE HAVE CONCRETE PHOTOS OF ITS EXISTENCE.
THE MYSTERY IS BEGINNING TO UNRAVEL. THE VEIL OBSCURING THIS KINGDOM FOR OVER 2,000 YEARS IS LIFTING!
WHO GIVES A CRAP?!
WHAT THE HELL DOES THAT HAVE TO DO WITH MY DAD?!
Y-YOUR HOLINESS...
PEOPLE ALL OVER THE WORLD USE JAPANESE CAMERAS NOWADAYS!
FUUTO...
LOOK AT THE NEXT PHOTO.

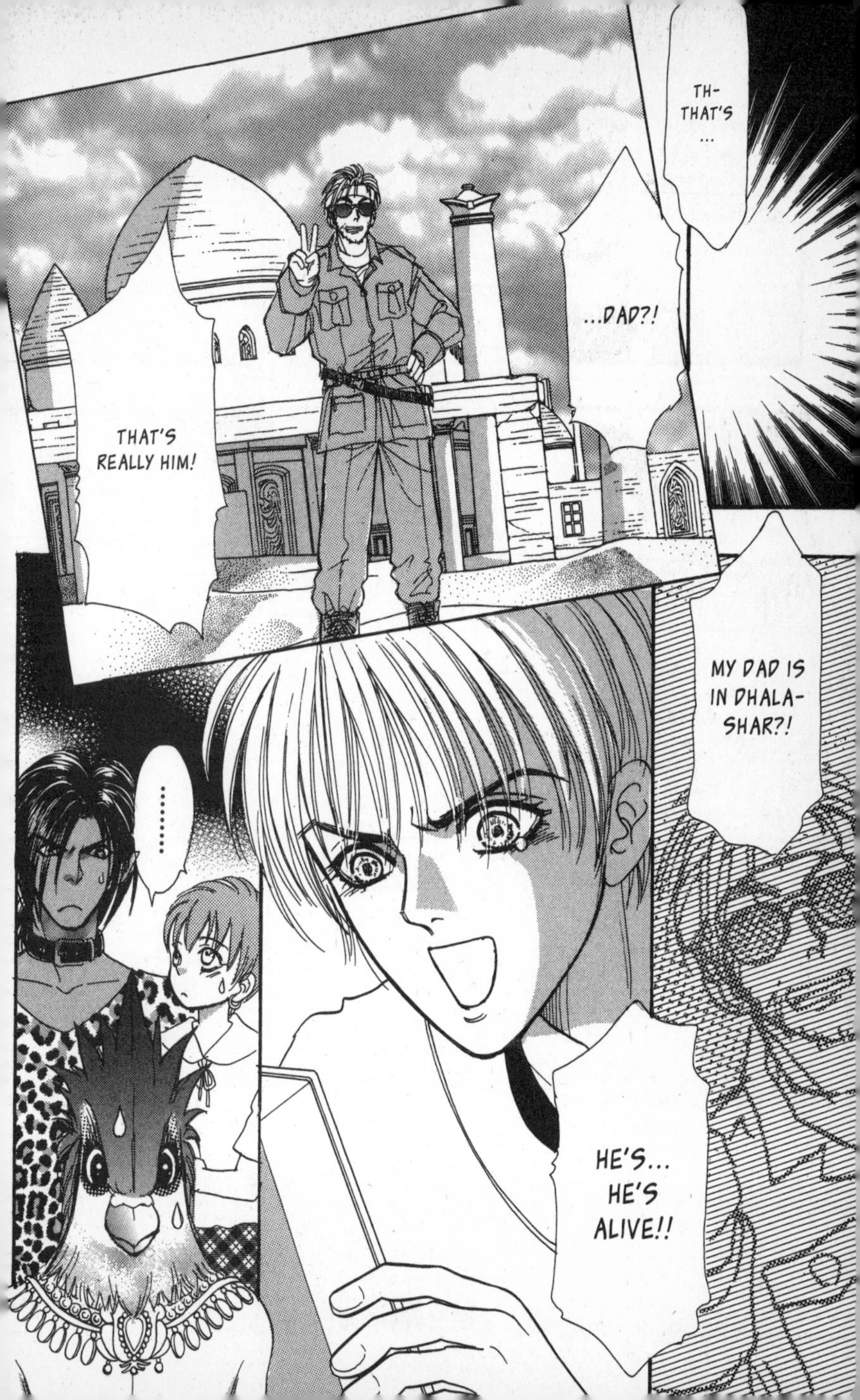
TH- THAT'S ...
...DAD?!
THAT'S REALLY HIM!
MY DAD IS IN DHALA-SHAR?!
......
HE'S... HE'S ALIVE!!

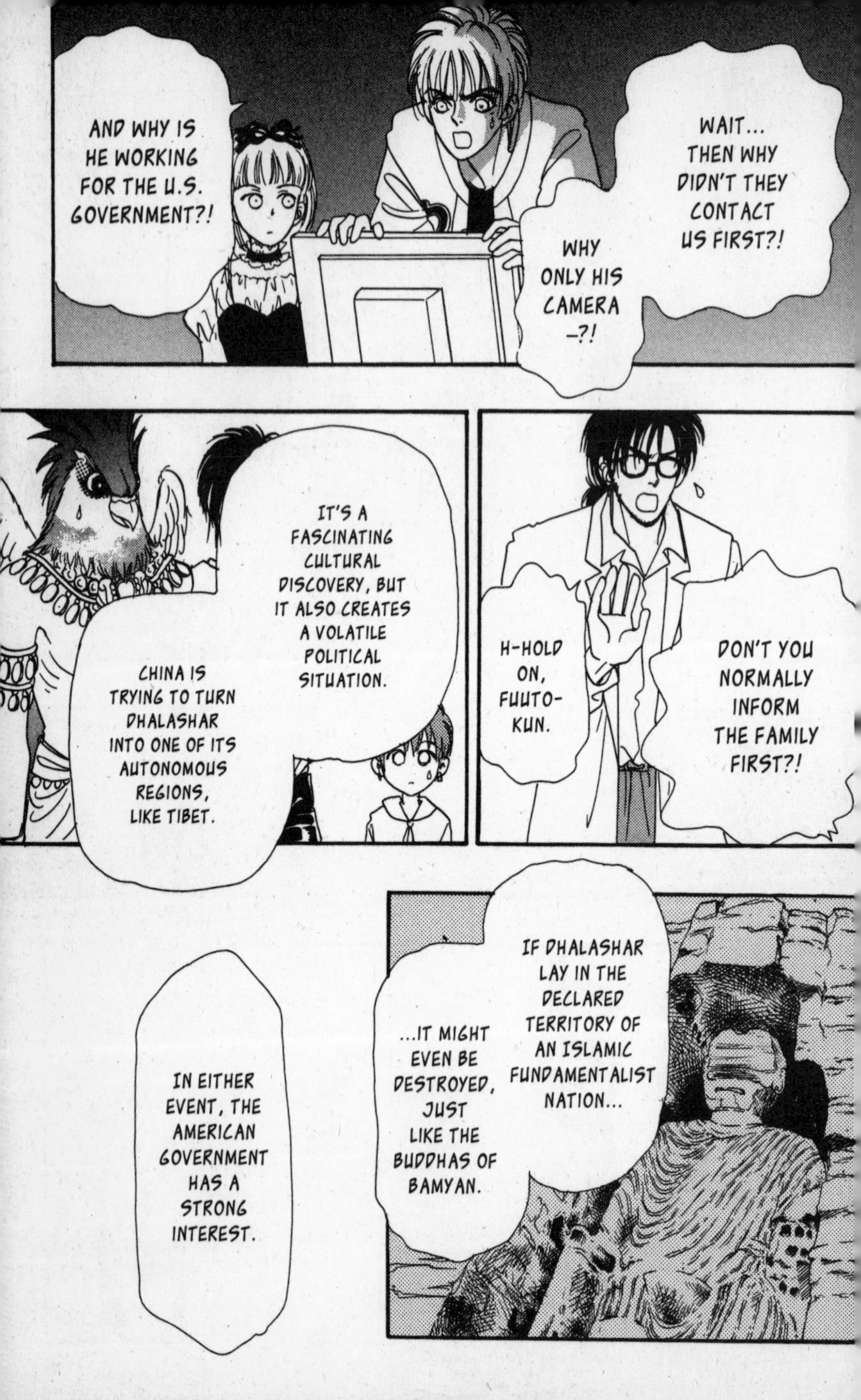
WAIT... THEN WHY DIDN'T THEY CONTACT US FIRST?!
WHY ONLY HIS CAMERA —?!
AND WHY IS HE WORKING FOR THE U.S. GOVERNMENT?!
DON'T YOU NORMALLY INFORM THE FAMILY FIRST?!
H-HOLD ON, FUUTO-KUN.
IT'S A FASCINATING CULTURAL DISCOVERY, BUT IT ALSO CREATES A VOLATILE POLITICAL SITUATION.
CHINA IS TRYING TO TURN DHALASHAR INTO ONE OF ITS AUTONOMOUS REGIONS, LIKE TIBET.
IF DHALASHAR LAY IN THE DECLARED TERRITORY OF AN ISLAMIC FUNDAMENTALIST NATION...
...IT MIGHT EVEN BE DESTROYED, JUST LIKE THE BUDDHAS OF BAMYAN.
IN EITHER EVENT, THE AMERICAN GOVERNMENT HAS A STRONG INTEREST.

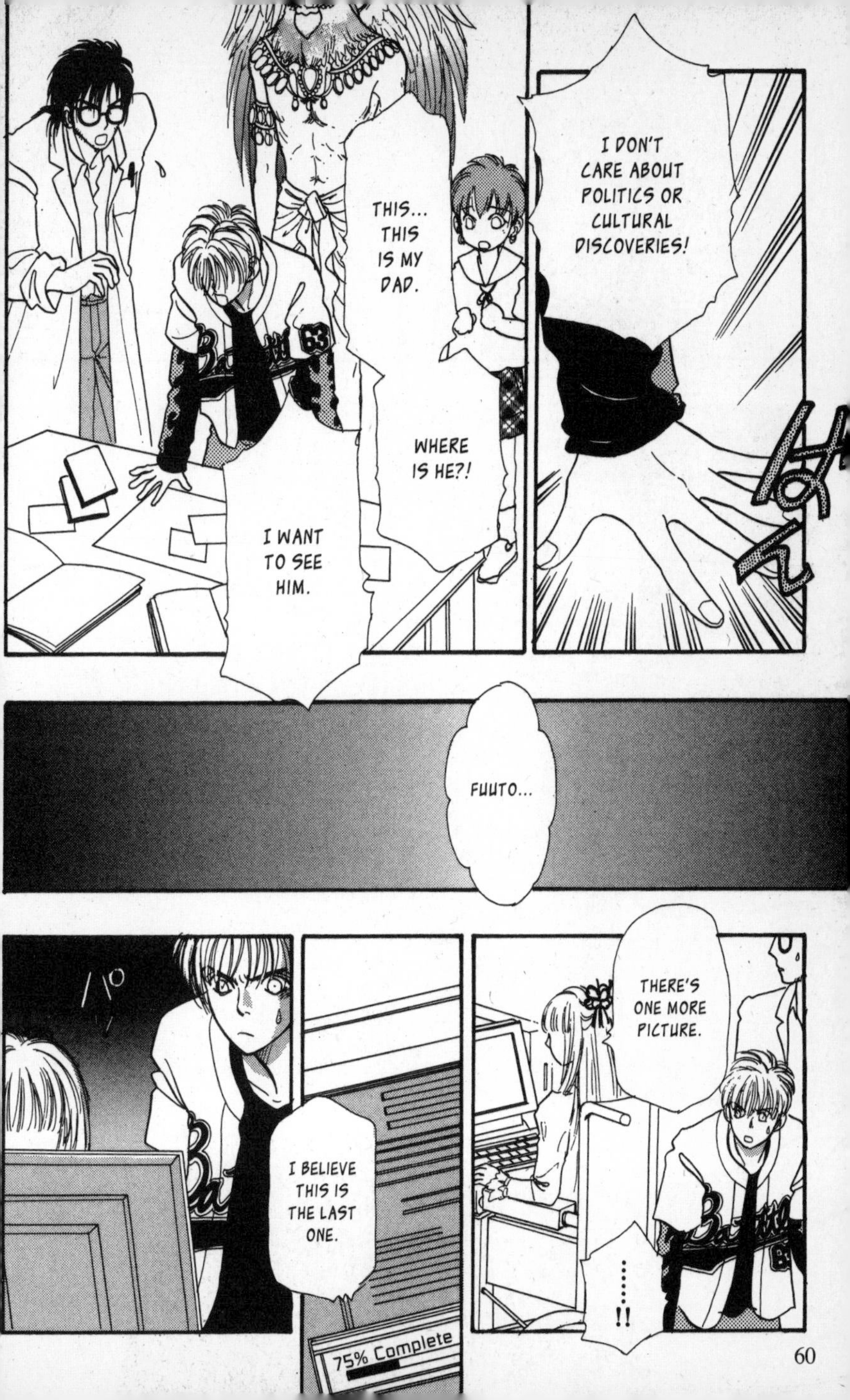
I DON'T CARE ABOUT POLITICS OR CULTURAL DISCOVERIES!
THIS... THIS IS MY DAD.
WHERE IS HE?!
I WANT TO SEE HIM.
FUUTO...
THERE'S ONE MORE PICTURE.
......!!
I BELIEVE THIS IS THE LAST ONE.
75% Complete

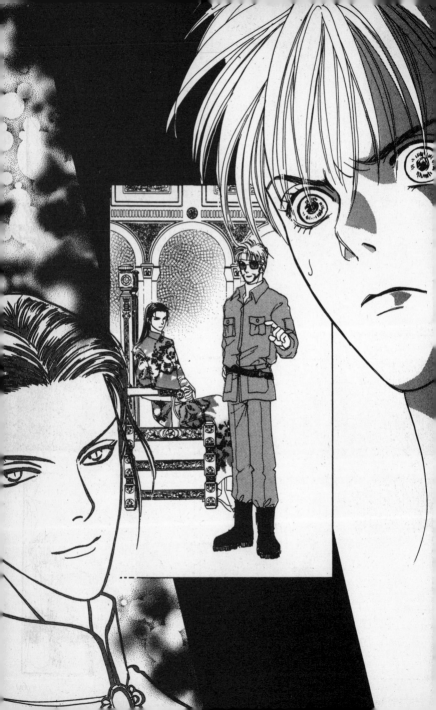

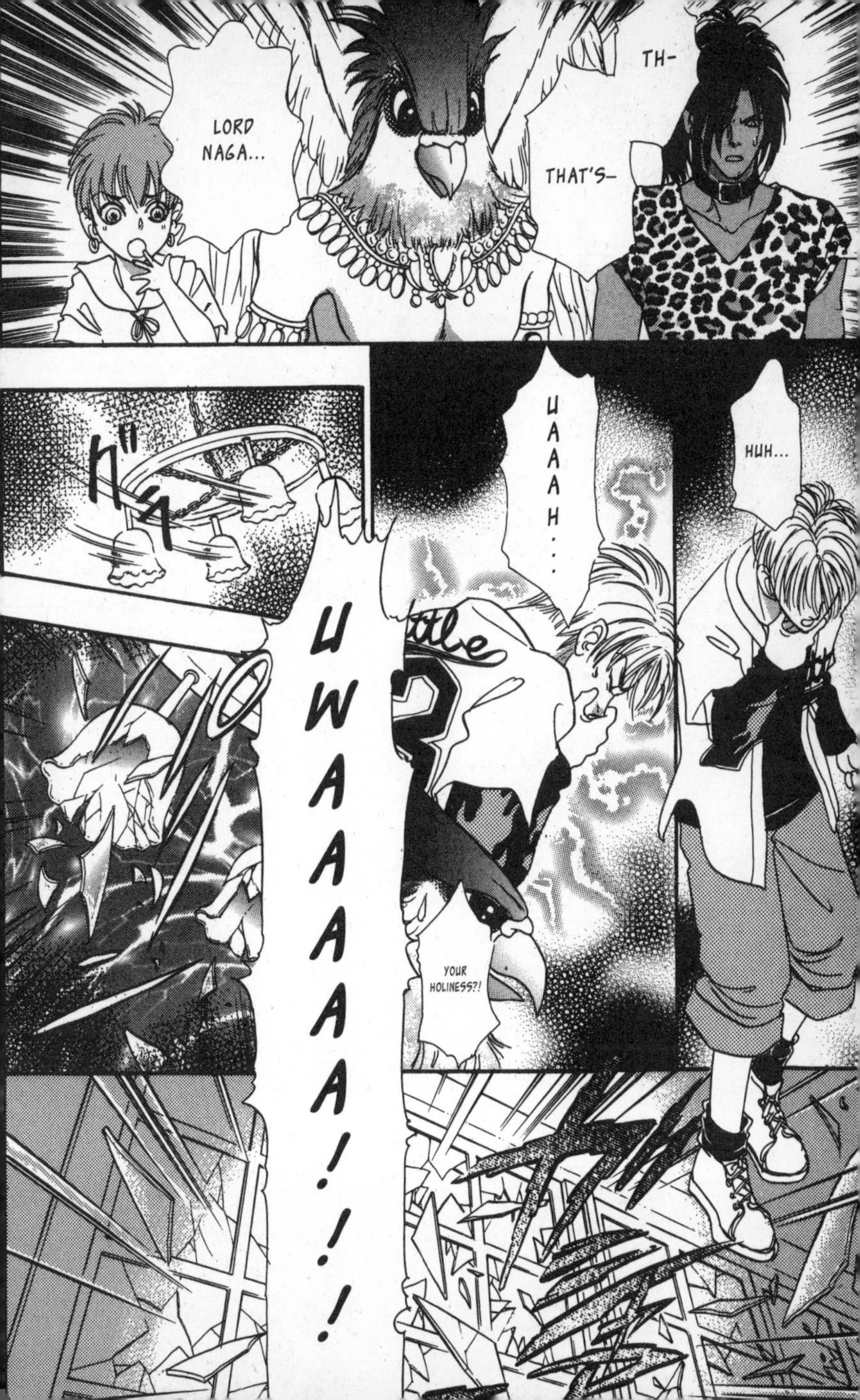
TH-
THAT'S—
LORD NAGA...
HUH...
UAAAAH...
UWAAAAA!!!
YOUR HOLINESS?!

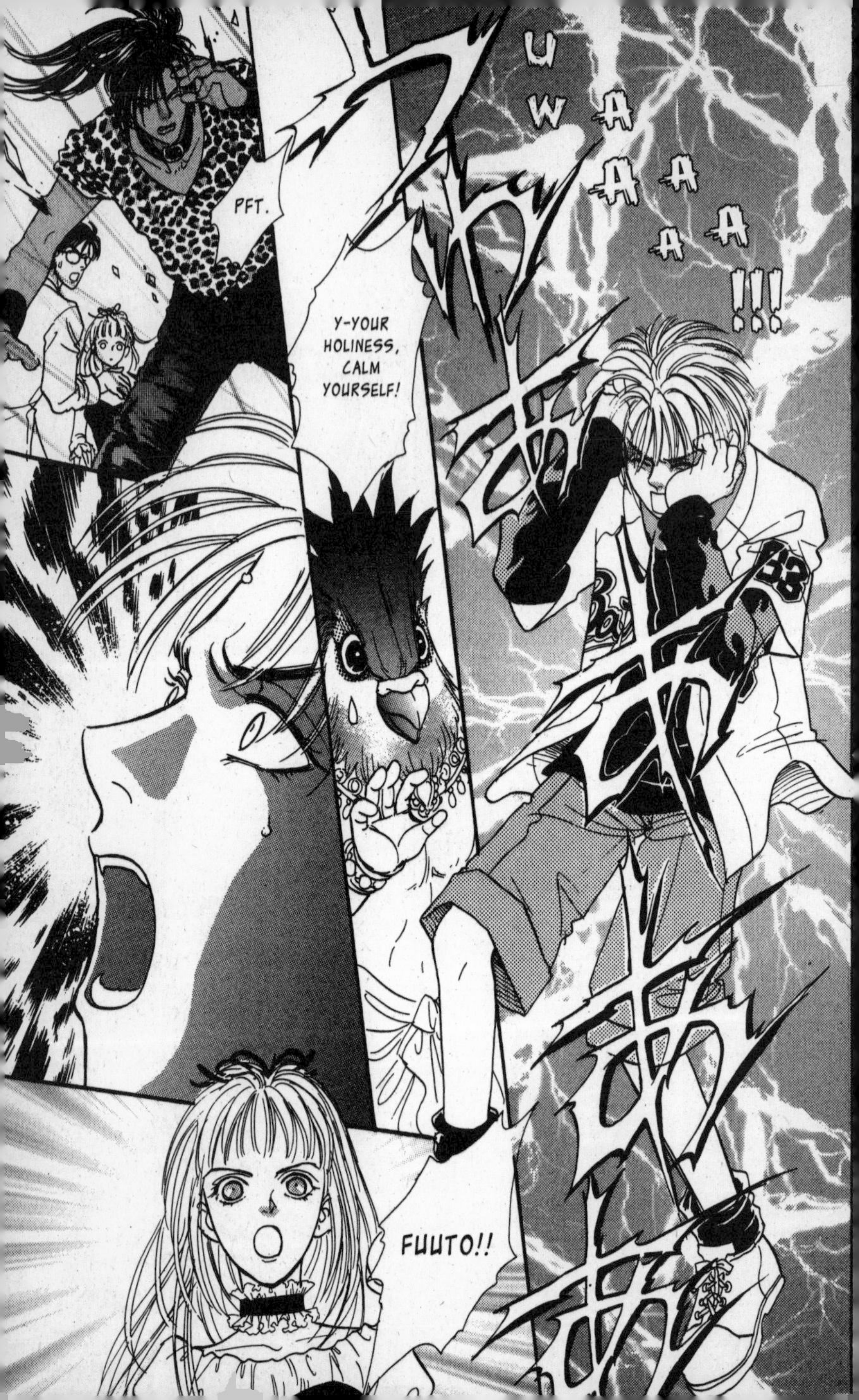
UWAAAAA!!!
Y-YOUR HOLINESS, CALM YOURSELF!
PFT.
FUUTO!!

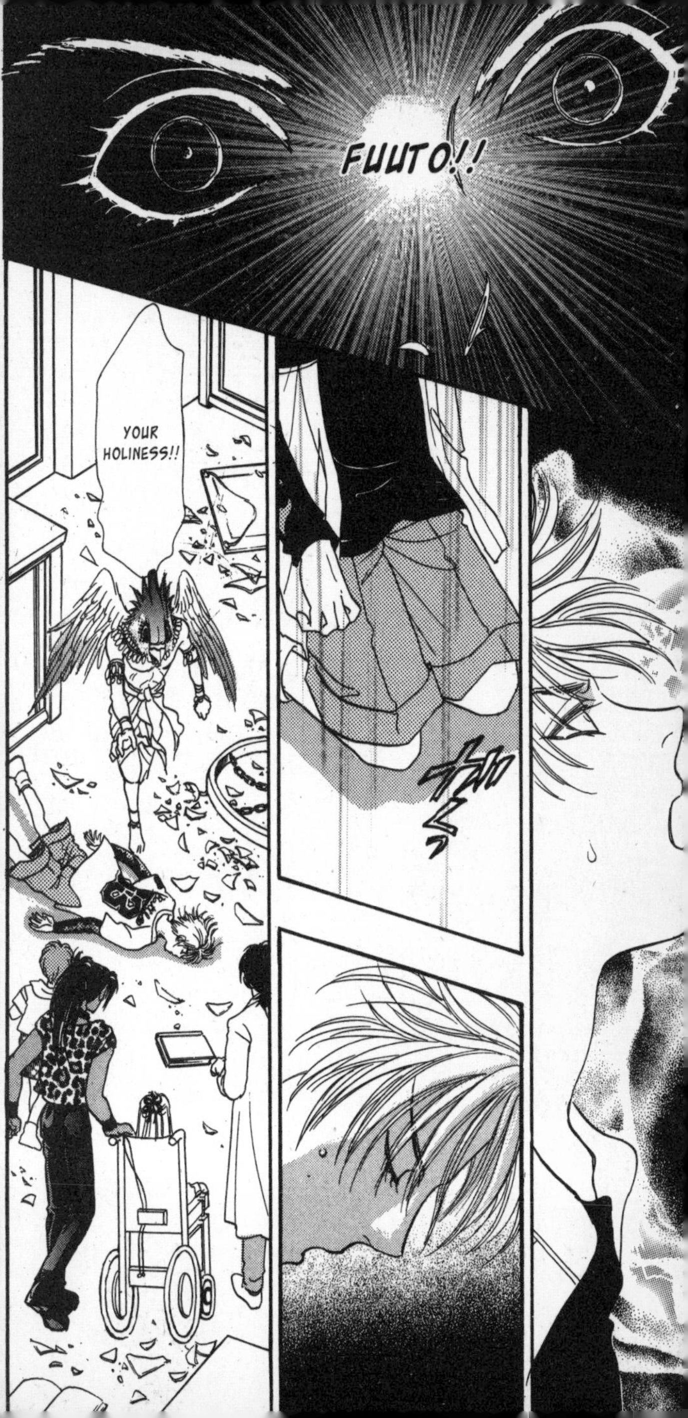
FUUTO!!
YOUR HOLINESS!!

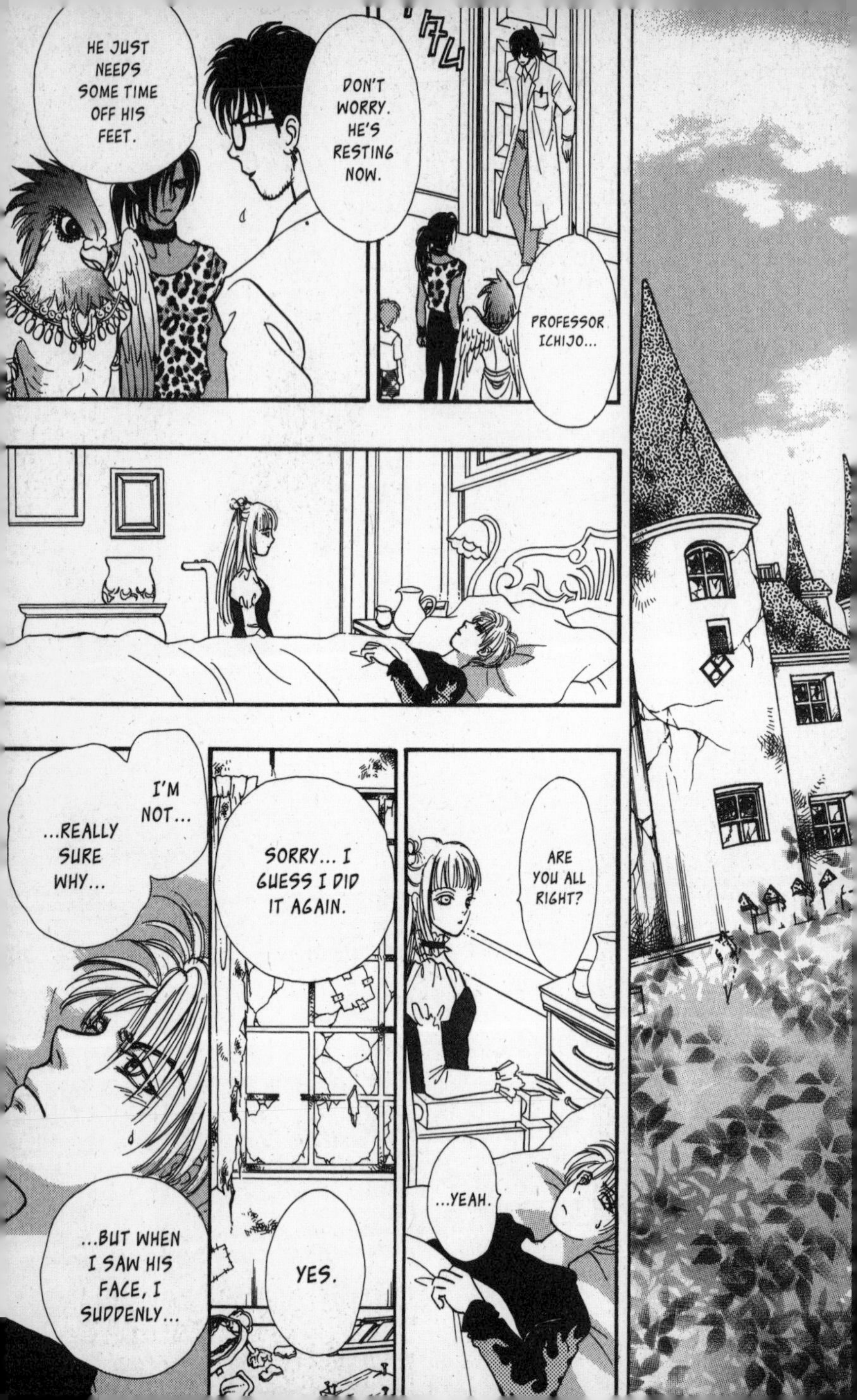
PROFESSOR ICHIJO...
DON'T WORRY. HE'S RESTING NOW.
HE JUST NEEDS SOME TIME OFF HIS FEET.
ARE YOU ALL RIGHT?
...YEAH.
SORRY... I GUESS I DID IT AGAIN.
YES.
I'M NOT...
...REALLY SURE WHY...
...BUT WHEN I SAW HIS FACE, I SUDDENLY...

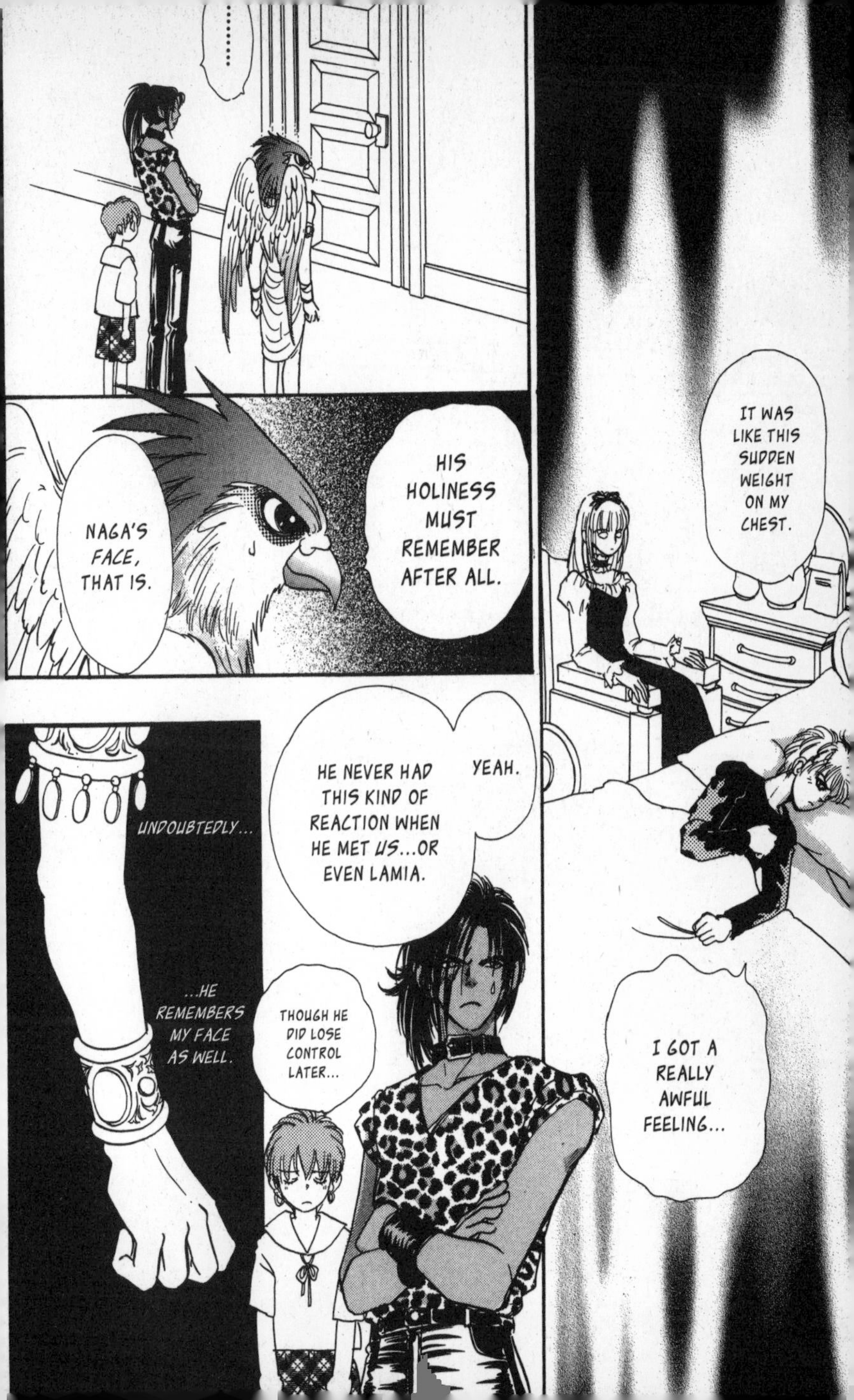
IT WAS LIKE THIS SUDDEN WEIGHT ON MY CHEST.
I GOT A REALLY AWFUL FEELING...
......
HIS HOLINESS MUST REMEMBER AFTER ALL.
NAGA'S FACE, THAT IS.
YEAH.
HE NEVER HAD THIS KIND OF REACTION WHEN HE MET *US*...OR EVEN LAMIA.
THOUGH HE DID LOSE CONTROL LATER...
UNDOUBTEDLY...
...HE REMEMBERS MY FACE AS WELL.

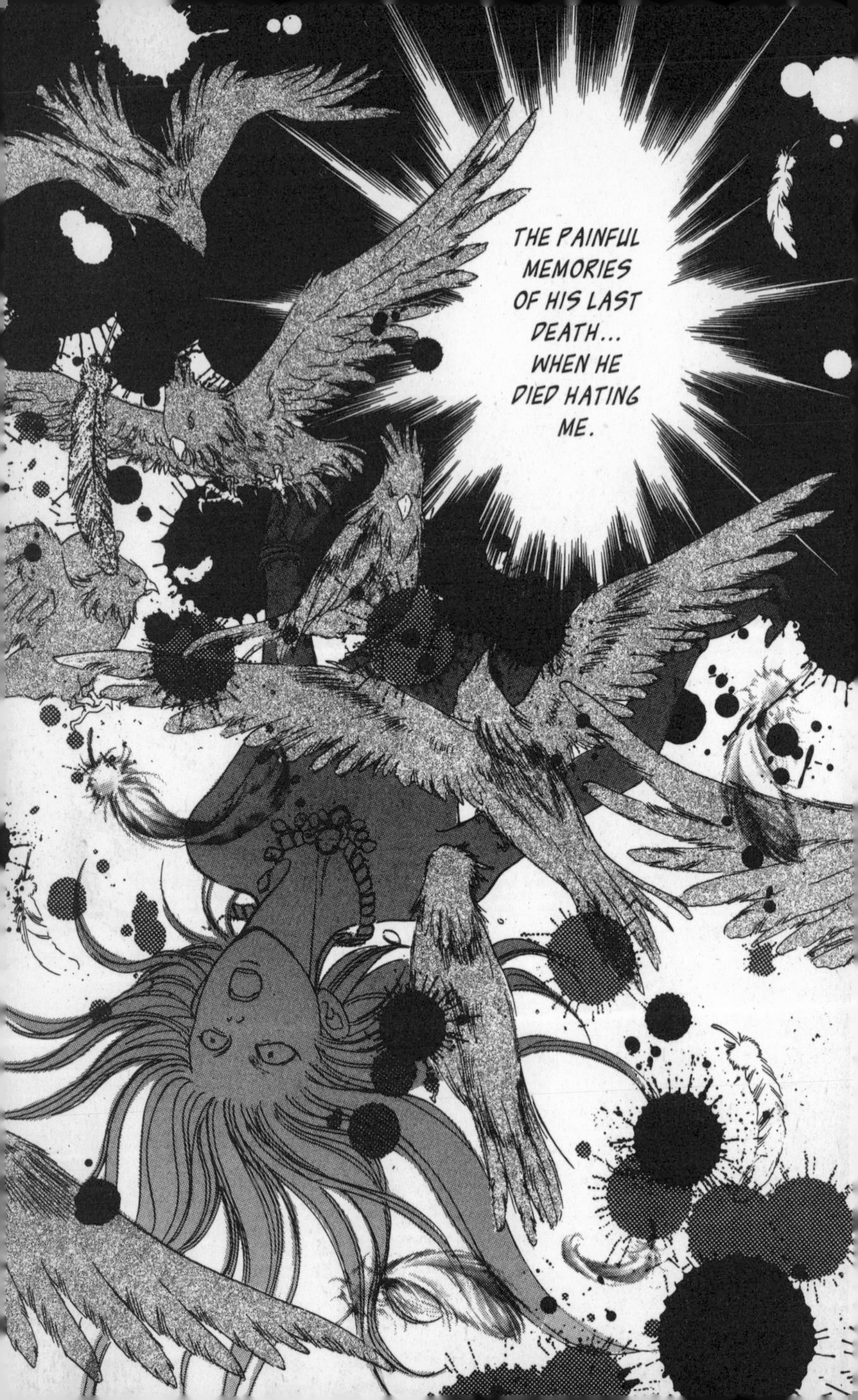
THE PAINFUL MEMORIES OF HIS LAST DEATH... WHEN HE DIED HATING ME.

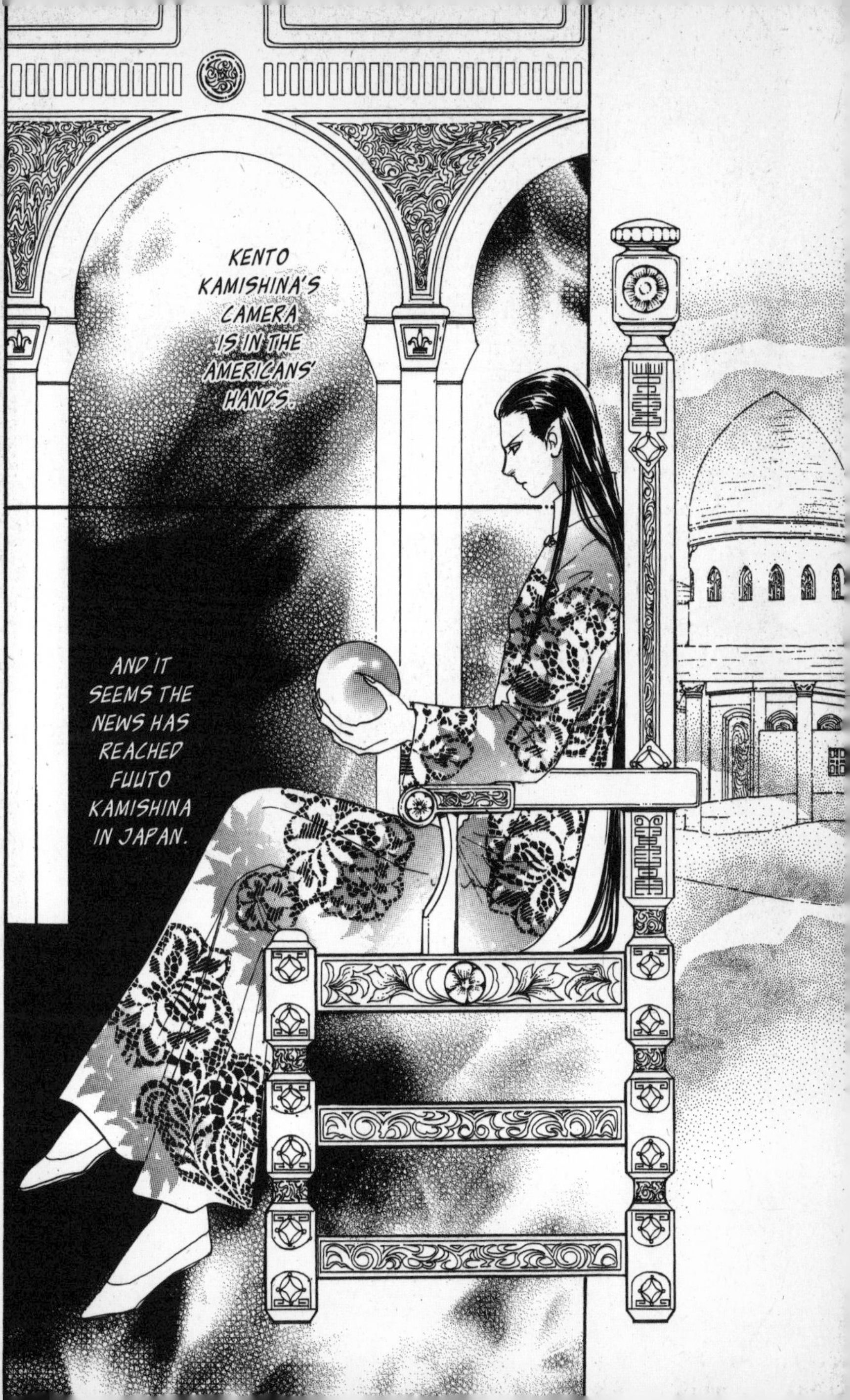
KENTO KAMISHINA'S CAMERA IS IN THE AMERICANS' HANDS.
AND IT SEEMS THE NEWS HAS REACHED FUUTO KAMISHINA IN JAPAN.

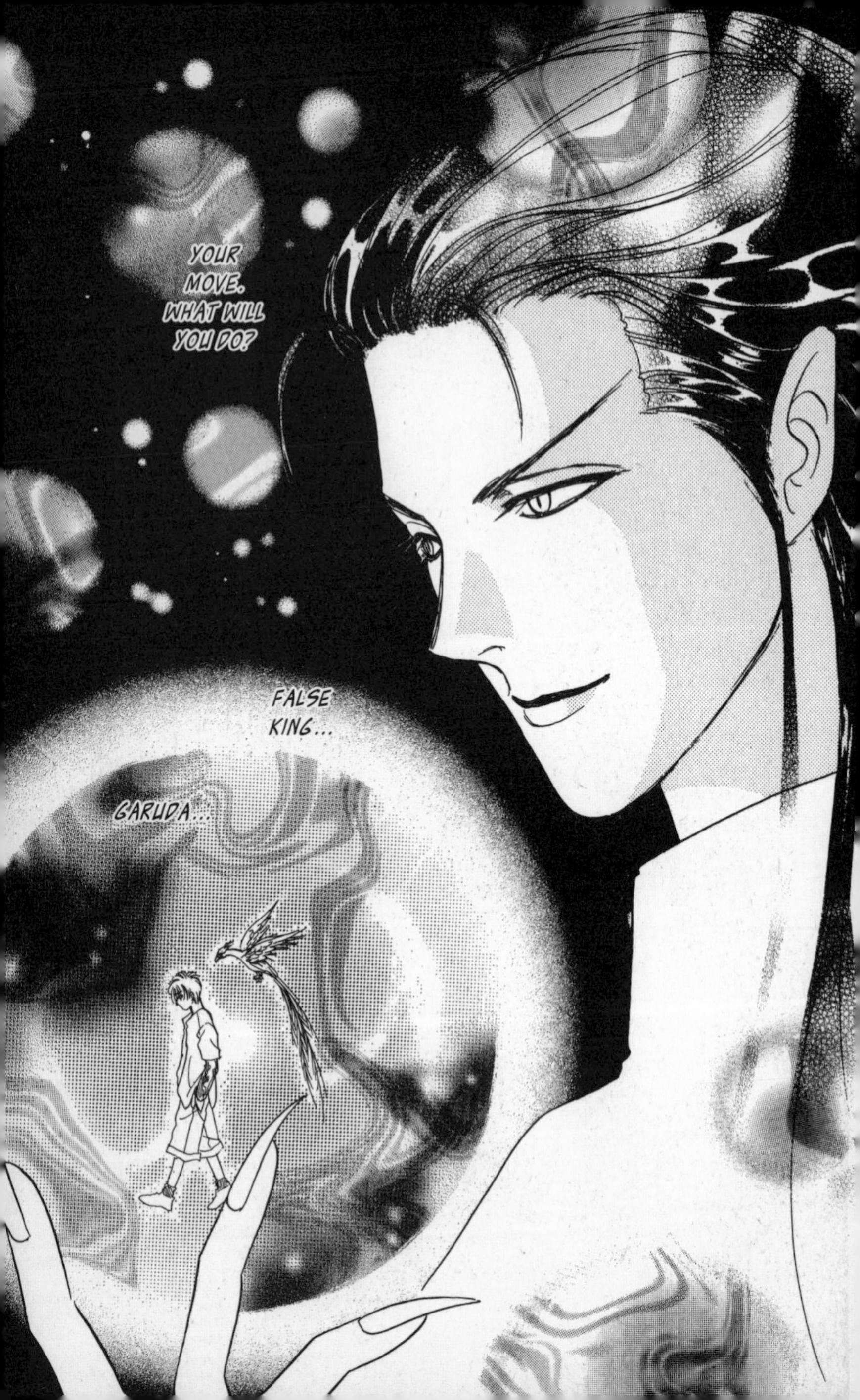
YOUR MOVE. WHAT WILL YOU DO?
FALSE KING...
GARUDA...

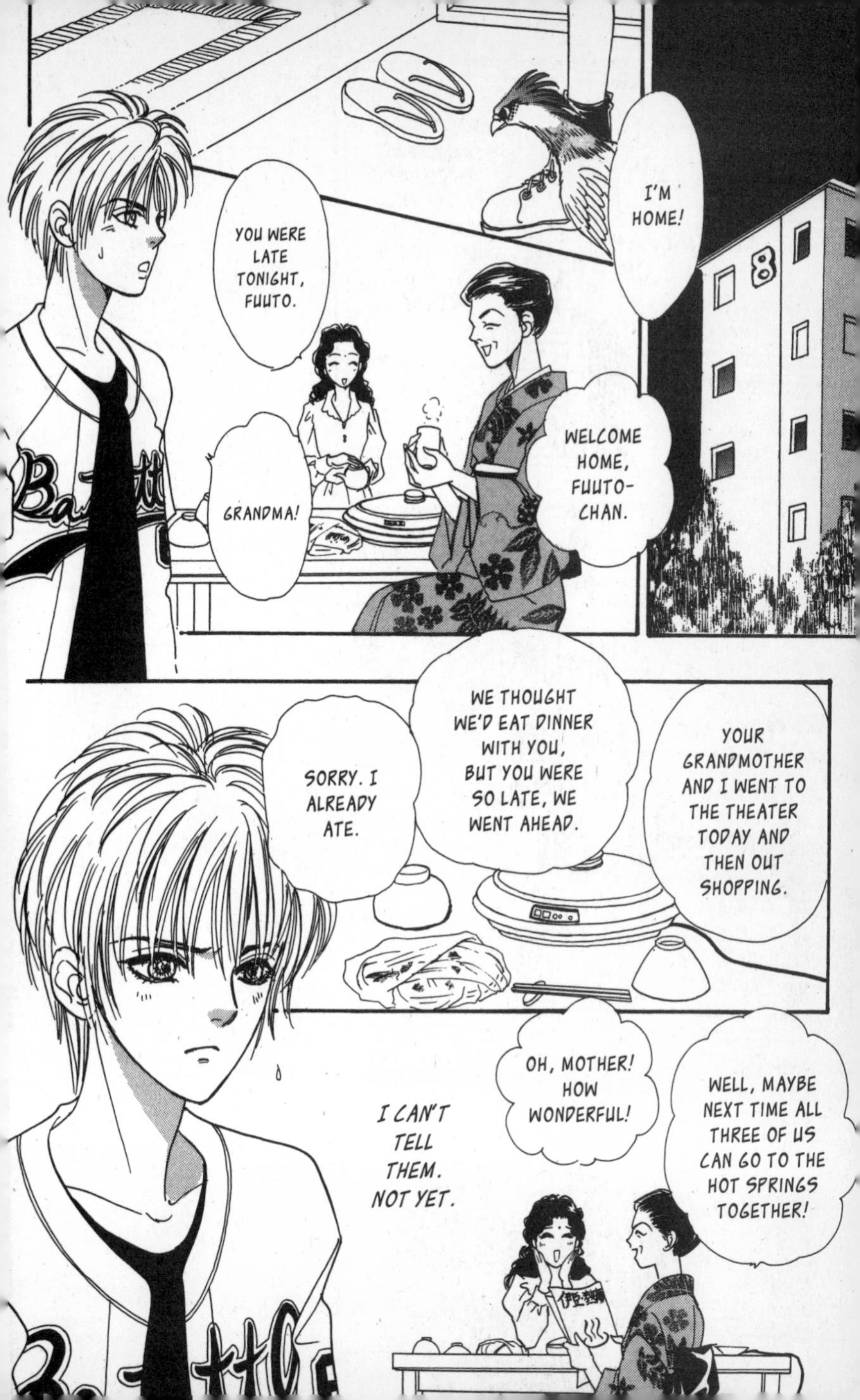
I'M HOME!
YOU WERE LATE TONIGHT, FUUTO.
GRANDMA!
WELCOME HOME, FUUTO-CHAN.
YOUR GRANDMOTHER AND I WENT TO THE THEATER TODAY AND THEN OUT SHOPPING.
WE THOUGHT WE'D EAT DINNER WITH YOU, BUT YOU WERE SO LATE, WE WENT AHEAD.
SORRY. I ALREADY ATE.
WELL, MAYBE NEXT TIME ALL THREE OF US CAN GO TO THE HOT SPRINGS TOGETHER!
OH, MOTHER! HOW WONDERFUL!
I CAN'T TELL THEM. NOT YET.

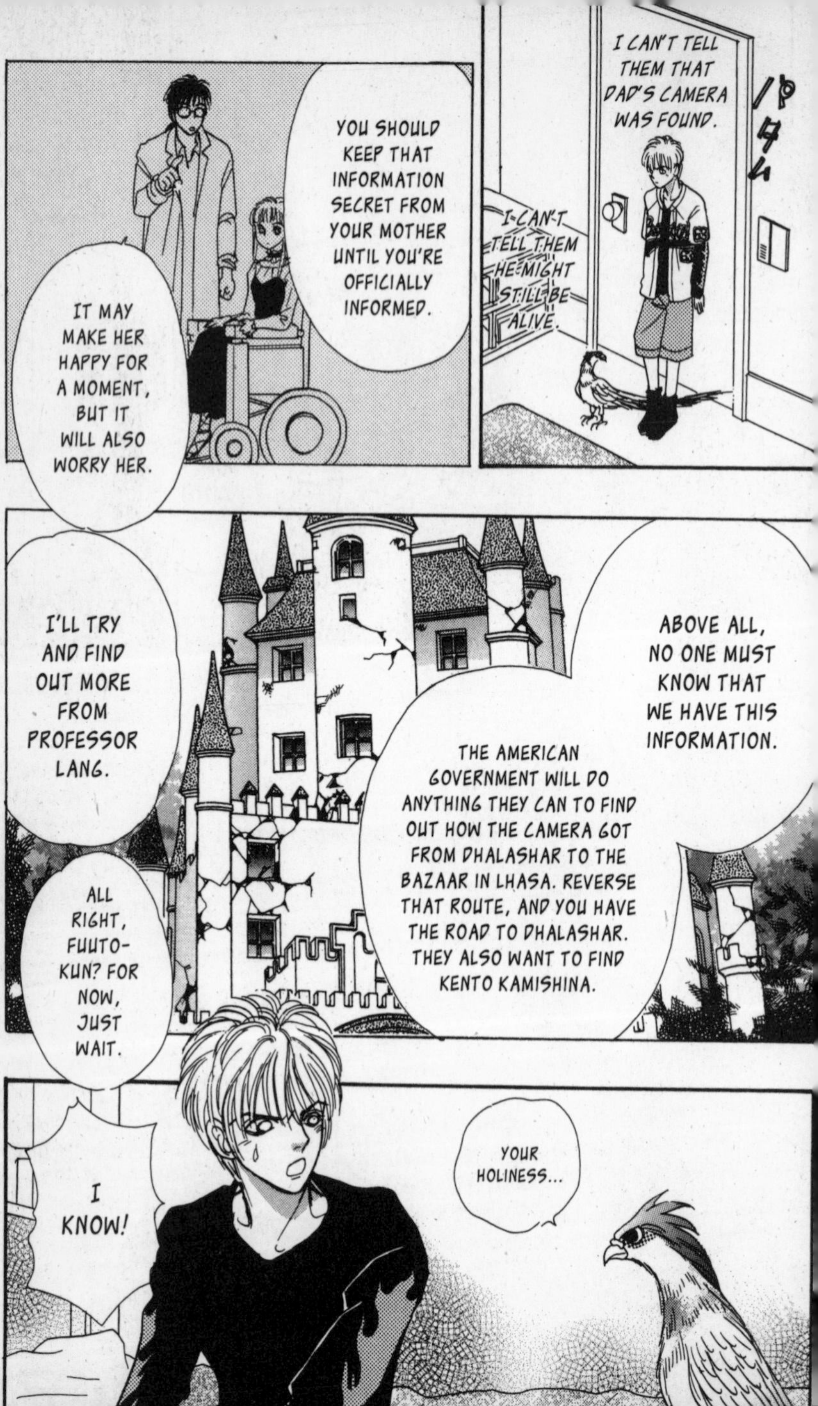

I CAN'T TELL THEM THAT DAD'S CAMERA WAS FOUND.
パタム
I CAN'T TELL THEM HE MIGHT STILL BE ALIVE.
YOU SHOULD KEEP THAT INFORMATION SECRET FROM YOUR MOTHER UNTIL YOU'RE OFFICIALLY INFORMED.
IT MAY MAKE HER HAPPY FOR A MOMENT, BUT IT WILL ALSO WORRY HER.
ABOVE ALL, NO ONE MUST KNOW THAT WE HAVE THIS INFORMATION.
THE AMERICAN GOVERNMENT WILL DO ANYTHING THEY CAN TO FIND OUT HOW THE CAMERA GOT FROM DHALASHAR TO THE BAZAAR IN LHASA. REVERSE THAT ROUTE, AND YOU HAVE THE ROAD TO DHALASHAR. THEY ALSO WANT TO FIND KENTO KAMISHINA.
I'LL TRY AND FIND OUT MORE FROM PROFESSOR LANG.
ALL RIGHT, FUUTO-KUN? FOR NOW, JUST WAIT.
YOUR HOLINESS...
I KNOW!

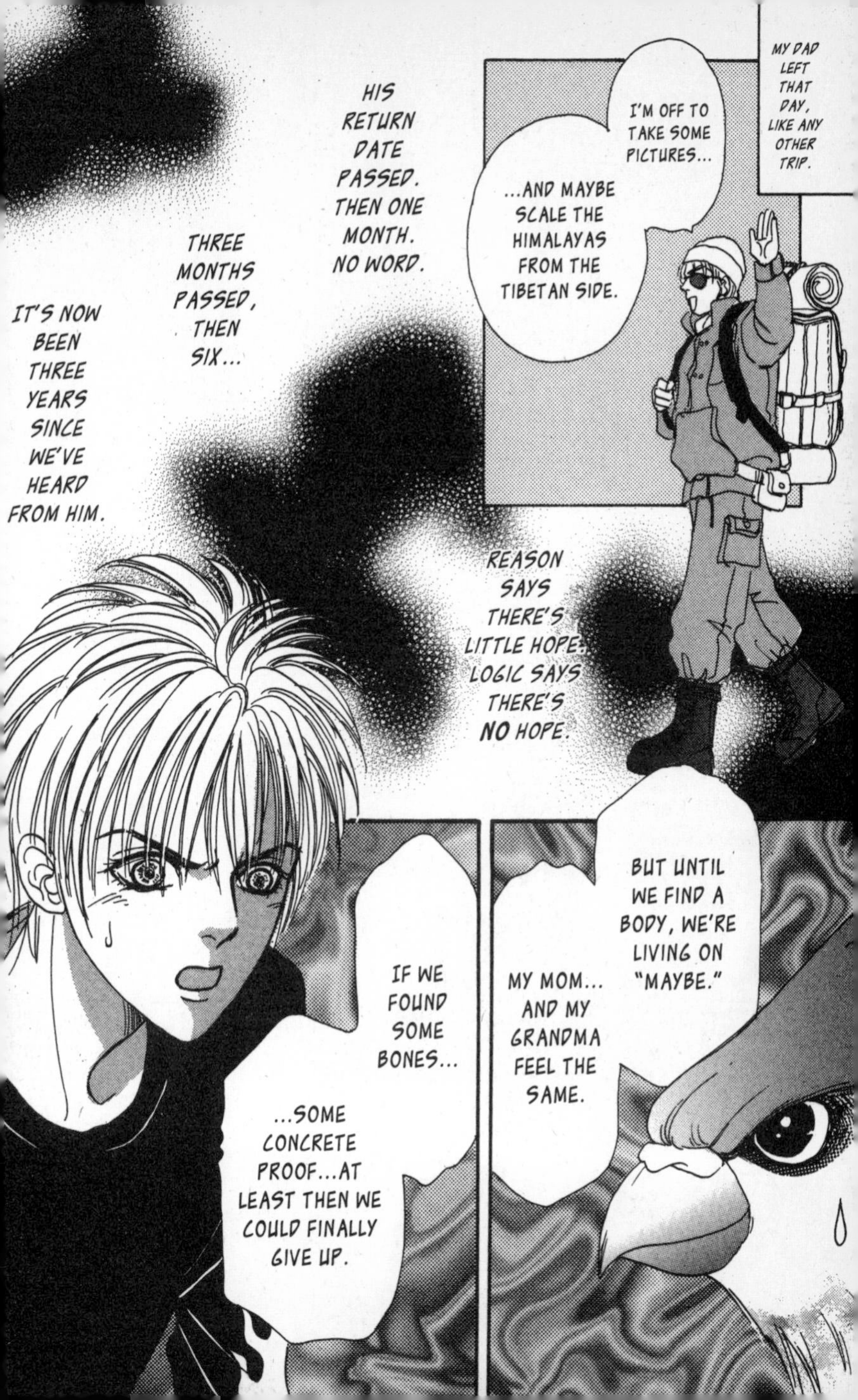
MY DAD LEFT THAT DAY, LIKE ANY OTHER TRIP.
I'M OFF TO TAKE SOME PICTURES...
...AND MAYBE SCALE THE HIMALAYAS FROM THE TIBETAN SIDE.
HIS RETURN DATE PASSED. THEN ONE MONTH. NO WORD.
THREE MONTHS PASSED, THEN SIX...
IT'S NOW BEEN THREE YEARS SINCE WE'VE HEARD FROM HIM.
REASON SAYS THERE'S LITTLE HOPE. LOGIC SAYS THERE'S NO HOPE.
BUT UNTIL WE FIND A BODY, WE'RE LIVING ON "MAYBE."
MY MOM... AND MY GRANDMA FEEL THE SAME.
IF WE FOUND SOME BONES...
...SOME CONCRETE PROOF...AT LEAST THEN WE COULD FINALLY GIVE UP.

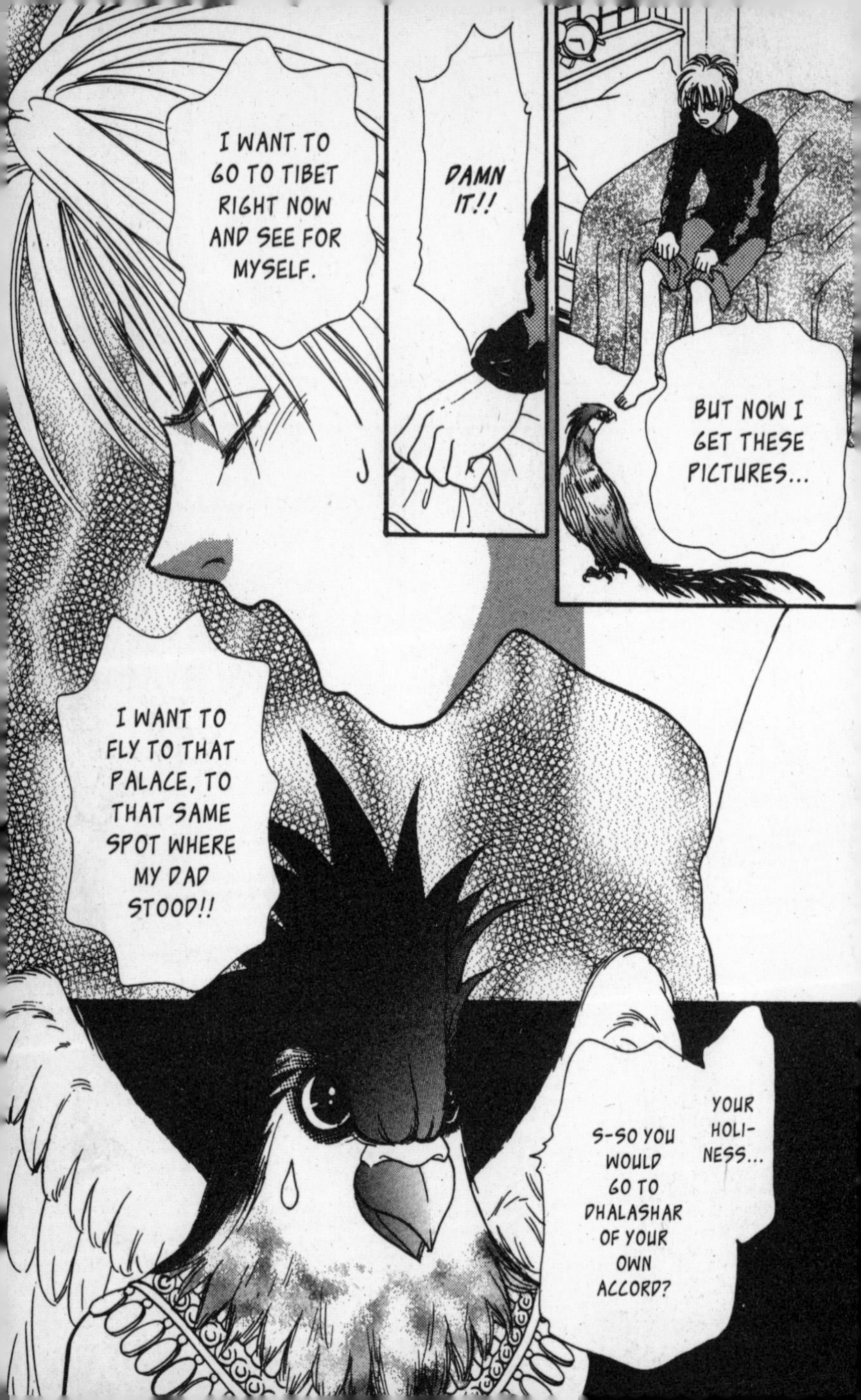
BUT NOW I GET THESE PICTURES...
DAMN IT!!
I WANT TO GO TO TIBET RIGHT NOW AND SEE FOR MYSELF.
I WANT TO FLY TO THAT PALACE, TO THAT SAME SPOT WHERE MY DAD STOOD!!
YOUR HOLI-NESS...
S-SO YOU WOULD GO TO DHALASHAR OF YOUR OWN ACCORD?

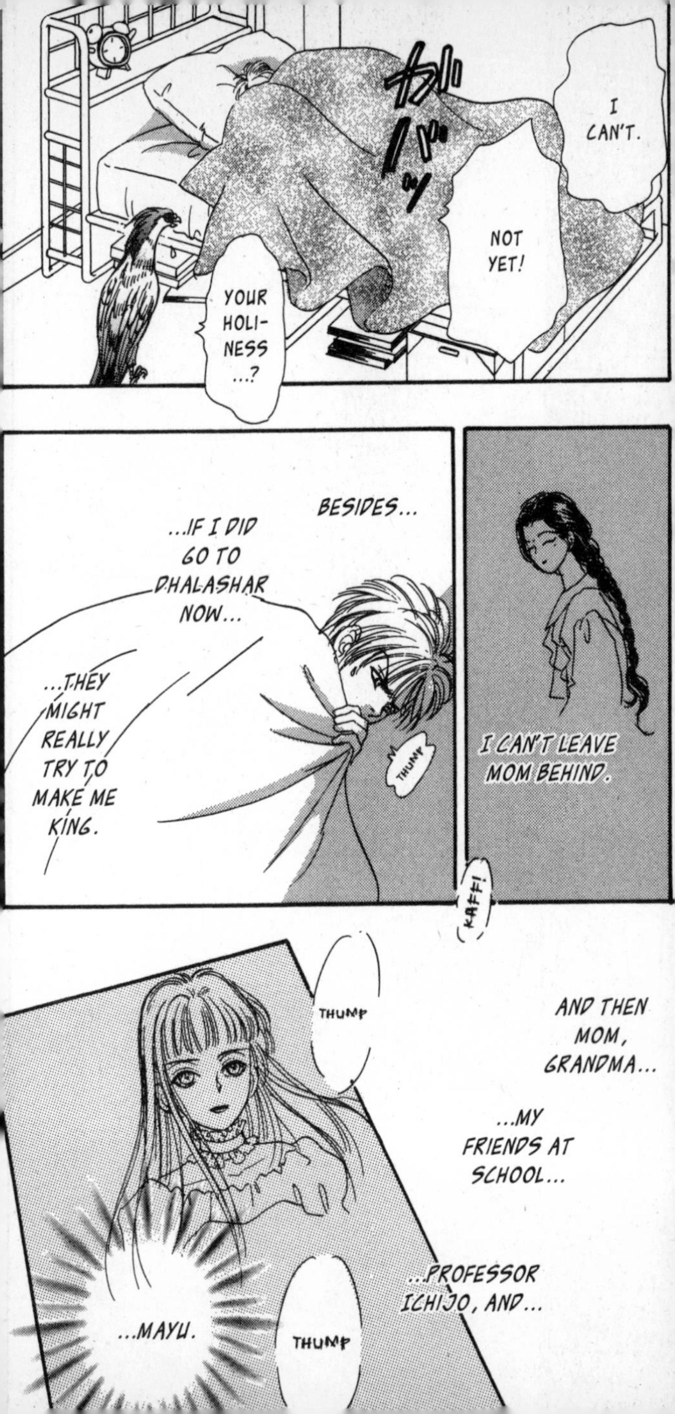
ガバッ
I CAN'T.
NOT YET!
YOUR HOLINESS...?
I CAN'T LEAVE MOM BEHIND.
BESIDES...
...IF I DID GO TO DHALASHAR NOW...
...THEY MIGHT REALLY TRY TO MAKE ME KING.
THUMP
KAFF!
AND THEN MOM, GRANDMA...
...MY FRIENDS AT SCHOOL...
...PROFESSOR ICHIJO, AND...
THUMP
...MAYU.
THUMP

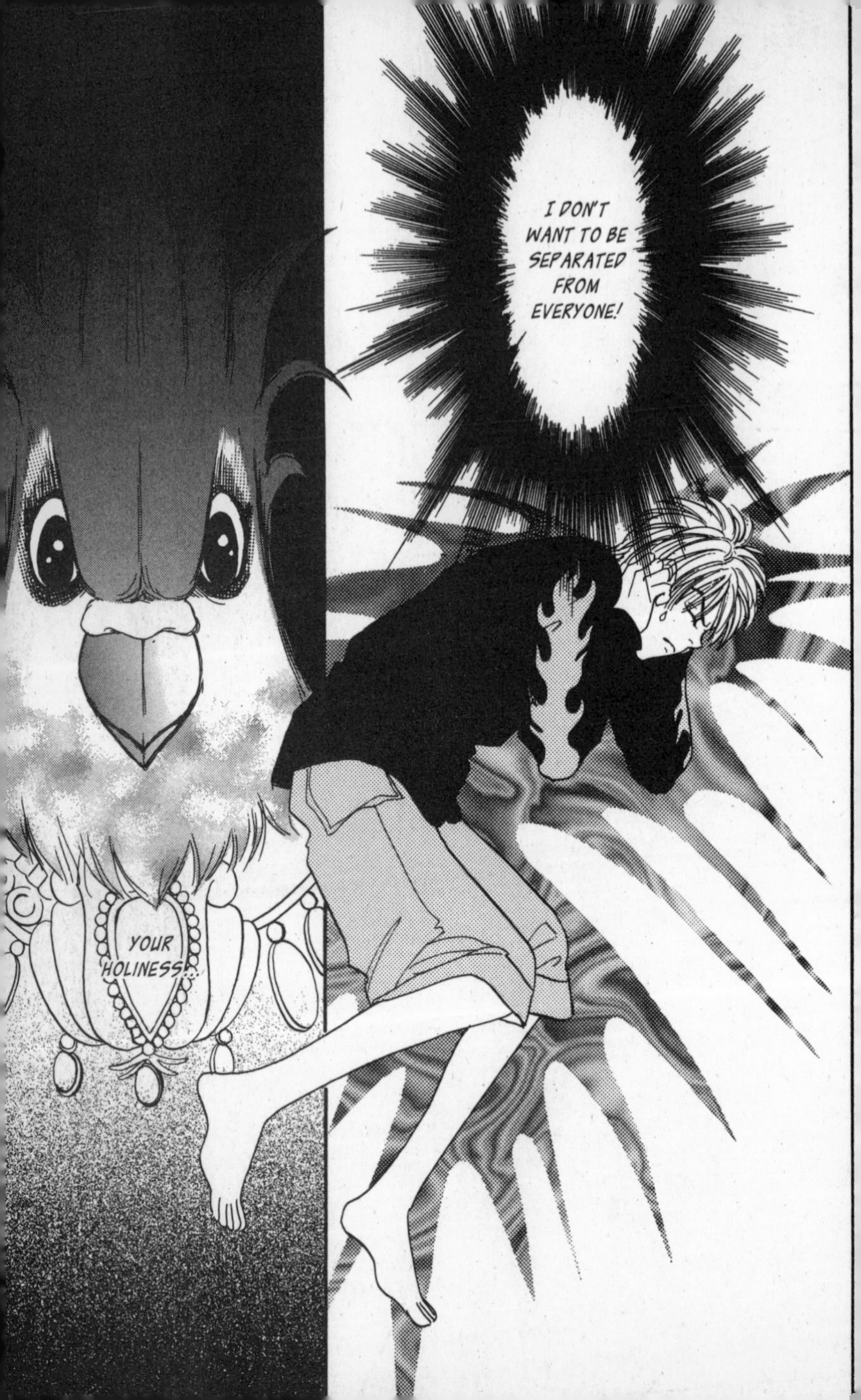
I DON'T WANT TO BE SEPARATED FROM EVERYONE!
YOUR HOLINESS...

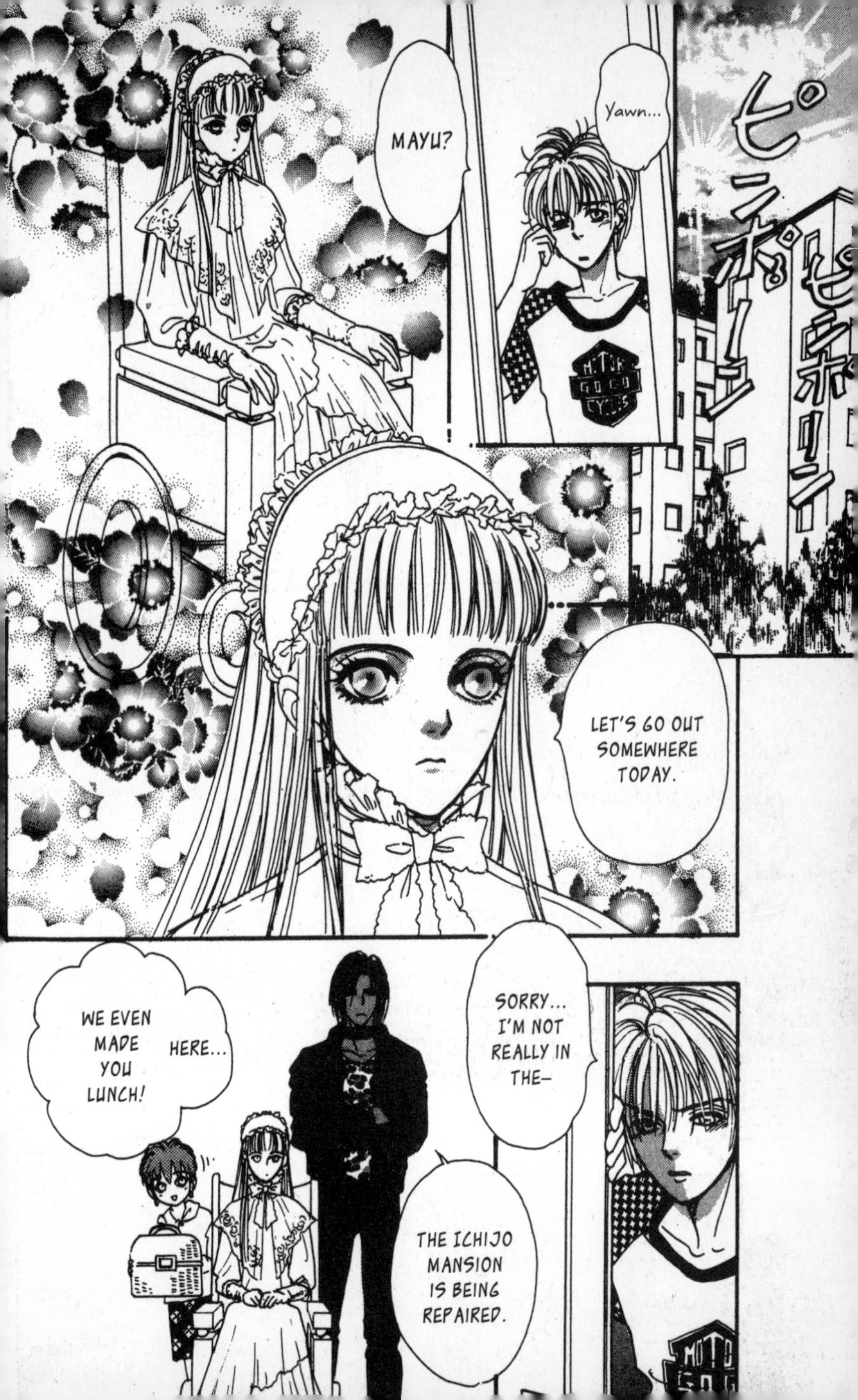
ピンポーン
Yawn...
MAYU?
...
...
LET'S GO OUT SOMEWHERE TODAY.
SORRY... I'M NOT REALLY IN THE–
THE ICHIJO MANSION IS BEING REPAIRED.
HERE...
WE EVEN MADE YOU LUNCH!

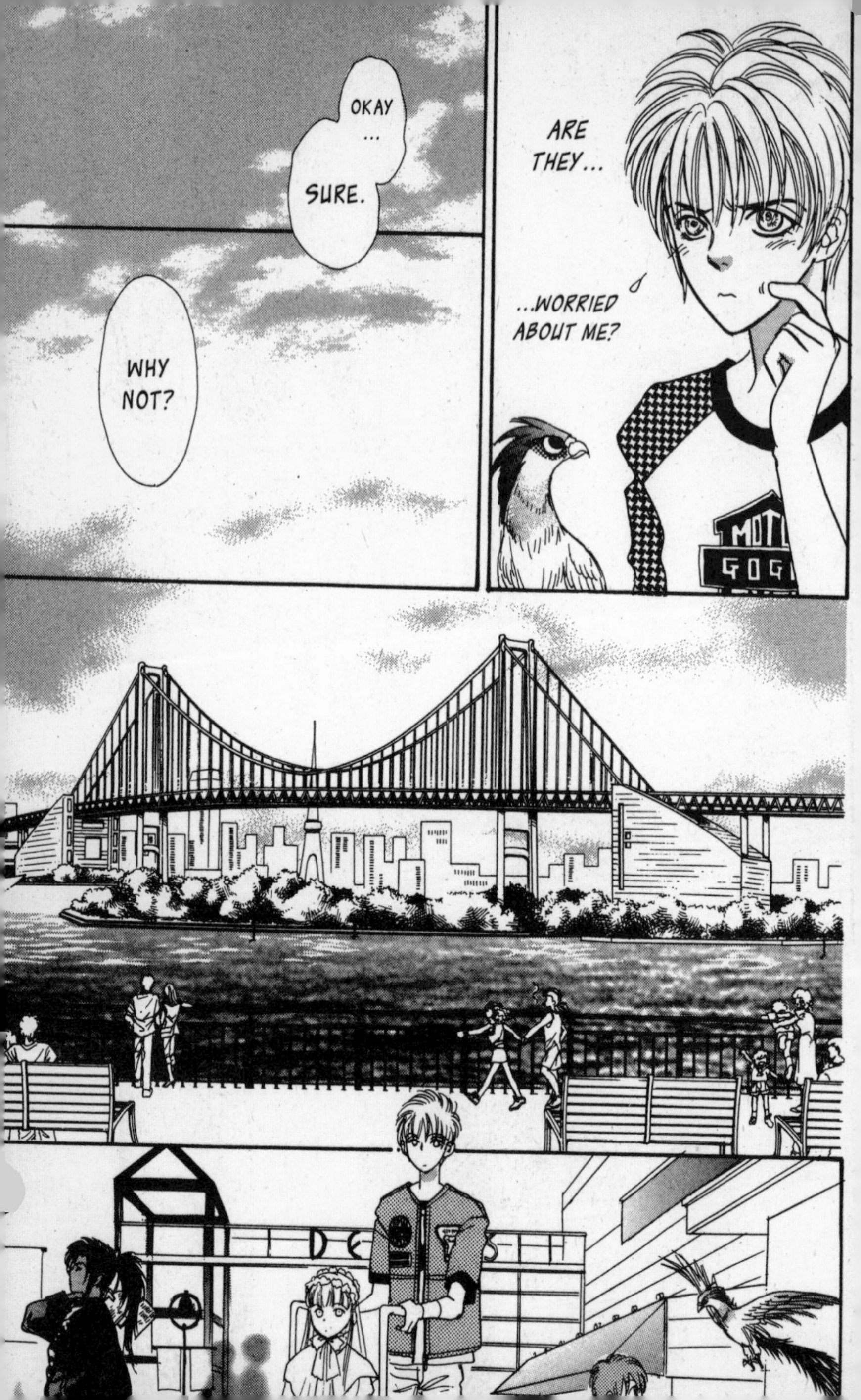
ARE THEY...
...WORRIED ABOUT ME?
OKAY ... SURE.
WHY NOT?

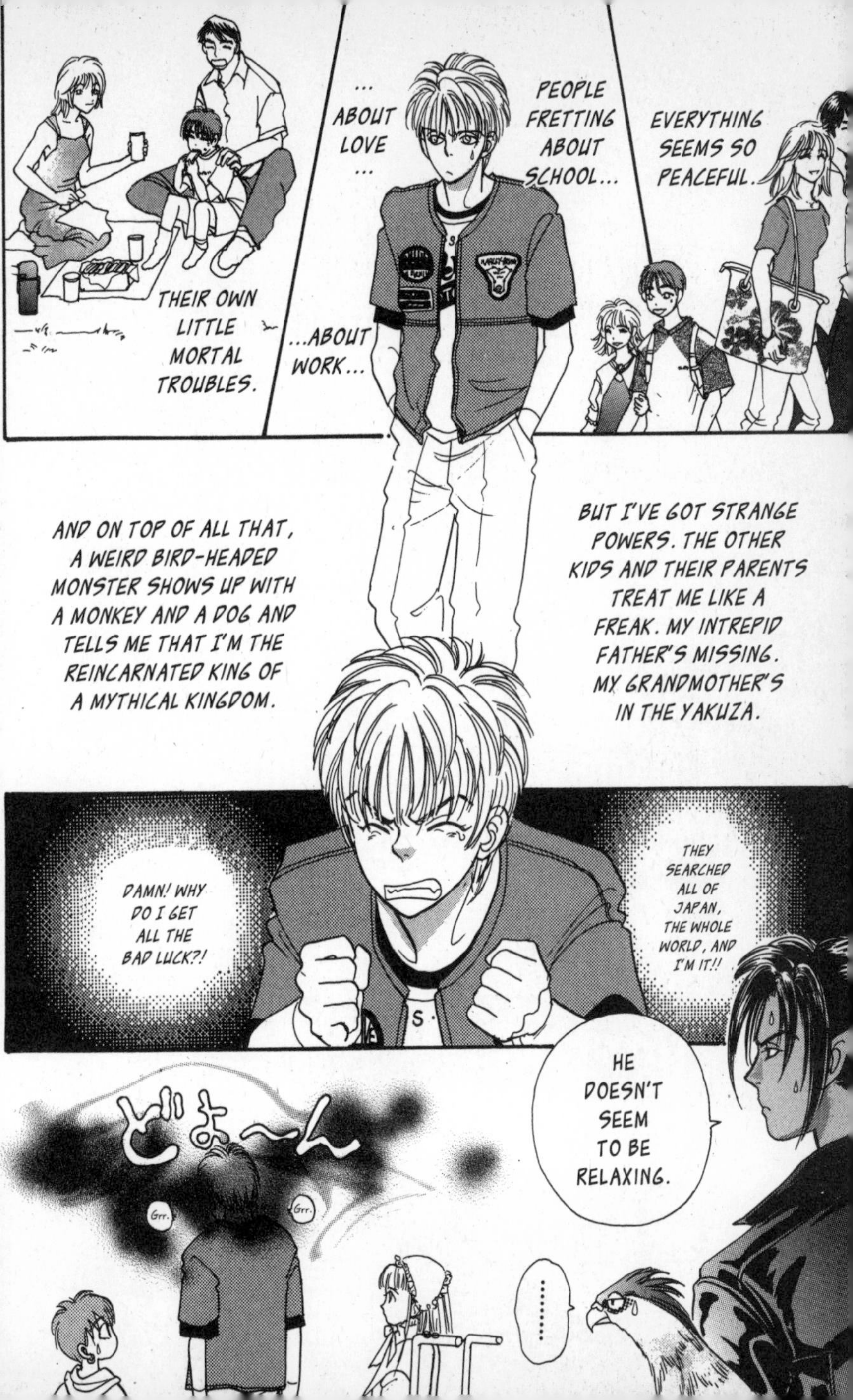
EVERYTHING SEEMS SO PEACEFUL.
PEOPLE FRETTING ABOUT SCHOOL...
... ABOUT LOVE ...
...ABOUT WORK...
THEIR OWN LITTLE MORTAL TROUBLES.
BUT I'VE GOT STRANGE POWERS. THE OTHER KIDS AND THEIR PARENTS TREAT ME LIKE A FREAK. MY INTREPID FATHER'S MISSING. MY GRANDMOTHER'S IN THE YAKUZA.
AND ON TOP OF ALL THAT, A WEIRD BIRD-HEADED MONSTER SHOWS UP WITH A MONKEY AND A DOG AND TELLS ME THAT I'M THE REINCARNATED KING OF A MYTHICAL KINGDOM.
THEY SEARCHED ALL OF JAPAN, THE WHOLE WORLD, AND I'M IT!!
DAMN! WHY DO I GET ALL THE BAD LUCK?!
HE DOESN'T SEEM TO BE RELAXING.
......
どよ〜ん
Grr.
Grr.

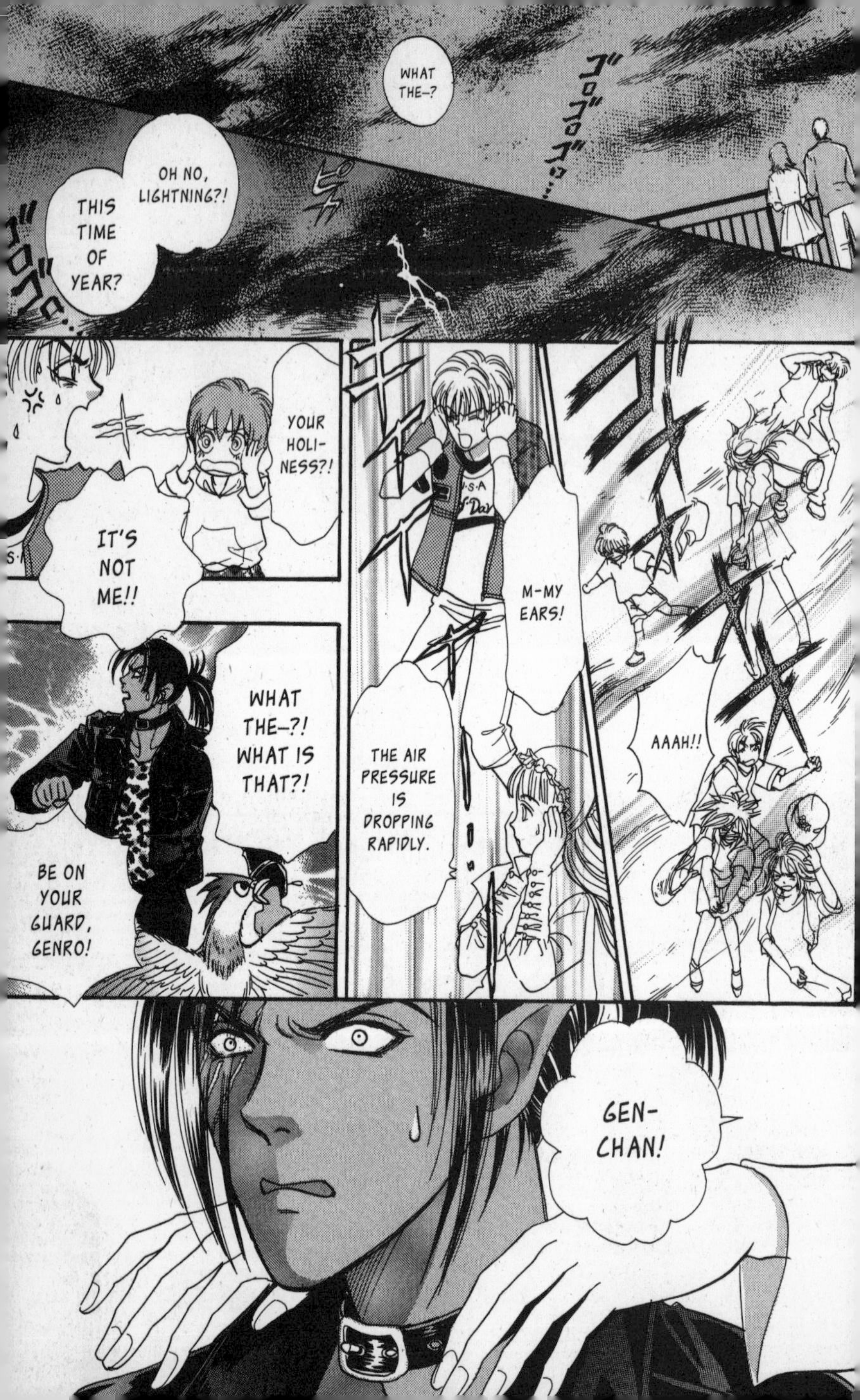

WHAT THE-?
OH NO, LIGHTNING?!
THIS TIME OF YEAR?
YOUR HOLINESS?!
IT'S NOT ME!!
M-MY EARS!
AAAH!!
THE AIR PRESSURE IS DROPPING RAPIDLY.
WHAT THE-?! WHAT IS THAT?!
BE ON YOUR GUARD, GENRO!
GEN-CHAN!

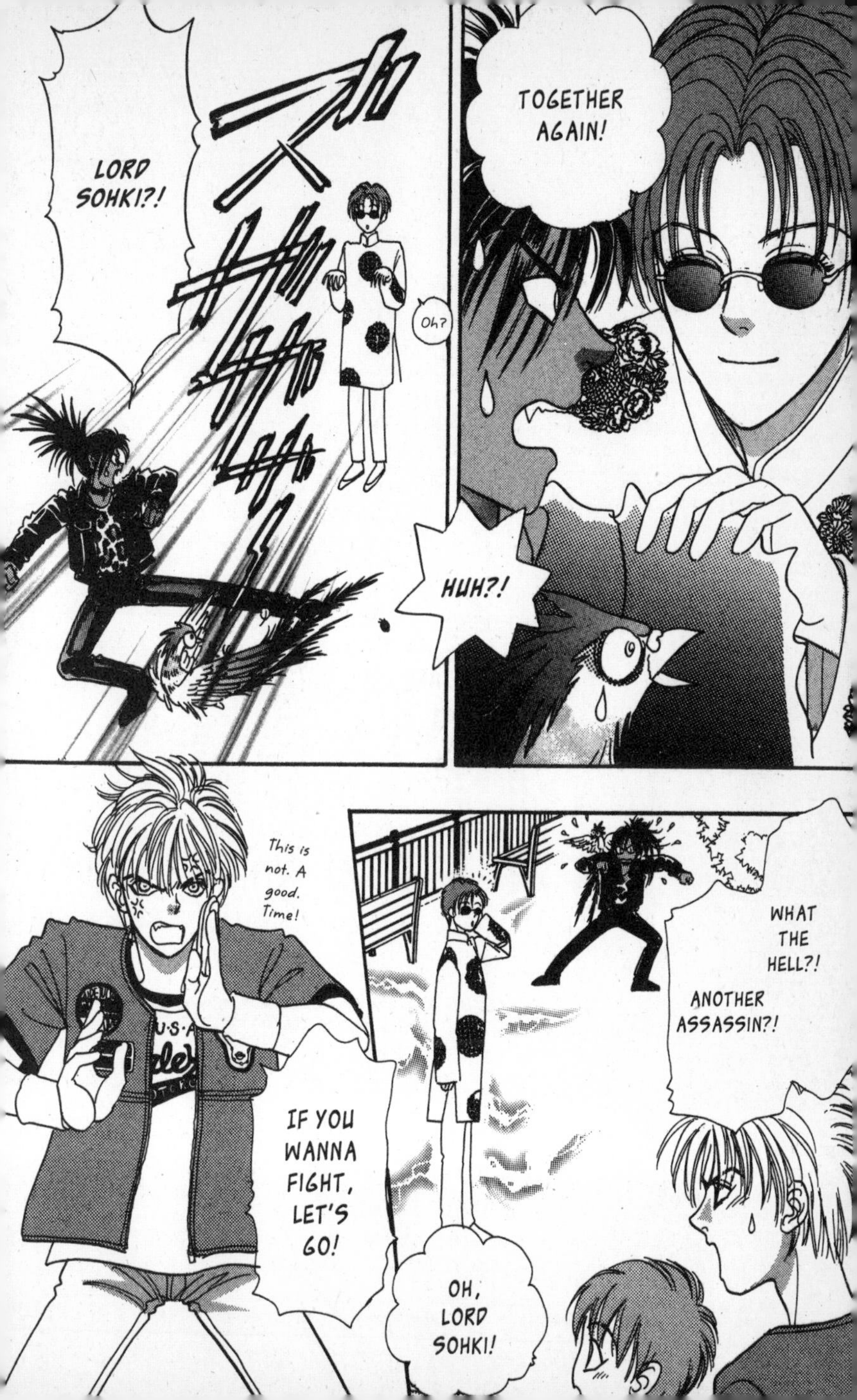
TOGETHER AGAIN!
HUH?!
LORD SOHKI?!
Oh?
WHAT THE HELL?!
ANOTHER ASSASSIN?!
OH, LORD SOHKI!
IF YOU WANNA FIGHT, LET'S GO!
This is not. A good. Time!

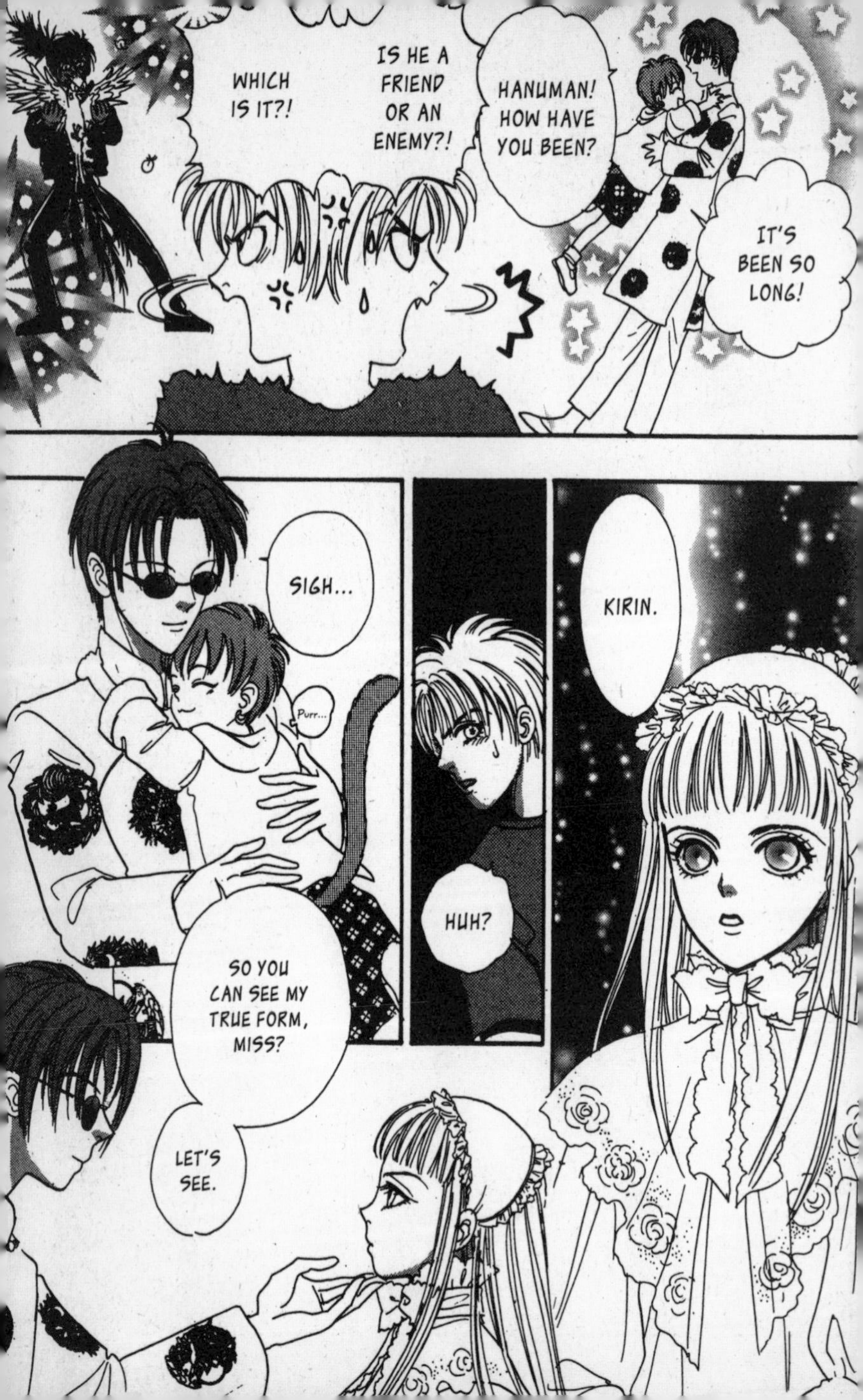
HANUMAN! HOW HAVE YOU BEEN?
IT'S BEEN SO LONG!
IS HE A FRIEND OR AN ENEMY?!
WHICH IS IT?!
KIRIN.
HUH?
SIGH...
Purr...
SO YOU CAN SEE MY TRUE FORM, MISS?
LET'S SEE.

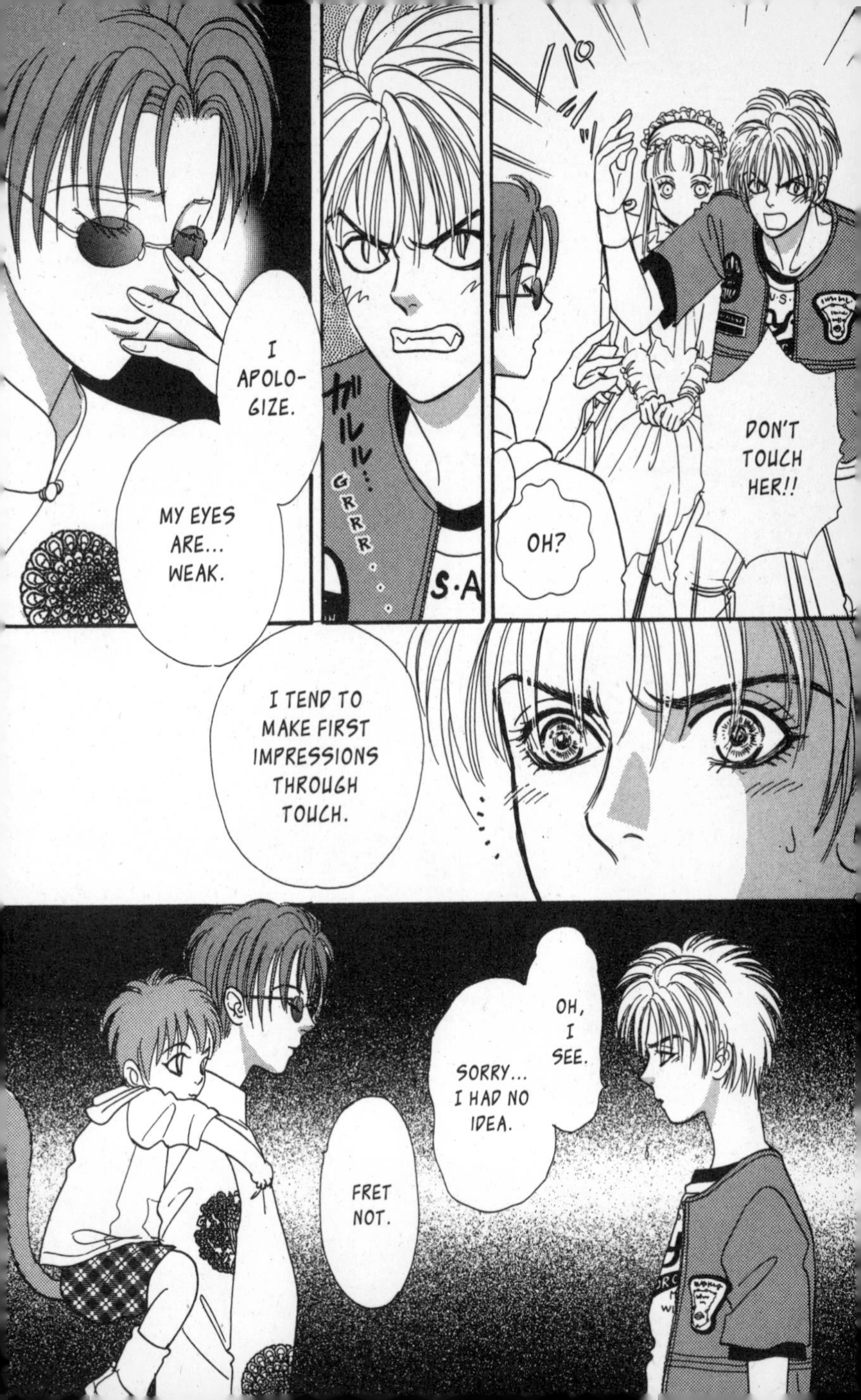
DON'T TOUCH HER!!
OH?
ガルル…
GRRR…
I APOLOGIZE.
MY EYES ARE... WEAK.
I TEND TO MAKE FIRST IMPRESSIONS THROUGH TOUCH.
OH, I SEE.
SORRY... I HAD NO IDEA.
FRET NOT.

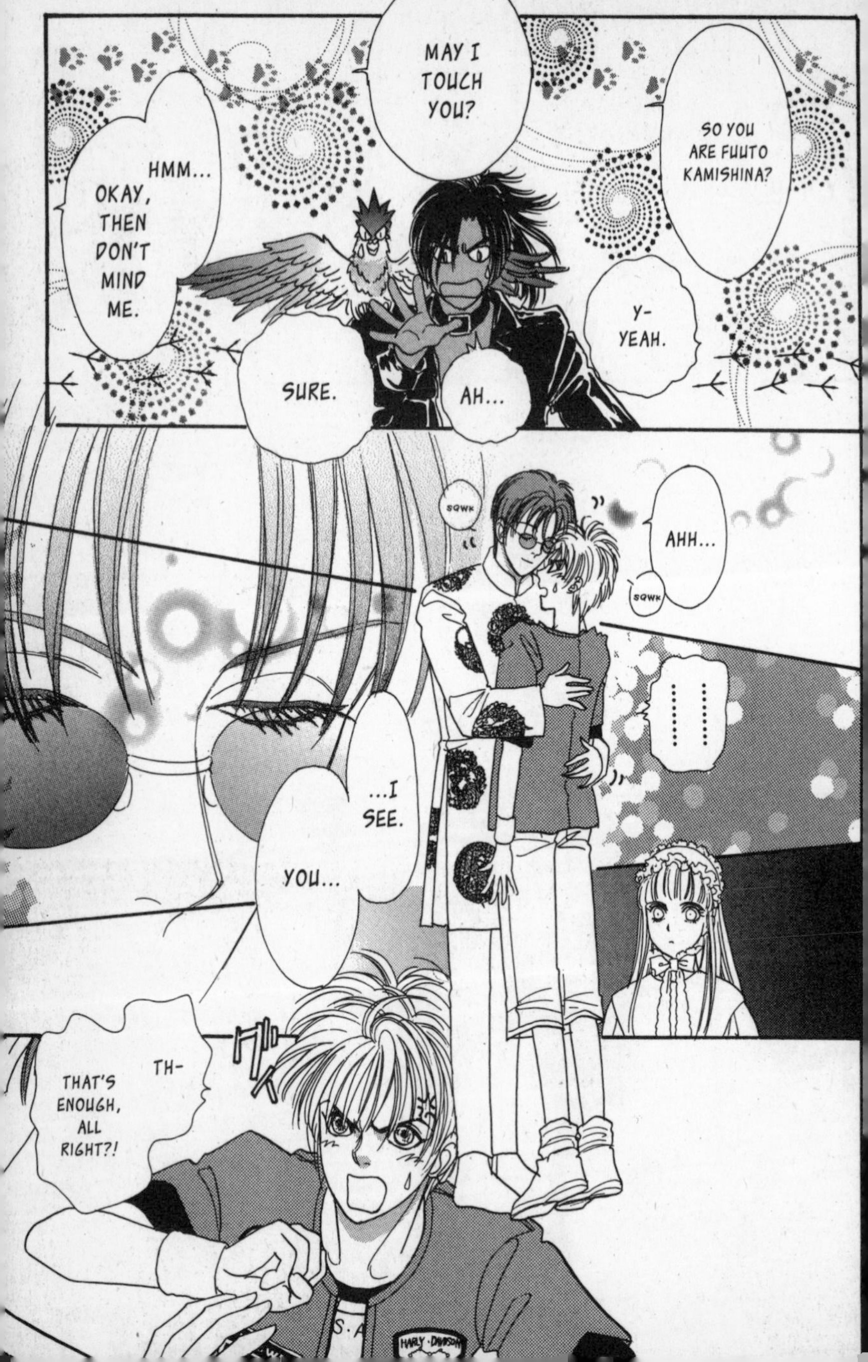
SO YOU ARE FUUTO KAMISHINA?
Y-YEAH.
MAY I TOUCH YOU?
AH...
SURE.
HMM... OKAY, THEN DON'T MIND ME.
SQWK
AHH...
SQWK
......
...I SEE.
YOU...
TH-
THAT'S ENOUGH, ALL RIGHT?!

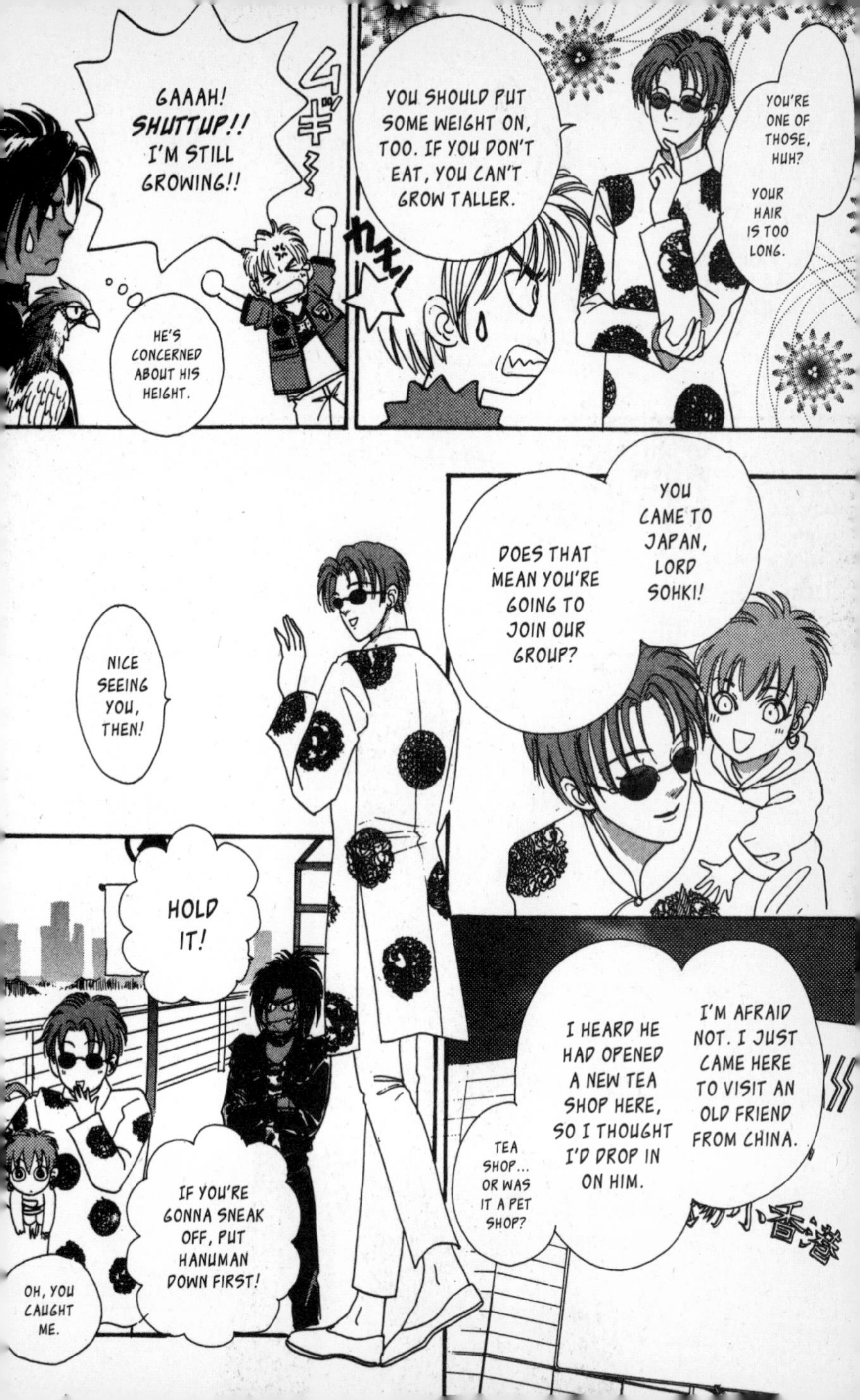

YOU'RE ONE OF THOSE, HUH?
YOUR HAIR IS TOO LONG.
YOU SHOULD PUT SOME WEIGHT ON, TOO. IF YOU DON'T EAT, YOU CAN'T GROW TALLER.
GAAAH! **SHUTTUP!!** I'M STILL GROWING!!
HE'S CONCERNED ABOUT HIS HEIGHT.
YOU CAME TO JAPAN, LORD SOHKI!
DOES THAT MEAN YOU'RE GOING TO JOIN OUR GROUP?
I'M AFRAID NOT. I JUST CAME HERE TO VISIT AN OLD FRIEND FROM CHINA.
I HEARD HE HAD OPENED A NEW TEA SHOP HERE, SO I THOUGHT I'D DROP IN ON HIM.
TEA SHOP... OR WAS IT A PET SHOP?
NICE SEEING YOU, THEN!
HOLD IT!
IF YOU'RE GONNA SNEAK OFF, PUT HANUMAN DOWN FIRST!
OH, YOU CAUGHT ME.

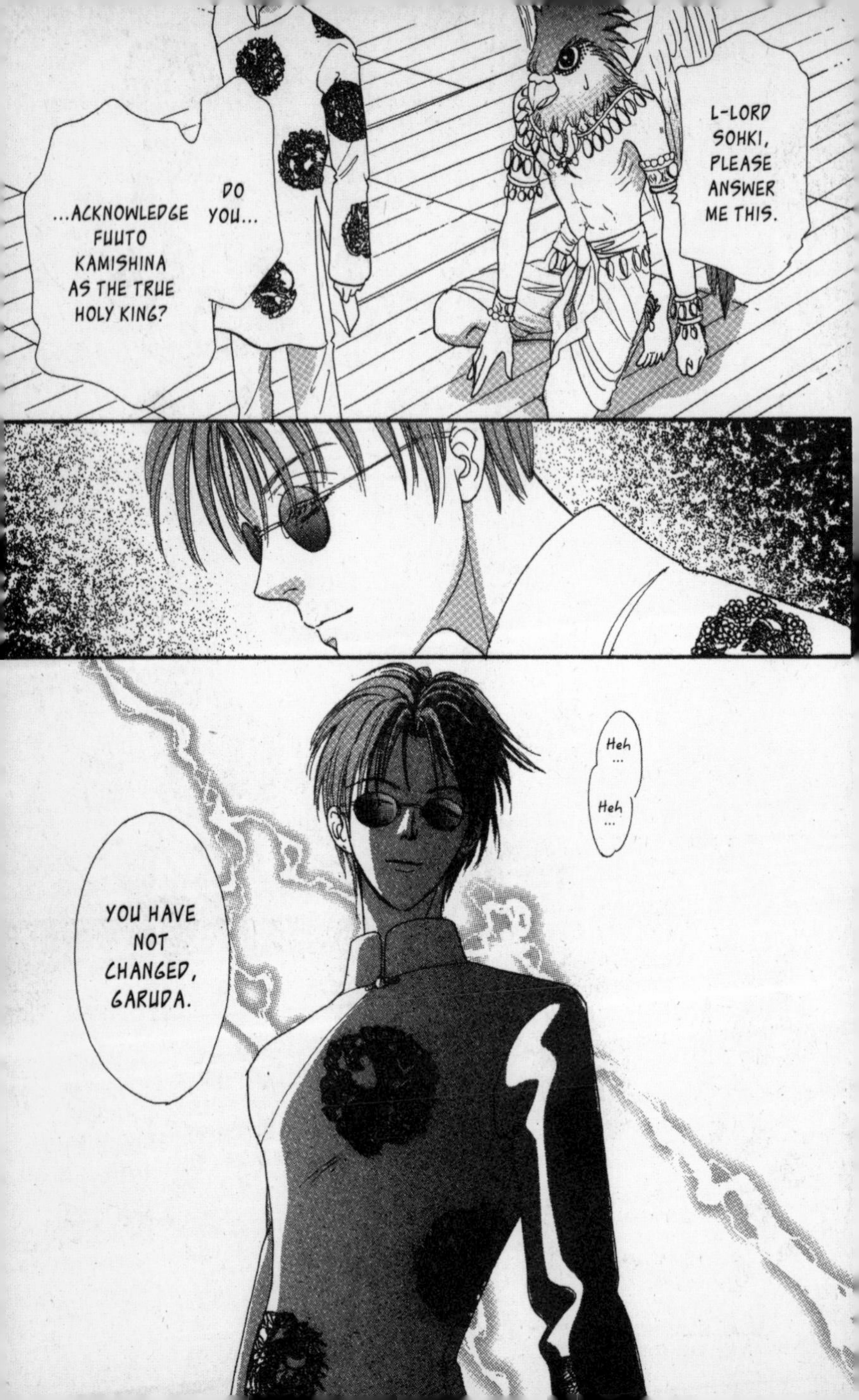
L-LORD SOHKI, PLEASE ANSWER ME THIS.
DO YOU...
...ACKNOWLEDGE FUUTO KAMISHINA AS THE TRUE HOLY KING?
Heh ... Heh ...
YOU HAVE NOT CHANGED, GARUDA.

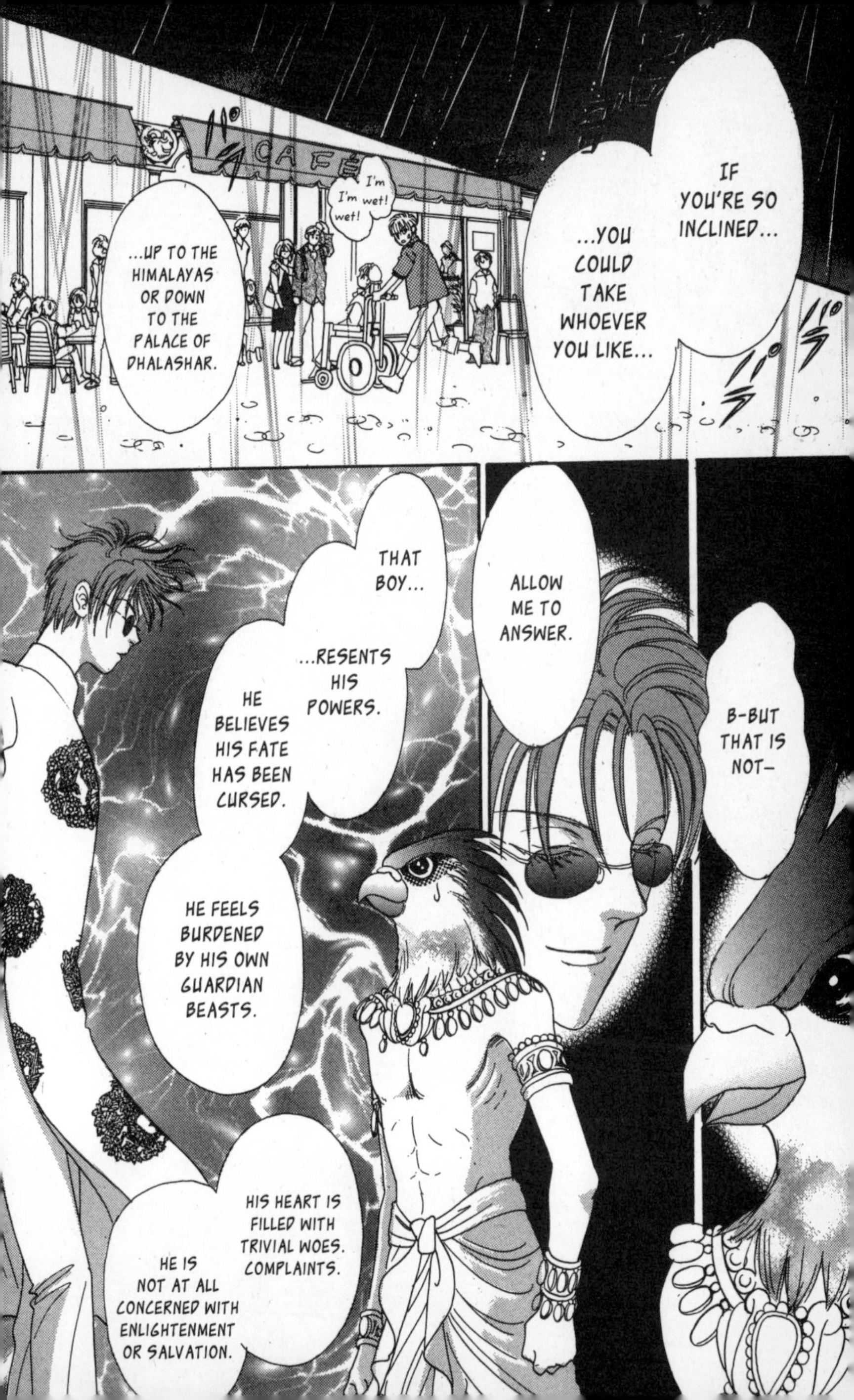
IF YOU'RE SO INCLINED...
...YOU COULD TAKE WHOEVER YOU LIKE...
...UP TO THE HIMALAYAS OR DOWN TO THE PALACE OF DHALASHAR.
CAFÉ
I'm wet! I'm wet!
B-BUT THAT IS NOT–
ALLOW ME TO ANSWER.
THAT BOY...
...RESENTS HIS POWERS.
HE BELIEVES HIS FATE HAS BEEN CURSED.
HE FEELS BURDENED BY HIS OWN GUARDIAN BEASTS.
HIS HEART IS FILLED WITH TRIVIAL WOES. COMPLAINTS.
HE IS NOT AT ALL CONCERNED WITH ENLIGHTENMENT OR SALVATION.

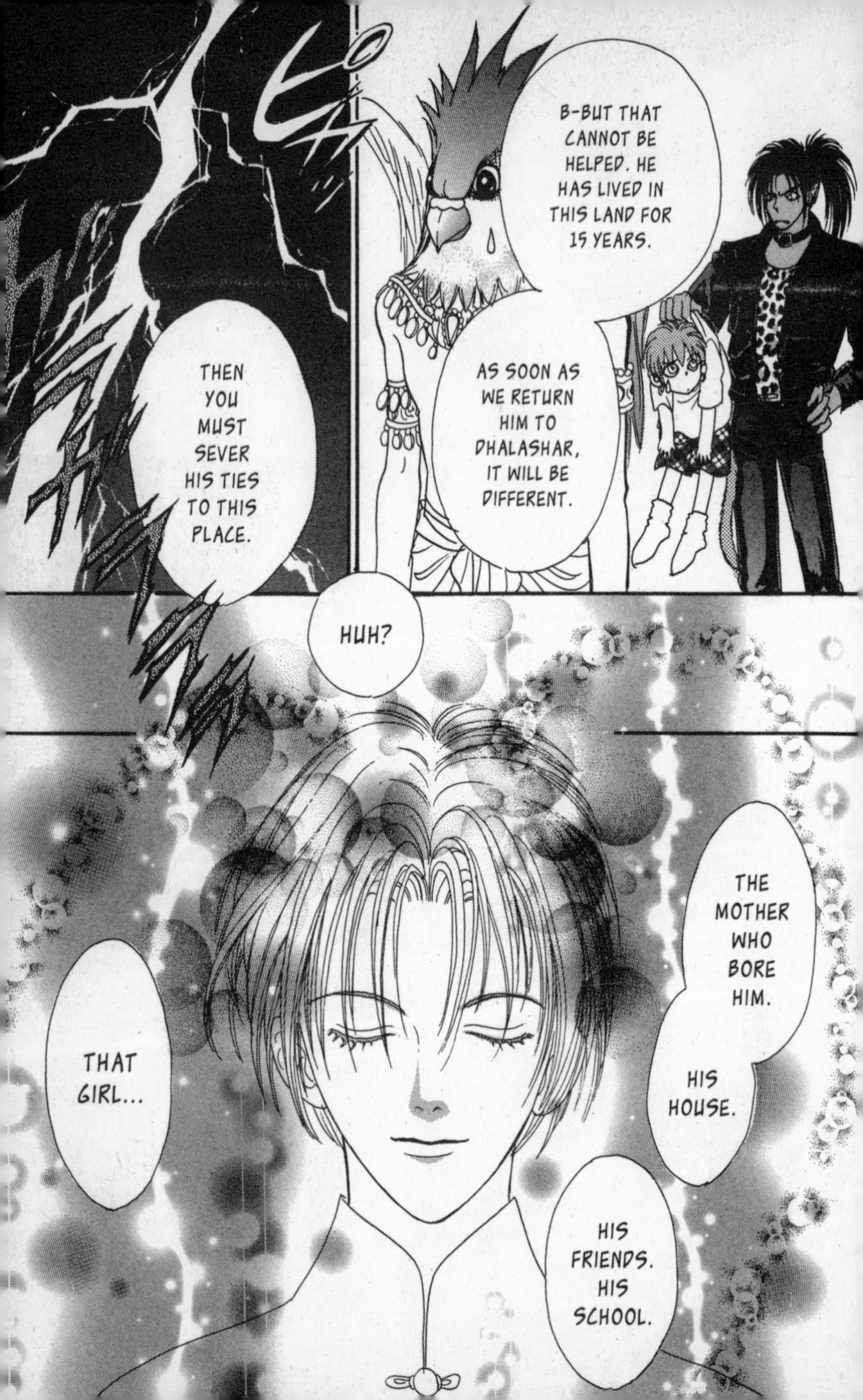
B-BUT THAT CANNOT BE HELPED. HE HAS LIVED IN THIS LAND FOR 15 YEARS.
AS SOON AS WE RETURN HIM TO DHALASHAR, IT WILL BE DIFFERENT.
THEN YOU MUST SEVER HIS TIES TO THIS PLACE.
HUH?
THE MOTHER WHO BORE HIM.
HIS HOUSE.
HIS FRIENDS. HIS SCHOOL.
THAT GIRL...

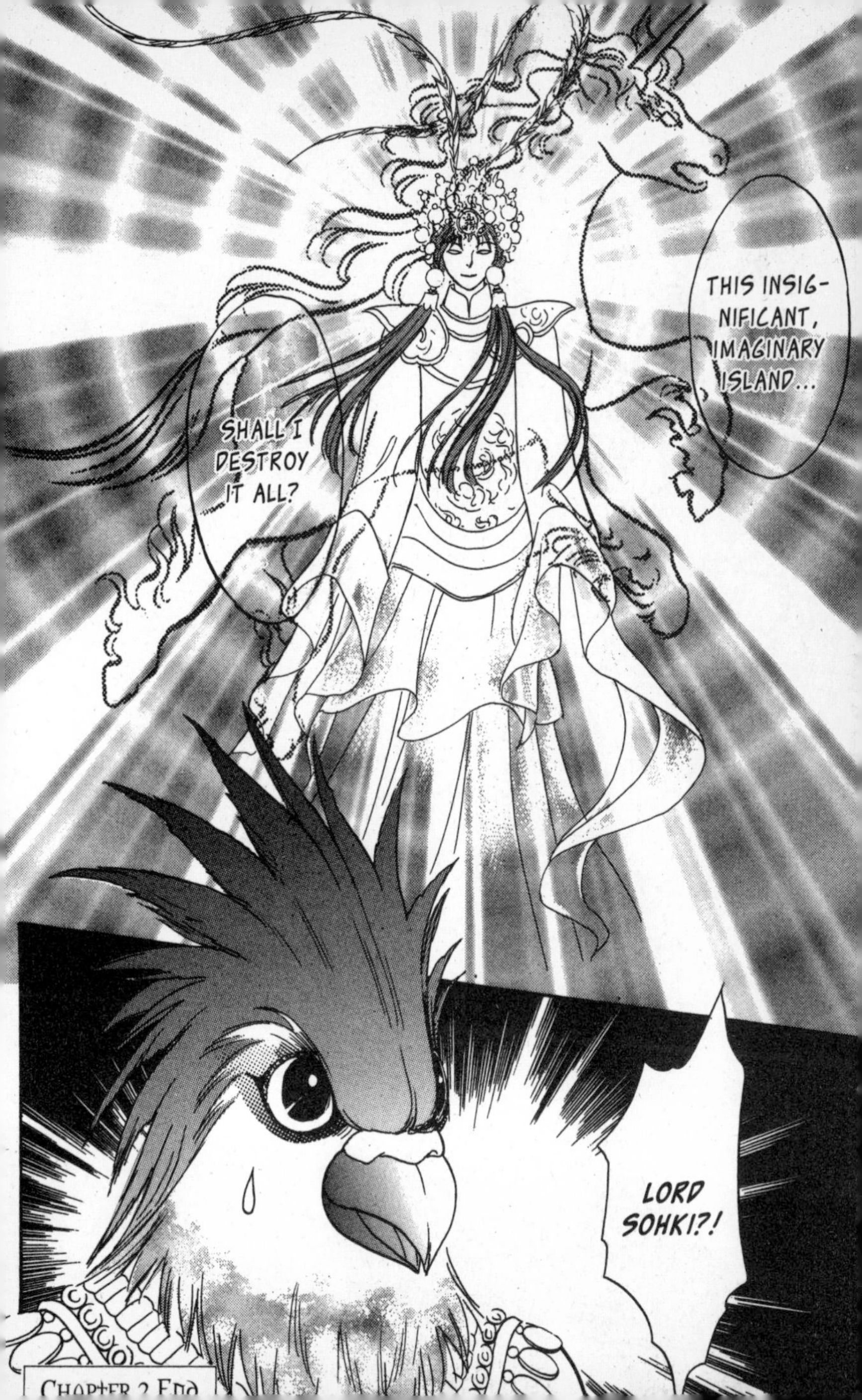
THIS INSIG-NIFICANT, IMAGINARY ISLAND...
SHALL I DESTROY IT ALL?
LORD SOHKI?!
Chapter 2 End

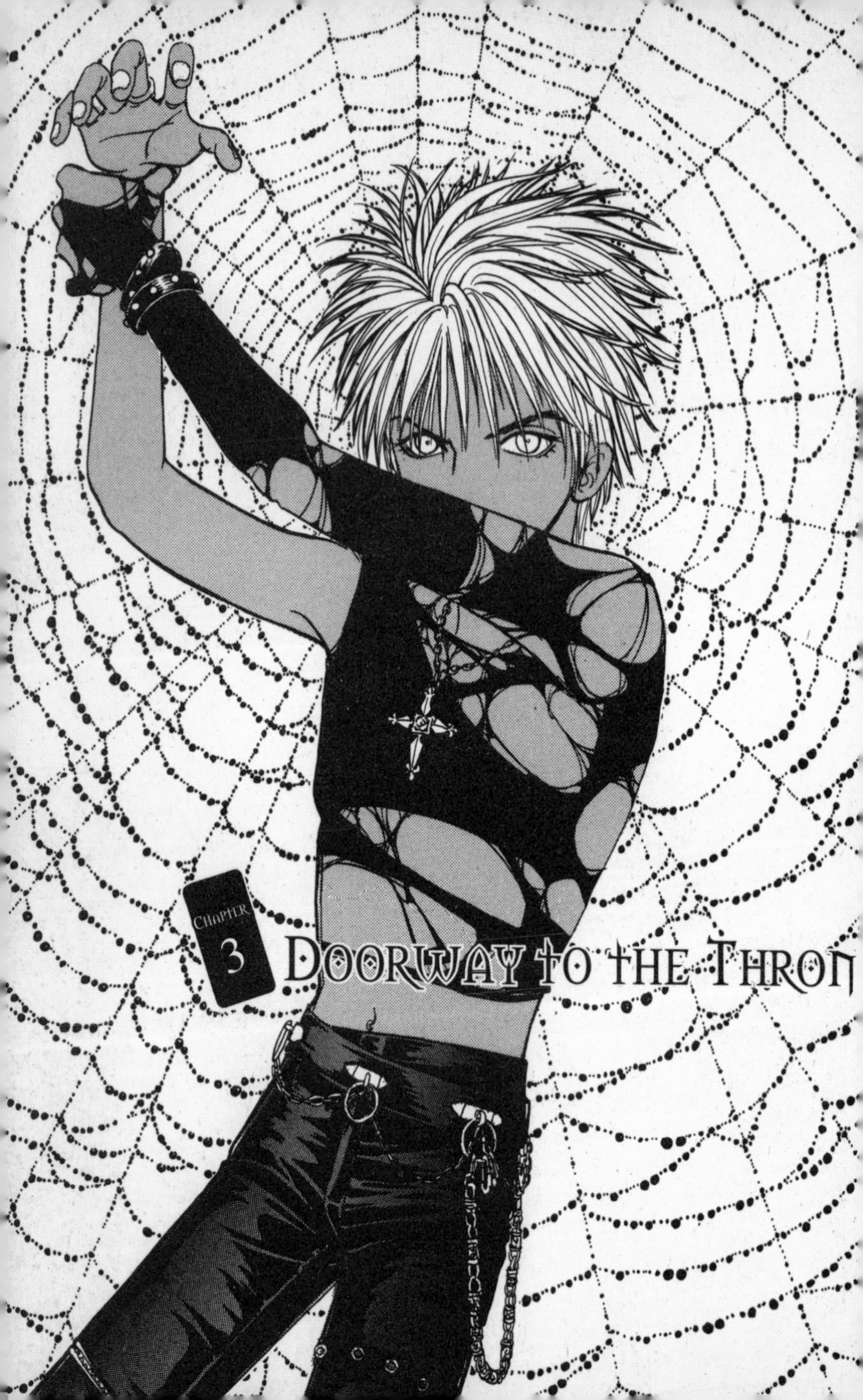

Chapter
3
Doorway to the Thron

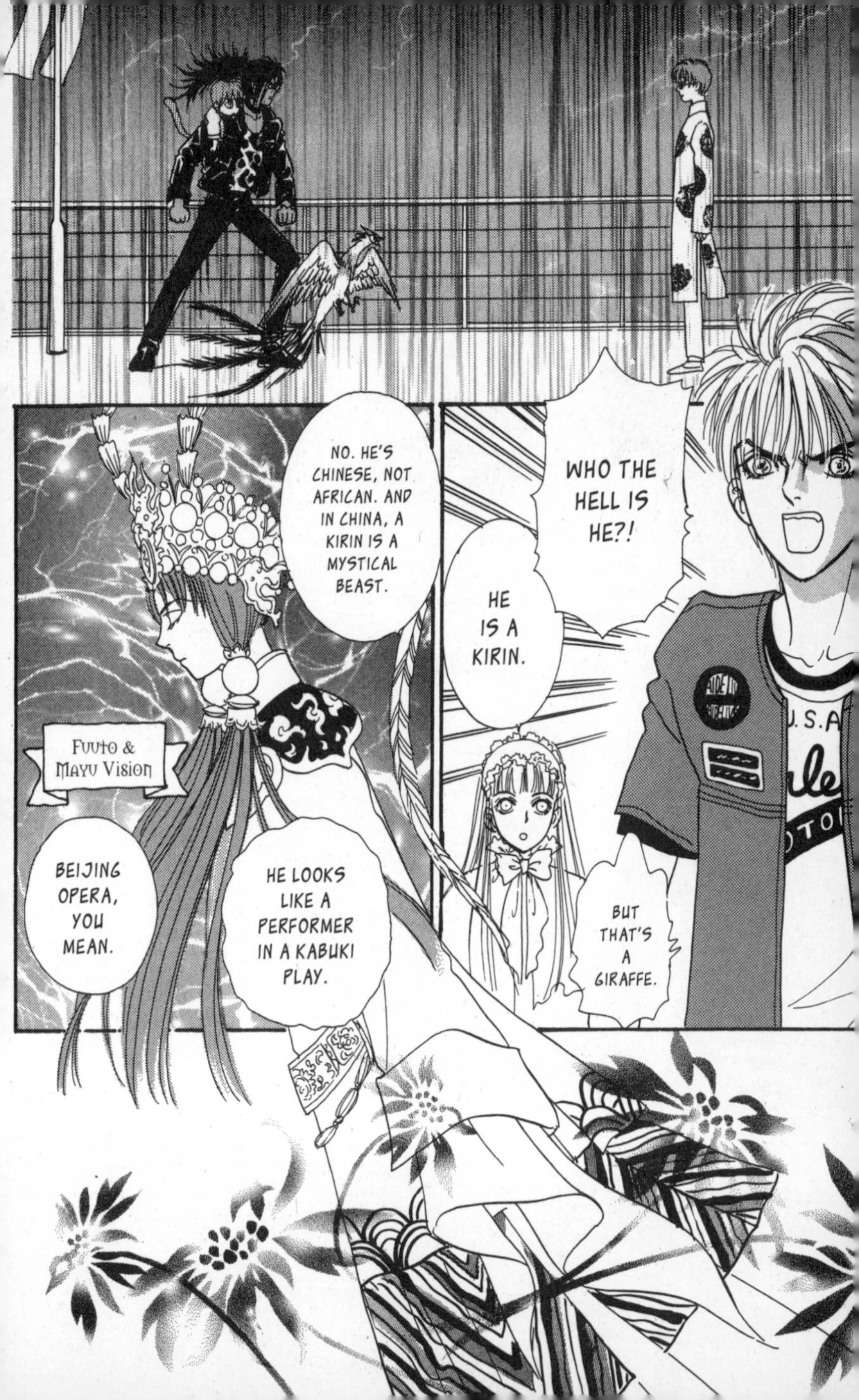
WHO THE HELL IS HE?!
HE IS A KIRIN.
BUT THAT'S A GIRAFFE.
NO. HE'S CHINESE, NOT AFRICAN. AND IN CHINA, A KIRIN IS A MYSTICAL BEAST.
FUUTO & MAYU VISION
HE LOOKS LIKE A PERFORMER IN A KABUKI PLAY.
BEIJING OPERA, YOU MEAN.

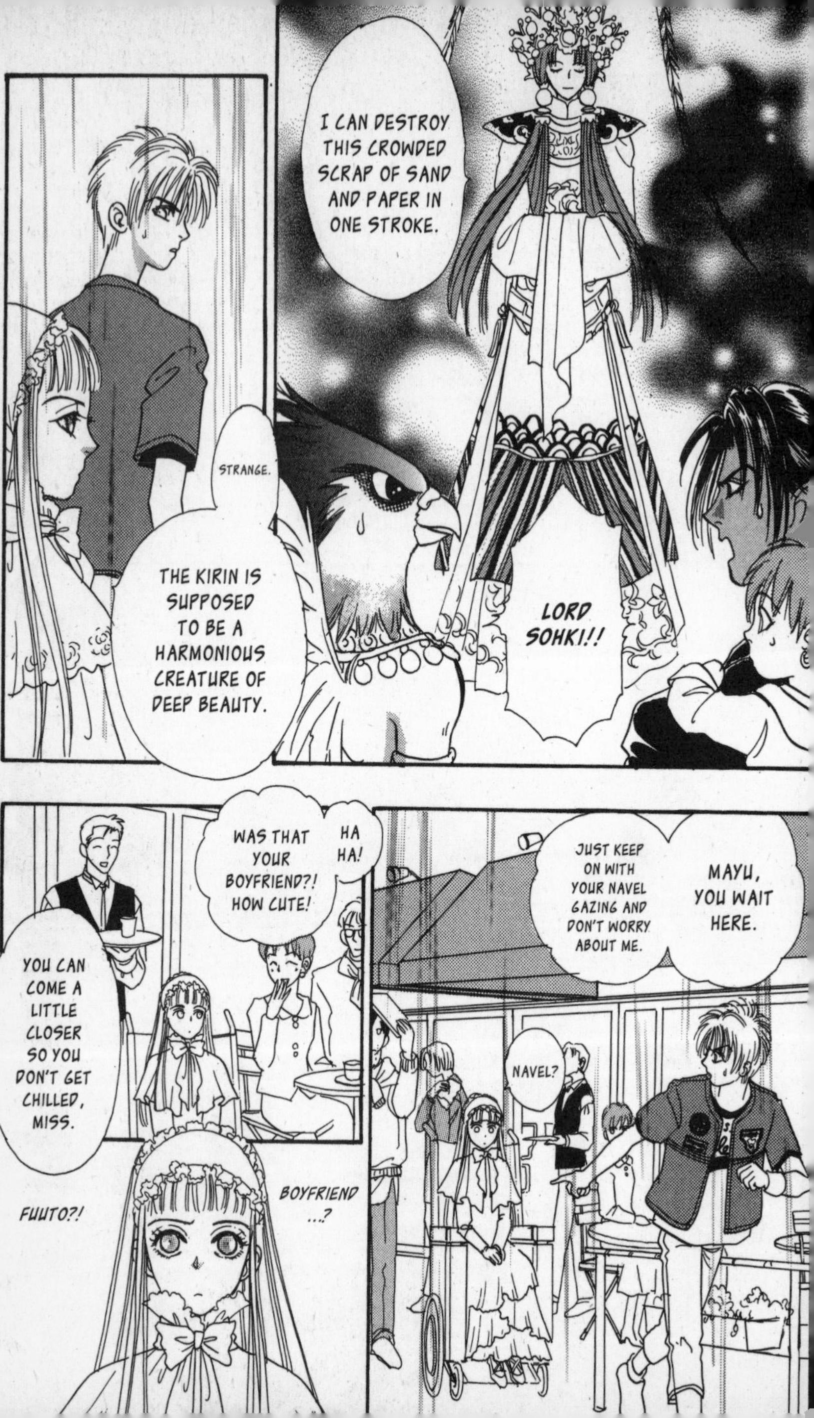
I CAN DESTROY THIS CROWDED SCRAP OF SAND AND PAPER IN ONE STROKE.
LORD SOHKI!!
STRANGE.
THE KIRIN IS SUPPOSED TO BE A HARMONIOUS CREATURE OF DEEP BEAUTY.
MAYU, YOU WAIT HERE.
JUST KEEP ON WITH YOUR NAVEL GAZING AND DON'T WORRY ABOUT ME.
NAVEL?
HA HA!
WAS THAT YOUR BOYFRIEND?! HOW CUTE!
YOU CAN COME A LITTLE CLOSER SO YOU DON'T GET CHILLED, MISS.
BOYFRIEND ...?
FUUTO?!

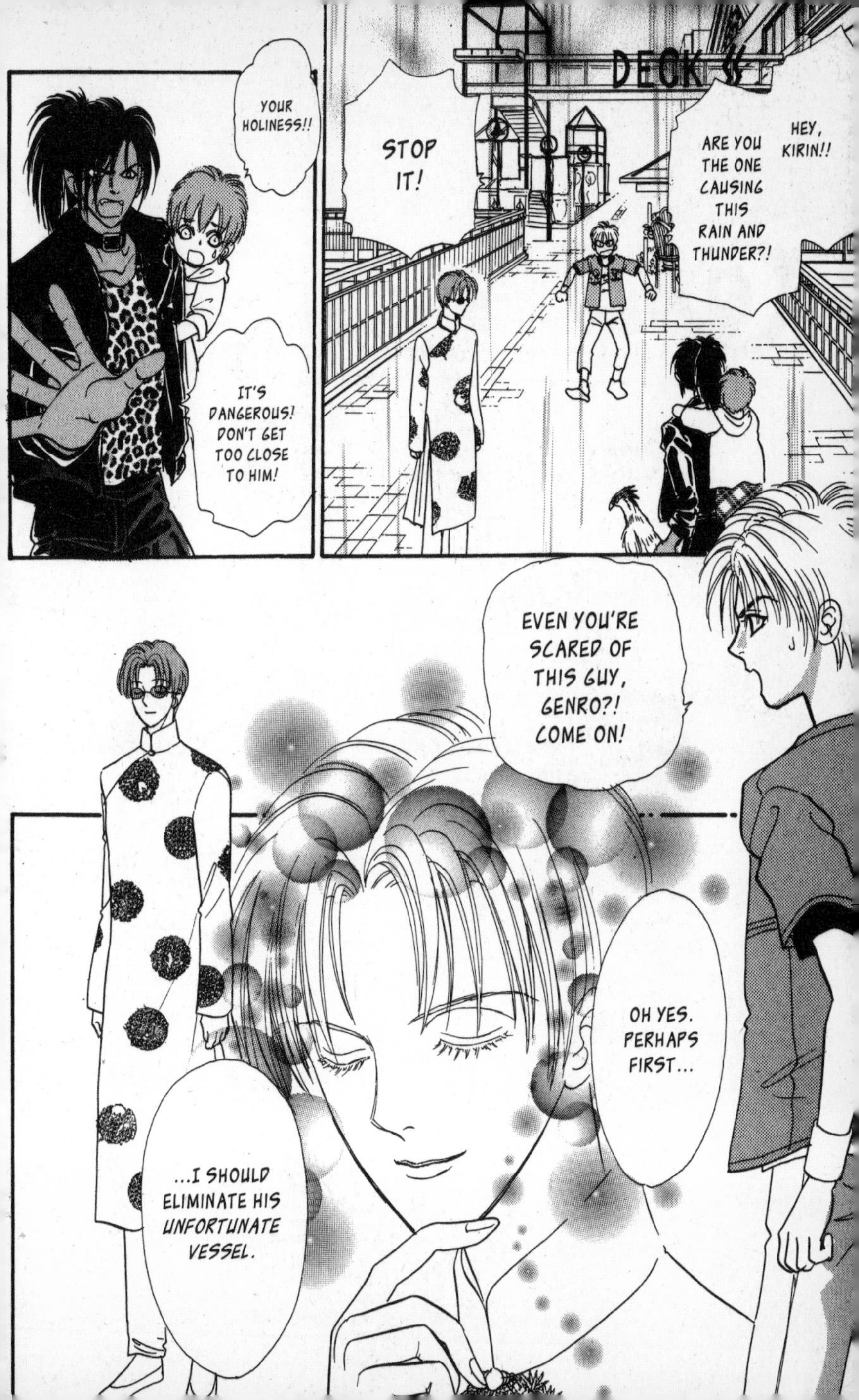

YOUR HOLINESS!!
IT'S DANGEROUS! DON'T GET TOO CLOSE TO HIM!
STOP IT!
DECK
HEY, KIRIN!!
ARE YOU THE ONE CAUSING THIS RAIN AND THUNDER?!
EVEN YOU'RE SCARED OF THIS GUY, GENRO?! COME ON!
OH YES. PERHAPS FIRST...
...I SHOULD ELIMINATE HIS UNFORTUNATE VESSEL.

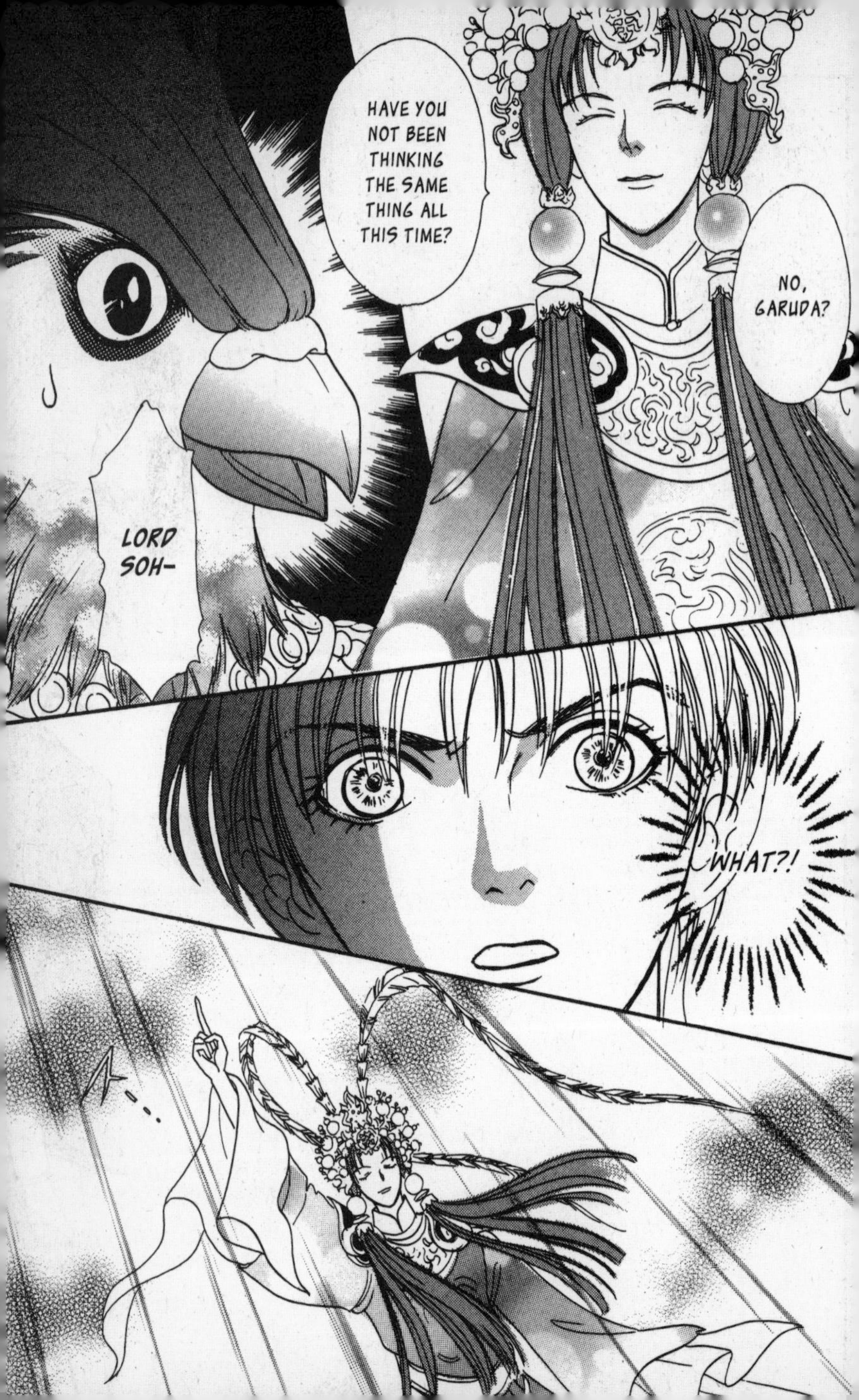
HAVE YOU NOT BEEN THINKING THE SAME THING ALL THIS TIME?
NO, GARUDA?
LORD SOH-
WHAT?!

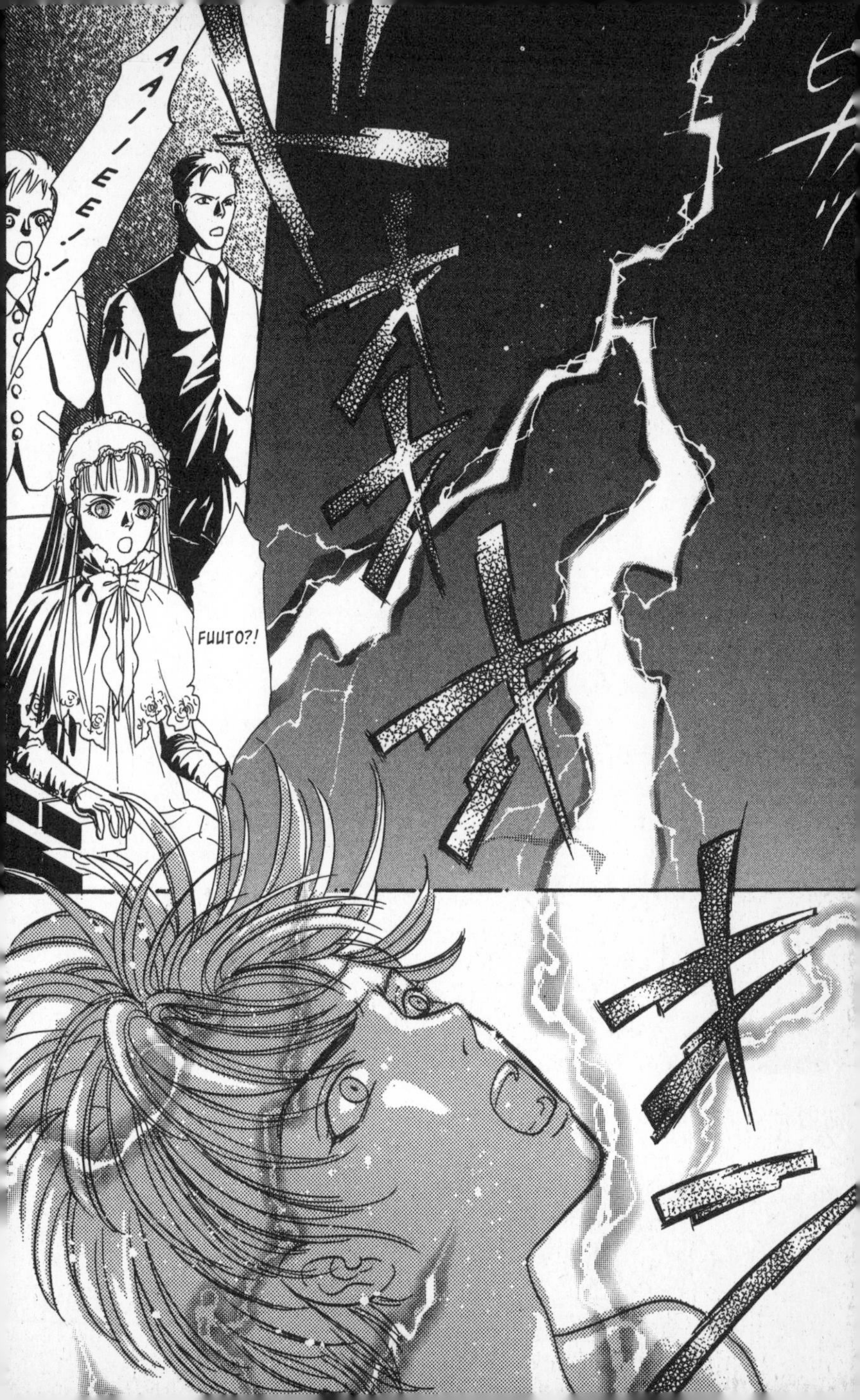
AAIIEEE?!
FUUTO?!

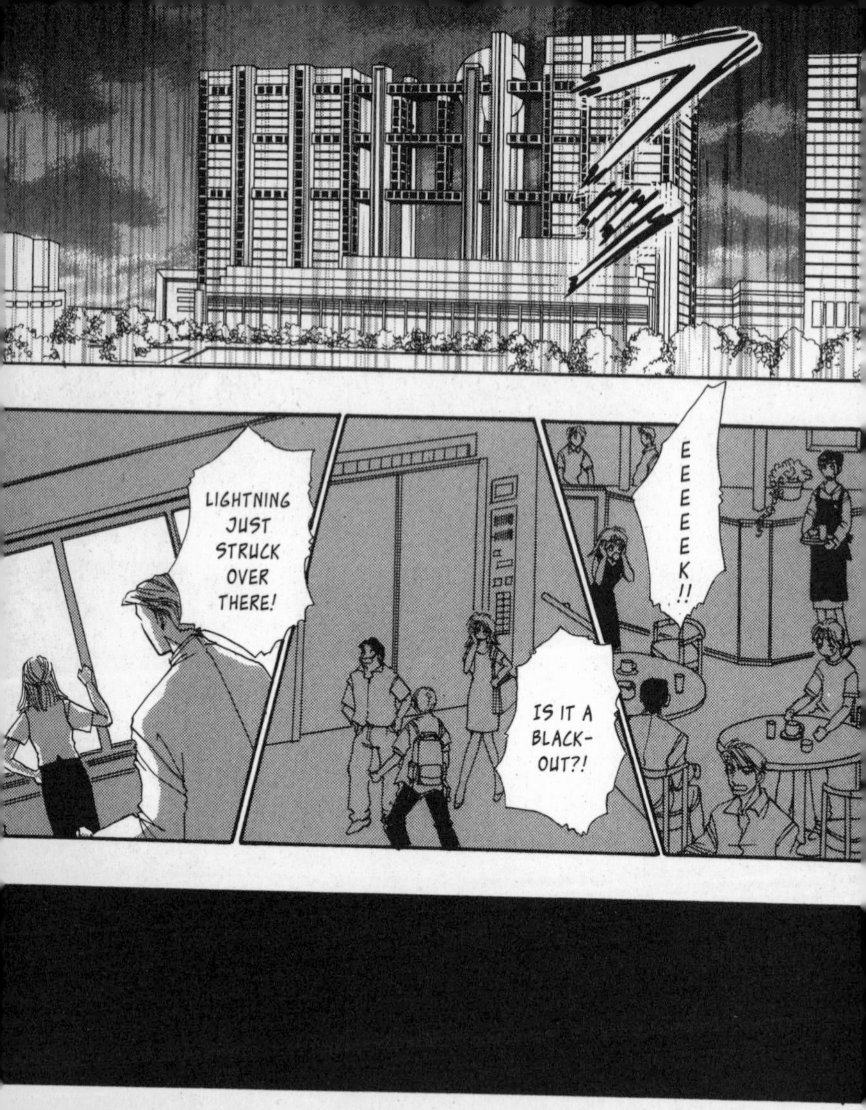
EEEEEK!!
IS IT A BLACK-OUT?!
LIGHTNING JUST STRUCK OVER THERE!

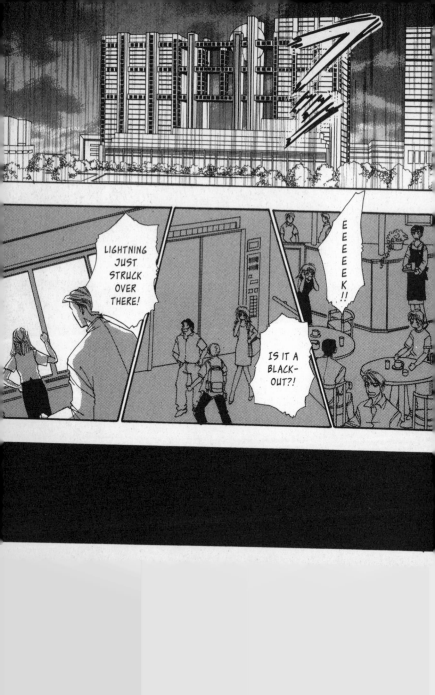

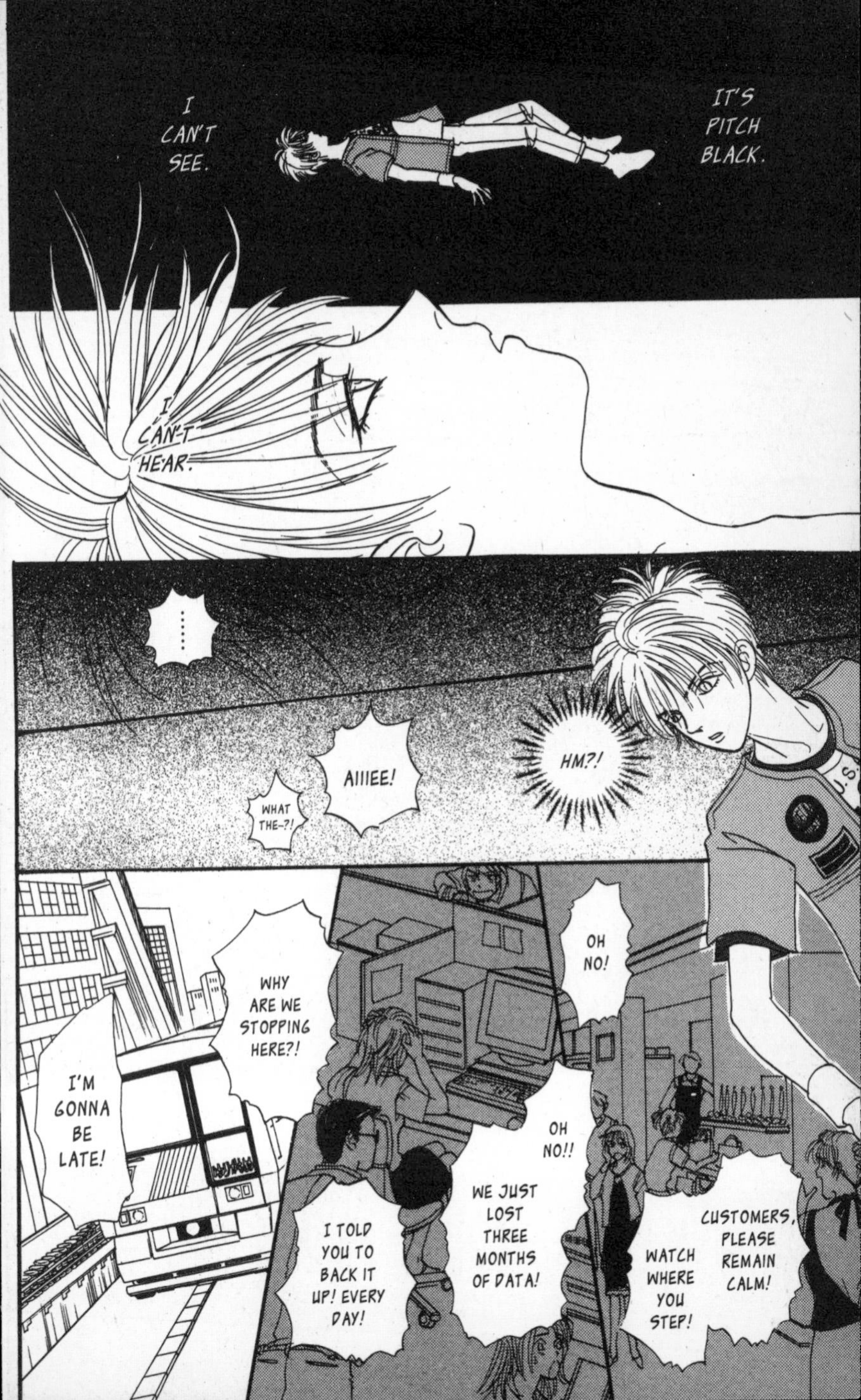
IT'S PITCH BLACK.
I CAN'T SEE.
I CAN'T HEAR.
......
HM?!
AIIIEE!
WHAT THE-?!
CUSTOMERS, PLEASE REMAIN CALM!
WATCH WHERE YOU STEP!
OH NO!!
WE JUST LOST THREE MONTHS OF DATA!
I TOLD YOU TO BACK IT UP! EVERY DAY!
OH NO!
WHY ARE WE STOPPING HERE?!
I'M GONNA BE LATE!

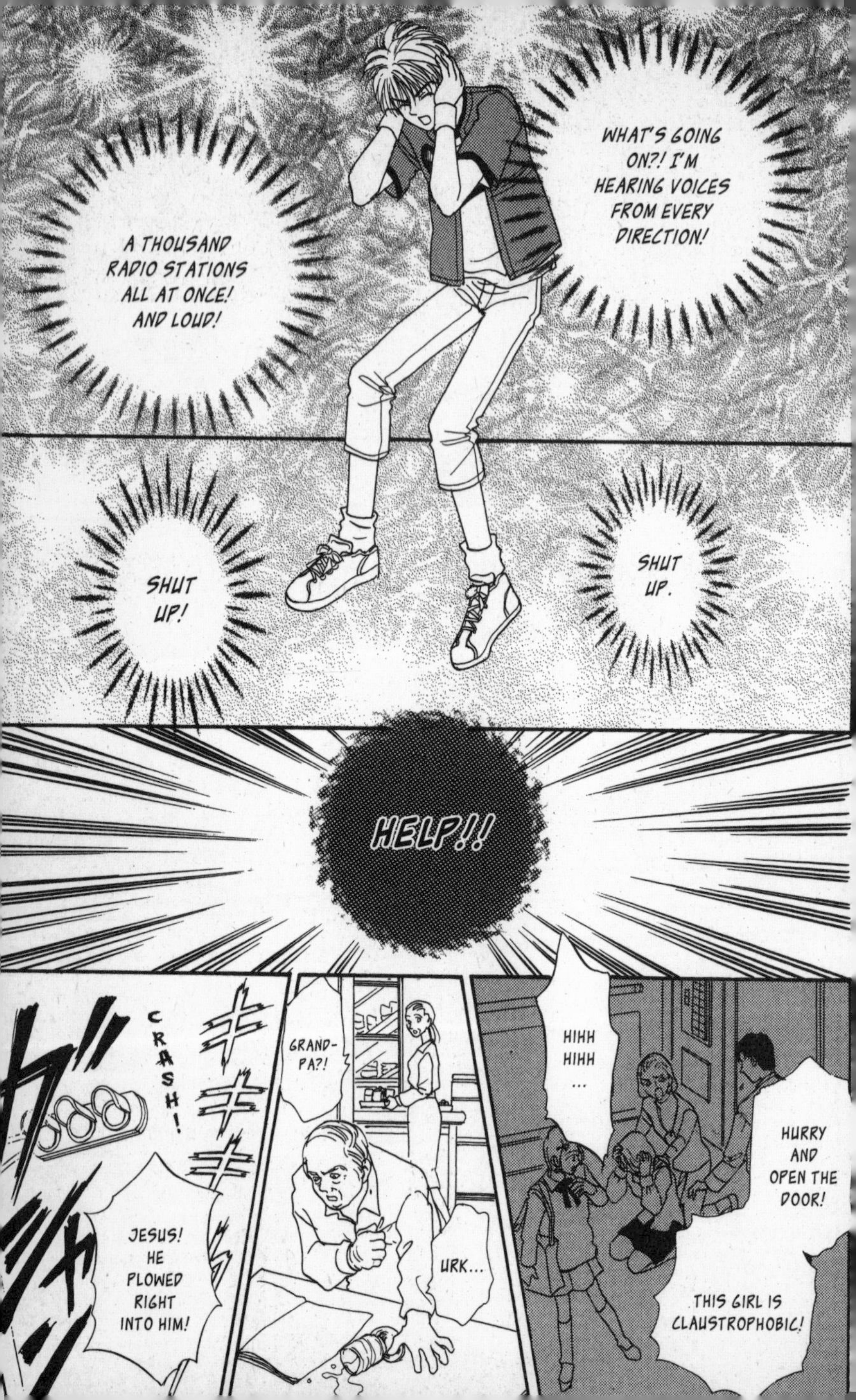
WHAT'S GOING ON?! I'M HEARING VOICES FROM EVERY DIRECTION!
A THOUSAND RADIO STATIONS ALL AT ONCE! AND LOUD!
SHUT UP.
SHUT UP!
HELP!!
HIHH HIHH ...
HURRY AND OPEN THE DOOR!
THIS GIRL IS CLAUSTROPHOBIC!
GRAND-PA?!
URK...
CRASH!
JESUS! HE PLOWED RIGHT INTO HIM!

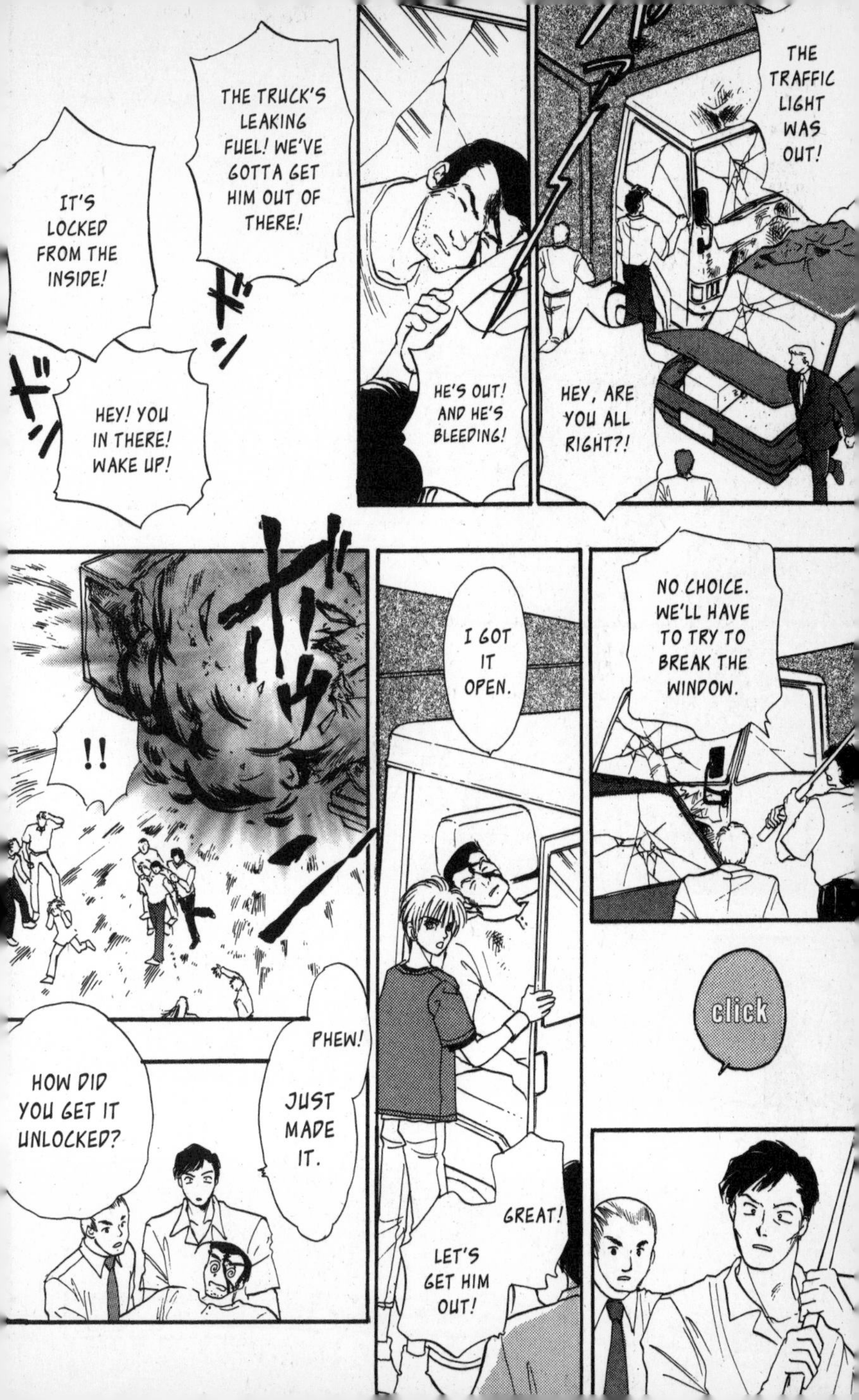
THE TRAFFIC LIGHT WAS OUT!
HEY, ARE YOU ALL RIGHT?!
HE'S OUT! AND HE'S BLEEDING!
THE TRUCK'S LEAKING FUEL! WE'VE GOTTA GET HIM OUT OF THERE!
IT'S LOCKED FROM THE INSIDE!
HEY! YOU IN THERE! WAKE UP!
NO CHOICE. WE'LL HAVE TO TRY TO BREAK THE WINDOW.
click
I GOT IT OPEN.
GREAT!
LET'S GET HIM OUT!
!!
PHEW!
JUST MADE IT.
HOW DID YOU GET IT UNLOCKED?

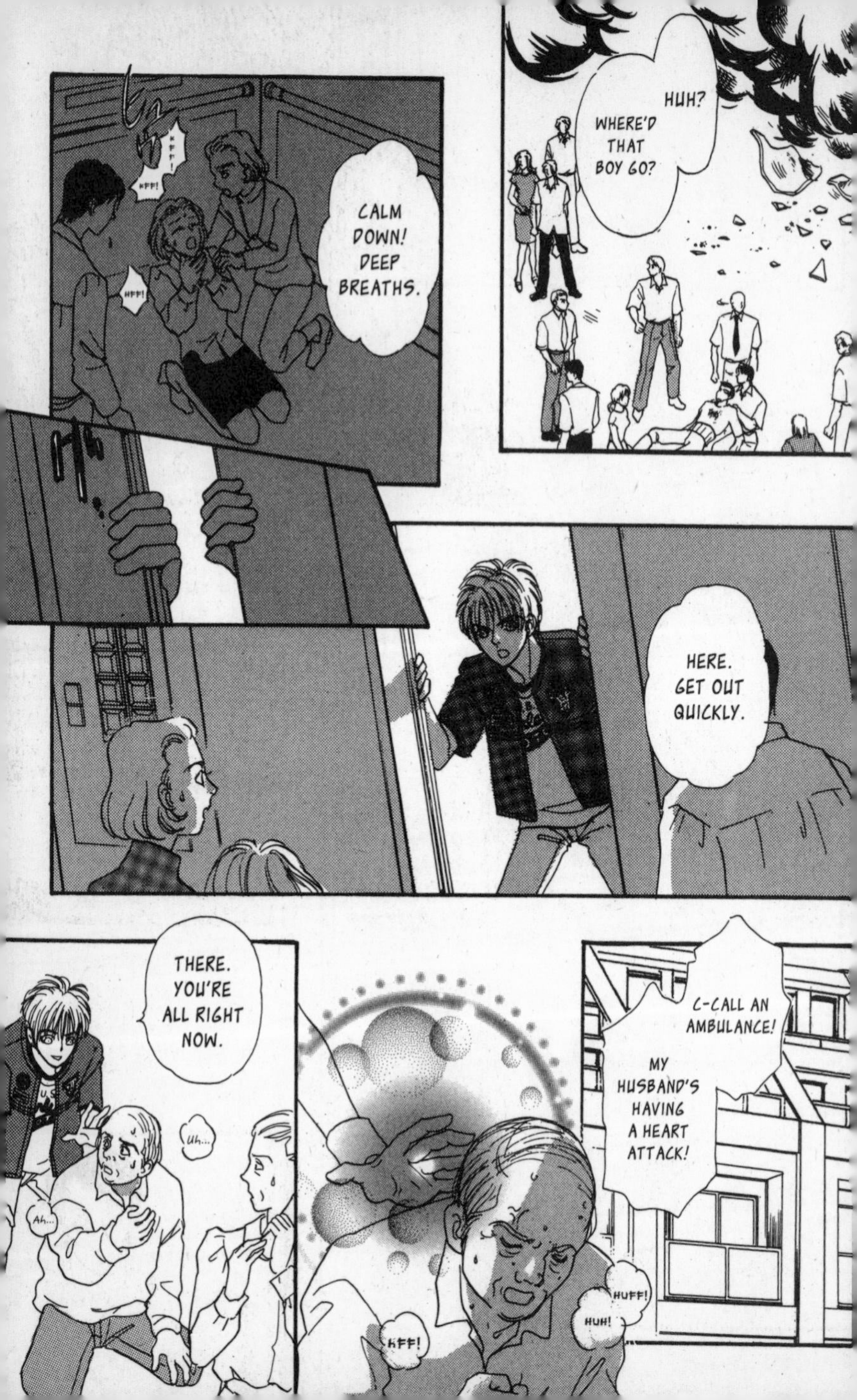
KFF!
HFF!
CALM DOWN! DEEP BREATHS.
HUH?
WHERE'D THAT BOY GO?
HERE. GET OUT QUICKLY.
THERE. YOU'RE ALL RIGHT NOW.
Uh...
Ah...
C-CALL AN AMBULANCE!
MY HUSBAND'S HAVING A HEART ATTACK!
HUFF!
HUH!
KFF!

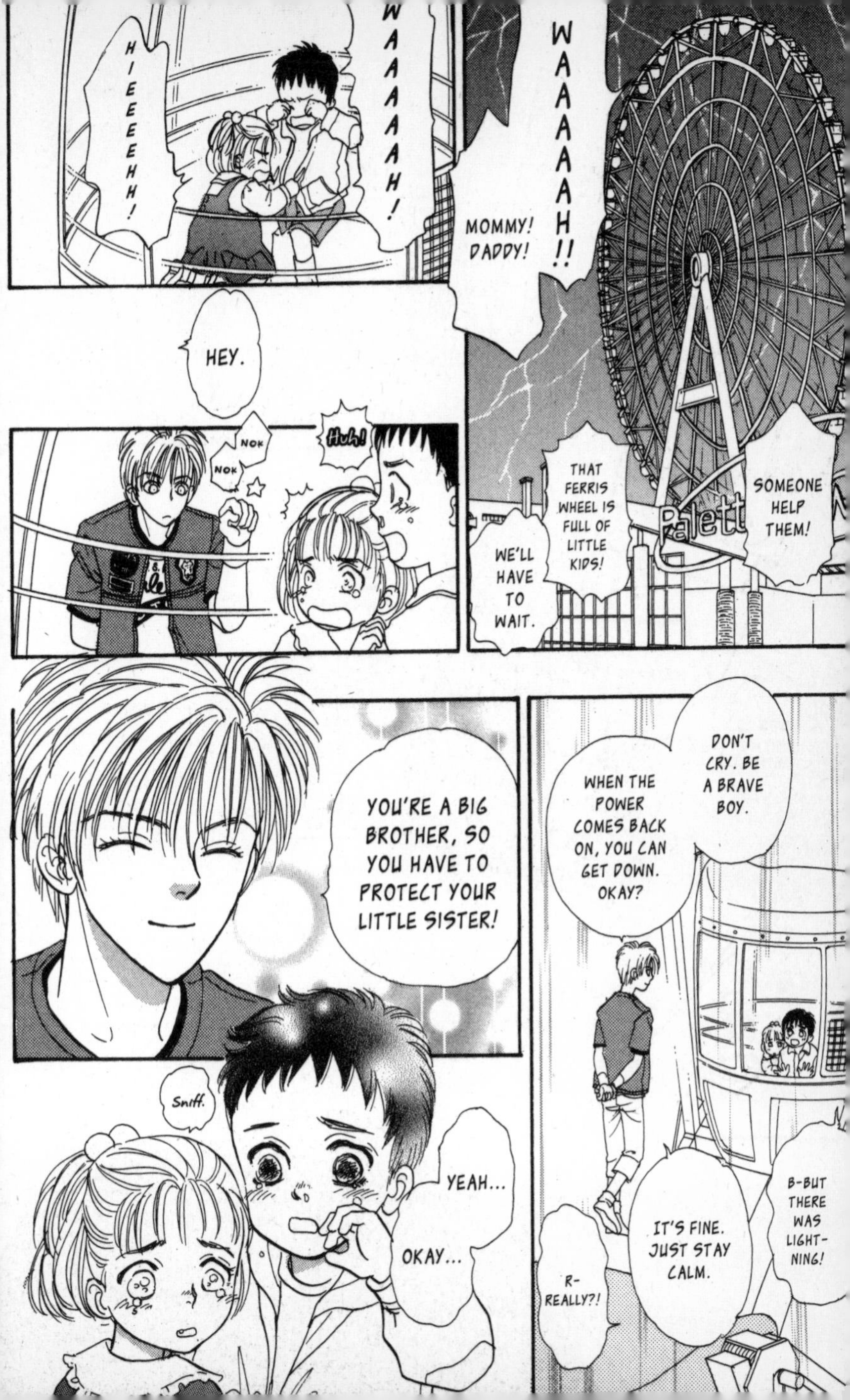

WAAAAAAAH!!
MOMMY! DADDY!
SOMEONE HELP THEM!
THAT FERRIS WHEEL IS FULL OF LITTLE KIDS!
WE'LL HAVE TO WAIT.
Palett
WAAAAAAAH!
HIEEEEEHH!
HEY.
Huh!
NOK
NOK
DON'T CRY. BE A BRAVE BOY.
WHEN THE POWER COMES BACK ON, YOU CAN GET DOWN. OKAY?
B-BUT THERE WAS LIGHT-NING!
IT'S FINE. JUST STAY CALM.
R-REALLY?!
YOU'RE A BIG BROTHER, SO YOU HAVE TO PROTECT YOUR LITTLE SISTER!
YEAH...
OKAY...
Sniff.

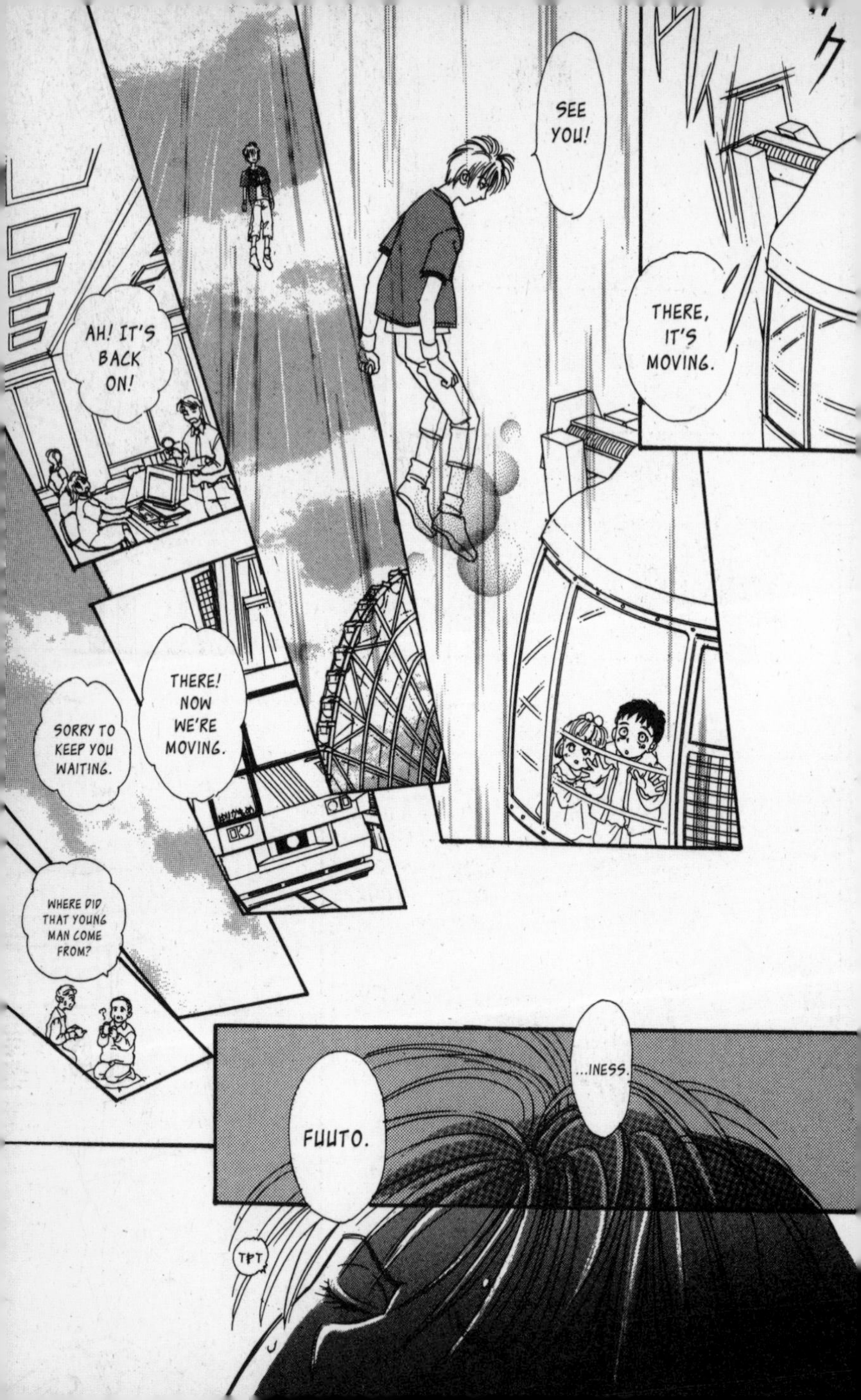
SEE YOU!
THERE, IT'S MOVING.
AH! IT'S BACK ON!
THERE! NOW WE'RE MOVING.
SORRY TO KEEP YOU WAITING.
WHERE DID THAT YOUNG MAN COME FROM?
...INESS.
FUUTO.
TPT

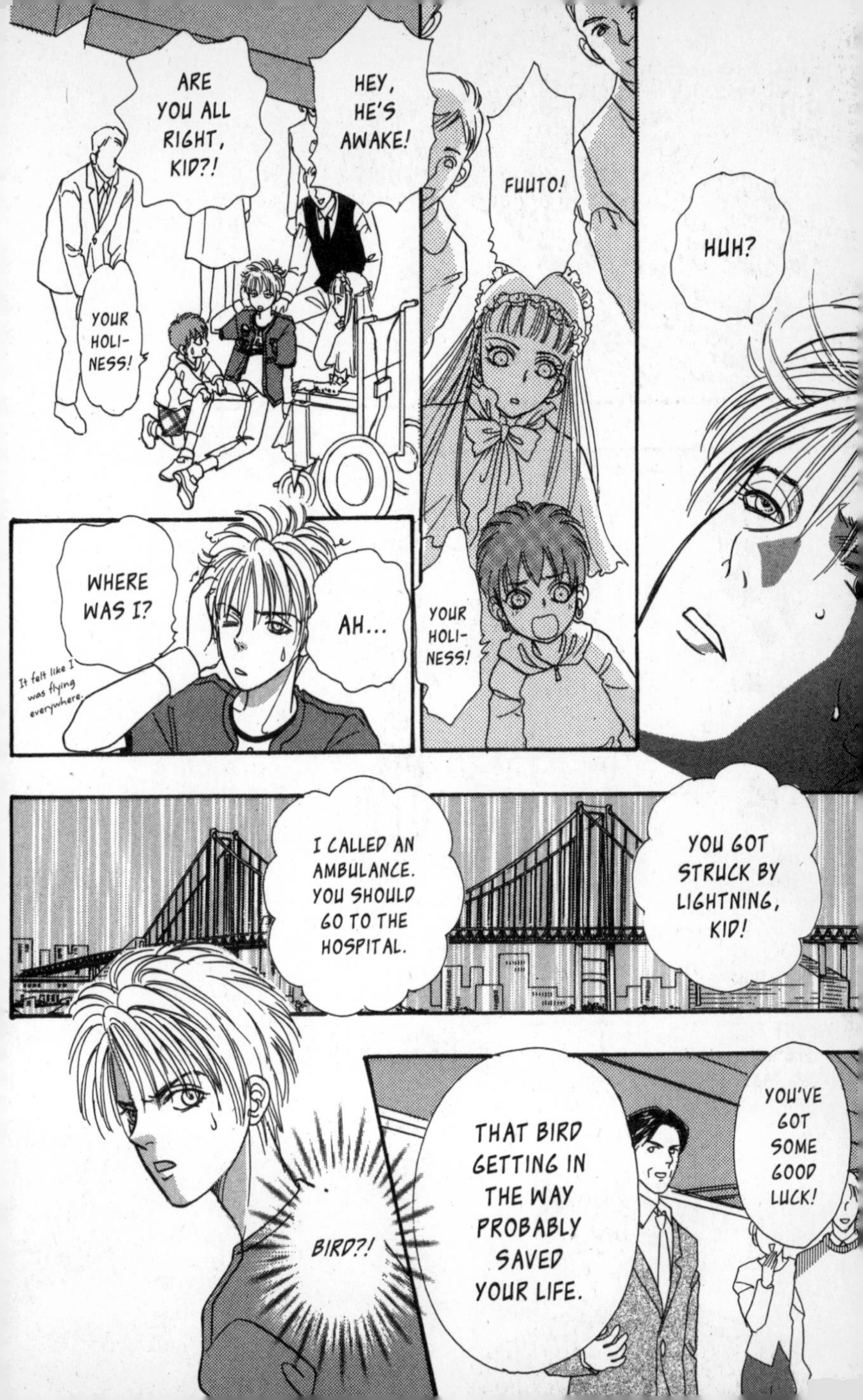
HEY, HE'S AWAKE!
ARE YOU ALL RIGHT, KID?!
YOUR HOLI-NESS!
AH...
WHERE WAS I?
It felt like I was flying everywhere.
FUUTO!
YOUR HOLI-NESS!
HUH?
YOU GOT STRUCK BY LIGHTNING, KID!
I CALLED AN AMBULANCE. YOU SHOULD GO TO THE HOSPITAL.
YOU'VE GOT SOME GOOD LUCK!
THAT BIRD GETTING IN THE WAY PROBABLY SAVED YOUR LIFE.
BIRD?!

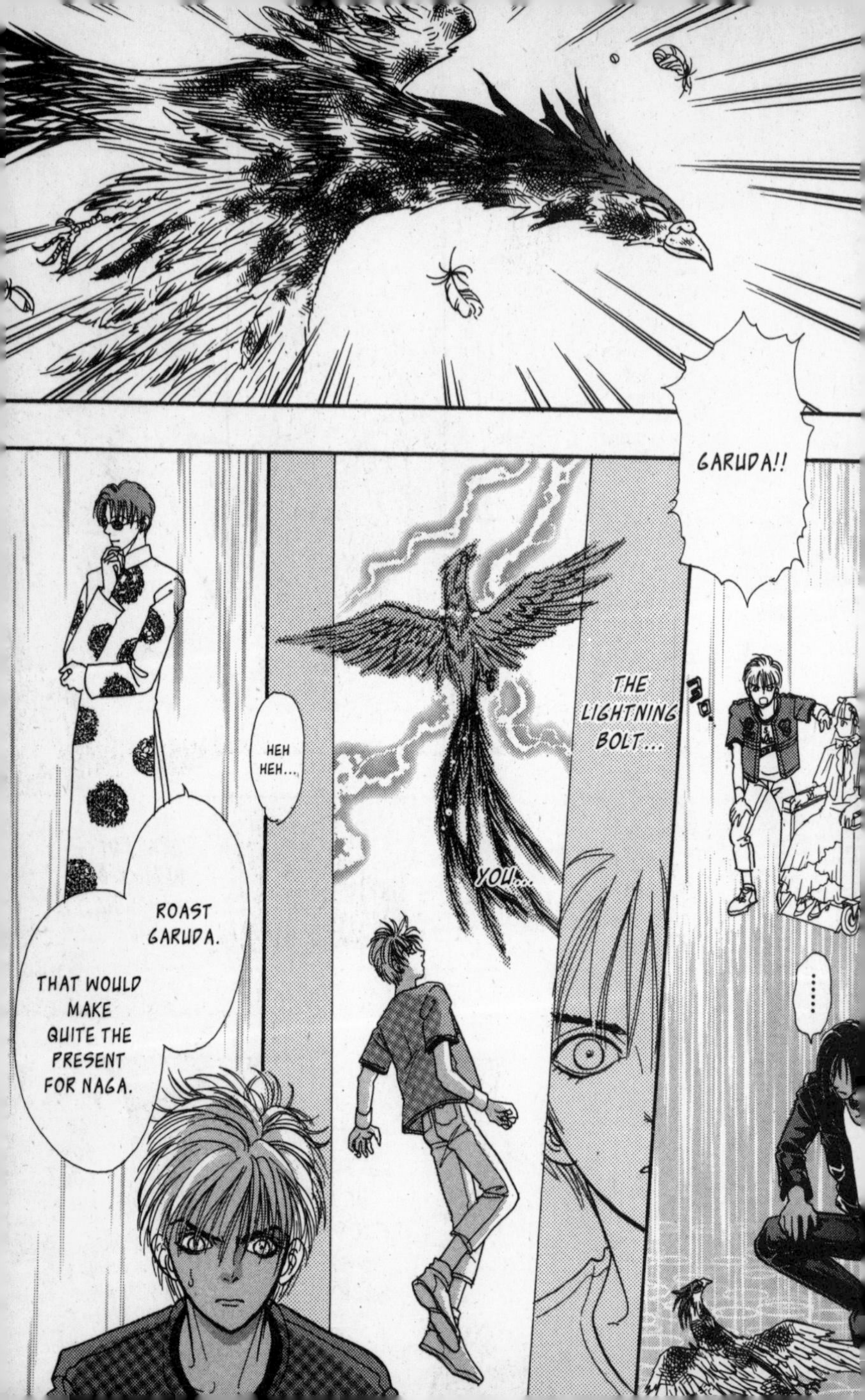
GARUDA!!
......
THE LIGHTNING BOLT...
YOU...
HEH HEH...
ROAST GARUDA.
THAT WOULD MAKE QUITE THE PRESENT FOR NAGA.

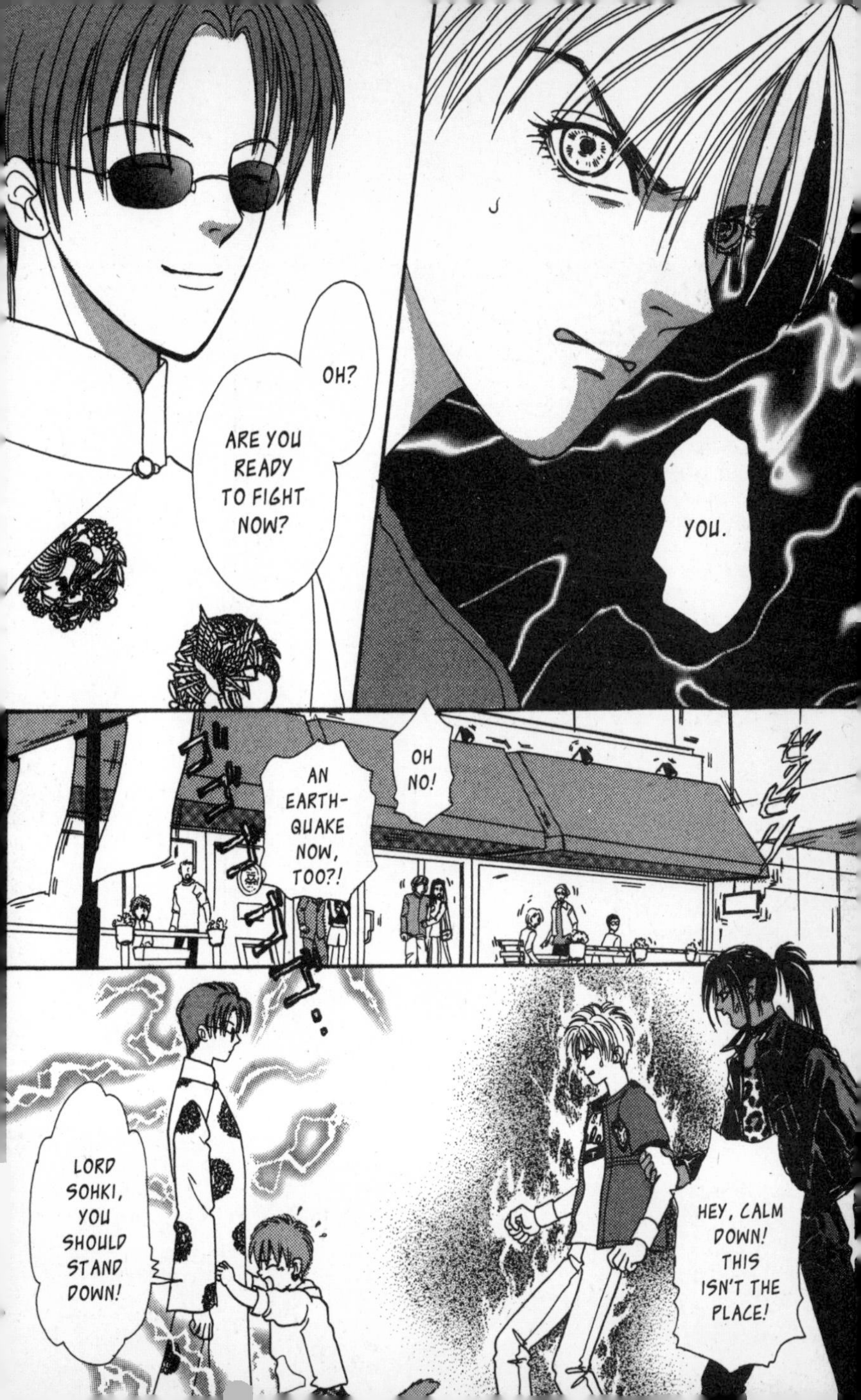
YOU.
OH?
ARE YOU READY TO FIGHT NOW?
OH NO!
AN EARTH-QUAKE NOW, TOO?!
HEY, CALM DOWN! THIS ISN'T THE PLACE!
LORD SOHKI, YOU SHOULD STAND DOWN!

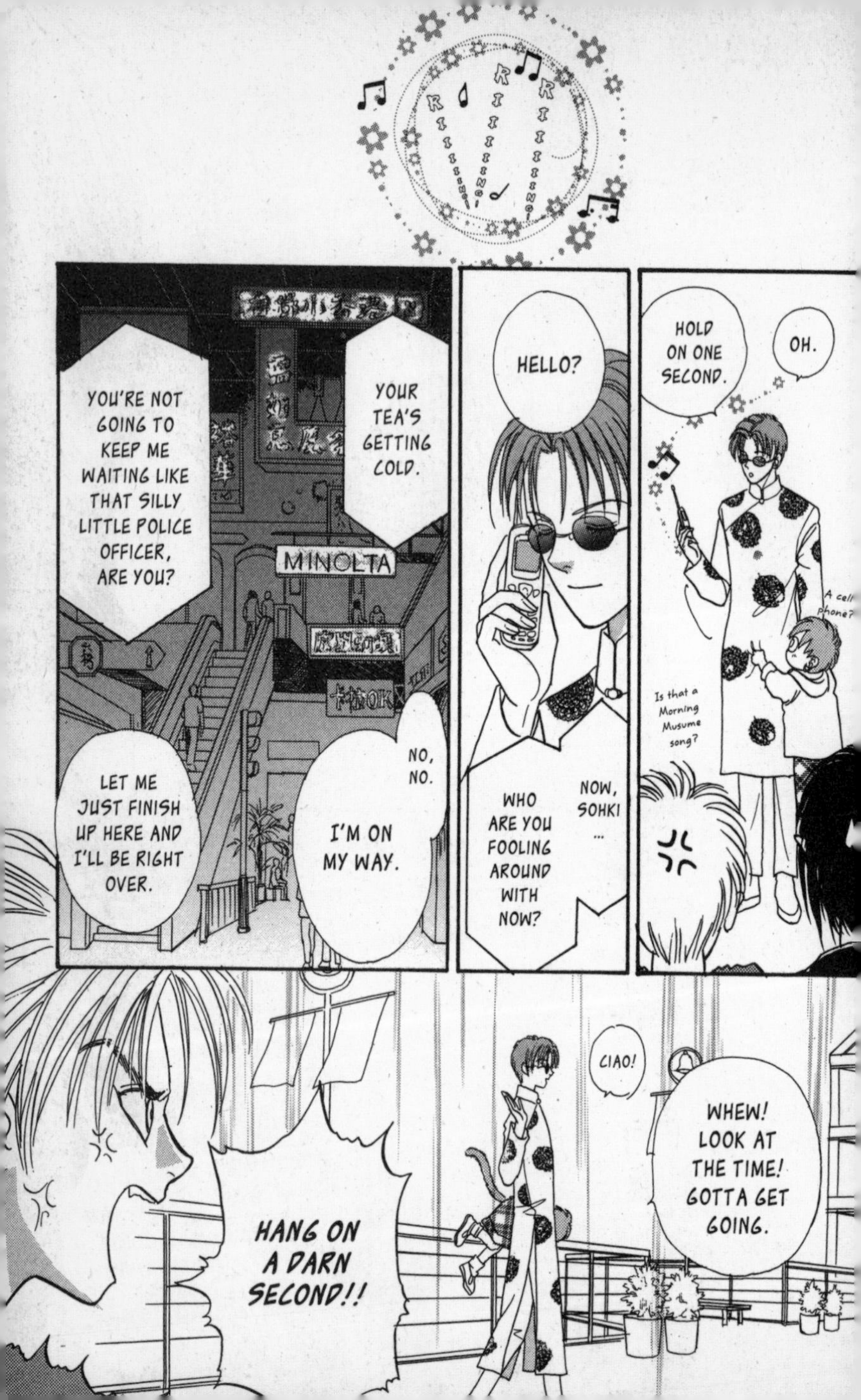
RIIIIIING!
RIIIIIING!
RIIIIIING!
OH.
HOLD ON ONE SECOND.
A cell phone?
Is that a Morning Musume song?
HELLO?
NOW, SOHKI ...
WHO ARE YOU FOOLING AROUND WITH NOW?
YOUR TEA'S GETTING COLD.
YOU'RE NOT GOING TO KEEP ME WAITING LIKE THAT SILLY LITTLE POLICE OFFICER, ARE YOU?
MINOLTA
NO, NO.
I'M ON MY WAY.
LET ME JUST FINISH UP HERE AND I'LL BE RIGHT OVER.
WHEW! LOOK AT THE TIME! GOTTA GET GOING.
CIAO!
HANG ON A DARN SECOND!!

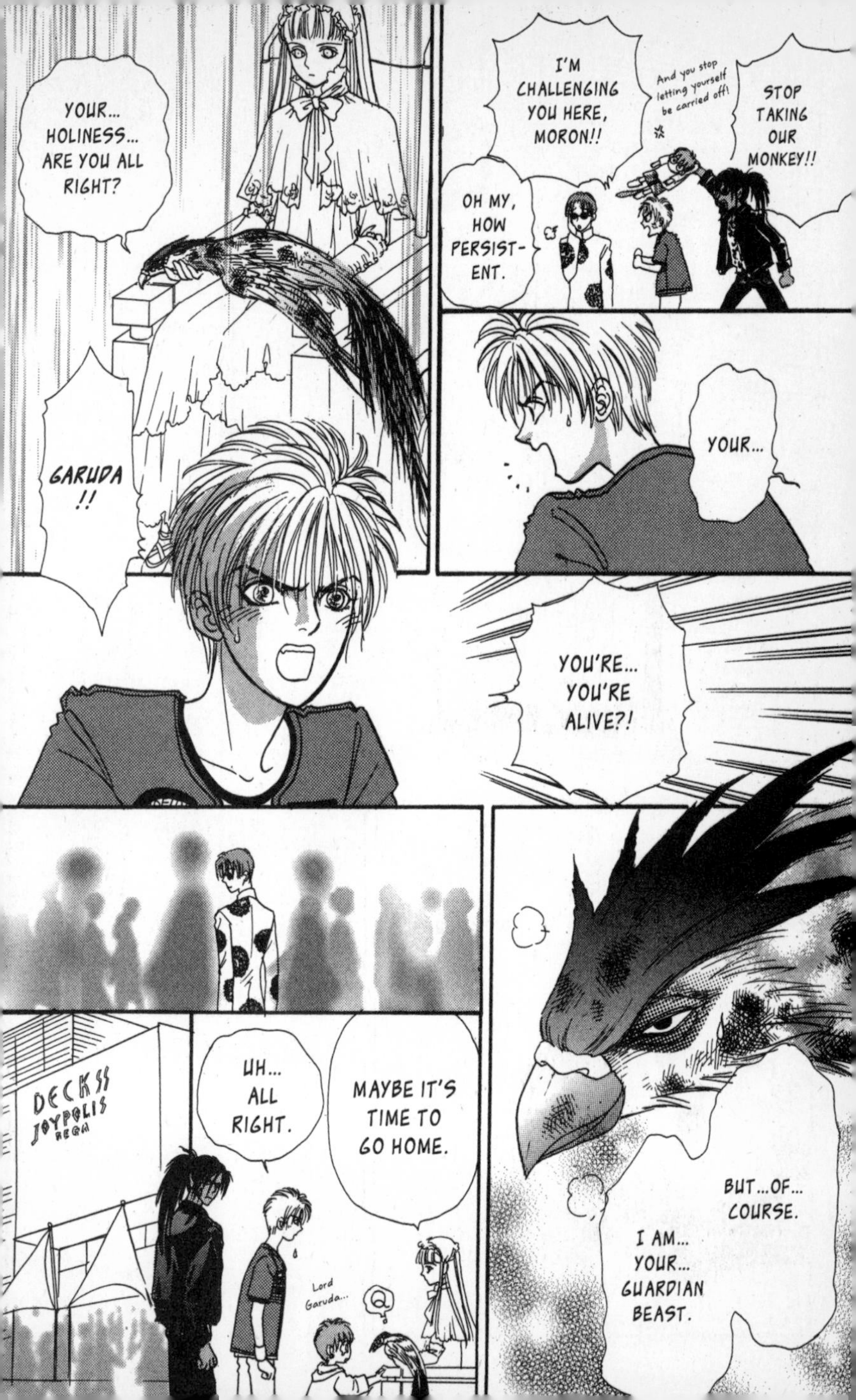
YOUR... HOLINESS... ARE YOU ALL RIGHT?
GARUDA!!
I'M CHALLENGING YOU HERE, MORON!!
And you stop letting yourself be carried off!
STOP TAKING OUR MONKEY!!
OH MY, HOW PERSIST-ENT.
YOUR...
YOU'RE... YOU'RE ALIVE?!
BUT...OF... COURSE.
I AM... YOUR... GUARDIAN BEAST.
JOYPOLIS
SEGA
MAYBE IT'S TIME TO GO HOME.
UH... ALL RIGHT.
Lord Garuda...

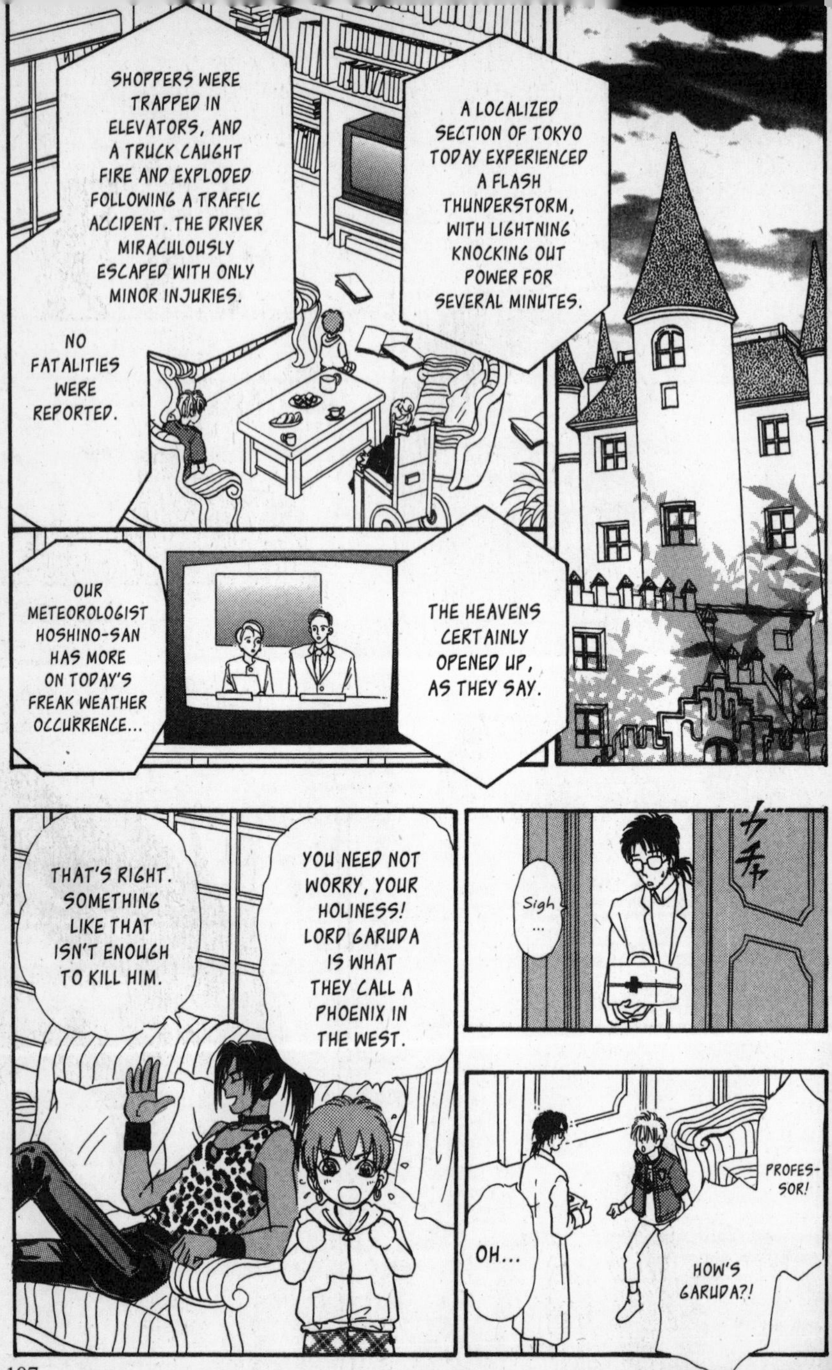
A LOCALIZED SECTION OF TOKYO TODAY EXPERIENCED A FLASH THUNDERSTORM, WITH LIGHTNING KNOCKING OUT POWER FOR SEVERAL MINUTES.
SHOPPERS WERE TRAPPED IN ELEVATORS, AND A TRUCK CAUGHT FIRE AND EXPLODED FOLLOWING A TRAFFIC ACCIDENT. THE DRIVER MIRACULOUSLY ESCAPED WITH ONLY MINOR INJURIES.
NO FATALITIES WERE REPORTED.
OUR METEOROLOGIST HOSHINO-SAN HAS MORE ON TODAY'S FREAK WEATHER OCCURRENCE...
THE HEAVENS CERTAINLY OPENED UP, AS THEY SAY.
THAT'S RIGHT. SOMETHING LIKE THAT ISN'T ENOUGH TO KILL HIM.
YOU NEED NOT WORRY, YOUR HOLINESS! LORD GARUDA IS WHAT THEY CALL A PHOENIX IN THE WEST.
Sigh ...
PROFES-SOR!
HOW'S GARUDA?!
OH...

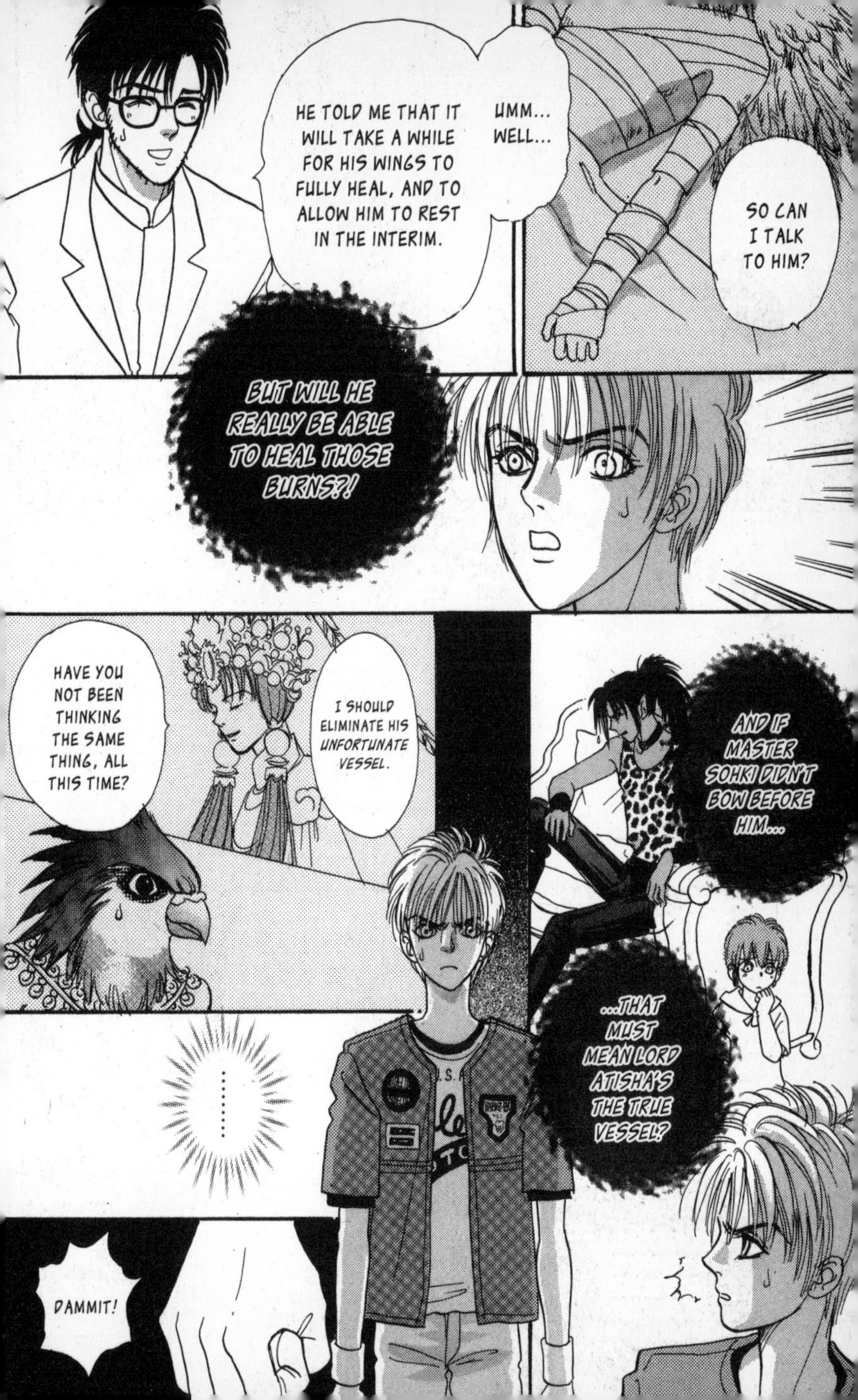
SO CAN I TALK TO HIM?
UMM... WELL...
HE TOLD ME THAT IT WILL TAKE A WHILE FOR HIS WINGS TO FULLY HEAL, AND TO ALLOW HIM TO REST IN THE INTERIM.
BUT WILL HE REALLY BE ABLE TO HEAL THOSE BURNS?!
AND IF MASTER SOHKI DIDN'T BOW BEFORE HIM...
...THAT MUST MEAN LORD ATISHA'S THE TRUE VESSEL?
I SHOULD ELIMINATE HIS UNFORTUNATE VESSEL.
HAVE YOU NOT BEEN THINKING THE SAME THING, ALL THIS TIME?
......
DAMMIT!

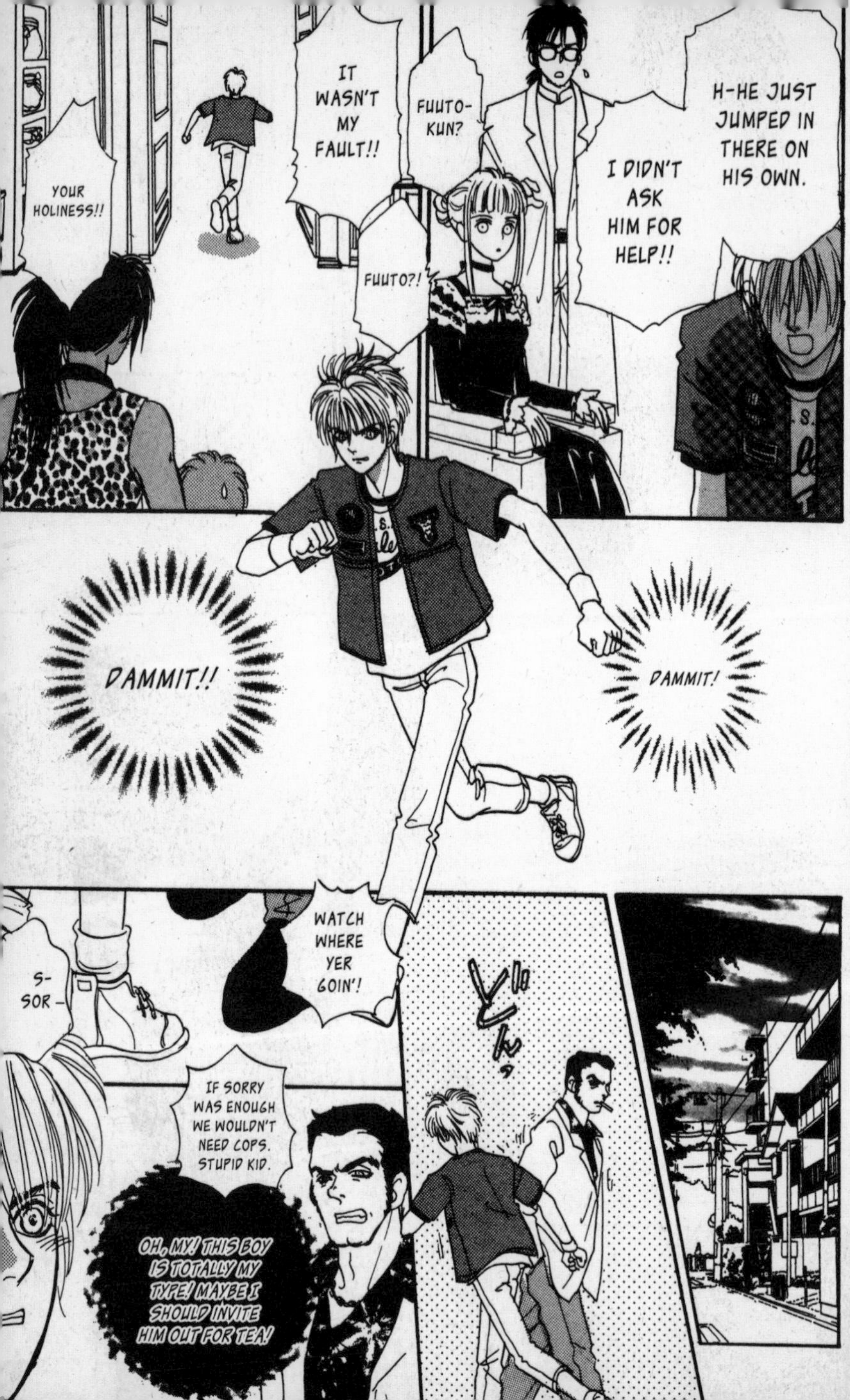
H-HE JUST JUMPED IN THERE ON HIS OWN.
I DIDN'T ASK HIM FOR HELP!!
FUUTO-KUN?
IT WASN'T MY FAULT!!
FUUTO?!
YOUR HOLINESS!!
DAMMIT!
DAMMIT!!
WATCH WHERE YER GOIN'!
S- SOR-
IF SORRY WAS ENOUGH WE WOULDN'T NEED COPS. STUPID KID.
OH, MY! THIS BOY IS TOTALLY MY TYPE! MAYBE I SHOULD INVITE HIM OUT FOR TEA!

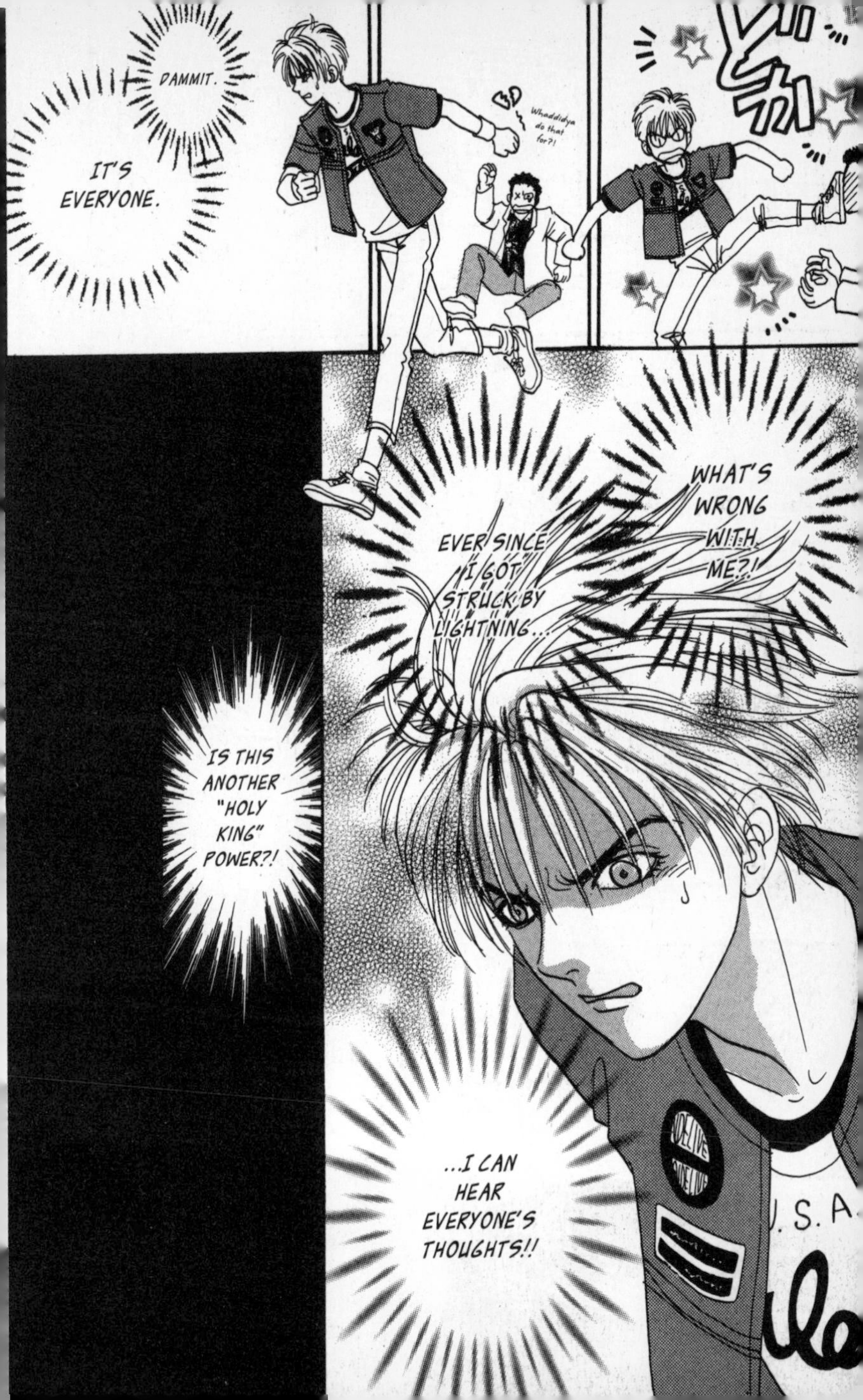
DAMMIT.
IT'S EVERYONE.
Whaddidya do that for?!
WHAT'S WRONG WITH ME?!
EVER SINCE I GOT STRUCK BY LIGHTNING...
IS THIS ANOTHER "HOLY KING" POWER?!
...I CAN HEAR EVERYONE'S THOUGHTS!!

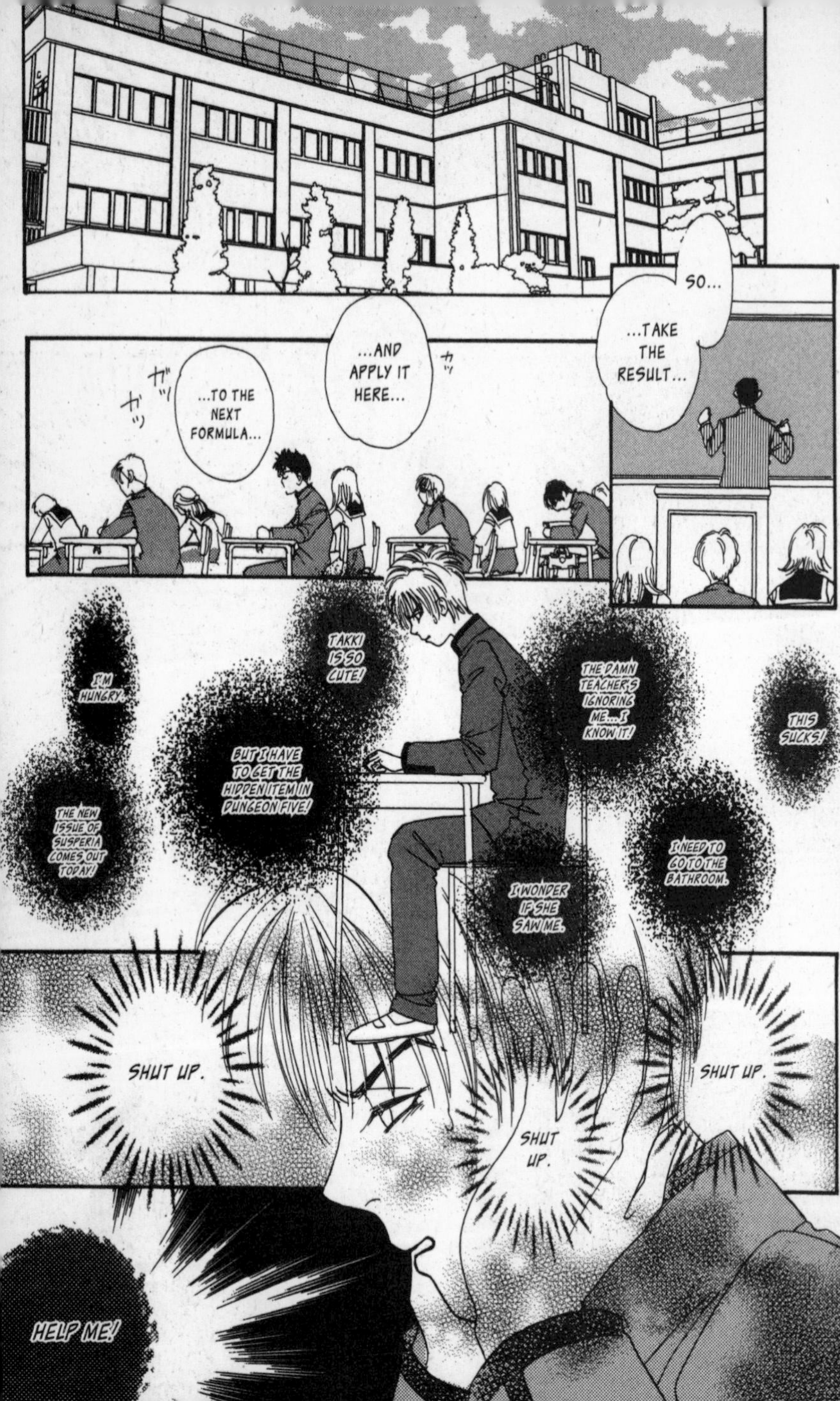
SO...
...TAKE THE RESULT...
...AND APPLY IT HERE...
...TO THE NEXT FORMULA...
THIS SUCKS!
THE DAMN TEACHER'S IGNORING ME... I KNOW IT!
TAKKI IS SO CUTE!
I'M HUNGRY.
I NEED TO GO TO THE BATHROOM.
I WONDER IF SHE SAW ME.
BUT I HAVE TO GET THE HIDDEN ITEM IN DUNGEON FIVE!
THE NEW ISSUE OF SUSPERIA COMES OUT TODAY!
SHUT UP.
SHUT UP.
SHUT UP.
HELP ME!

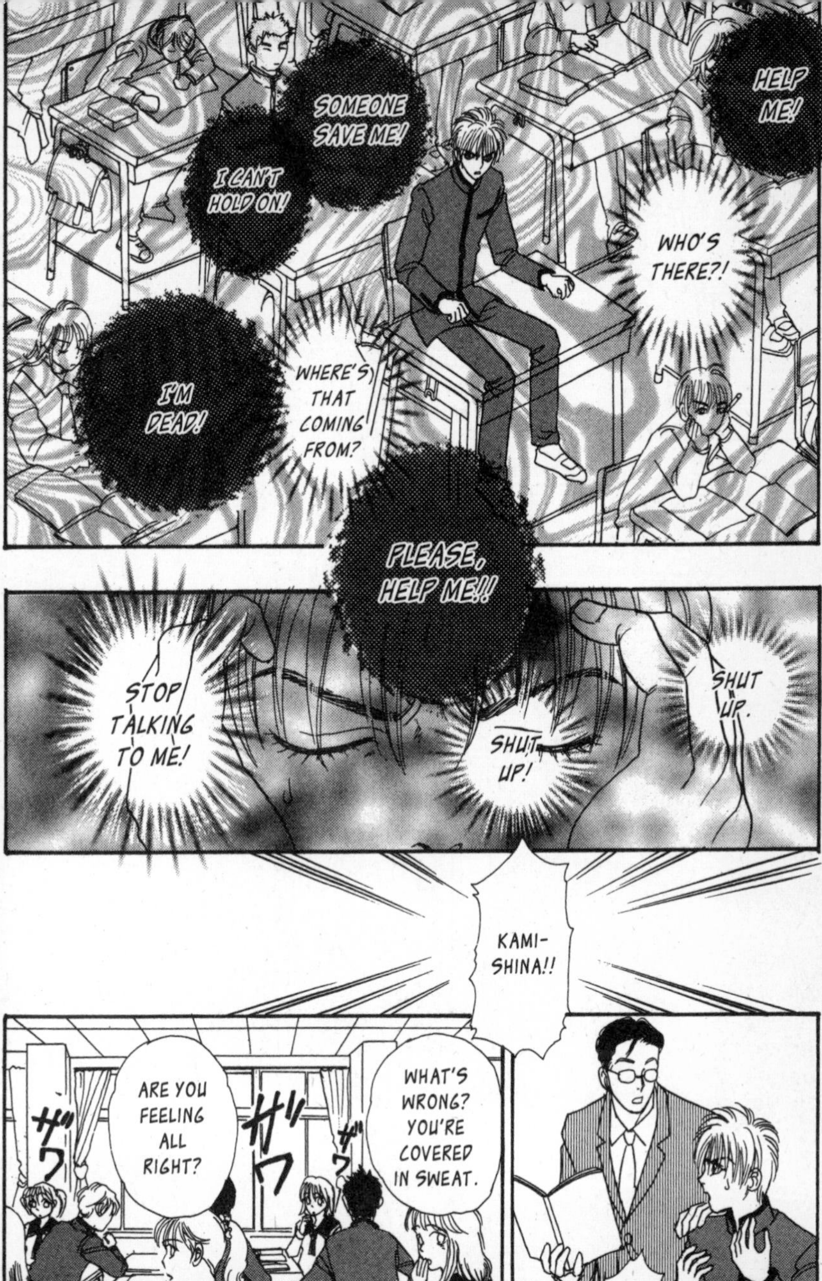
HELP ME!
WHO'S THERE?!
SOMEONE SAVE ME!
I CAN'T HOLD ON!
WHERE'S THAT COMING FROM?
I'M DEAD!
PLEASE, HELP ME!!
SHUT UP.
SHUT UP!
STOP TALKING TO ME!
KAMI-SHINA!!
AH!
WHAT'S WRONG? YOU'RE COVERED IN SWEAT.
ザワ
ザワ
ARE YOU FEELING ALL RIGHT?
ザワ

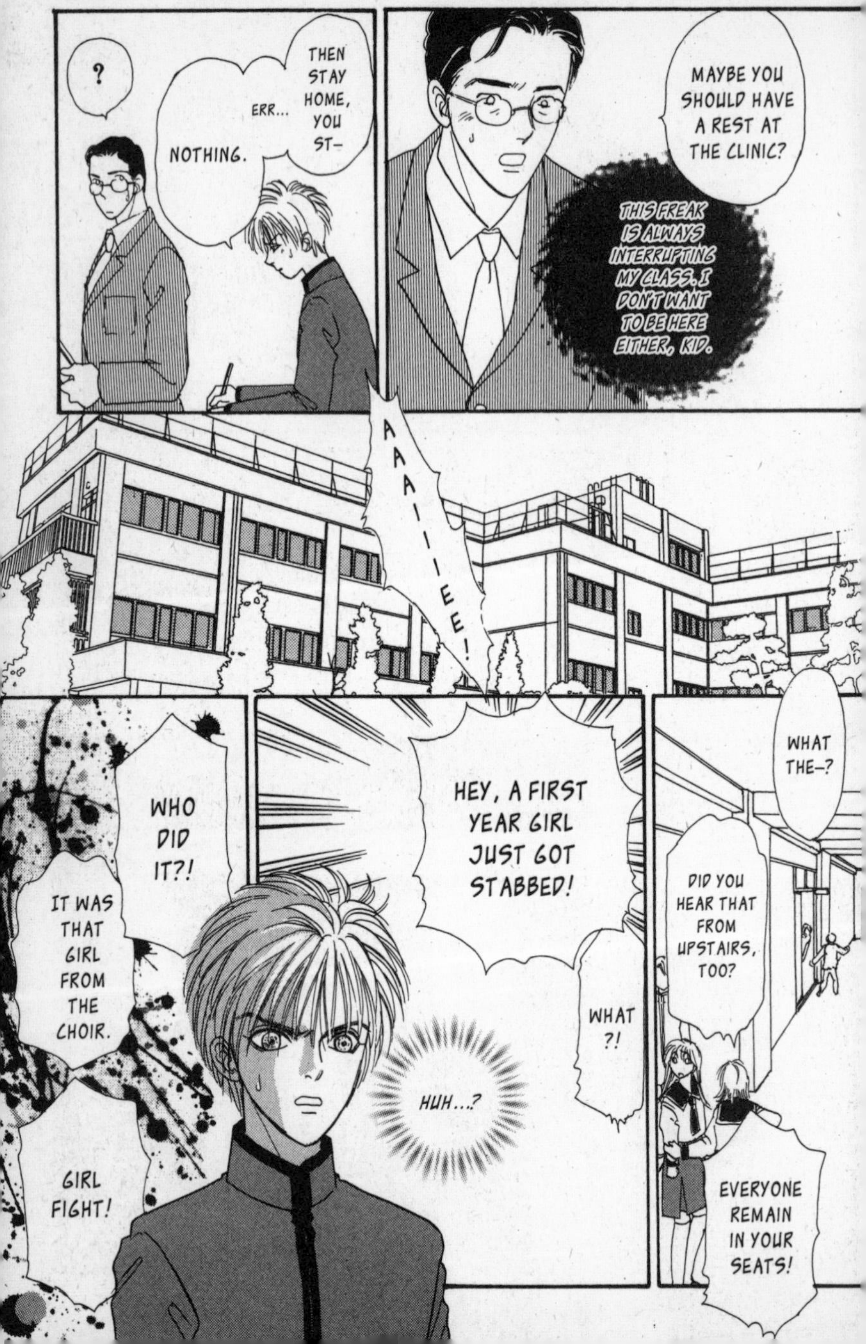
MAYBE YOU SHOULD HAVE A REST AT THE CLINIC?
THIS FREAK IS ALWAYS INTERRUPTING MY CLASS. I DON'T WANT TO BE HERE EITHER, KID.
THEN STAY HOME, YOU ST—
ERR...
NOTHING.
?
AAAIIIEE!
WHAT THE—?
DID YOU HEAR THAT FROM UPSTAIRS, TOO?
EVERYONE REMAIN IN YOUR SEATS!
HEY, A FIRST YEAR GIRL JUST GOT STABBED!
WHAT?!
HUH...?
WHO DID IT?!
IT WAS THAT GIRL FROM THE CHOIR.
GIRL FIGHT!

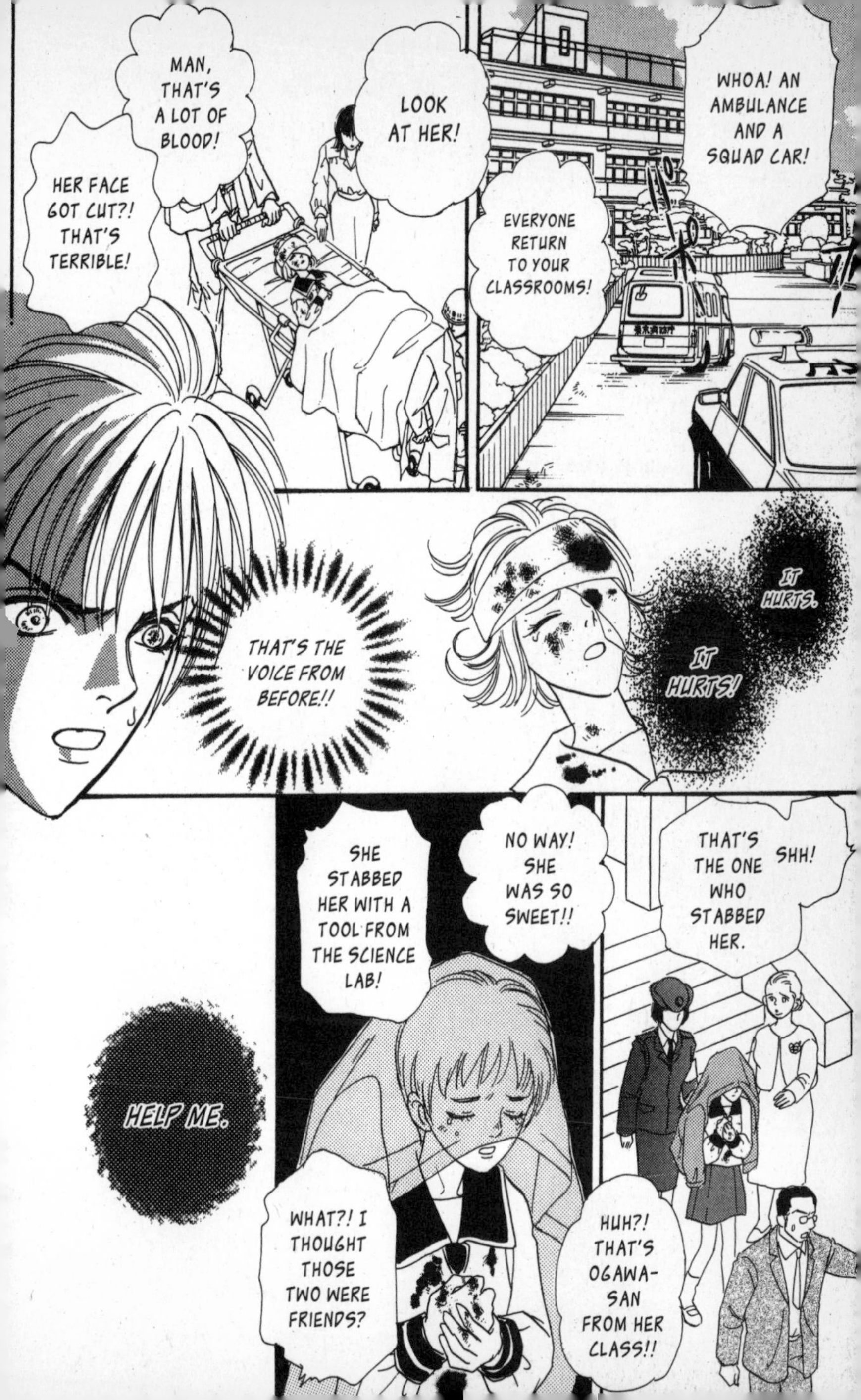
WHOA! AN AMBULANCE AND A SQUAD CAR!
EVERYONE RETURN TO YOUR CLASSROOMS!
LOOK AT HER!
MAN, THAT'S A LOT OF BLOOD!
HER FACE GOT CUT?! THAT'S TERRIBLE!
IT HURTS.
IT HURTS!
THAT'S THE VOICE FROM BEFORE!!
THAT'S THE ONE WHO STABBED HER.
SHH!
HUH?! THAT'S OGAWA-SAN FROM HER CLASS!!
NO WAY! SHE WAS SO SWEET!!
SHE STABBED HER WITH A TOOL FROM THE SCIENCE LAB!
WHAT?! I THOUGHT THOSE TWO WERE FRIENDS?
HELP ME.

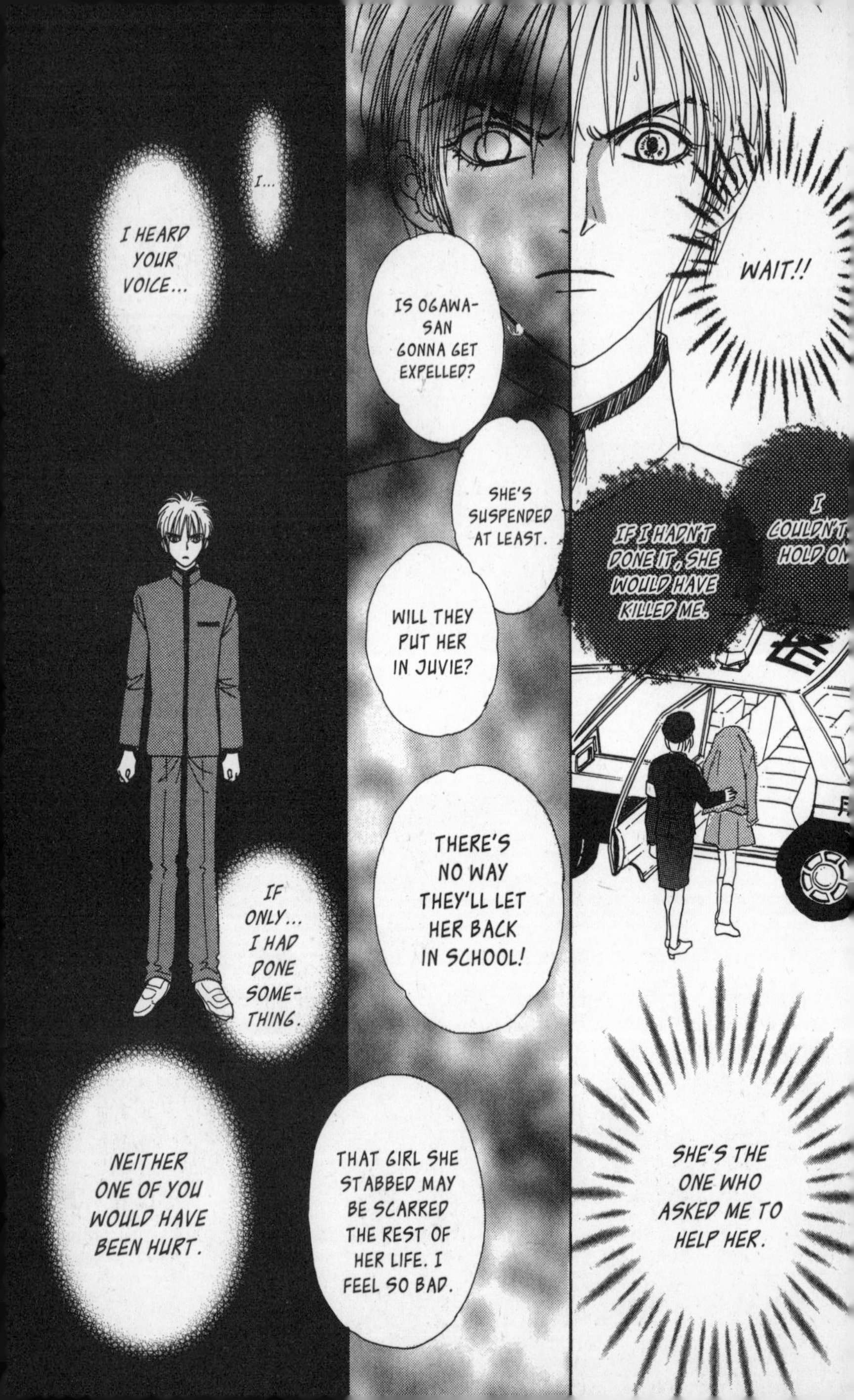
WAIT!!
I COULDN'T HOLD O
IF I HADN'T DONE IT, SHE WOULD HAVE KILLED ME.
SHE'S THE ONE WHO ASKED ME TO HELP HER.
IS OGAWA-SAN GONNA GET EXPELLED?
SHE'S SUSPENDED AT LEAST.
WILL THEY PUT HER IN JUVIE?
THERE'S NO WAY THEY'LL LET HER BACK IN SCHOOL!
THAT GIRL SHE STABBED MAY BE SCARRED THE REST OF HER LIFE. I FEEL SO BAD.
I...
I HEARD YOUR VOICE...
IF ONLY... I HAD DONE SOME-THING.
NEITHER ONE OF YOU WOULD HAVE BEEN HURT.

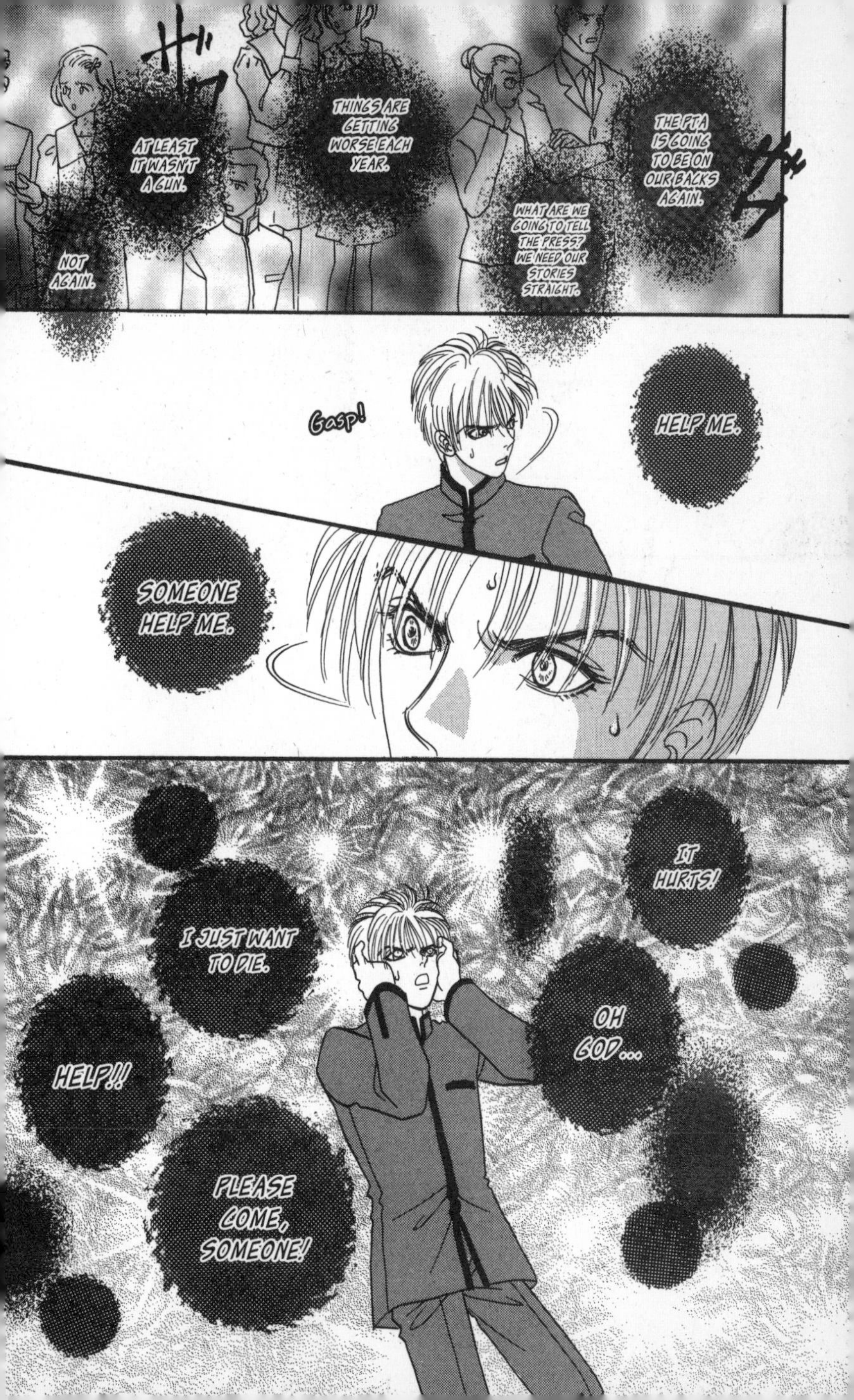
THE PTA IS GOING TO BE ON OUR BACKS AGAIN.
WHAT ARE WE GOING TO TELL THE PRESS? WE NEED OUR STORIES STRAIGHT.
THINGS ARE GETTING WORSE EACH YEAR.
AT LEAST IT WASN'T A GUN.
NOT AGAIN.
HELP ME.
Gasp!
SOMEONE HELP ME.
IT HURTS!
OH GOD...
I JUST WANT TO DIE.
HELP!!
PLEASE COME, SOMEONE!

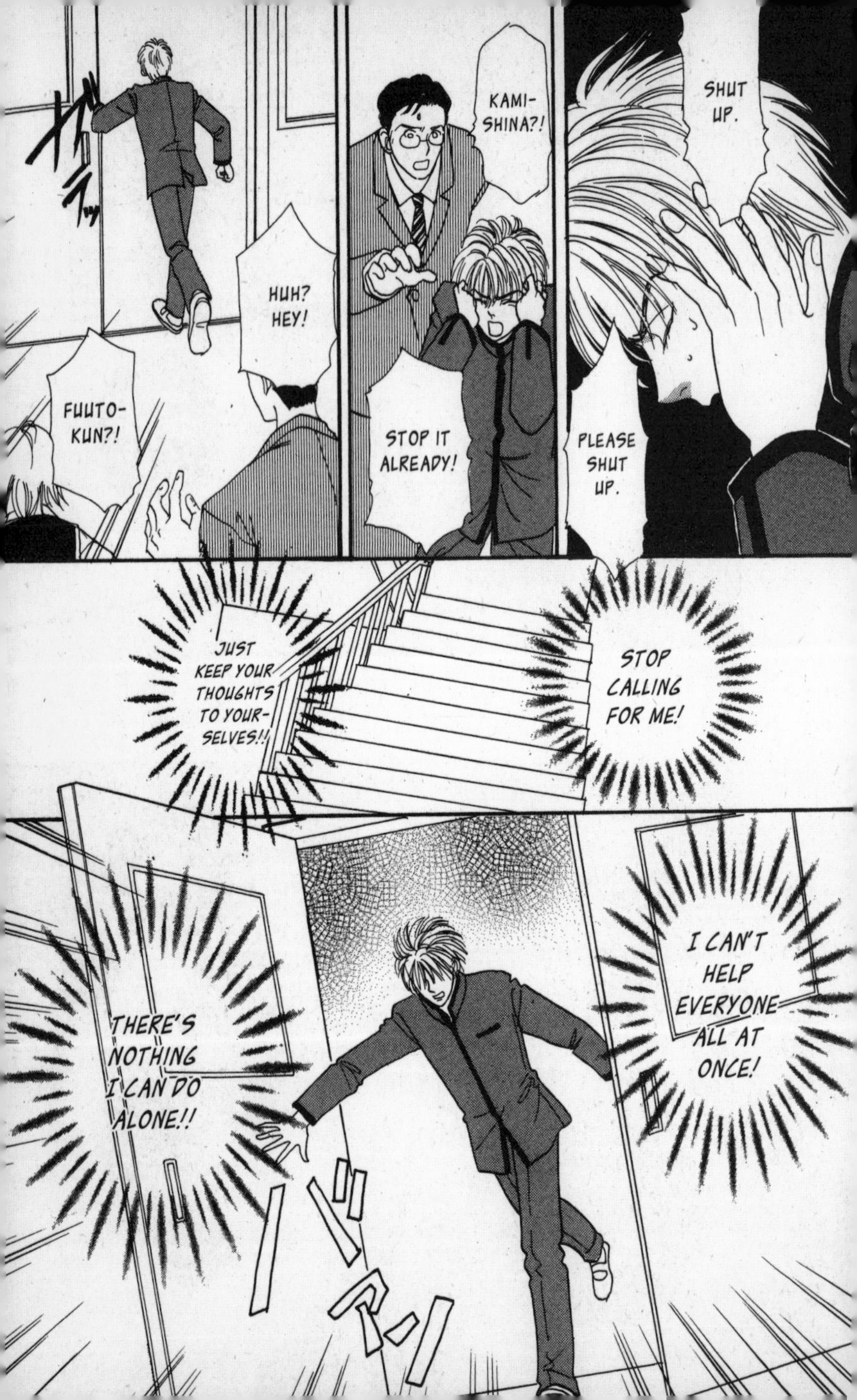
FUUTO-KUN?!
HUH? HEY!
KAMI-SHINA?!
STOP IT ALREADY!
SHUT UP.
PLEASE SHUT UP.
JUST KEEP YOUR THOUGHTS TO YOUR-SELVES!!
STOP CALLING FOR ME!
THERE'S NOTHING I CAN DO ALONE!!
I CAN'T HELP EVERYONE ALL AT ONCE!

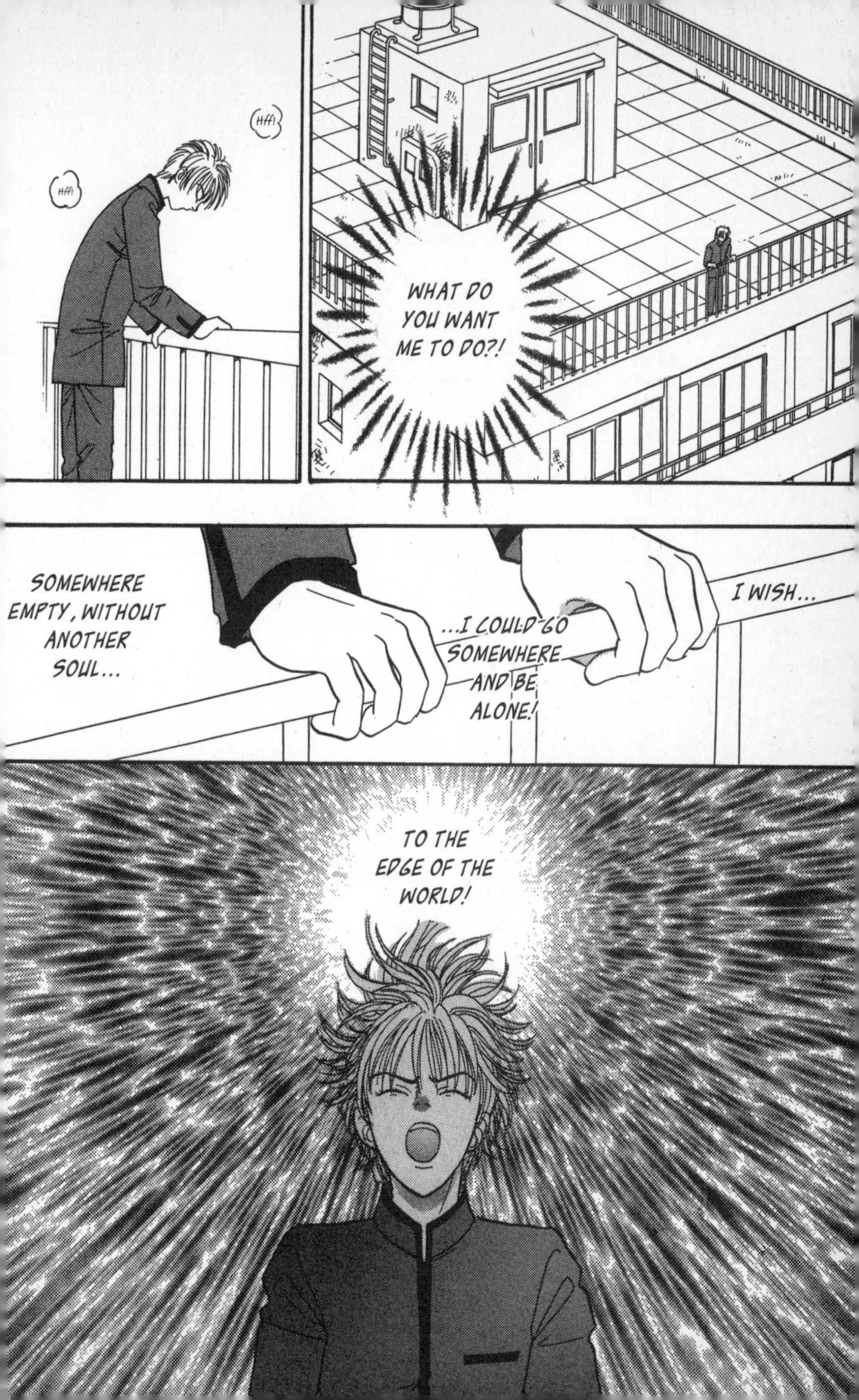
HFF!
HFF!
WHAT DO YOU WANT ME TO DO?!
I WISH...
...I COULD GO SOMEWHERE AND BE ALONE!
SOMEWHERE EMPTY, WITHOUT ANOTHER SOUL...
TO THE EDGE OF THE WORLD!

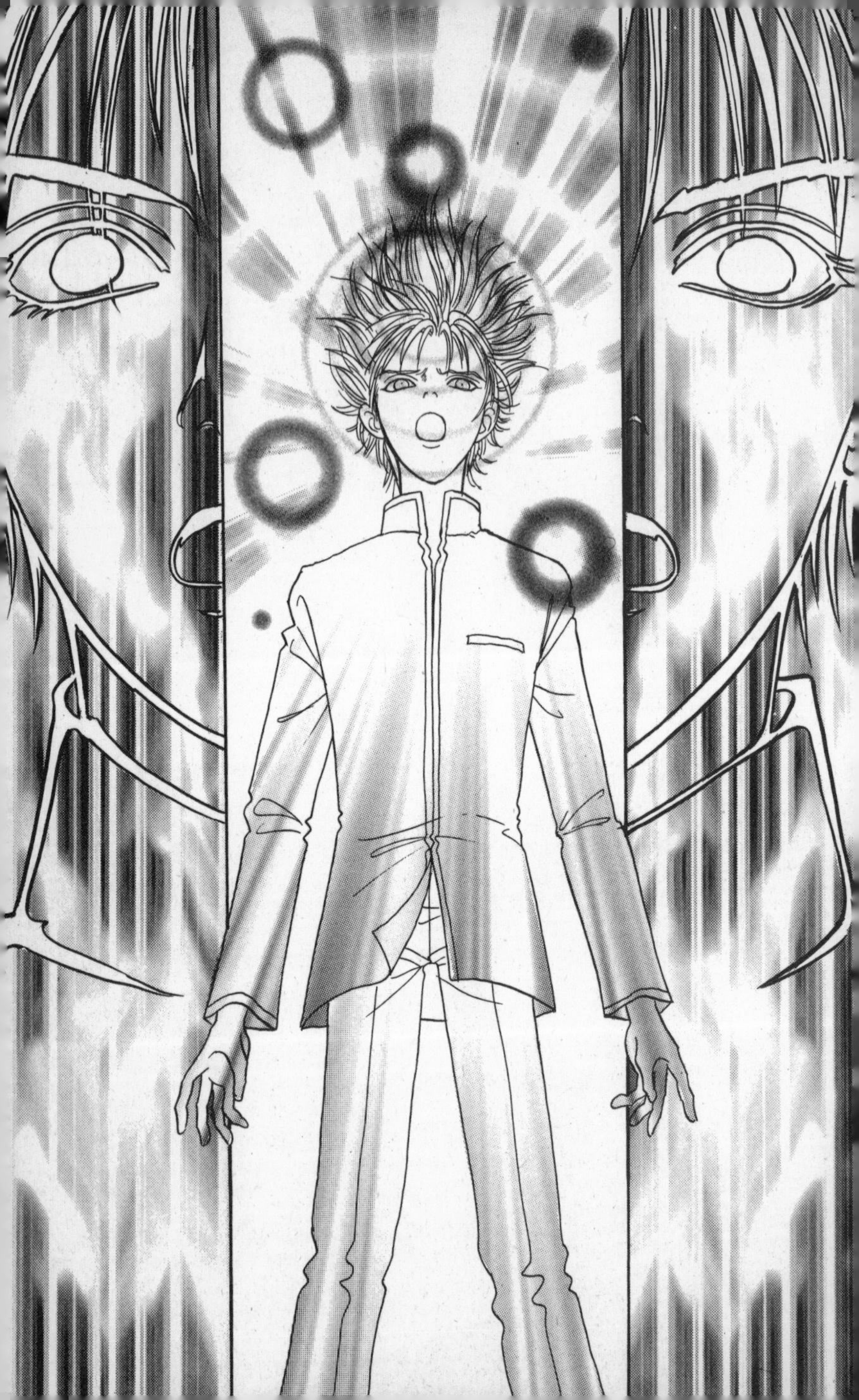

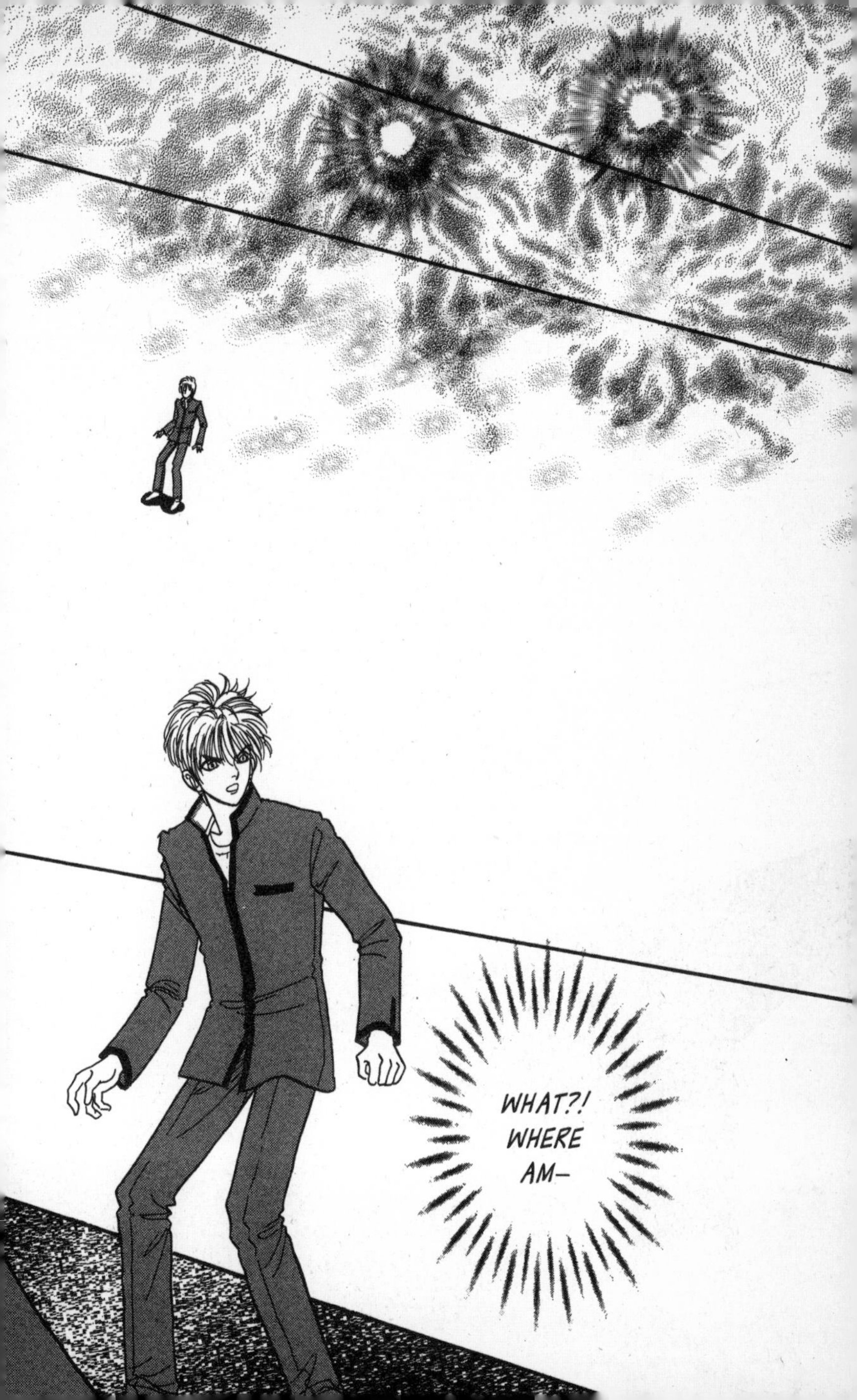
WHAT?! WHERE AM–

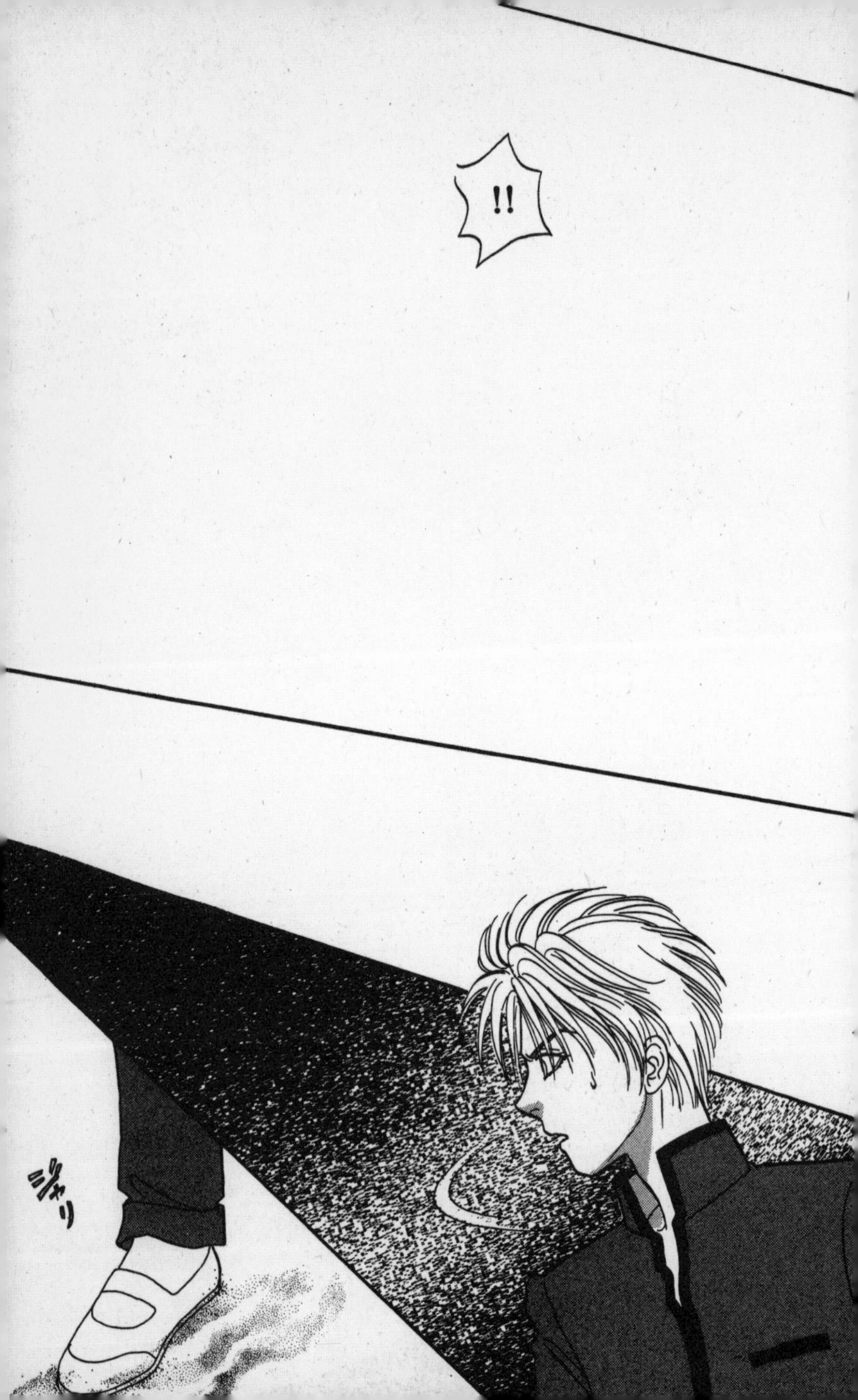
!!
ジャリ

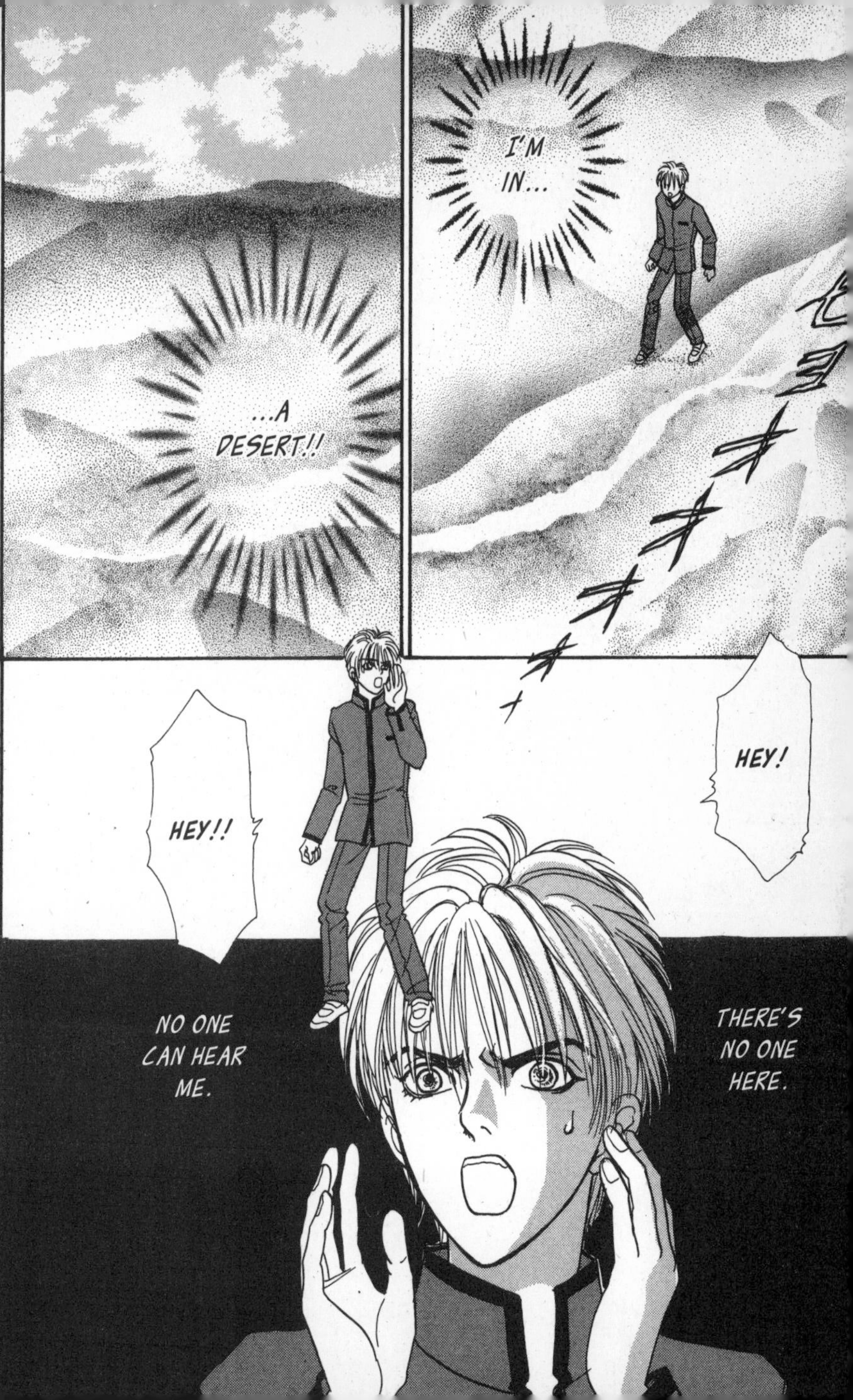
I'M IN...
...A DESERT!!
HEY!
HEY!!
THERE'S NO ONE HERE.
NO ONE CAN HEAR ME.

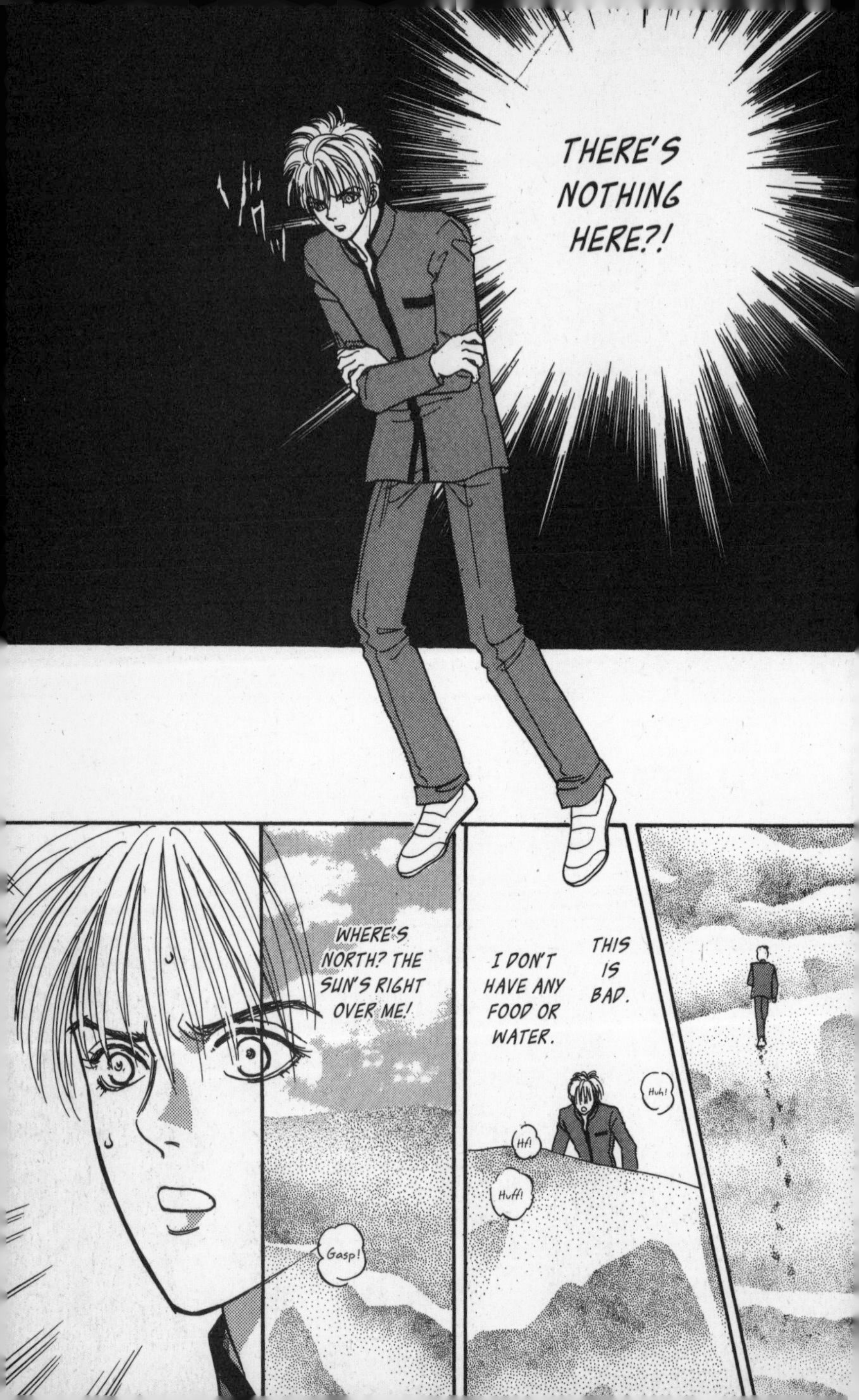
THERE'S NOTHING HERE?!
Huh!
THIS IS BAD.
I DON'T HAVE ANY FOOD OR WATER.
Hf!
Huff!
WHERE'S NORTH? THE SUN'S RIGHT OVER ME!
Gasp!

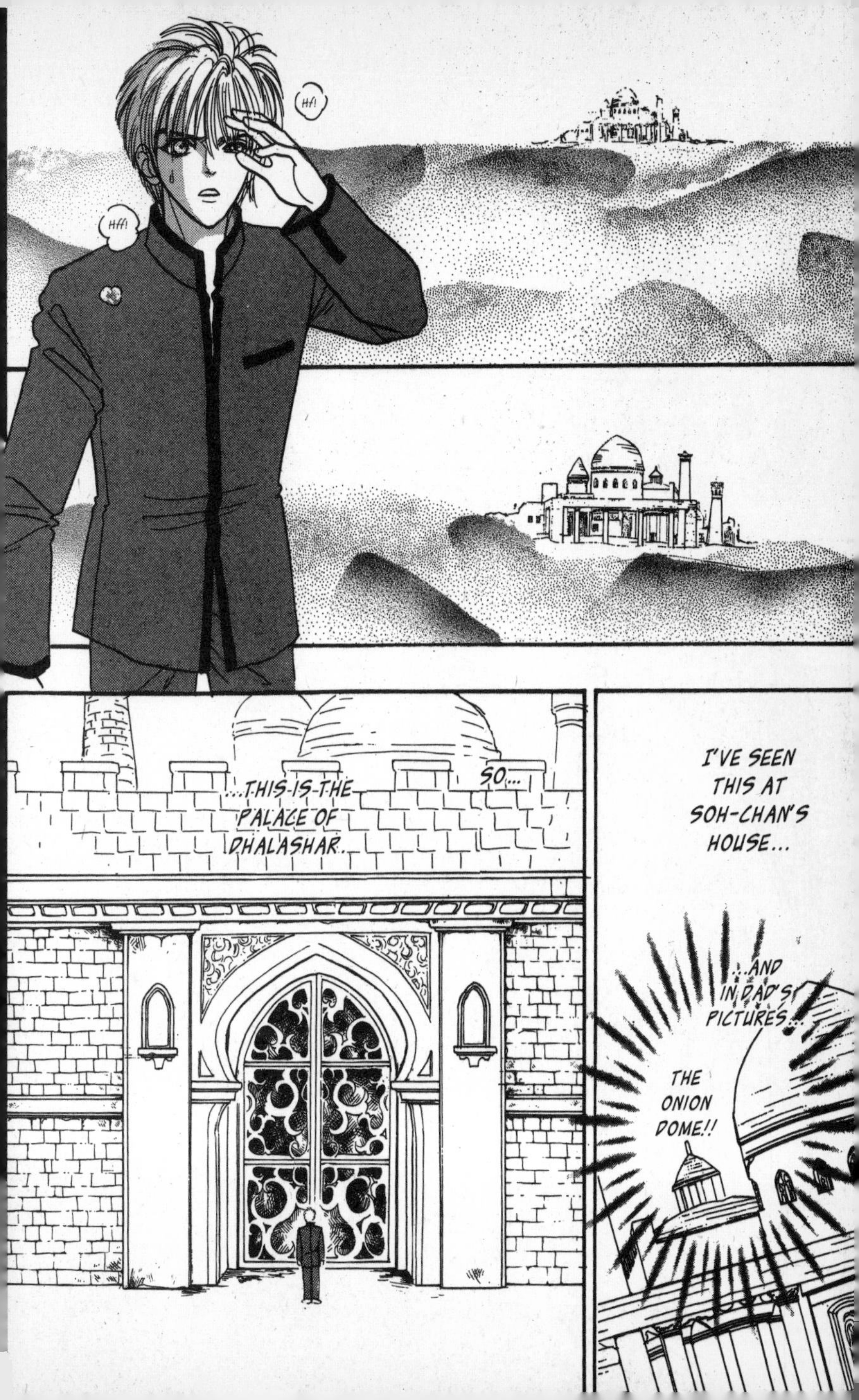
HF!
HF!
SO...
...THIS IS THE PALACE OF DHALASHAR.
I'VE SEEN THIS AT SOH-CHAN'S HOUSE...
...AND IN DAD'S PICTURES...
THE ONION DOME!!

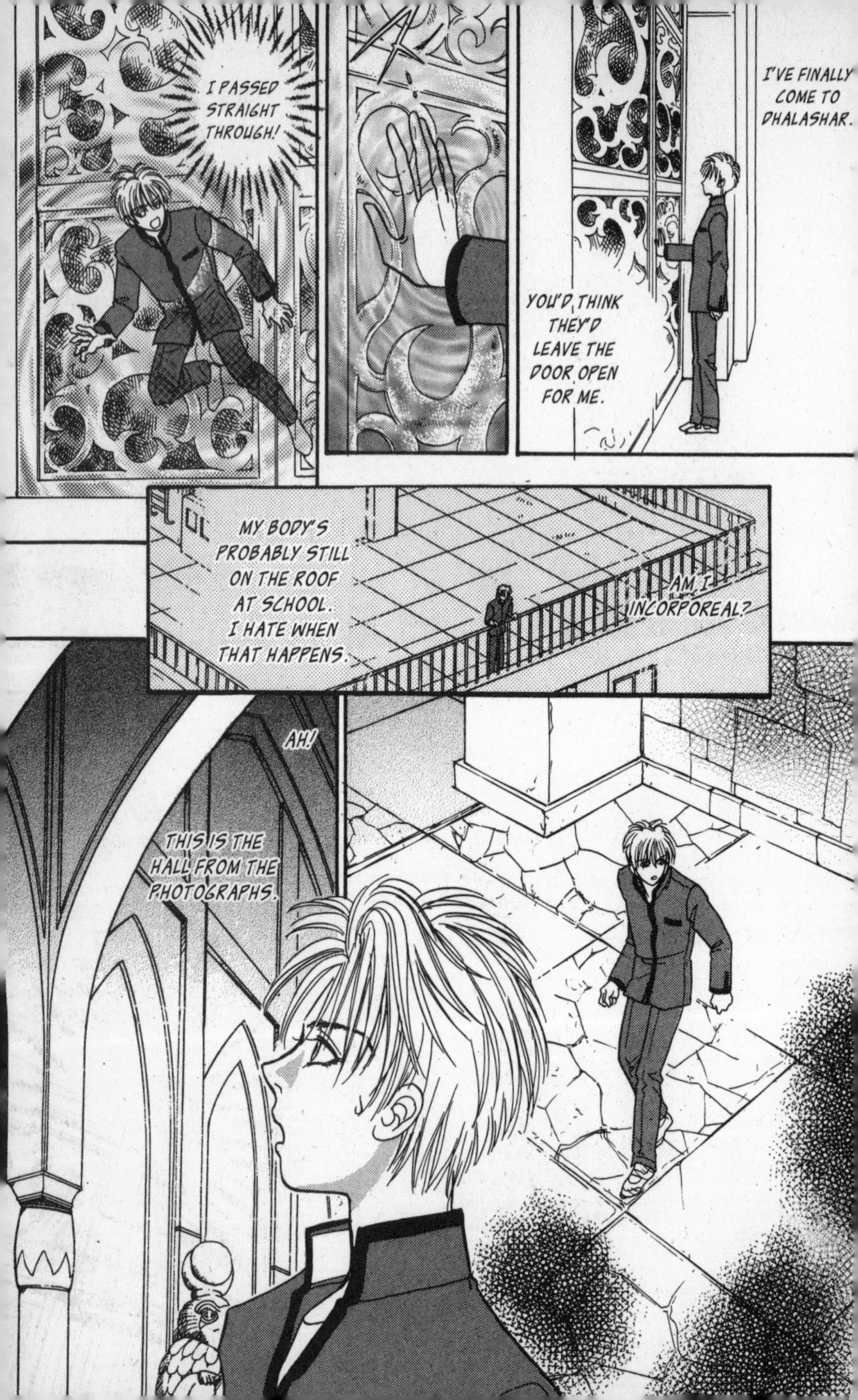
I'VE FINALLY COME TO DHALASHAR.
YOU'D THINK THEY'D LEAVE THE DOOR OPEN FOR ME.
I PASSED STRAIGHT THROUGH!
AM I INCORPOREAL?
MY BODY'S PROBABLY STILL ON THE ROOF AT SCHOOL. I HATE WHEN THAT HAPPENS.
AH!
THIS IS THE HALL FROM THE PHOTOGRAPHS.

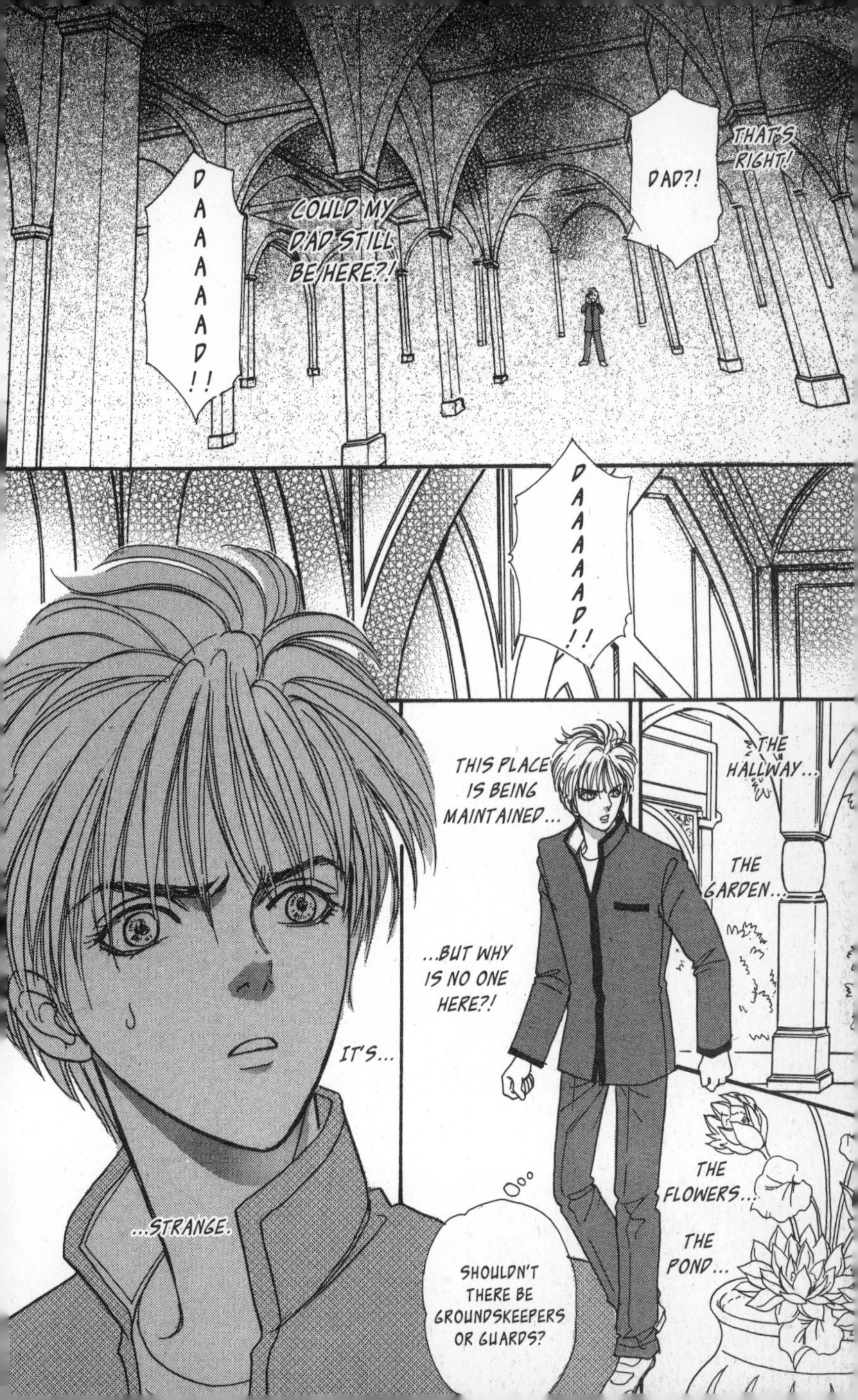
THAT'S RIGHT!
DAD?!
COULD MY DAD STILL BE HERE?!
DAAAAAD!!
DAAAAAD!!
THE HALLWAY...
THE GARDEN...
THE FLOWERS...
THE POND...
THIS PLACE IS BEING MAINTAINED...
...BUT WHY IS NO ONE HERE?!
SHOULDN'T THERE BE GROUNDSKEEPERS OR GUARDS?
IT'S...
...STRANGE.

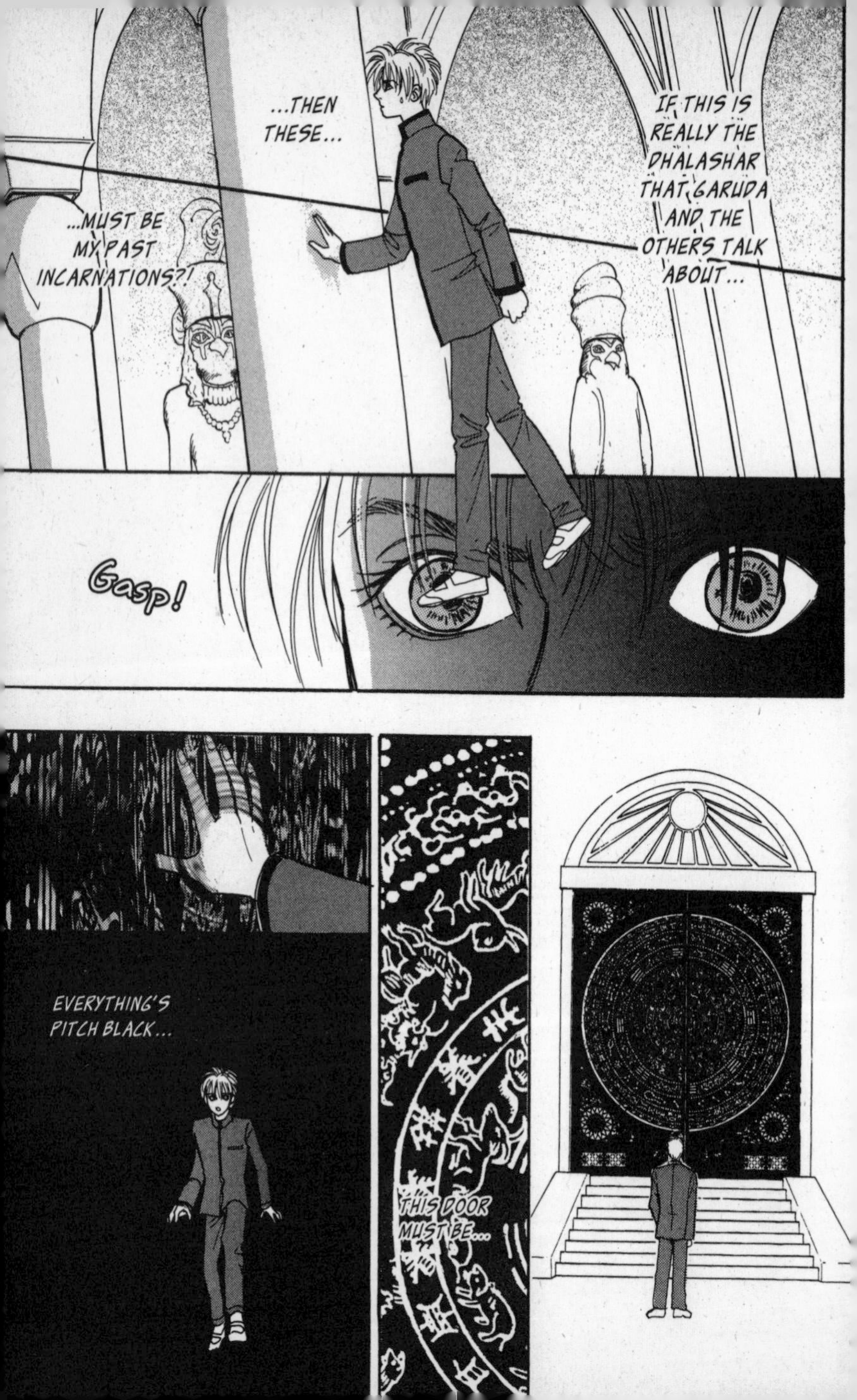
IF THIS IS REALLY THE DHALASHAR THAT GARUDA AND THE OTHERS TALK ABOUT...
...THEN THESE...
...MUST BE MY PAST INCARNATIONS?!
Gasp!
THIS DOOR MUST BE...
EVERYTHING'S PITCH BLACK...

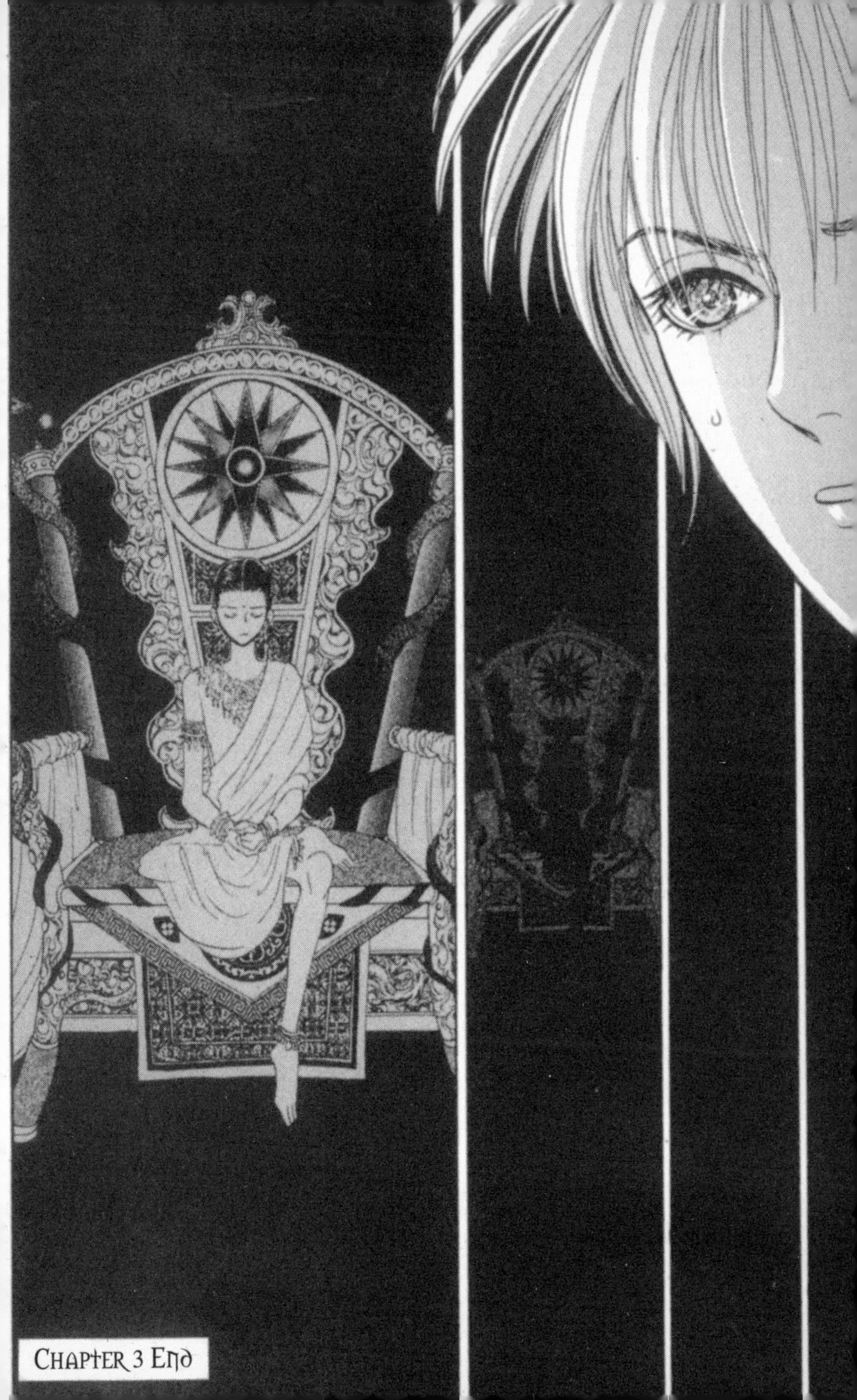
Chapter 3 End

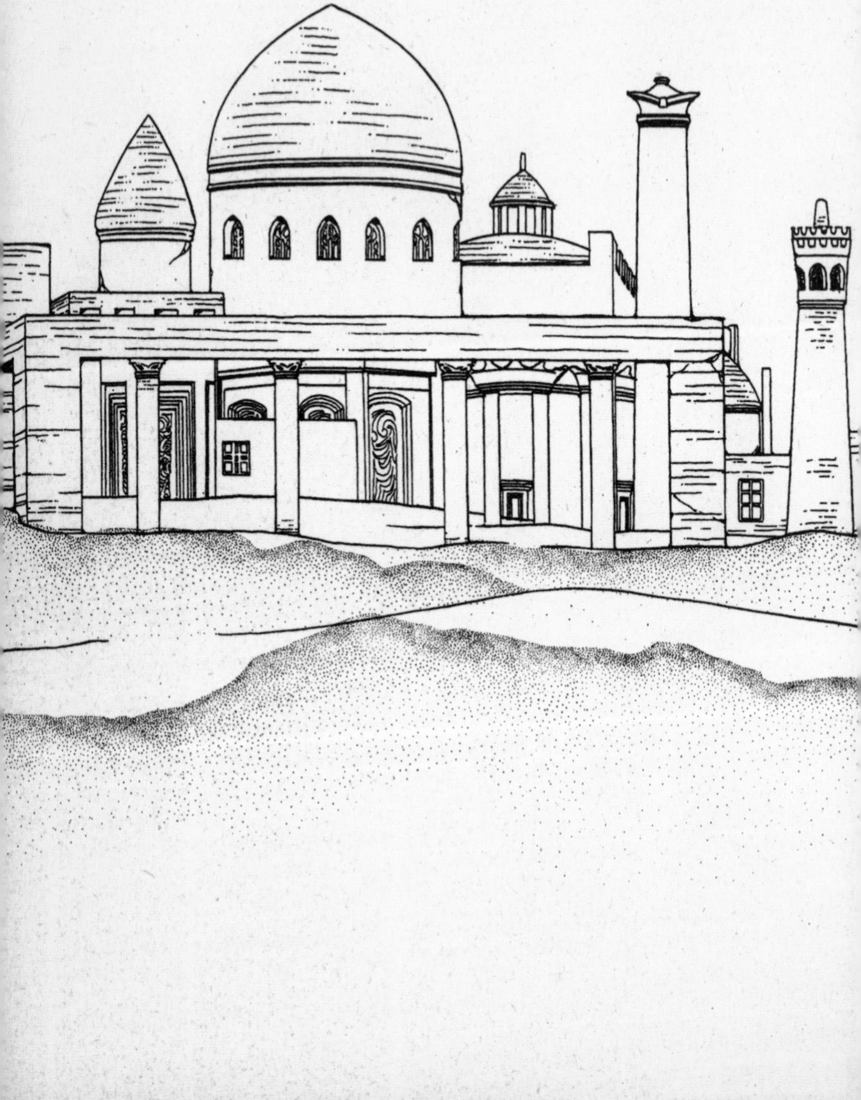

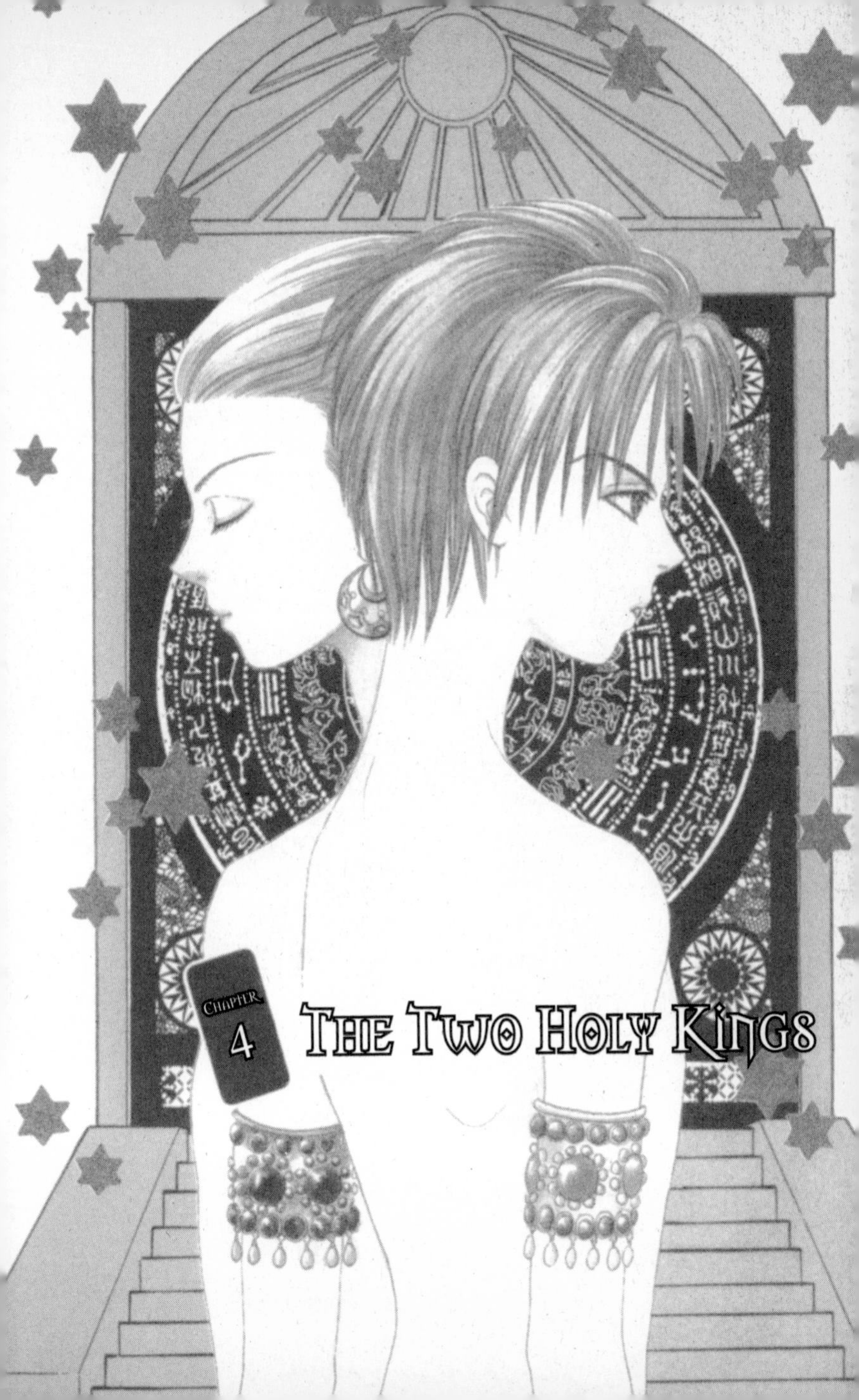
Chapter
4
The Two Holy Kings

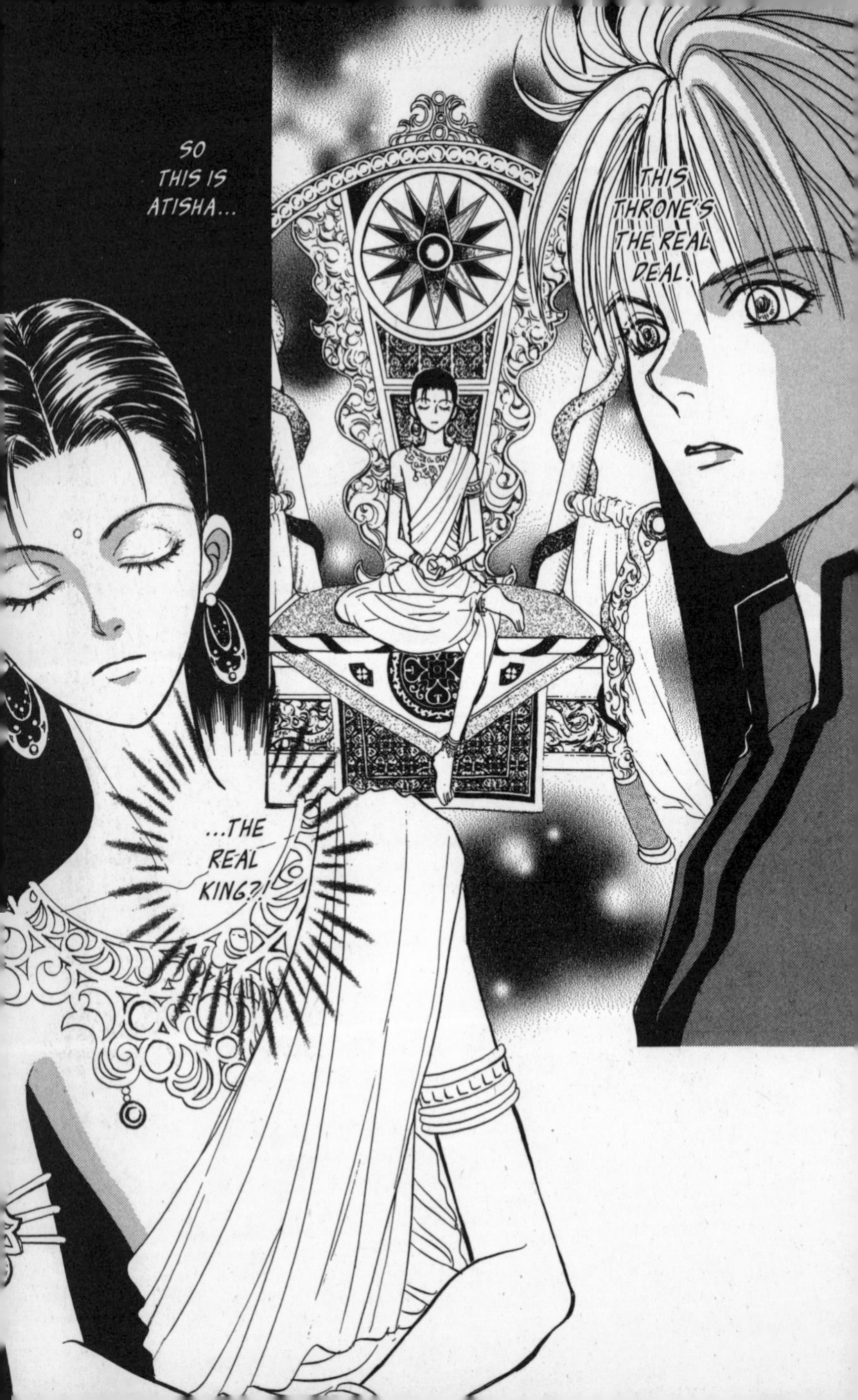
THIS THRONE'S THE REAL DEAL!
SO THIS IS ATISHA...
...THE REAL KING?!

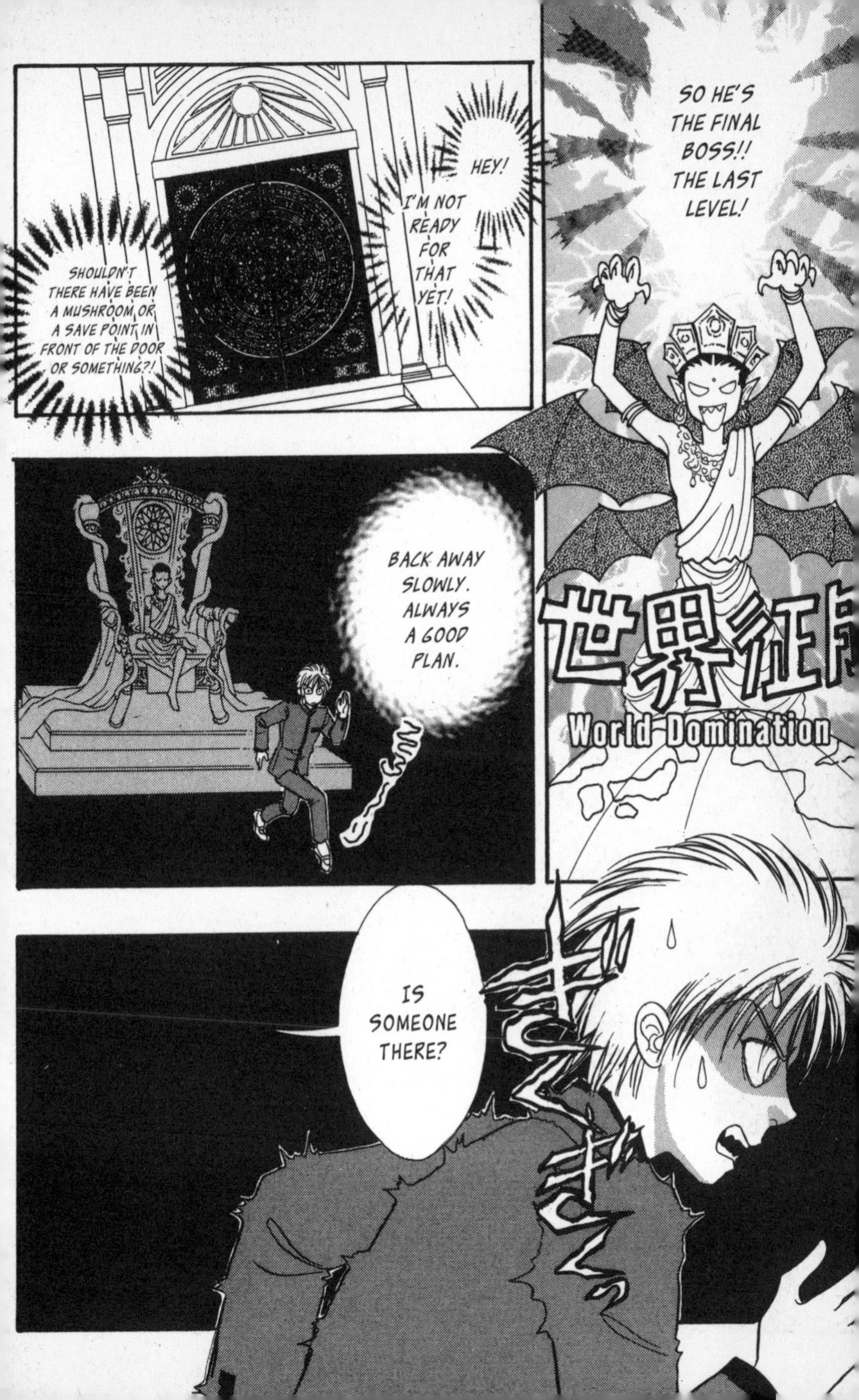
SO HE'S THE FINAL BOSS!! THE LAST LEVEL!
世界征
World Domination
HEY!
I'M NOT READY FOR THAT YET!
SHOULDN'T THERE HAVE BEEN A MUSHROOM OR A SAVE POINT IN FRONT OF THE DOOR OR SOMETHING?!
BACK AWAY SLOWLY. ALWAYS A GOOD PLAN.
IS SOMEONE THERE?

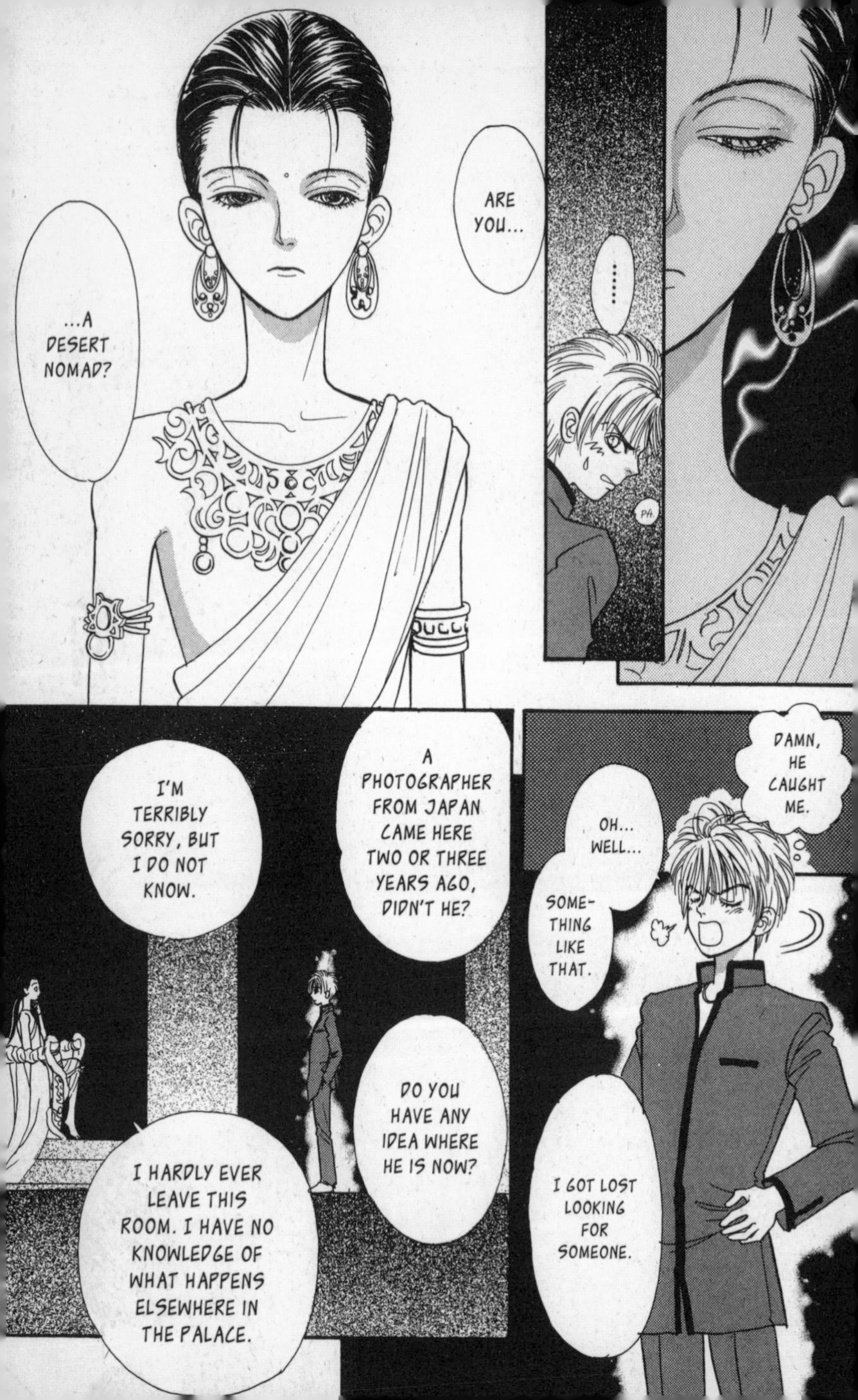
......
ARE YOU...
...A DESERT NOMAD?
DAMN, HE CAUGHT ME.
OH... WELL...
SOME-THING LIKE THAT.
I GOT LOST LOOKING FOR SOMEONE.
A PHOTOGRAPHER FROM JAPAN CAME HERE TWO OR THREE YEARS AGO, DIDN'T HE?
I'M TERRIBLY SORRY, BUT I DO NOT KNOW.
DO YOU HAVE ANY IDEA WHERE HE IS NOW?
I HARDLY EVER LEAVE THIS ROOM. I HAVE NO KNOWLEDGE OF WHAT HAPPENS ELSEWHERE IN THE PALACE.

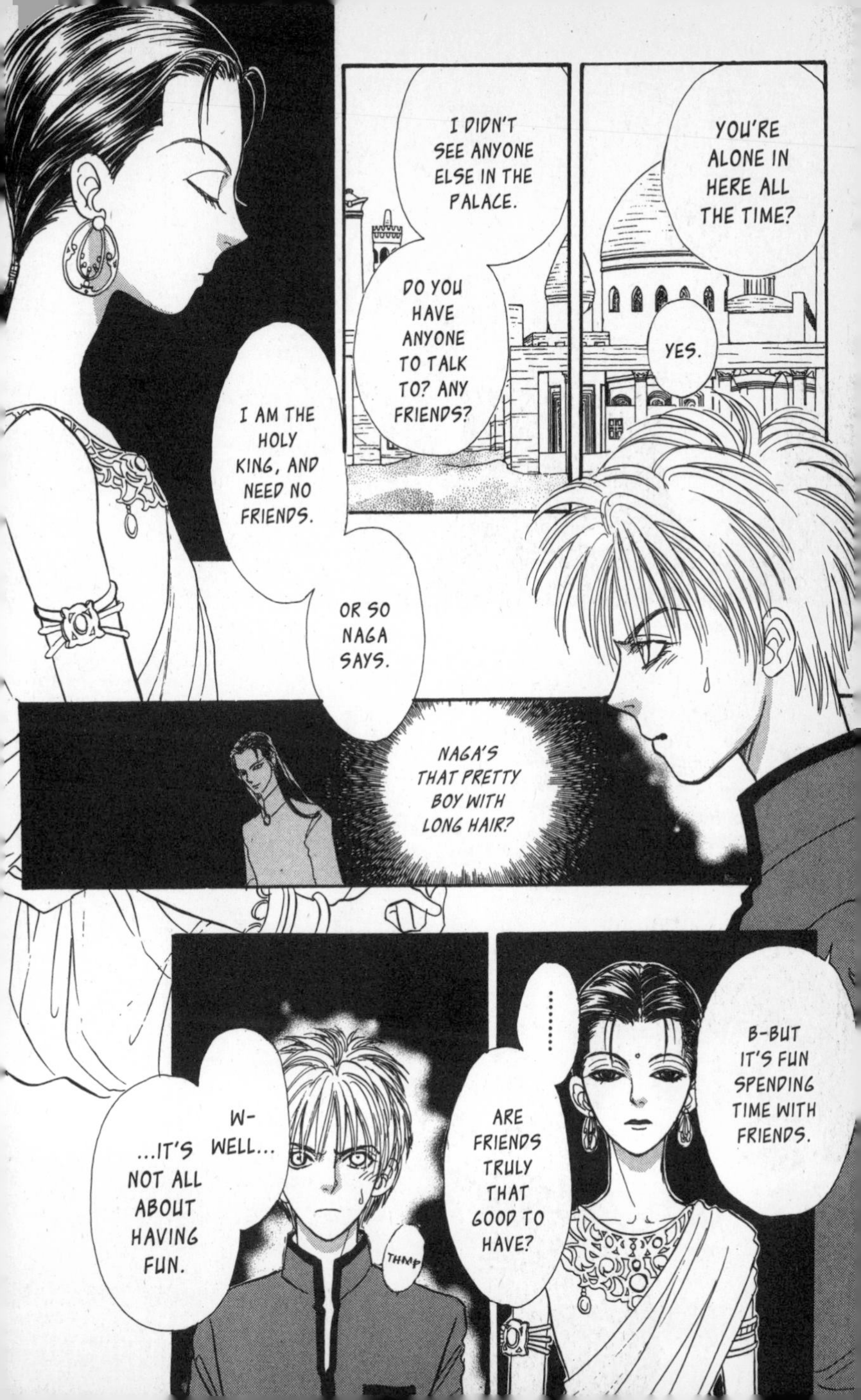
YOU'RE ALONE IN HERE ALL THE TIME?
YES.
I DIDN'T SEE ANYONE ELSE IN THE PALACE.
DO YOU HAVE ANYONE TO TALK TO? ANY FRIENDS?
I AM THE HOLY KING, AND NEED NO FRIENDS.
OR SO NAGA SAYS.
NAGA'S THAT PRETTY BOY WITH LONG HAIR?
B-BUT IT'S FUN SPENDING TIME WITH FRIENDS.
......
ARE FRIENDS TRULY THAT GOOD TO HAVE?
W-WELL...
...IT'S NOT ALL ABOUT HAVING FUN.
THMP

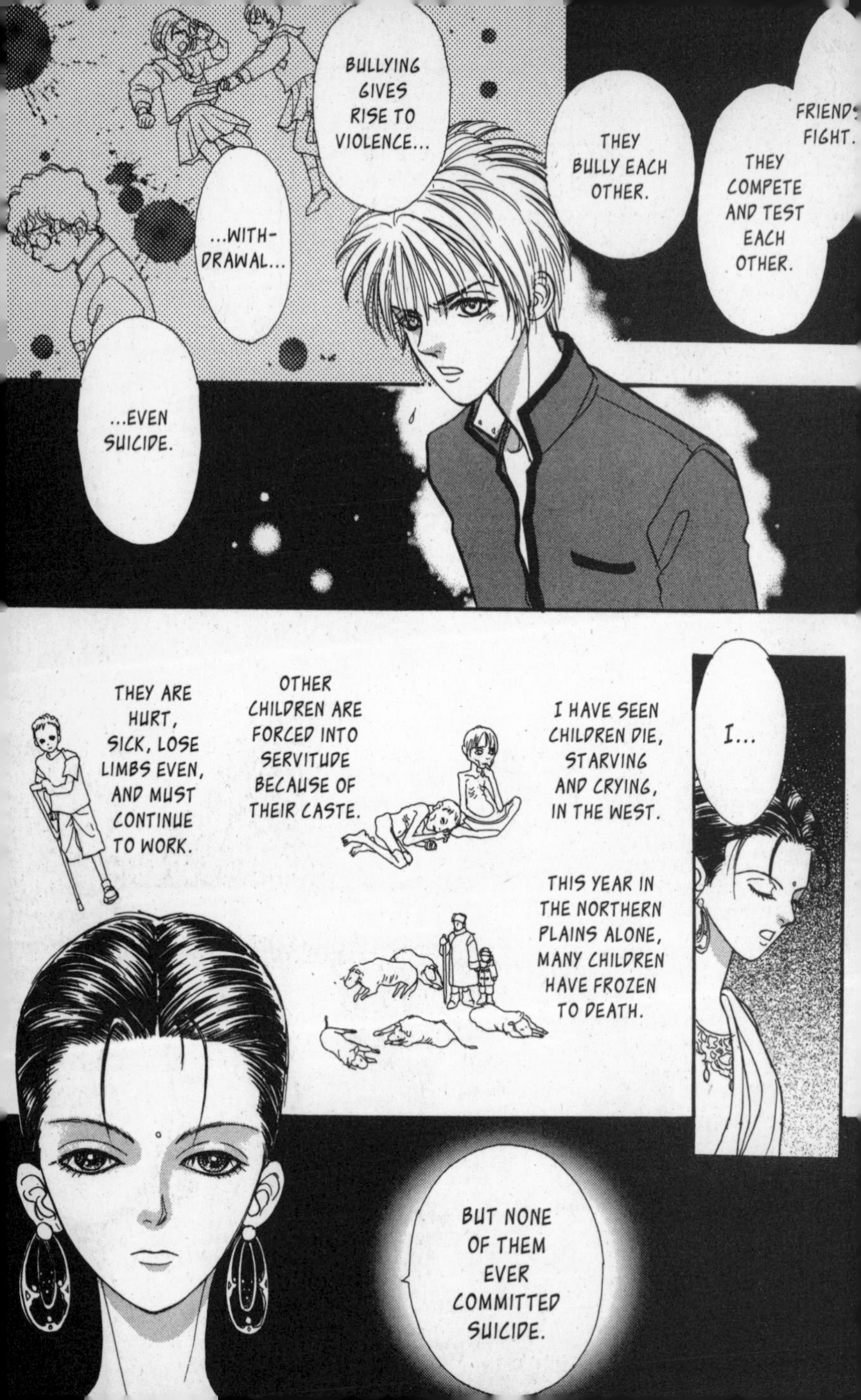
FRIEND FIGHT.
THEY COMPETE AND TEST EACH OTHER.
THEY BULLY EACH OTHER.
BULLYING GIVES RISE TO VIOLENCE...
...WITH-DRAWAL...
...EVEN SUICIDE.
I...
I HAVE SEEN CHILDREN DIE, STARVING AND CRYING, IN THE WEST.
THIS YEAR IN THE NORTHERN PLAINS ALONE, MANY CHILDREN HAVE FROZEN TO DEATH.
OTHER CHILDREN ARE FORCED INTO SERVITUDE BECAUSE OF THEIR CASTE.
THEY ARE HURT, SICK, LOSE LIMBS EVEN, AND MUST CONTINUE TO WORK.
BUT NONE OF THEM EVER COMMITTED SUICIDE.

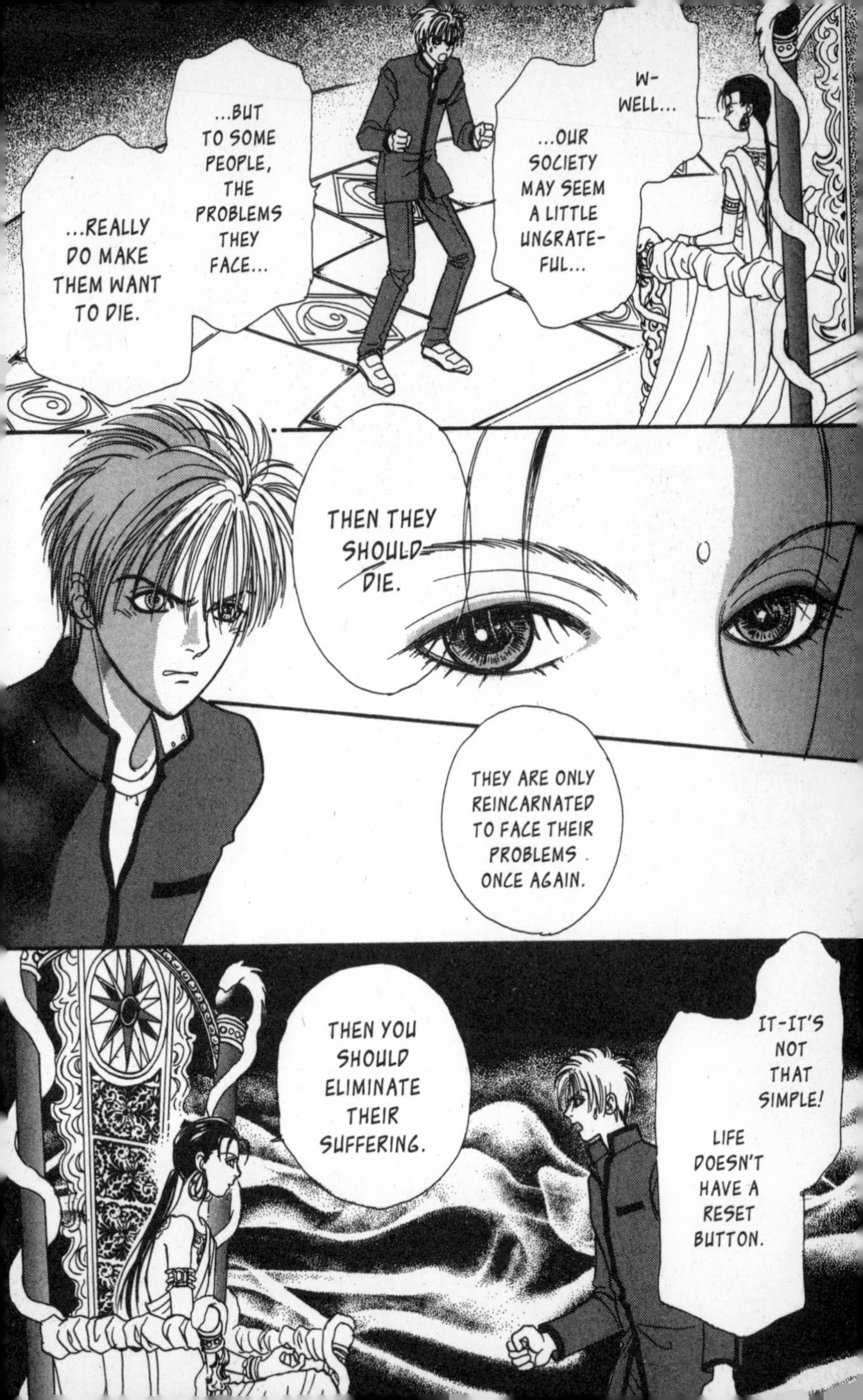
W-WELL...
...OUR SOCIETY MAY SEEM A LITTLE UNGRATE-FUL...
...BUT TO SOME PEOPLE, THE PROBLEMS THEY FACE...
...REALLY DO MAKE THEM WANT TO DIE.
THEN THEY SHOULD DIE.
THEY ARE ONLY REINCARNATED TO FACE THEIR PROBLEMS ONCE AGAIN.
IT-IT'S NOT THAT SIMPLE!
LIFE DOESN'T HAVE A RESET BUTTON.
THEN YOU SHOULD ELIMINATE THEIR SUFFERING.

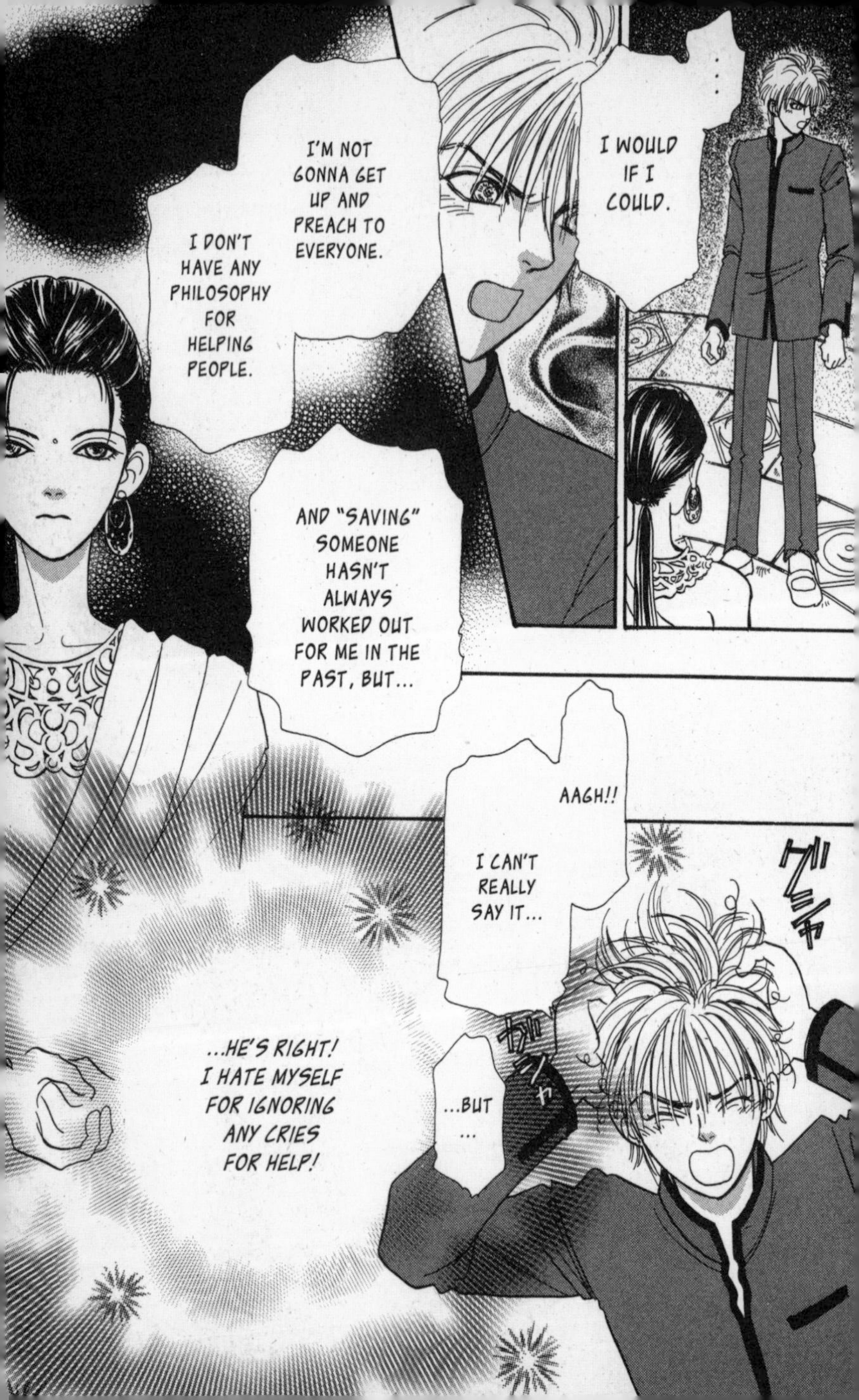
...
I WOULD IF I COULD.
I'M NOT GONNA GET UP AND PREACH TO EVERYONE.
I DON'T HAVE ANY PHILOSOPHY FOR HELPING PEOPLE.
AND "SAVING" SOMEONE HASN'T ALWAYS WORKED OUT FOR ME IN THE PAST, BUT...
AAGH!!
I CAN'T REALLY SAY IT...
...BUT ...
...HE'S RIGHT! I HATE MYSELF FOR IGNORING ANY CRIES FOR HELP!

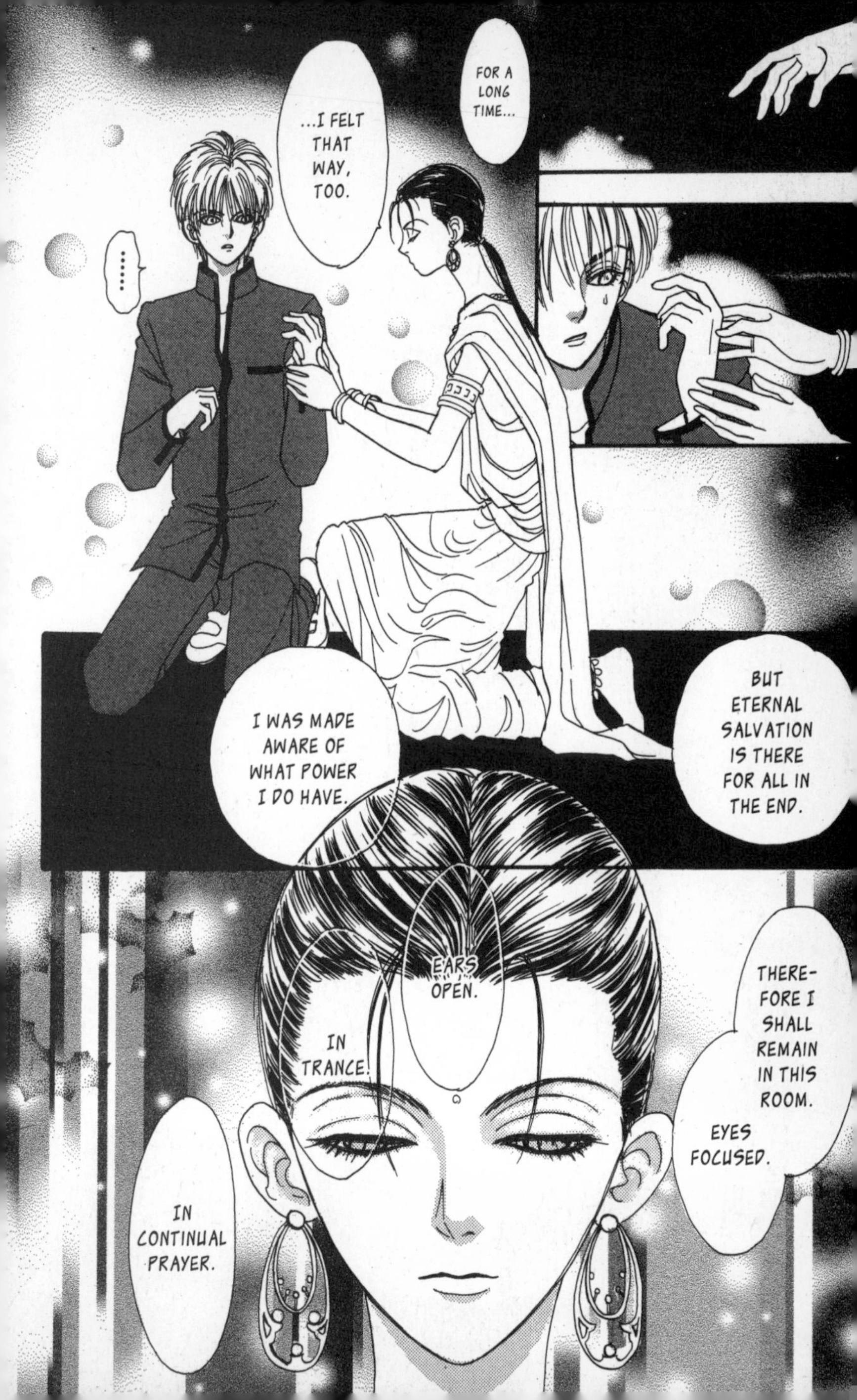

FOR A LONG TIME...
...I FELT THAT WAY, TOO.
......
BUT ETERNAL SALVATION IS THERE FOR ALL IN THE END.
I WAS MADE AWARE OF WHAT POWER I DO HAVE.
THERE-FORE I SHALL REMAIN IN THIS ROOM.
EYES FOCUSED.
EARS OPEN.
IN TRANCE.
IN CONTINUAL PRAYER.

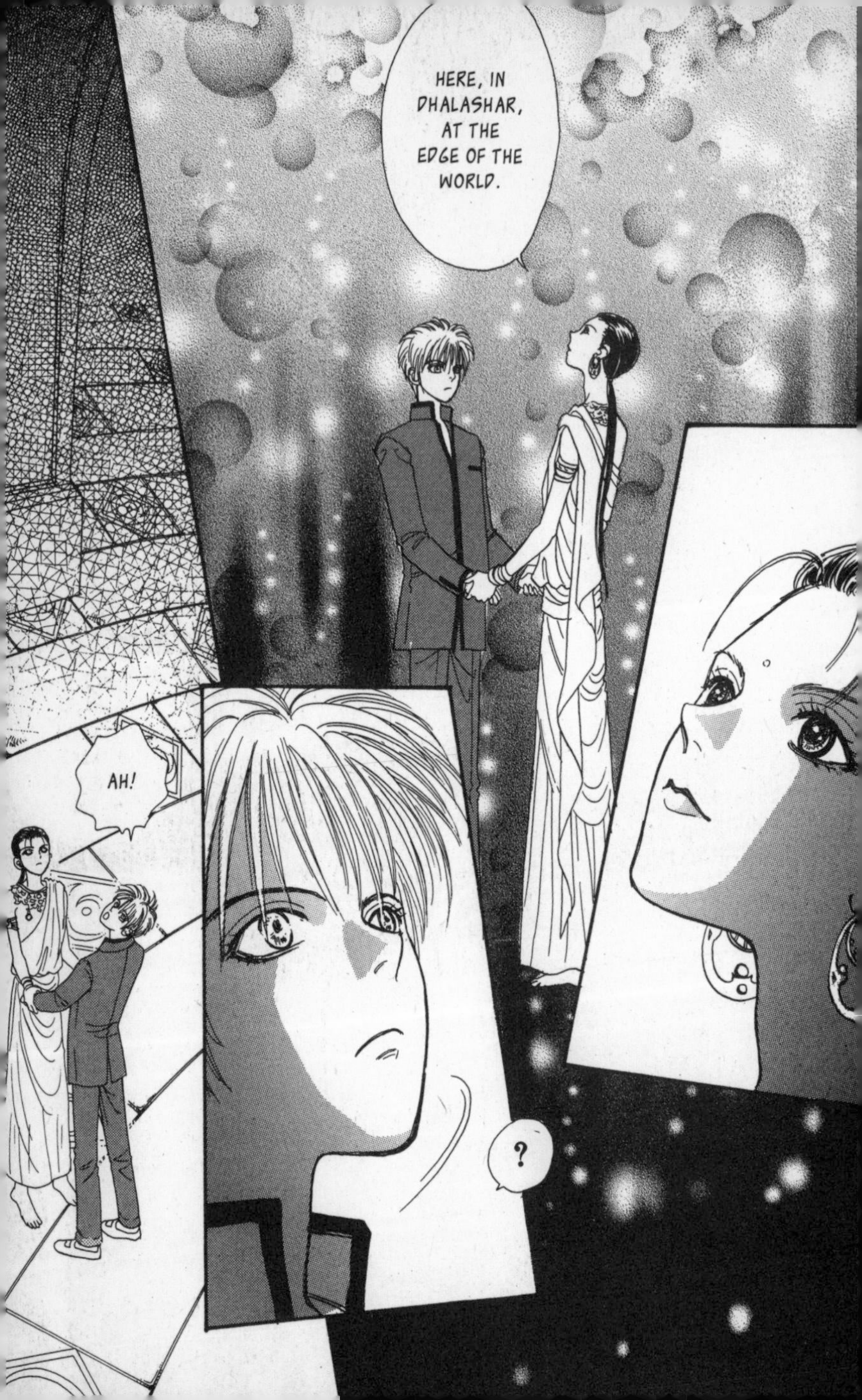
HERE, IN DHALASHAR, AT THE EDGE OF THE WORLD.
AH!
?

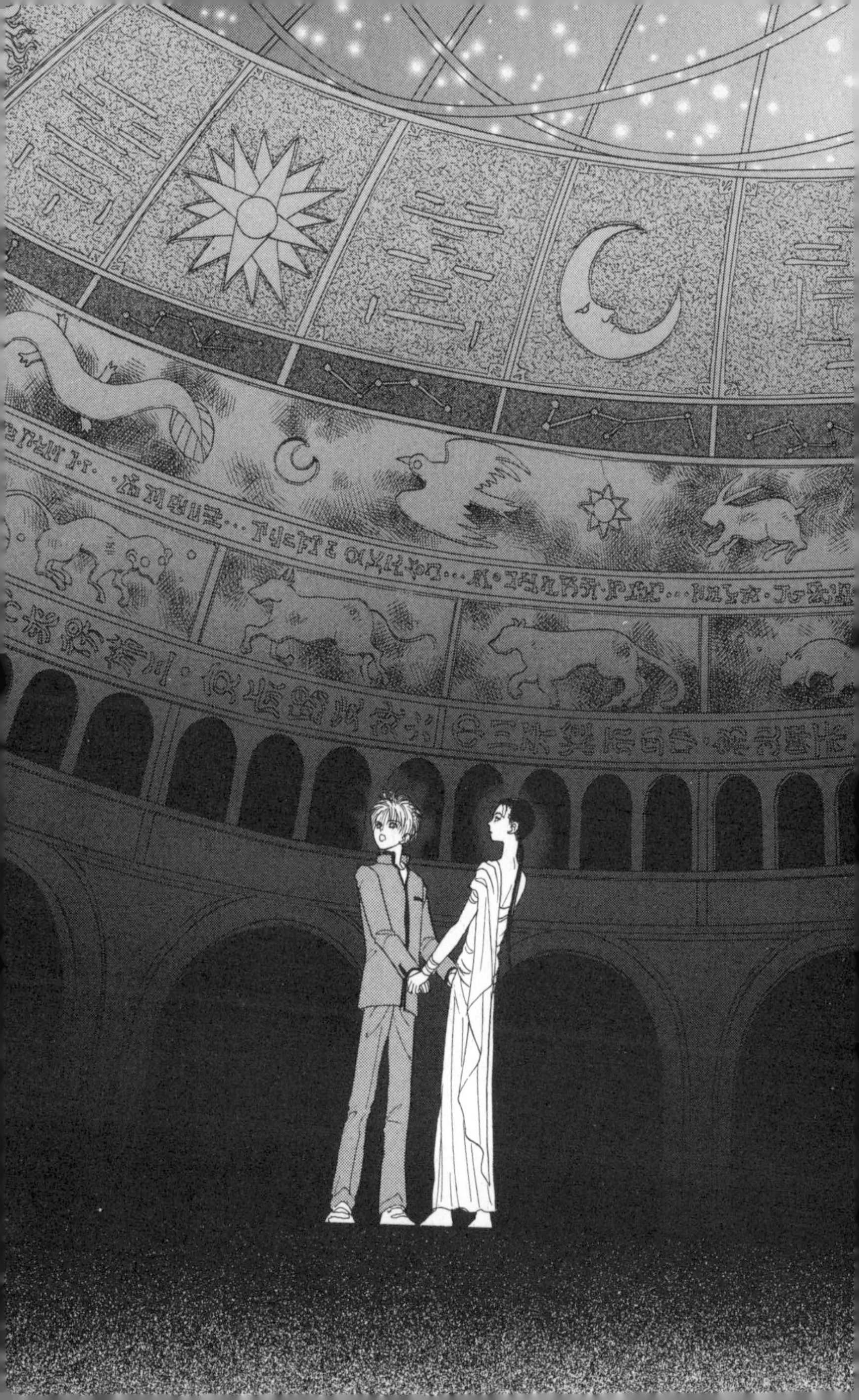

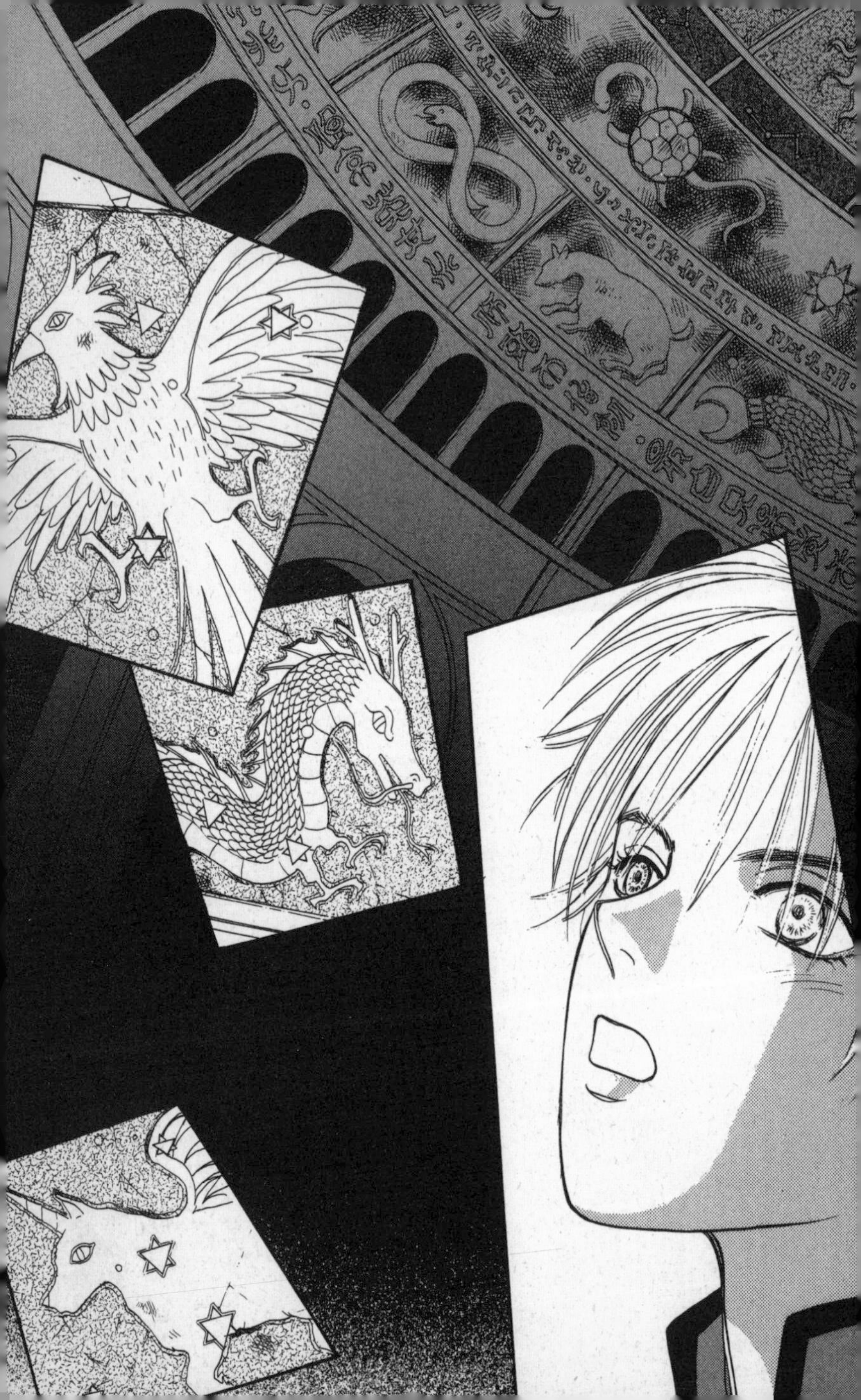

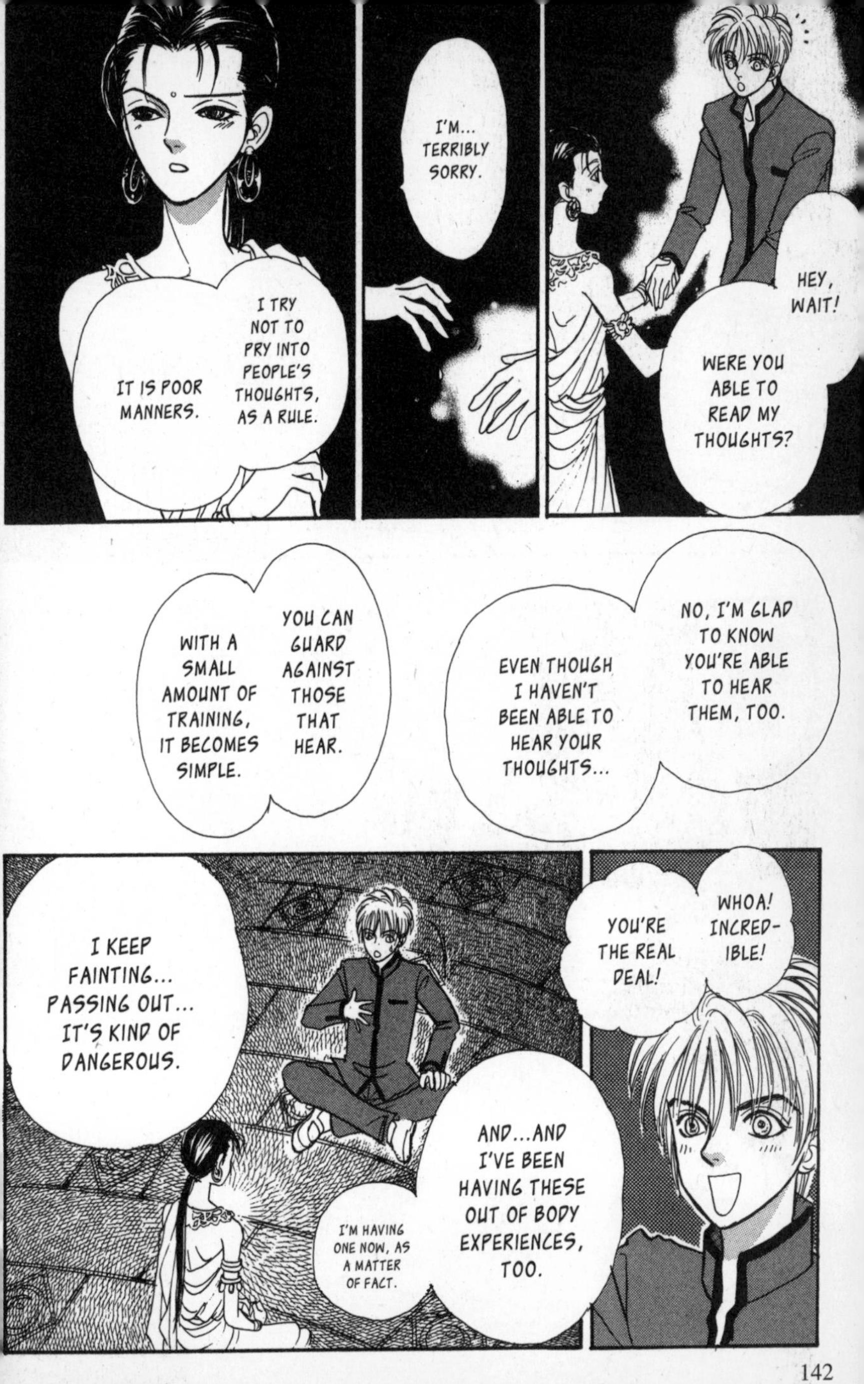
HEY, WAIT!
WERE YOU ABLE TO READ MY THOUGHTS?
I'M... TERRIBLY SORRY.
I TRY NOT TO PRY INTO PEOPLE'S THOUGHTS, AS A RULE.
IT IS POOR MANNERS.
NO, I'M GLAD TO KNOW YOU'RE ABLE TO HEAR THEM, TOO.
EVEN THOUGH I HAVEN'T BEEN ABLE TO HEAR YOUR THOUGHTS...
YOU CAN GUARD AGAINST THOSE THAT HEAR.
WITH A SMALL AMOUNT OF TRAINING, IT BECOMES SIMPLE.
WHOA! INCRED-IBLE!
YOU'RE THE REAL DEAL!
I KEEP FAINTING... PASSING OUT... IT'S KIND OF DANGEROUS.
AND...AND I'VE BEEN HAVING THESE OUT OF BODY EXPERIENCES, TOO.
I'M HAVING ONE NOW, AS A MATTER OF FACT.

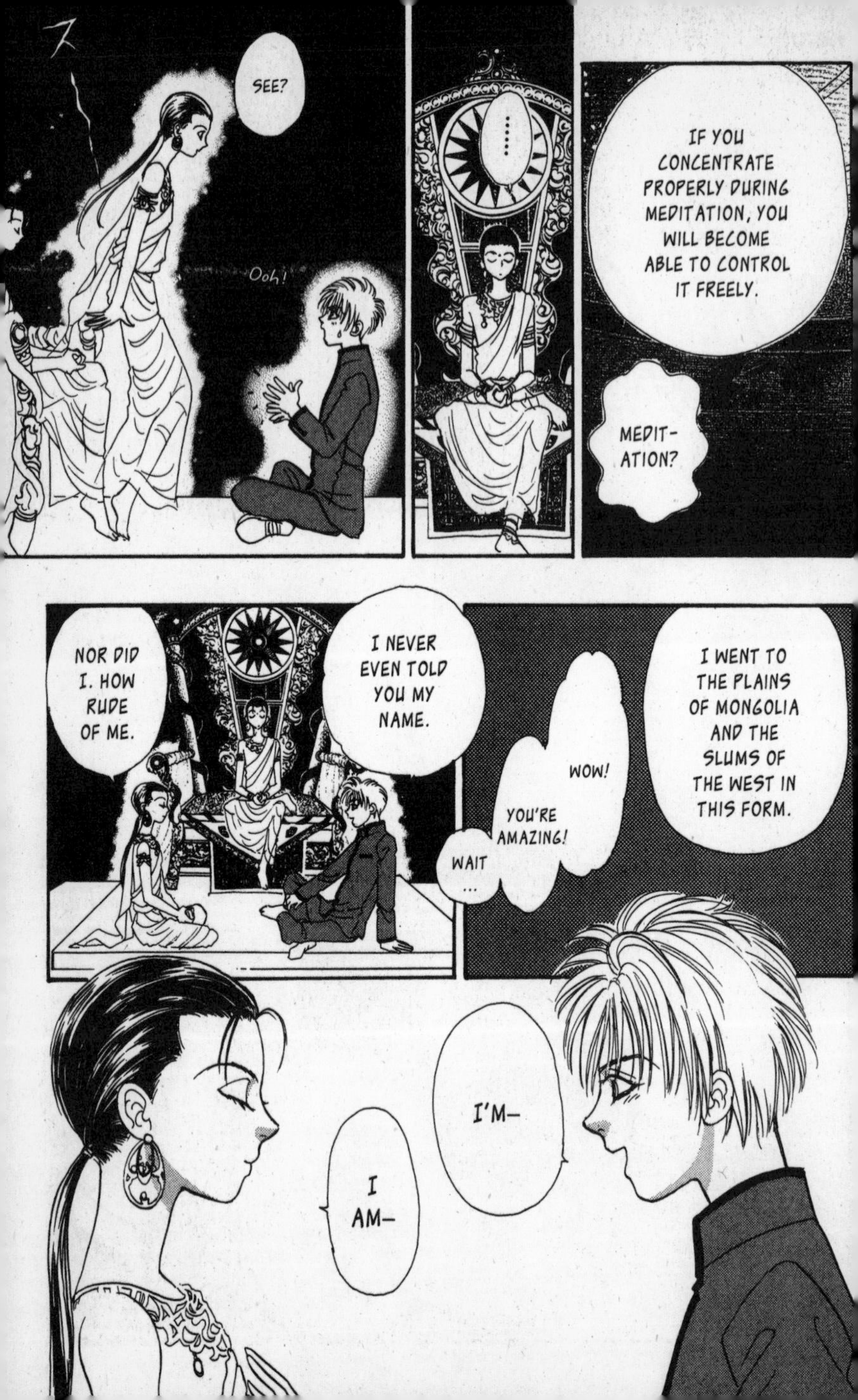
IF YOU CONCENTRATE PROPERLY DURING MEDITATION, YOU WILL BECOME ABLE TO CONTROL IT FREELY.
MEDIT-ATION?
......
SEE?
Ooh!
I WENT TO THE PLAINS OF MONGOLIA AND THE SLUMS OF THE WEST IN THIS FORM.
WOW!
YOU'RE AMAZING!
WAIT ...
I NEVER EVEN TOLD YOU MY NAME.
NOR DID I. HOW RUDE OF ME.
I'M—
I AM—

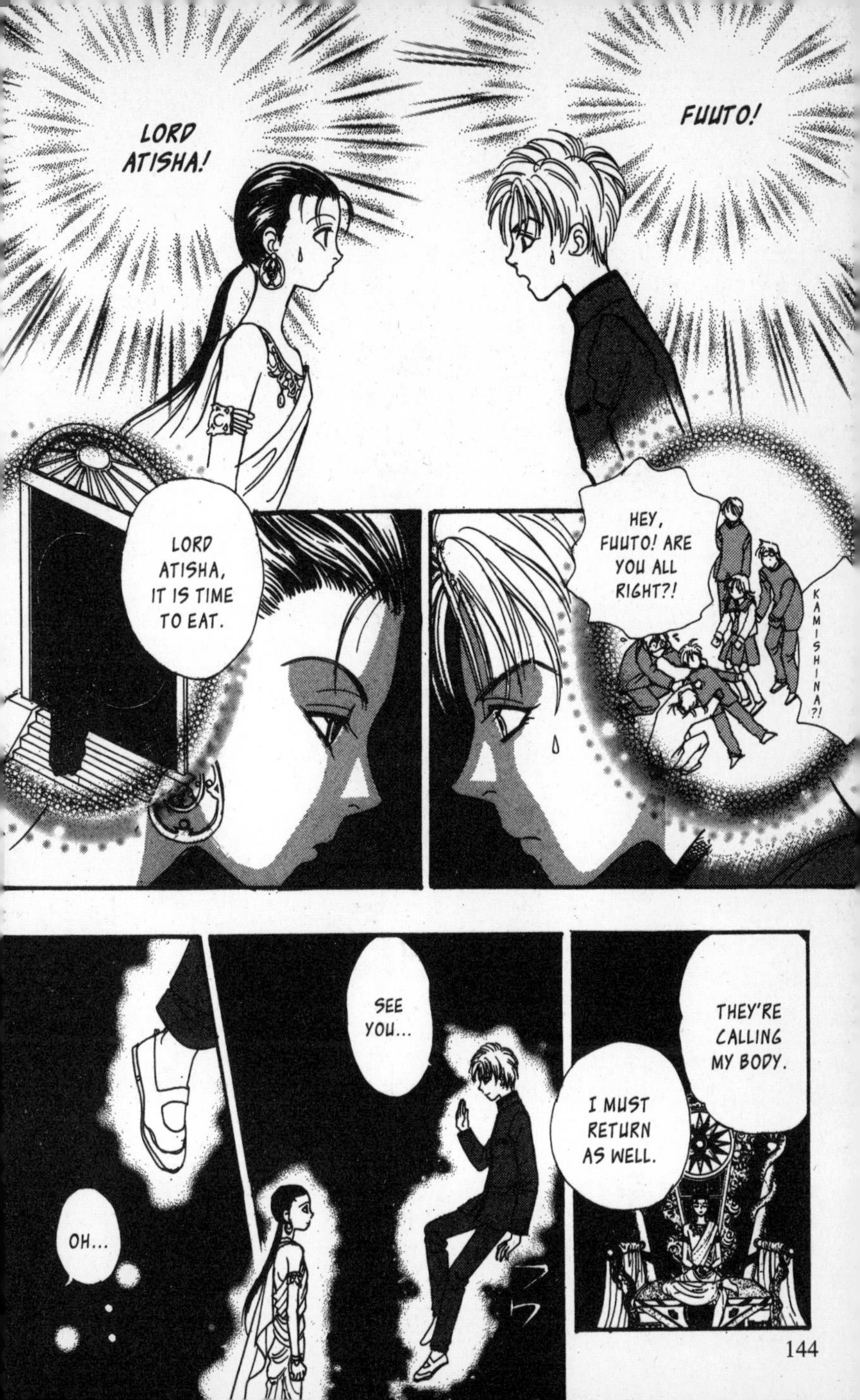
LORD ATISHA!
FUUTO!
LORD ATISHA, IT IS TIME TO EAT.
HEY, FUUTO! ARE YOU ALL RIGHT?!
KAMISHINA?!
OH...
SEE YOU...
THEY'RE CALLING MY BODY.
I MUST RETURN AS WELL.

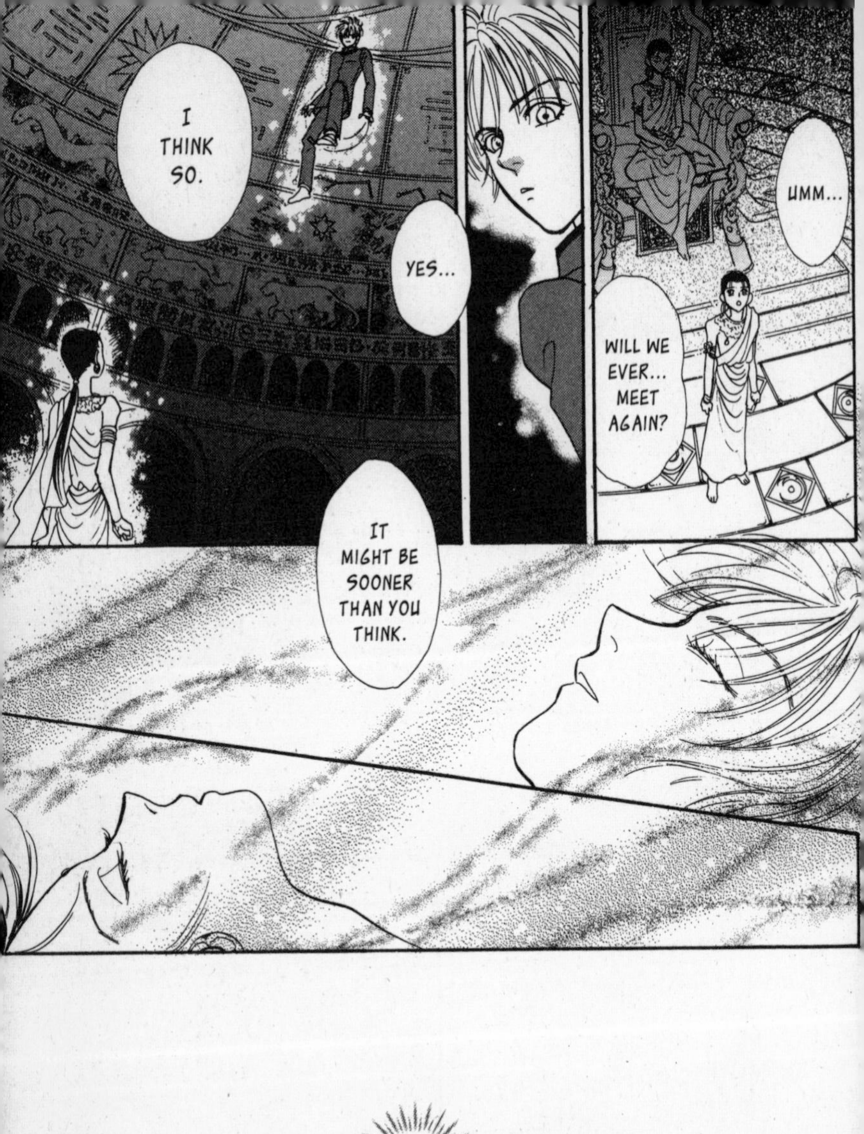
UMM...
WILL WE EVER... MEET AGAIN?
YES...
I THINK SO.
IT MIGHT BE SOONER THAN YOU THINK.

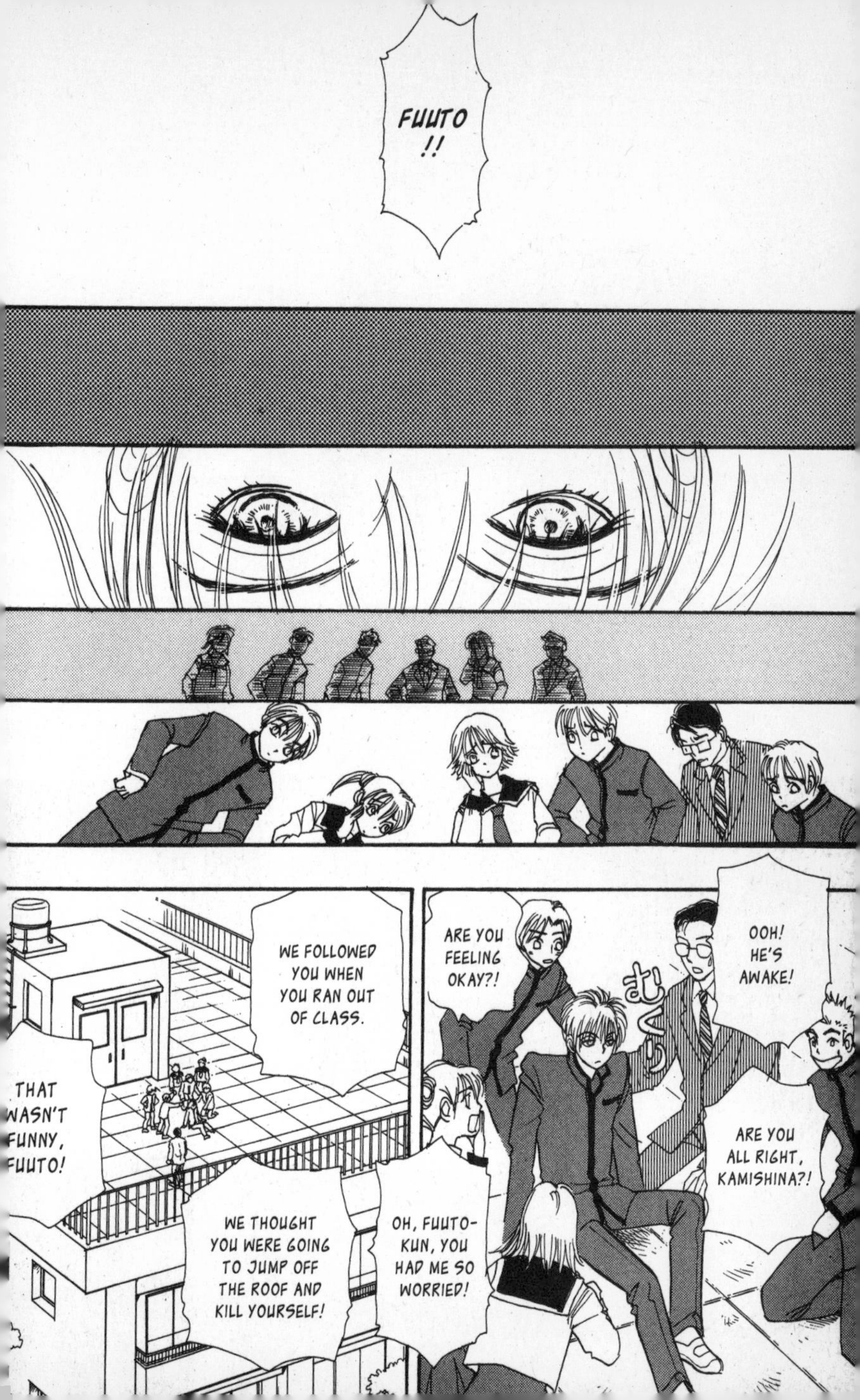

FUUTO !!
OOH! HE'S AWAKE!
ARE YOU FEELING OKAY?!
むくり
ARE YOU ALL RIGHT, KAMISHINA?!
OH, FUUTO-KUN, YOU HAD ME SO WORRIED!
WE FOLLOWED YOU WHEN YOU RAN OUT OF CLASS.
THAT WASN'T FUNNY, FUUTO!
WE THOUGHT YOU WERE GOING TO JUMP OFF THE ROOF AND KILL YOURSELF!

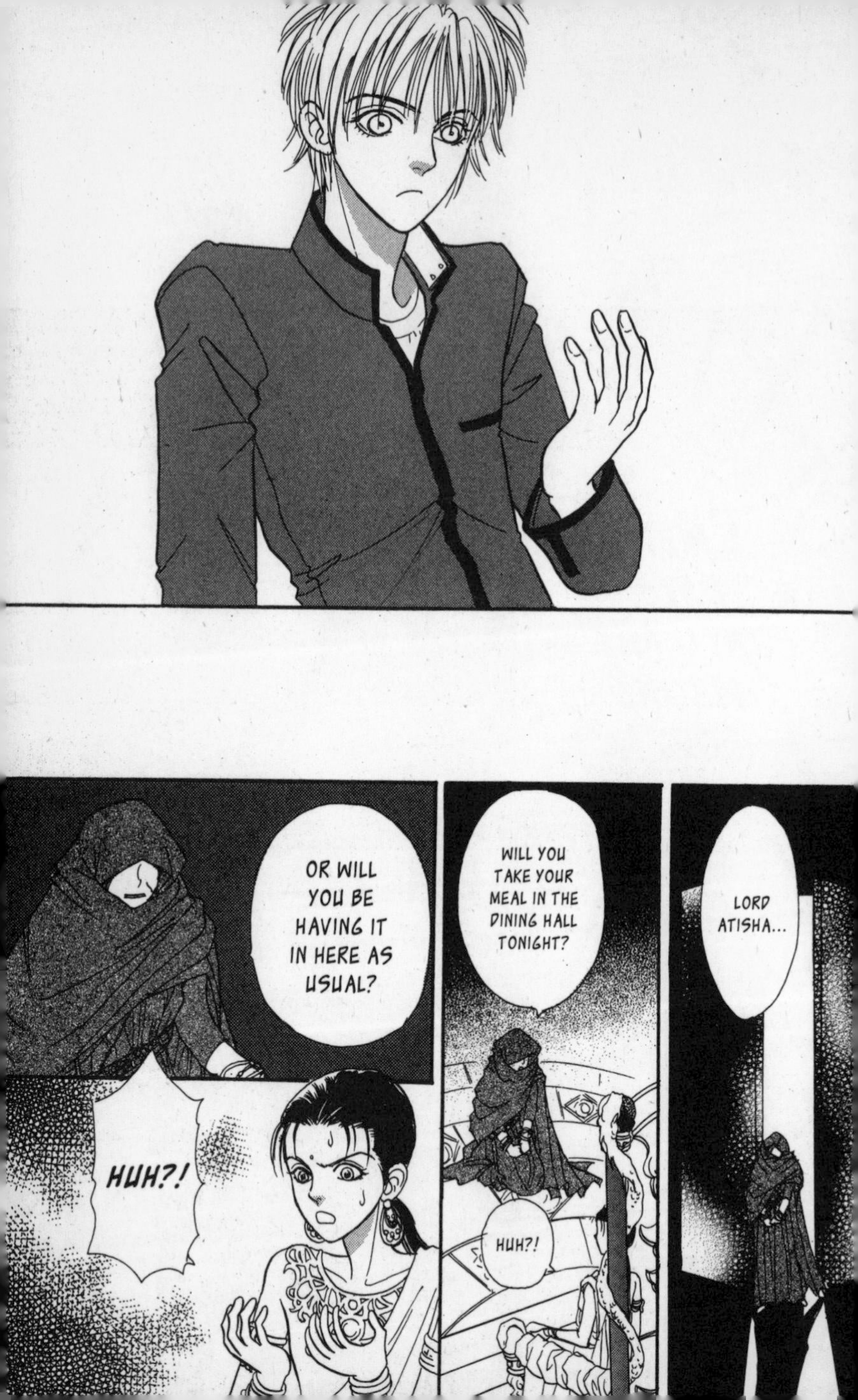
LORD ATISHA...
WILL YOU TAKE YOUR MEAL IN THE DINING HALL TONIGHT?
HUH?!
OR WILL YOU BE HAVING IT IN HERE AS USUAL?
HUH?!

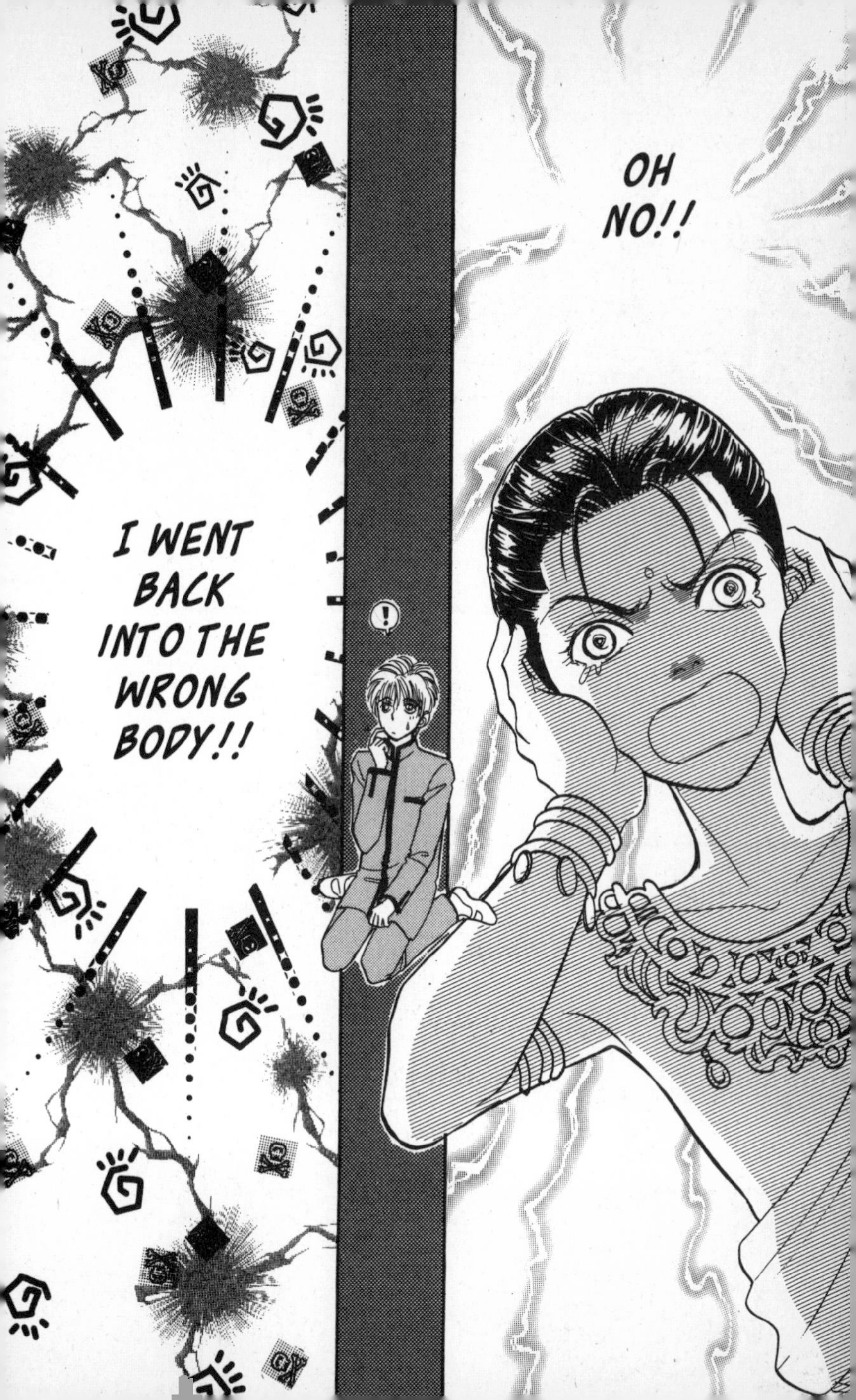
OH NO!!
!
I WENT BACK INTO THE WRONG BODY!!

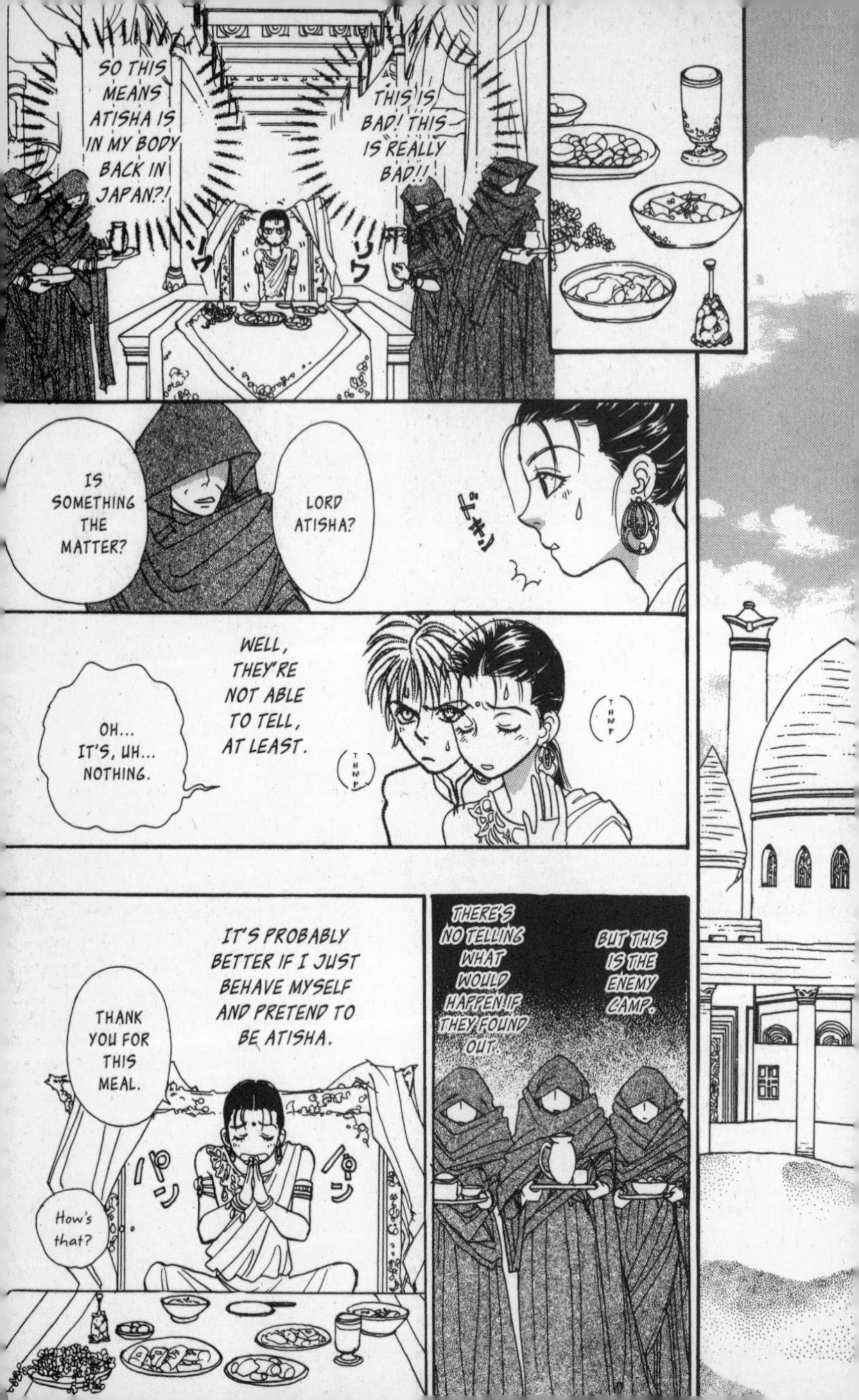
THIS IS BAD! THIS IS REALLY BAD!!
SO THIS MEANS ATISHA IS IN MY BODY BACK IN JAPAN?!
LORD ATISHA?
IS SOMETHING THE MATTER?
THMP
WELL, THEY'RE NOT ABLE TO TELL, AT LEAST.
THMP
OH... IT'S, UH... NOTHING.
BUT THIS IS THE ENEMY CAMP.
THERE'S NO TELLING WHAT WOULD HAPPEN IF THEY FOUND OUT.
IT'S PROBABLY BETTER IF I JUST BEHAVE MYSELF AND PRETEND TO BE ATISHA.
THANK YOU FOR THIS MEAL.
How's that?

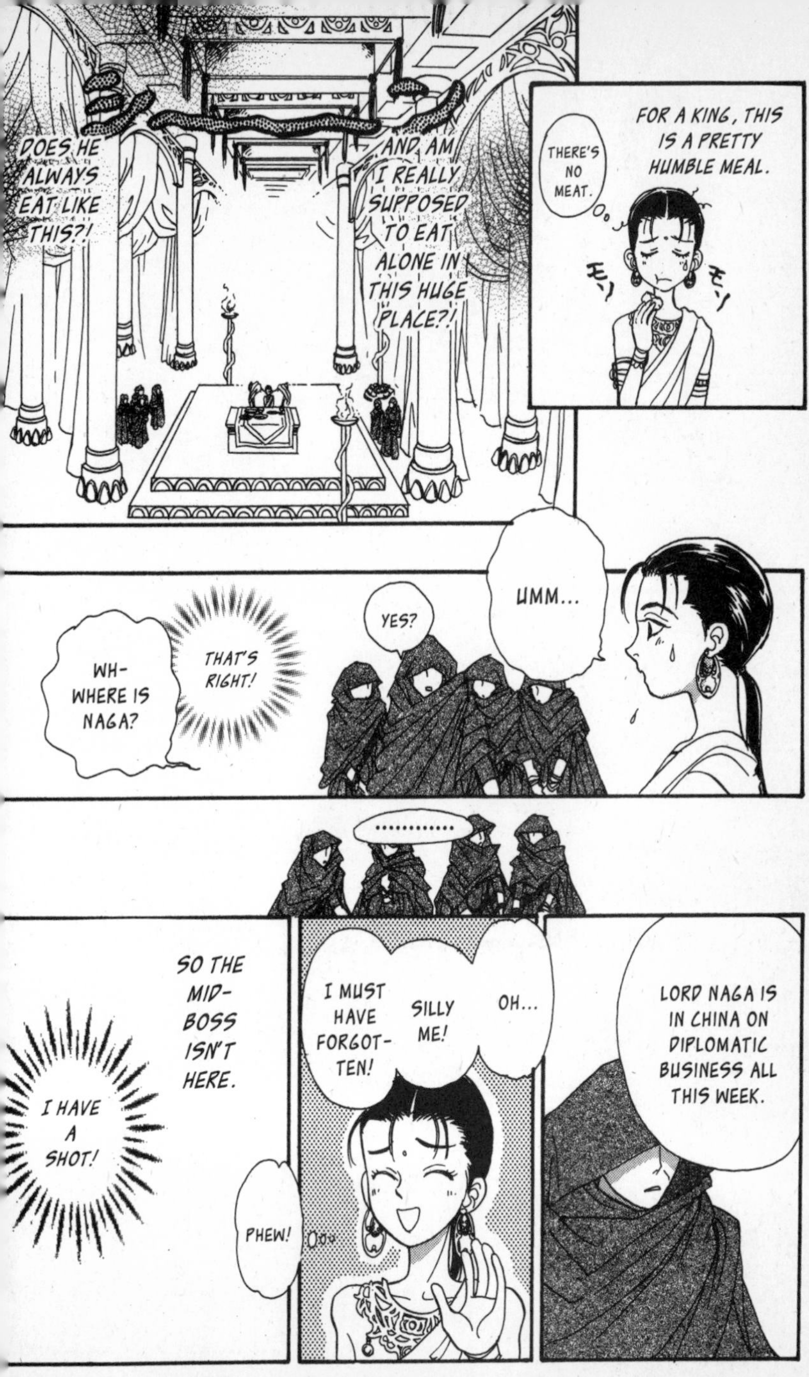
FOR A KING, THIS IS A PRETTY HUMBLE MEAL.
THERE'S NO MEAT.
モソ
モソ
AND AM I REALLY SUPPOSED TO EAT ALONE IN THIS HUGE PLACE?!
DOES HE ALWAYS EAT LIKE THIS?!
UMM...
YES?
THAT'S RIGHT!
WH- WHERE IS NAGA?
....
LORD NAGA IS IN CHINA ON DIPLOMATIC BUSINESS ALL THIS WEEK.
OH...
SILLY ME!
I MUST HAVE FORGOT- TEN!
PHEW!
SO THE MID- BOSS ISN'T HERE.
I HAVE A SHOT!

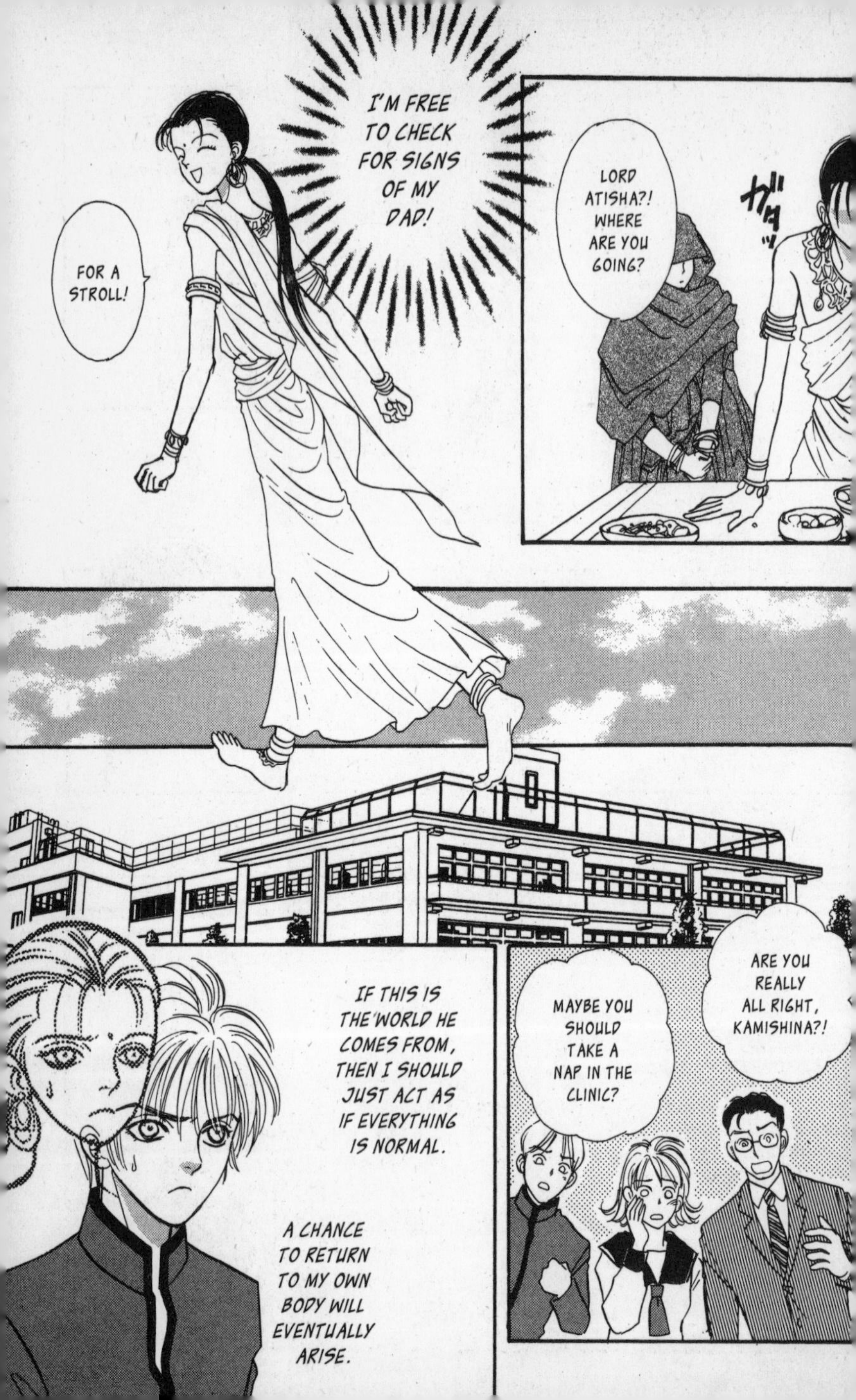
LORD ATISHA?! WHERE ARE YOU GOING?
ガタッ
FOR A STROLL!
I'M FREE TO CHECK FOR SIGNS OF MY DAD!
ARE YOU REALLY ALL RIGHT, KAMISHINA?!
MAYBE YOU SHOULD TAKE A NAP IN THE CLINIC?
IF THIS IS THE WORLD HE COMES FROM, THEN I SHOULD JUST ACT AS IF EVERYTHING IS NORMAL.
A CHANCE TO RETURN TO MY OWN BODY WILL EVENTUALLY ARISE.

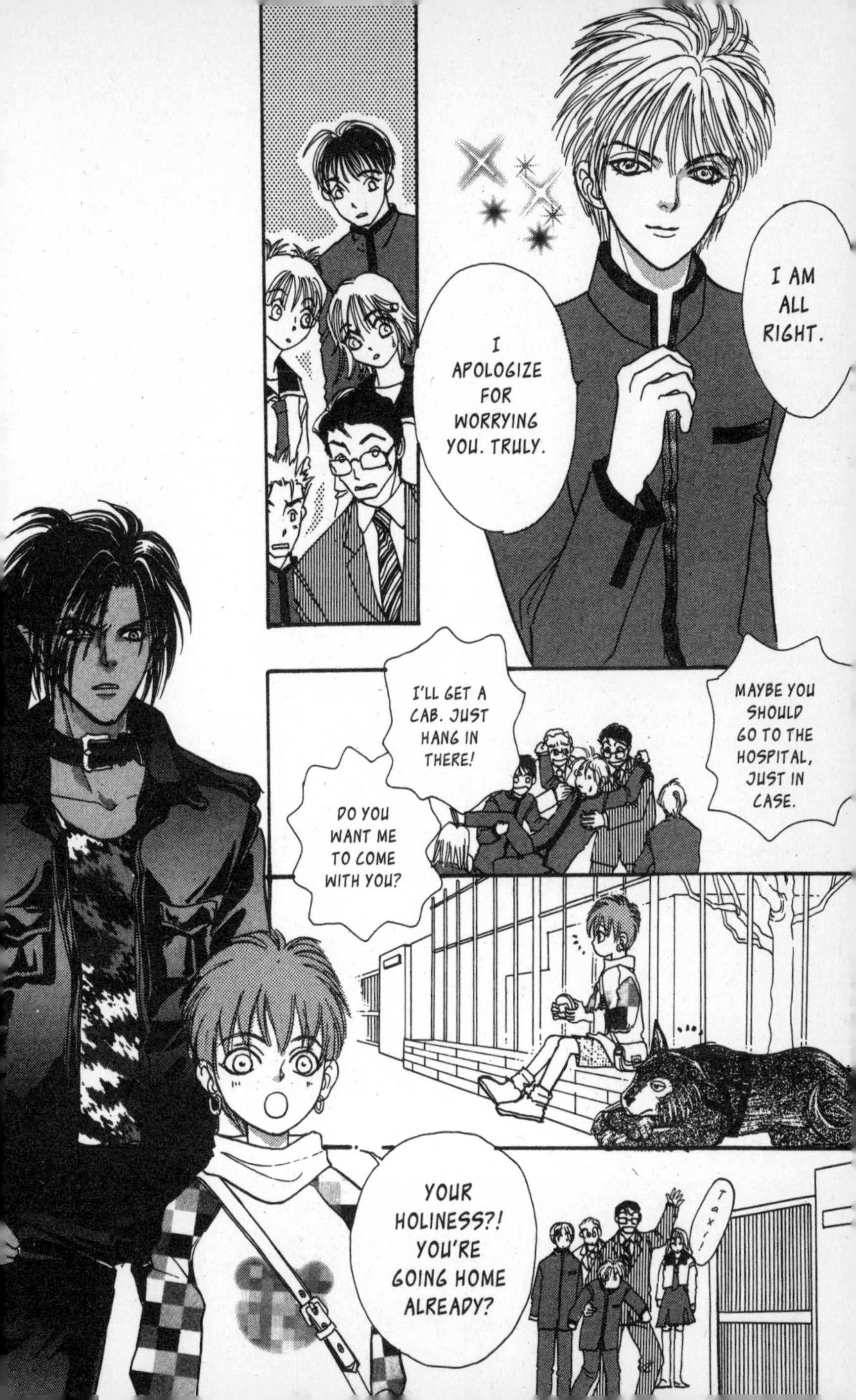
I AM ALL RIGHT.
I APOLOGIZE FOR WORRYING YOU. TRULY.
MAYBE YOU SHOULD GO TO THE HOSPITAL, JUST IN CASE.
I'LL GET A CAB. JUST HANG IN THERE!
DO YOU WANT ME TO COME WITH YOU?
Taxi-!
YOUR HOLINESS?! YOU'RE GOING HOME ALREADY?

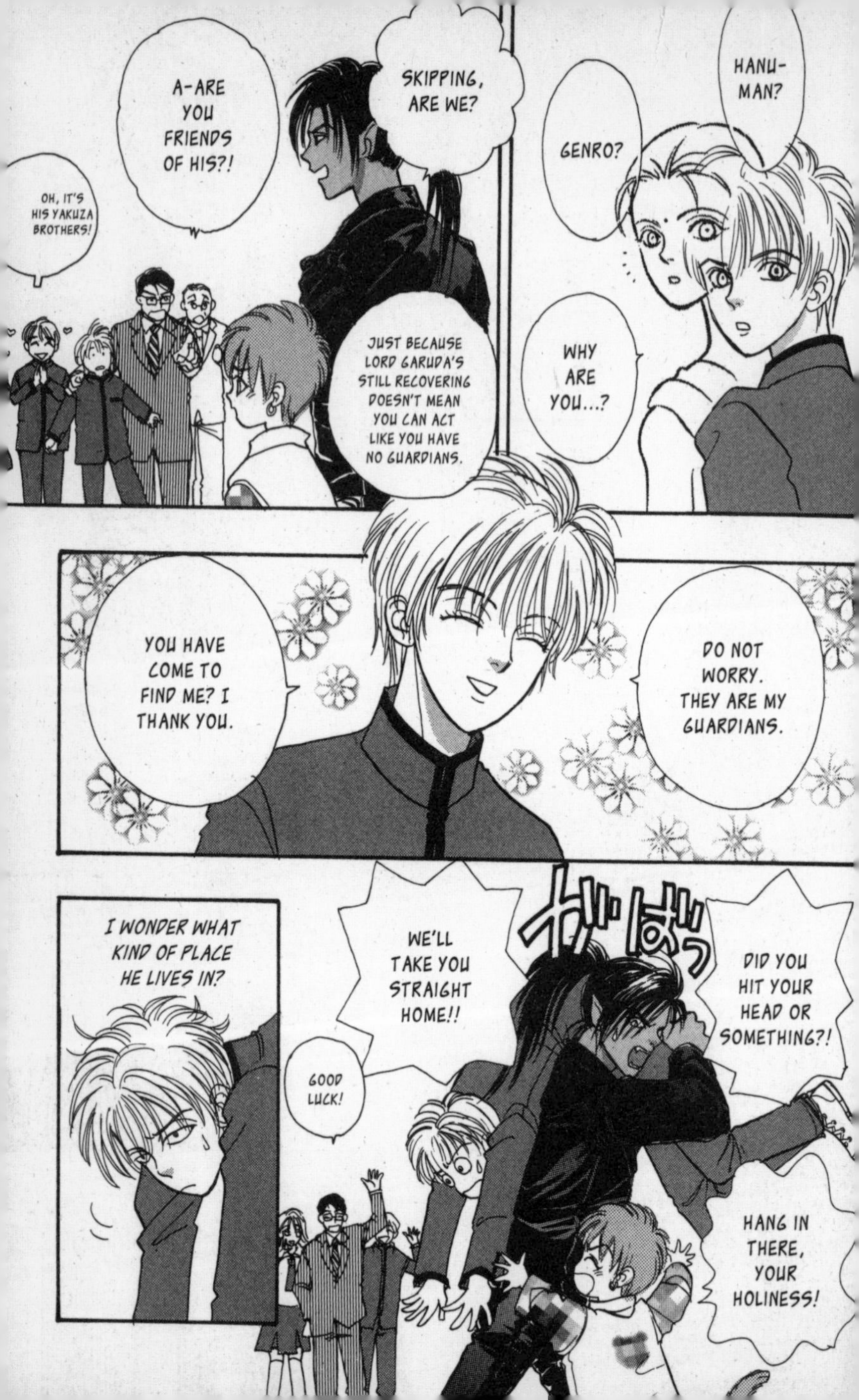
HANU-MAN?
GENRO?
WHY ARE YOU...?
SKIPPING, ARE WE?
JUST BECAUSE LORD GARUDA'S STILL RECOVERING DOESN'T MEAN YOU CAN ACT LIKE YOU HAVE NO GUARDIANS.
A-ARE YOU FRIENDS OF HIS?!
OH, IT'S HIS YAKUZA BROTHERS!
DO NOT WORRY. THEY ARE MY GUARDIANS.
YOU HAVE COME TO FIND ME? I THANK YOU.
DID YOU HIT YOUR HEAD OR SOMETHING?!
WE'LL TAKE YOU STRAIGHT HOME!!
HANG IN THERE, YOUR HOLINESS!
GOOD LUCK!
I WONDER WHAT KIND OF PLACE HE LIVES IN?

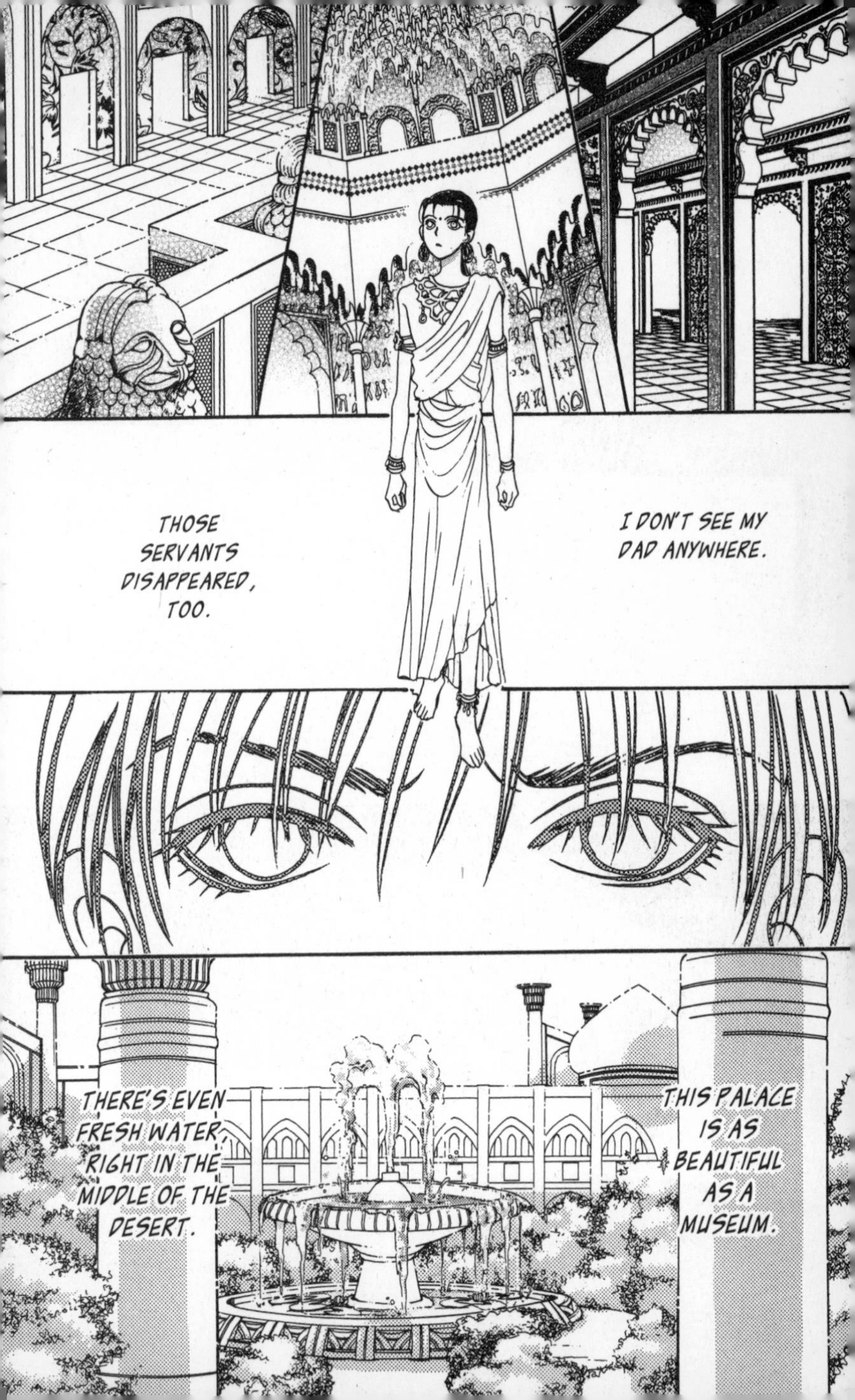
I DON'T SEE MY DAD ANYWHERE.
THOSE SERVANTS DISAPPEARED, TOO.
THIS PALACE IS AS BEAUTIFUL AS A MUSEUM.
THERE'S EVEN FRESH WATER, RIGHT IN THE MIDDLE OF THE DESERT.

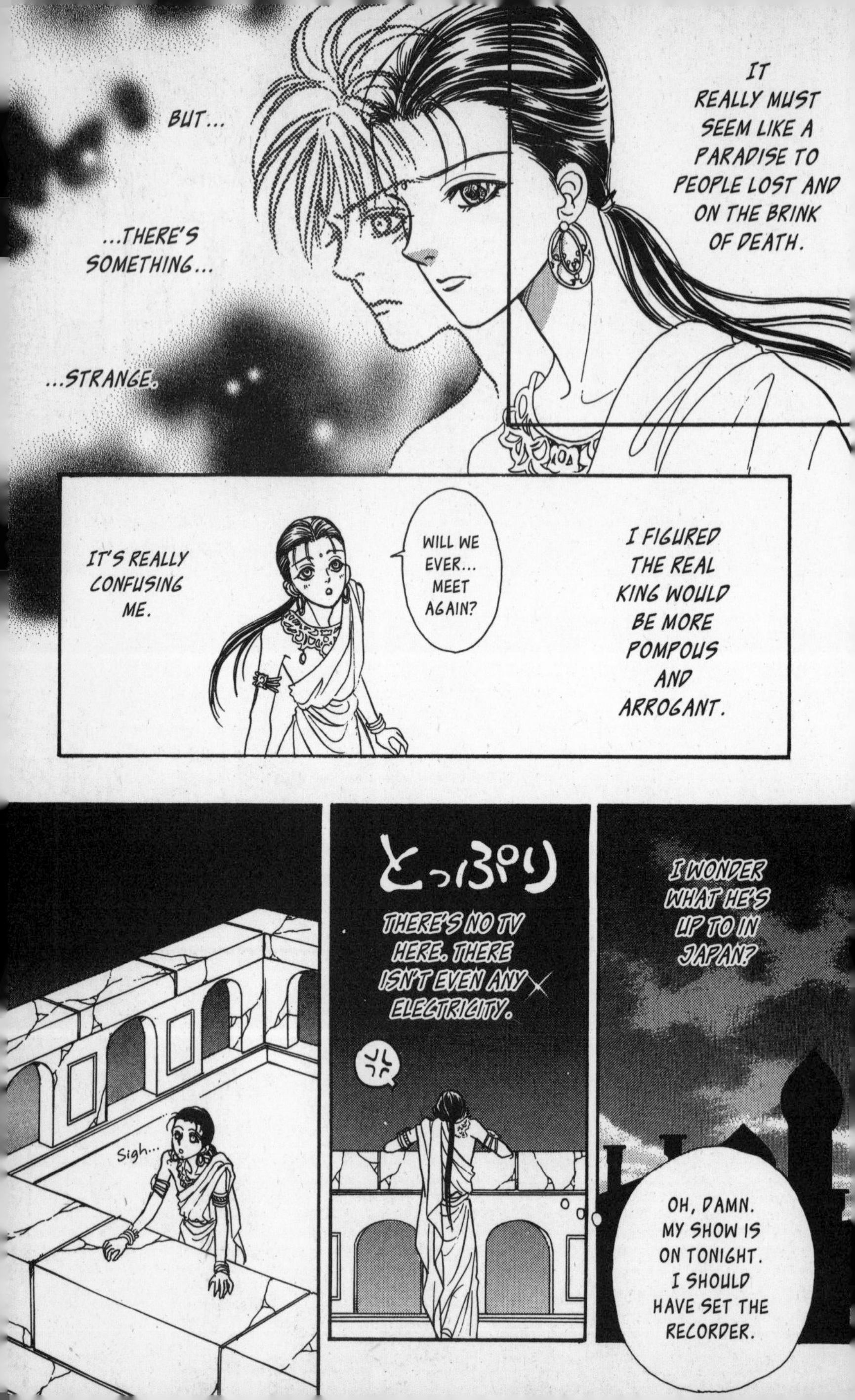
IT REALLY MUST SEEM LIKE A PARADISE TO PEOPLE LOST AND ON THE BRINK OF DEATH.
BUT...
...THERE'S SOMETHING...
...STRANGE.
IT'S REALLY CONFUSING ME.
WILL WE EVER... MEET AGAIN?
I FIGURED THE REAL KING WOULD BE MORE POMPOUS AND ARROGANT.
Sigh...
とっぷり
THERE'S NO TV HERE. THERE ISN'T EVEN ANY ELECTRICITY.
I WONDER WHAT HE'S UP TO IN JAPAN?
OH, DAMN. MY SHOW IS ON TONIGHT. I SHOULD HAVE SET THE RECORDER.

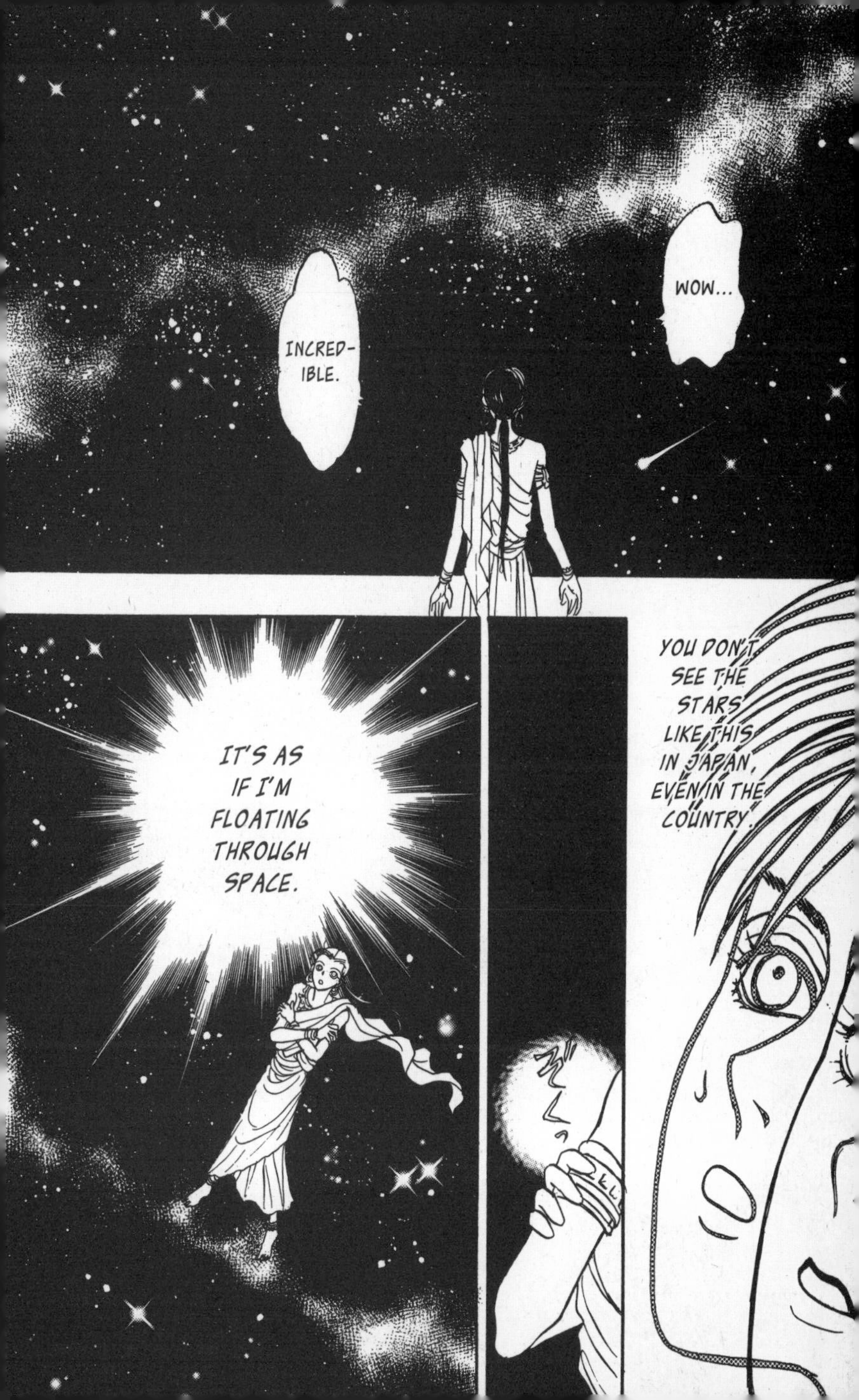
WOW...
INCRED-IBLE.
YOU DON'T SEE THE STARS LIKE THIS IN JAPAN, EVEN IN THE COUNTRY.
IT'S AS IF I'M FLOATING THROUGH SPACE.

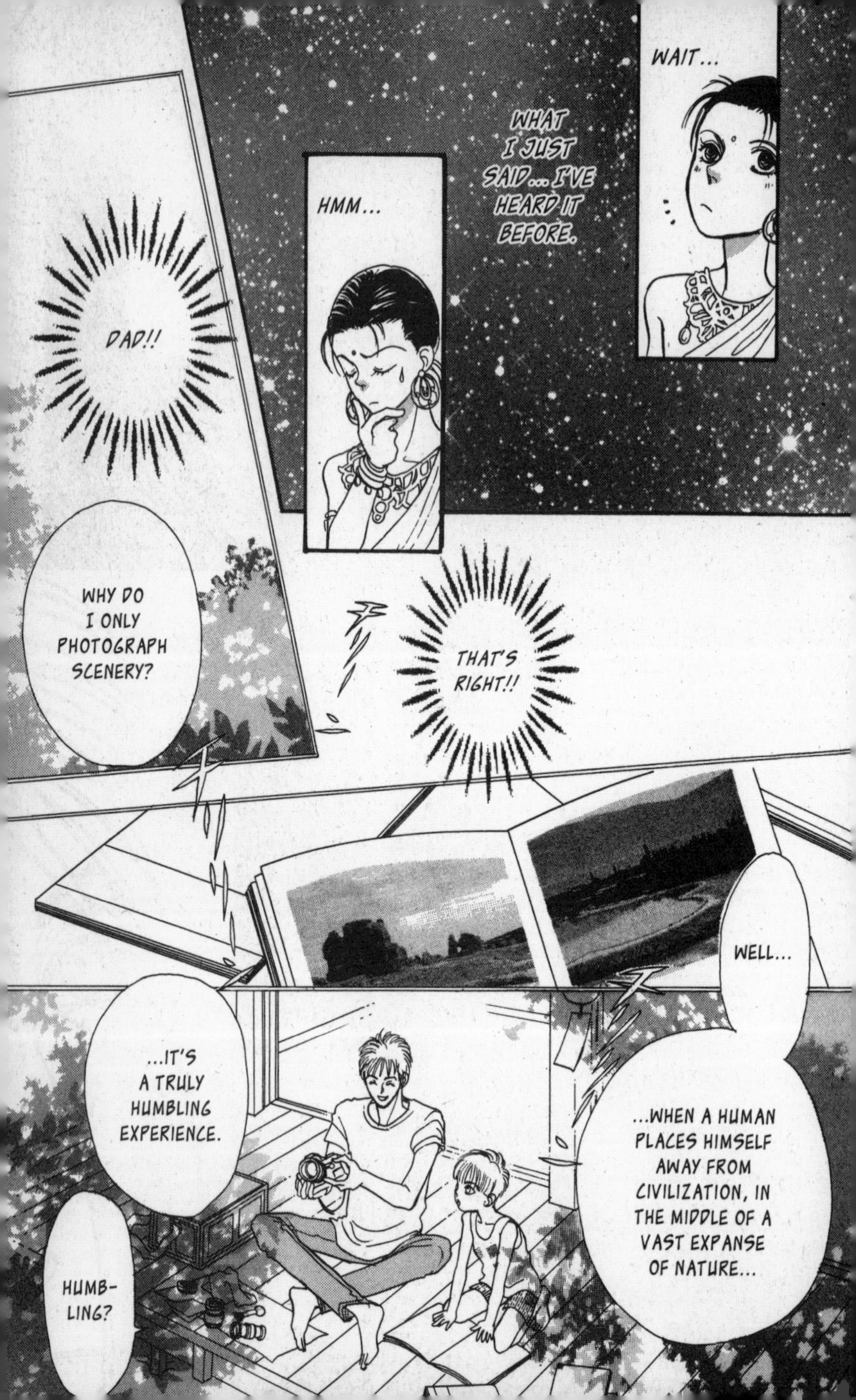
WAIT...
WHAT I JUST SAID... I'VE HEARD IT BEFORE.
HMM...
DAD!!
THAT'S RIGHT!!
WHY DO I ONLY PHOTOGRAPH SCENERY?
WELL...
...WHEN A HUMAN PLACES HIMSELF AWAY FROM CIVILIZATION, IN THE MIDDLE OF A VAST EXPANSE OF NATURE...
...IT'S A TRULY HUMBLING EXPERIENCE.
HUMB-LING?

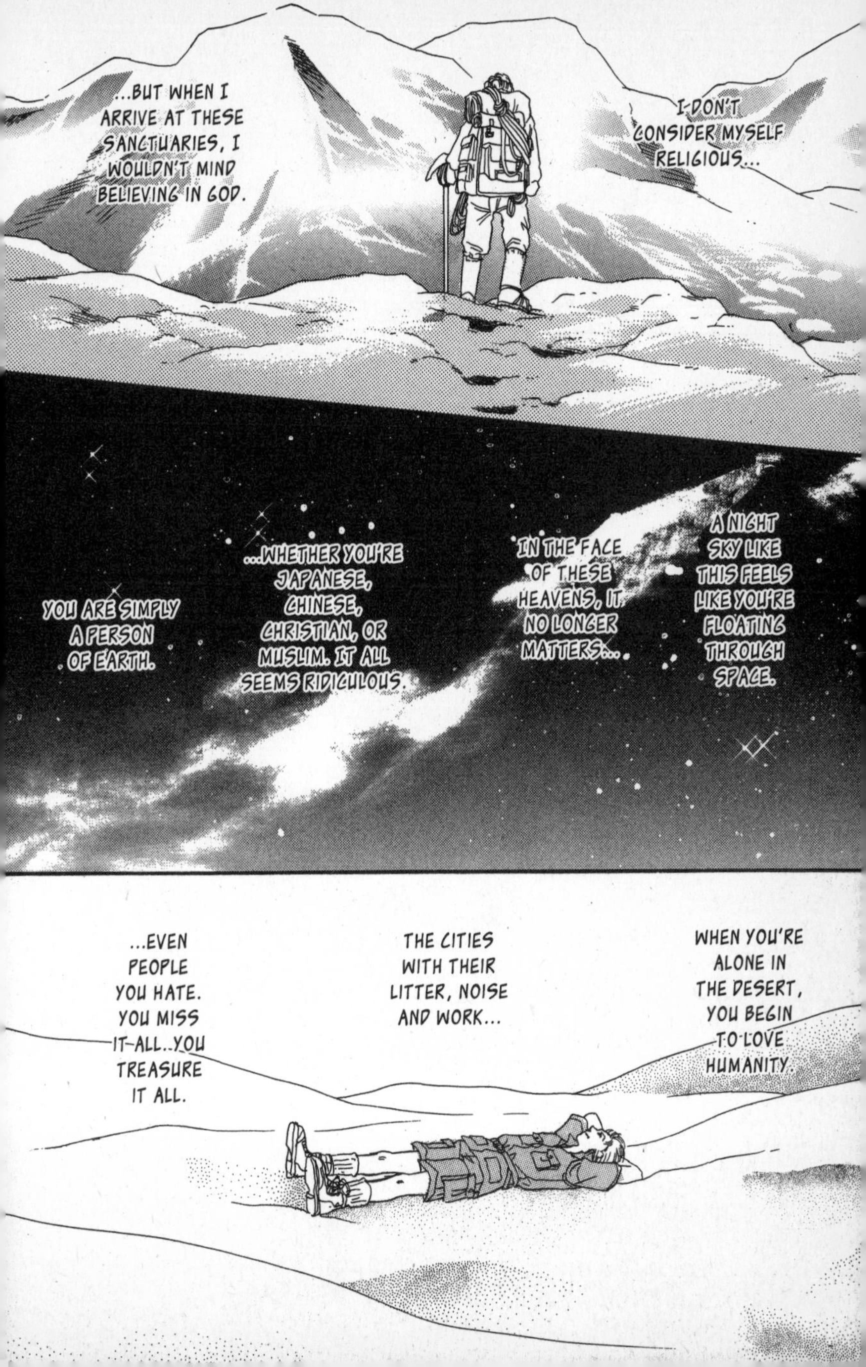
I DON'T CONSIDER MYSELF RELIGIOUS...
...BUT WHEN I ARRIVE AT THESE SANCTUARIES, I WOULDN'T MIND BELIEVING IN GOD.
A NIGHT SKY LIKE THIS FEELS LIKE YOU'RE FLOATING THROUGH SPACE.
IN THE FACE OF THESE HEAVENS, IT NO LONGER MATTERS...
...WHETHER YOU'RE JAPANESE, CHINESE, CHRISTIAN, OR MUSLIM. IT ALL SEEMS RIDICULOUS.
YOU ARE SIMPLY A PERSON OF EARTH.
WHEN YOU'RE ALONE IN THE DESERT, YOU BEGIN TO LOVE HUMANITY.
THE CITIES WITH THEIR LITTER, NOISE AND WORK...
...EVEN PEOPLE YOU HATE. YOU MISS IT ALL..YOU TREASURE IT ALL.

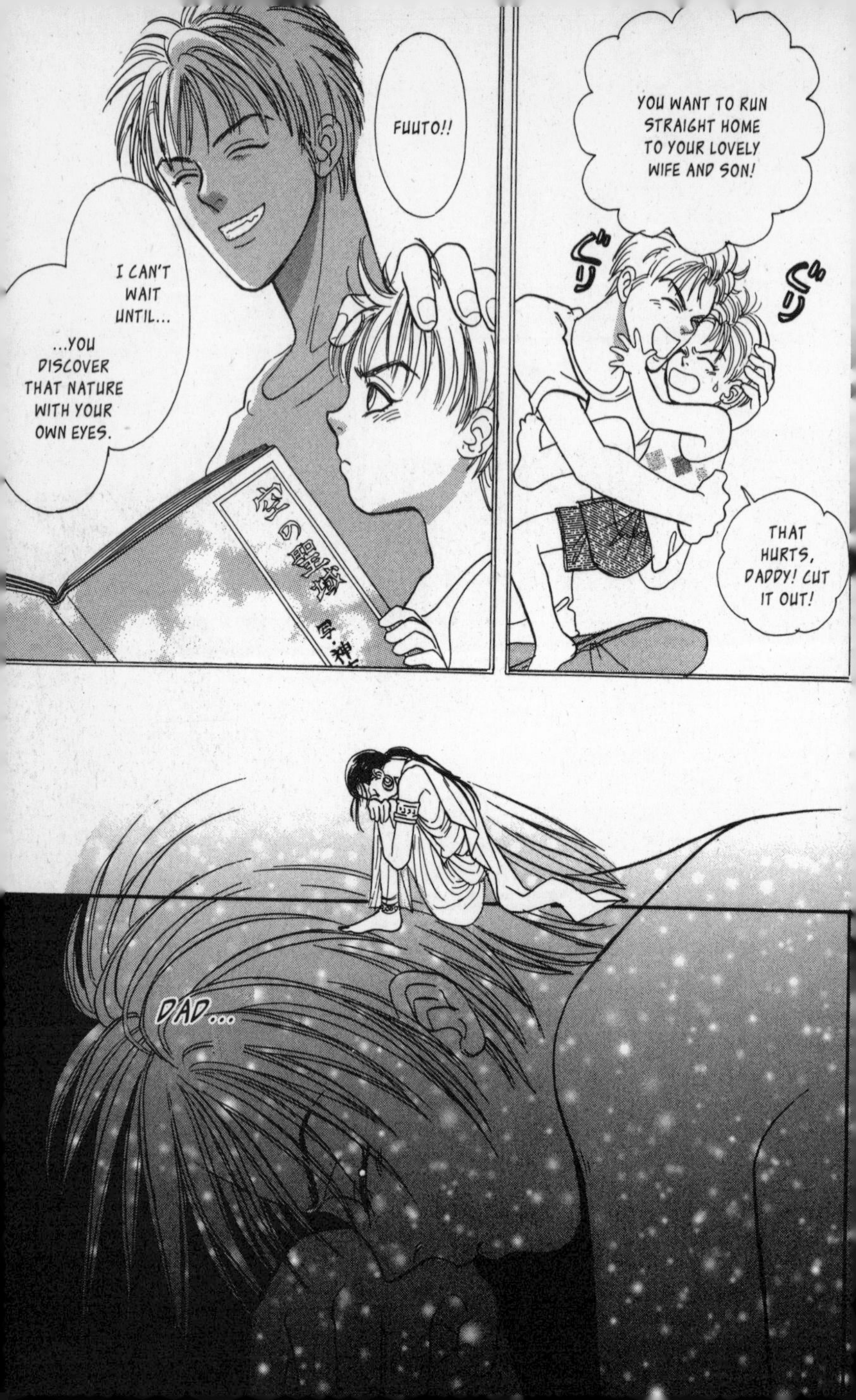
YOU WANT TO RUN STRAIGHT HOME TO YOUR LOVELY WIFE AND SON!
ぐり
ぐり
THAT HURTS, DADDY! CUT IT OUT!
FUUTO!!
I CAN'T WAIT UNTIL...
...YOU DISCOVER THAT NATURE WITH YOUR OWN EYES.
DAD...

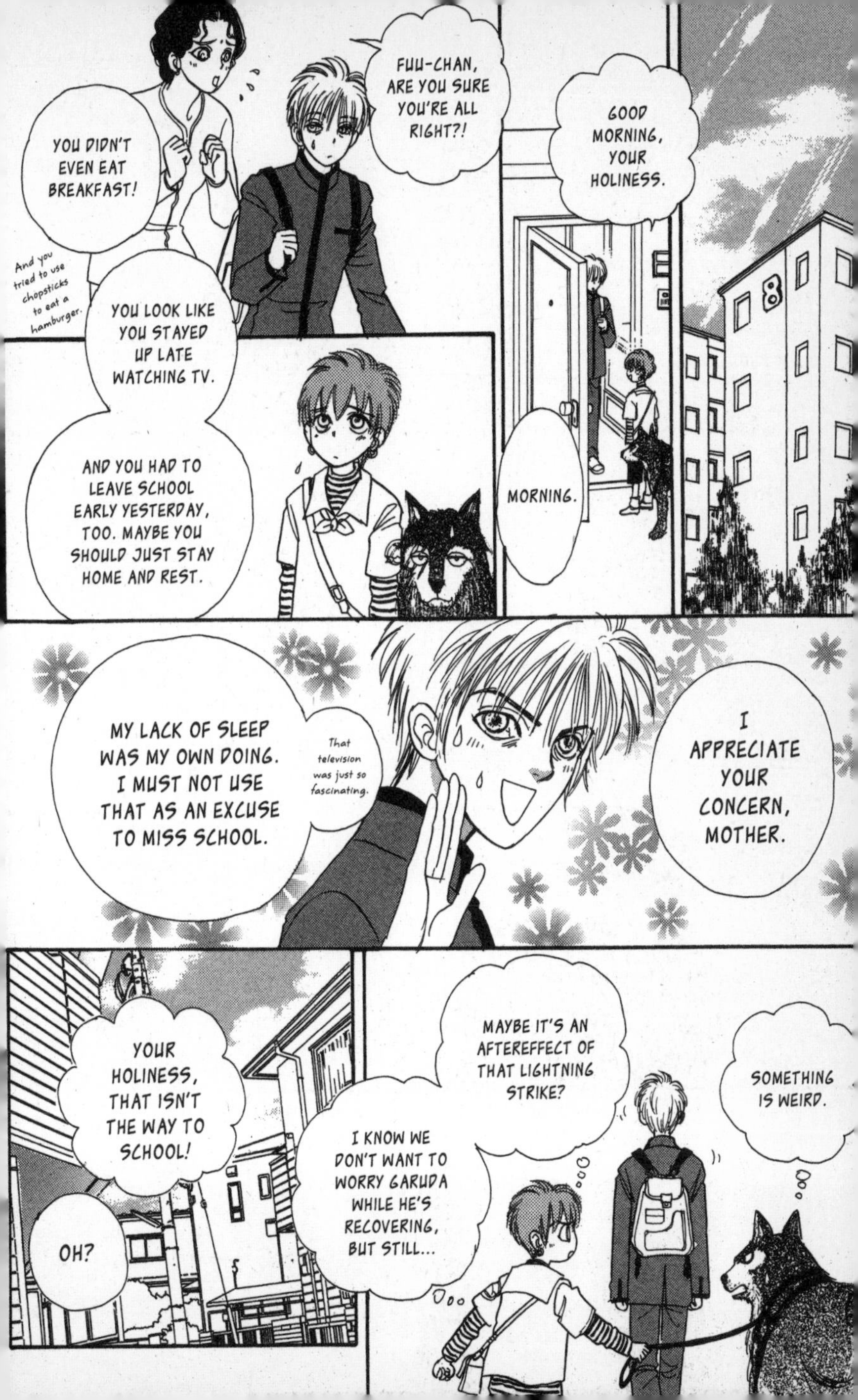
GOOD MORNING, YOUR HOLINESS.
MORNING.
FUU-CHAN, ARE YOU SURE YOU'RE ALL RIGHT?!
YOU DIDN'T EVEN EAT BREAKFAST!
And you tried to use chopsticks to eat a hamburger.
YOU LOOK LIKE YOU STAYED UP LATE WATCHING TV.
AND YOU HAD TO LEAVE SCHOOL EARLY YESTERDAY, TOO. MAYBE YOU SHOULD JUST STAY HOME AND REST.
I APPRECIATE YOUR CONCERN, MOTHER.
MY LACK OF SLEEP WAS MY OWN DOING. I MUST NOT USE THAT AS AN EXCUSE TO MISS SCHOOL.
That television was just so fascinating.
SOMETHING IS WEIRD.
MAYBE IT'S AN AFTEREFFECT OF THAT LIGHTNING STRIKE?
I KNOW WE DON'T WANT TO WORRY GARUDA WHILE HE'S RECOVERING, BUT STILL...
YOUR HOLINESS, THAT ISN'T THE WAY TO SCHOOL!
OH?

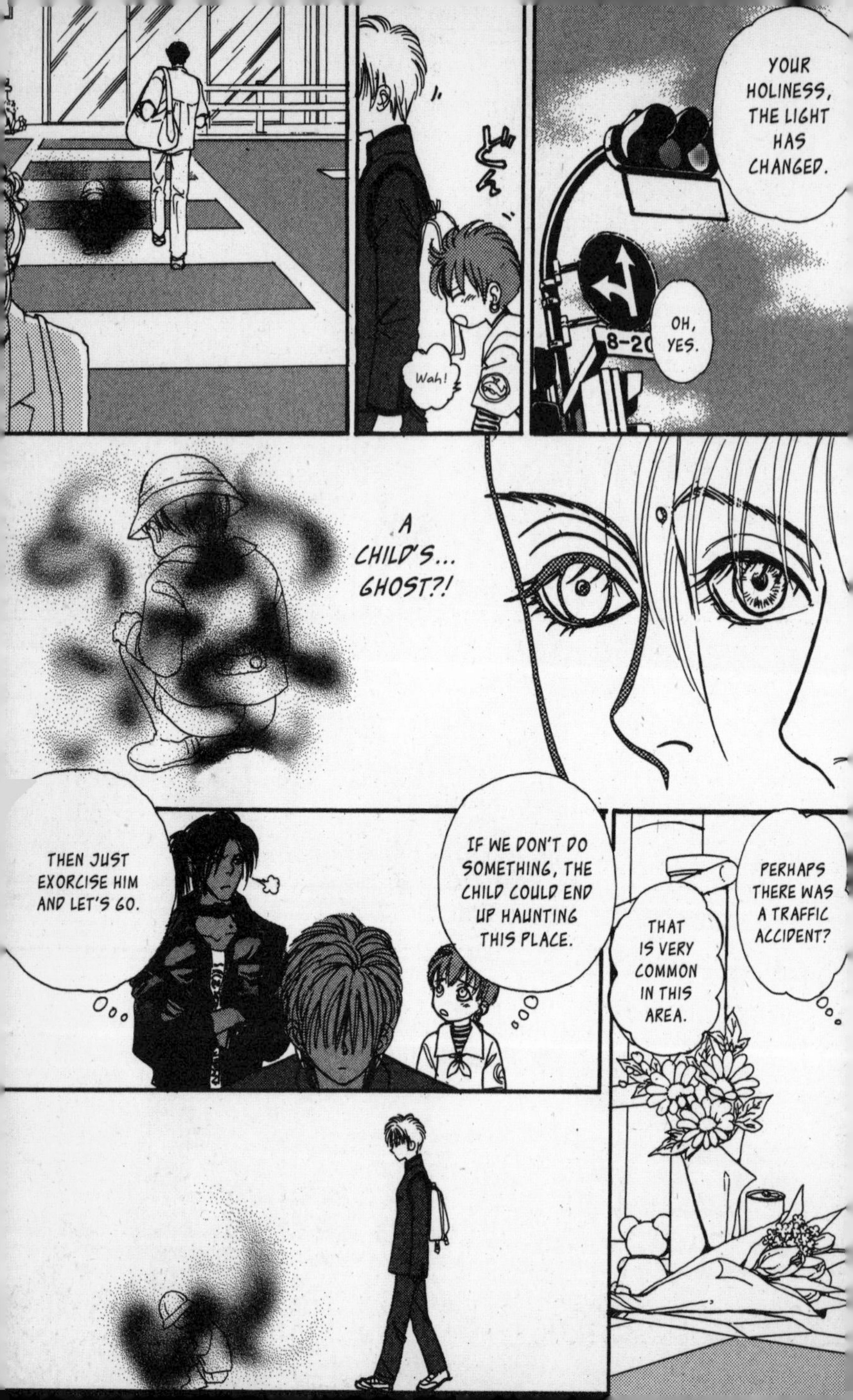
YOUR HOLINESS, THE LIGHT HAS CHANGED.
OH, YES.
8-20
Wah!
A CHILD'S... GHOST?!
PERHAPS THERE WAS A TRAFFIC ACCIDENT?
THAT IS VERY COMMON IN THIS AREA.
IF WE DON'T DO SOMETHING, THE CHILD COULD END UP HAUNTING THIS PLACE.
THEN JUST EXORCISE HIM AND LET'S GO.

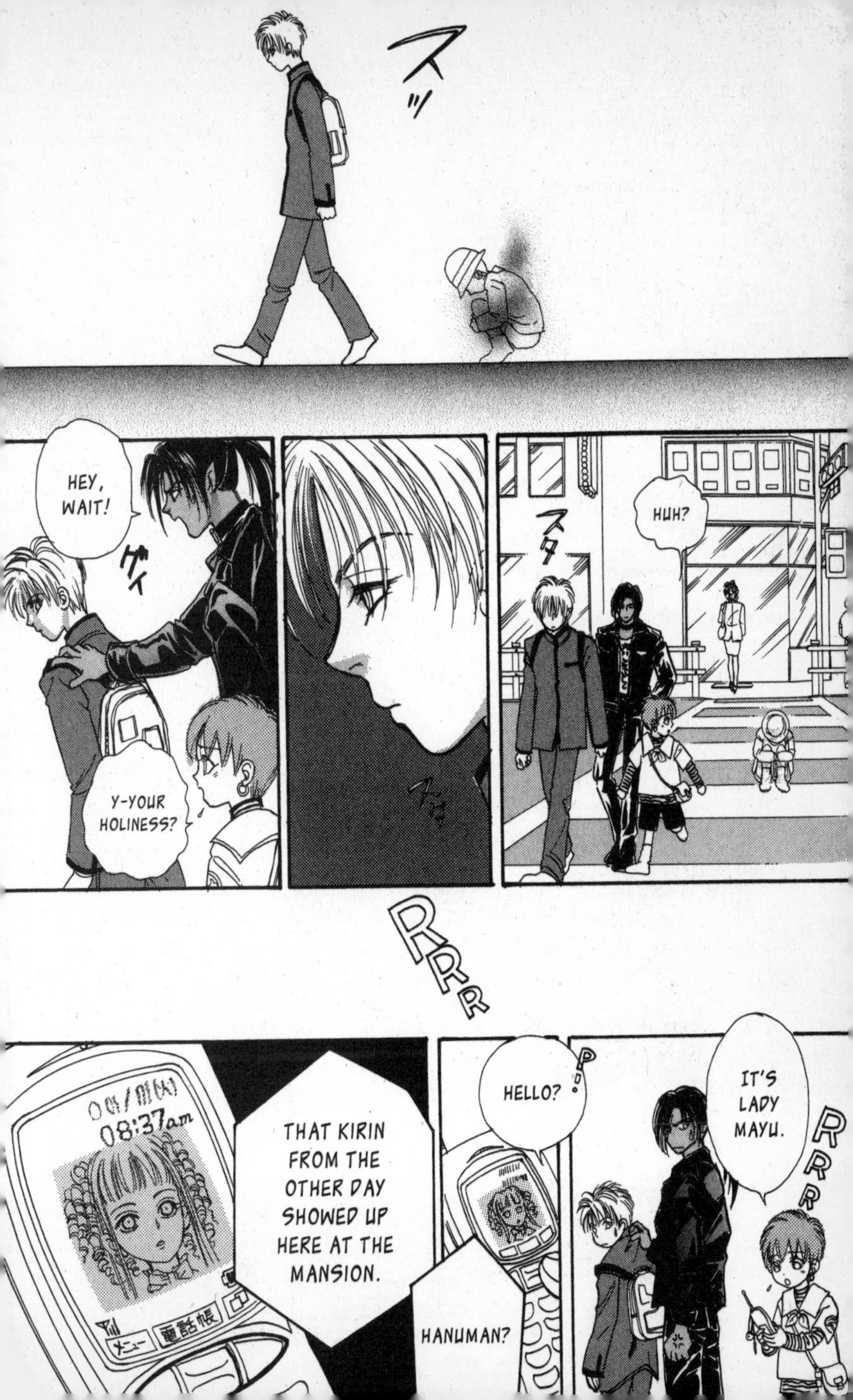
スッ
スタ
HUH?
HEY, WAIT!
グイ
Y-YOUR HOLINESS?
RRR
IT'S LADY MAYU.
RRR
HELLO?
08:37am
メニュー
電話帳
THAT KIRIN FROM THE OTHER DAY SHOWED UP HERE AT THE MANSION.
HANUMAN?

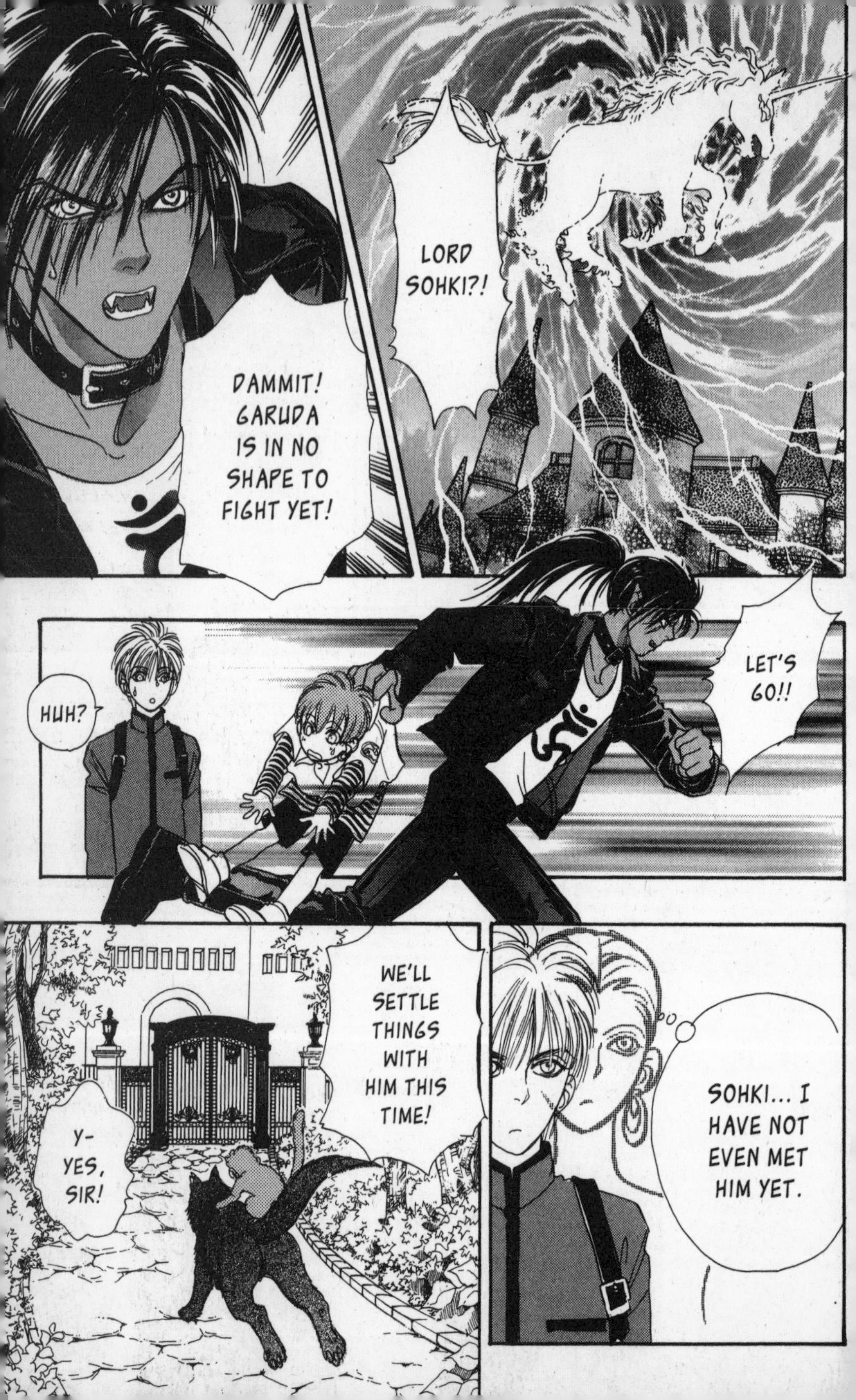
DAMMIT! GARUDA IS IN NO SHAPE TO FIGHT YET!
LORD SOHKI?!
HUH?
LET'S GO!!
WE'LL SETTLE THINGS WITH HIM THIS TIME!
Y-YES, SIR!
SOHKI... I HAVE NOT EVEN MET HIM YET.

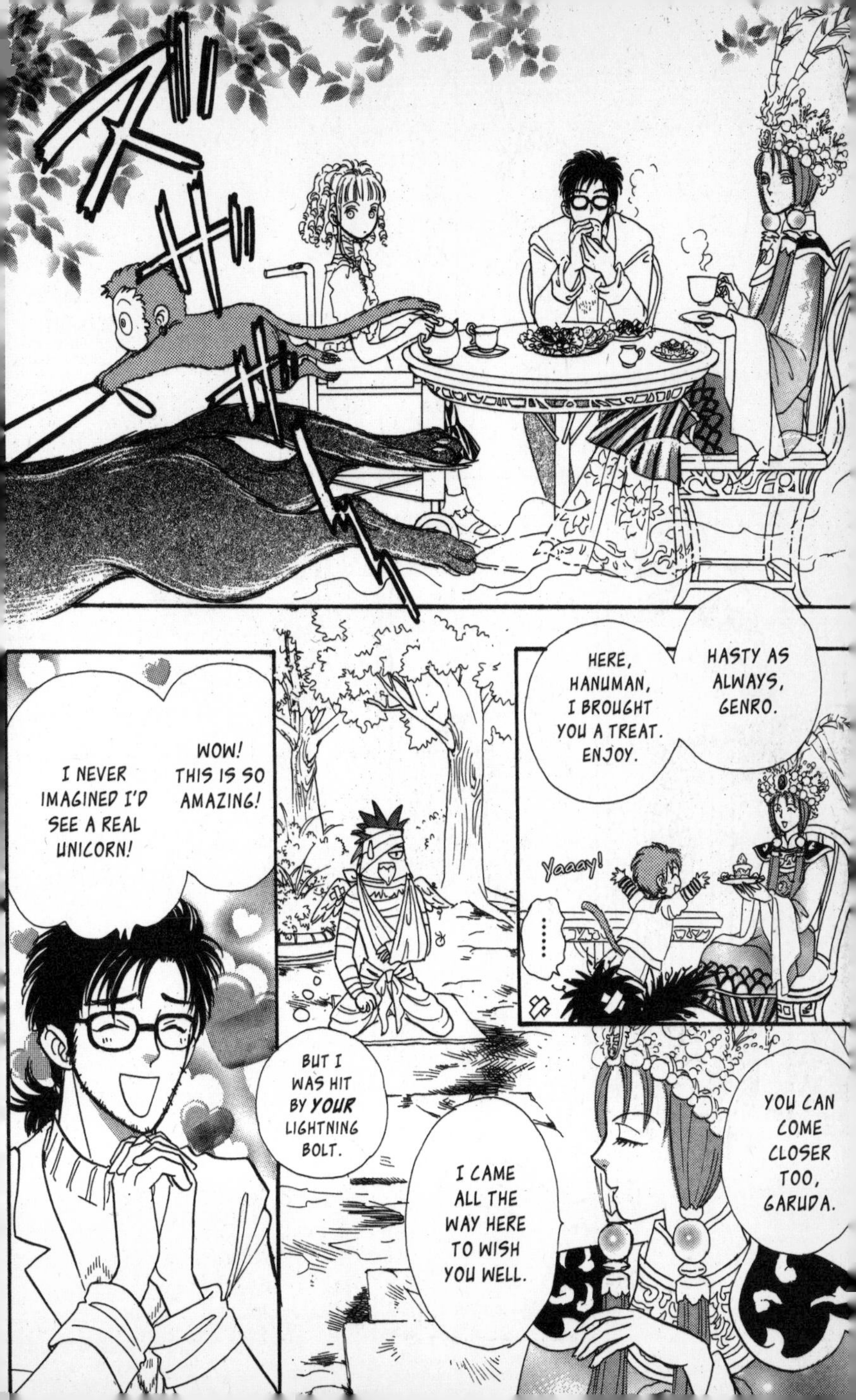
HASTY AS ALWAYS, GENRO.
HERE, HANUMAN, I BROUGHT YOU A TREAT. ENJOY.
Yaaay!
......
YOU CAN COME CLOSER TOO, GARUDA.
I CAME ALL THE WAY HERE TO WISH YOU WELL.
BUT I WAS HIT BY *YOUR* LIGHTNING BOLT.
WOW! THIS IS SO AMAZING!
I NEVER IMAGINED I'D SEE A REAL UNICORN!

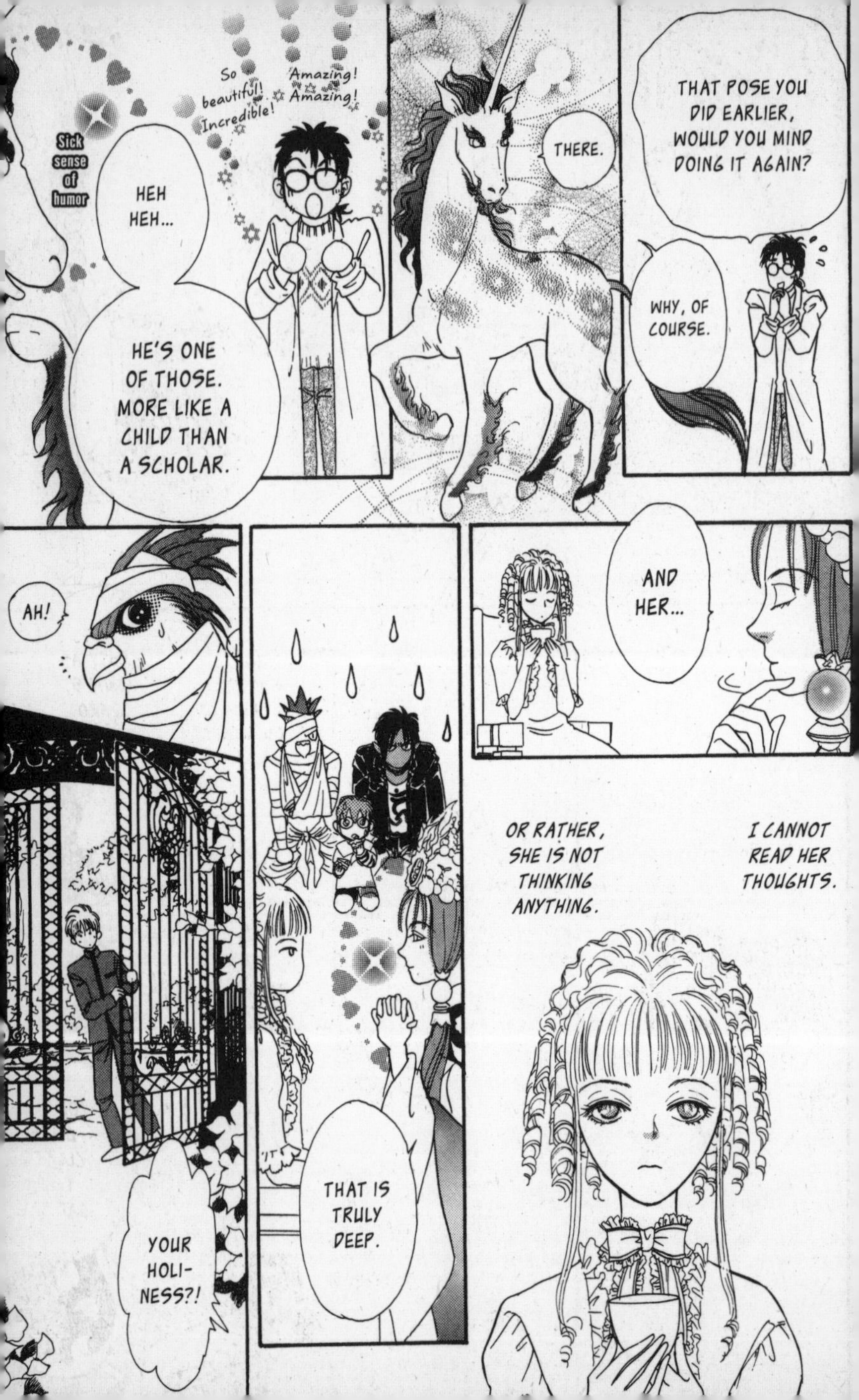

THAT POSE YOU DID EARLIER, WOULD YOU MIND DOING IT AGAIN?
WHY, OF COURSE.
THERE.
Amazing! Amazing!
So beautiful! Incredible!
HEH HEH...
HE'S ONE OF THOSE. MORE LIKE A CHILD THAN A SCHOLAR.
Sick sense of humor
AND HER...
I CANNOT READ HER THOUGHTS.
OR RATHER, SHE IS NOT THINKING ANYTHING.
THAT IS TRULY DEEP.
AH!
YOUR HOLI-NESS?!

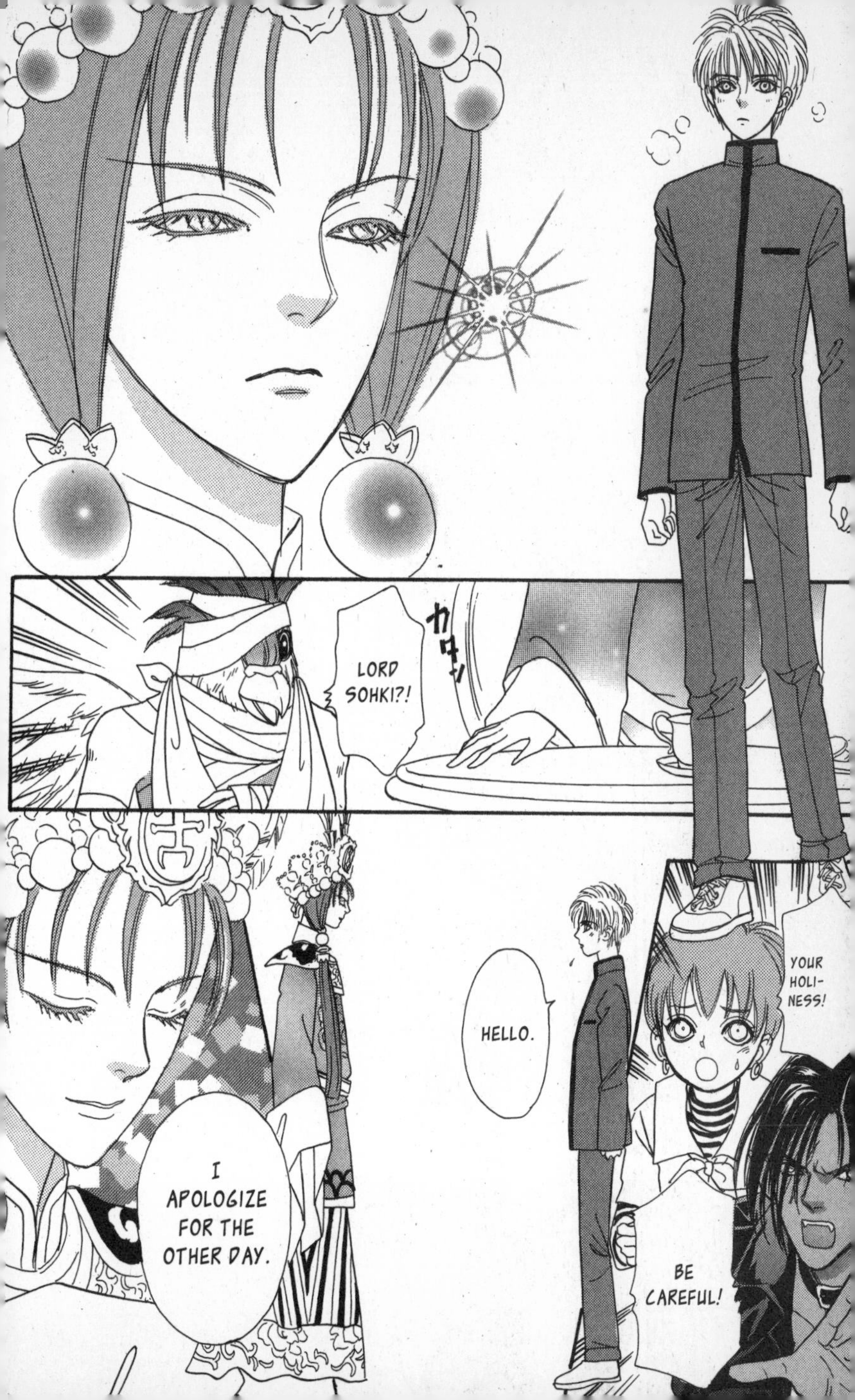
LORD SOHKI?!
YOUR HOLINESS!
BE CAREFUL!
HELLO.
I APOLOGIZE FOR THE OTHER DAY.

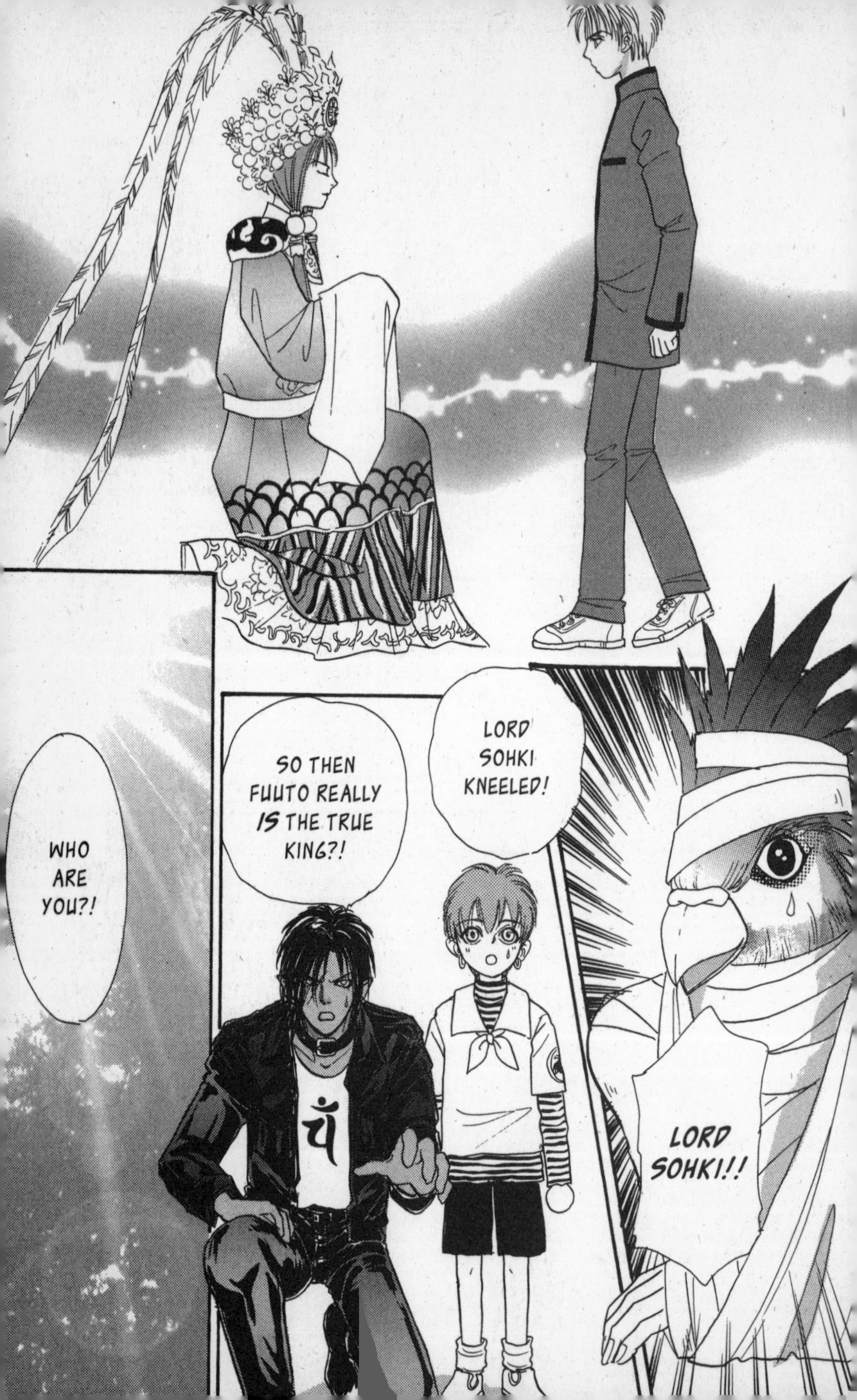
LORD SOHKI!!
LORD SOHKI KNEELED!
SO THEN FUUTO REALLY *IS* THE TRUE KING?!
WHO ARE YOU?!

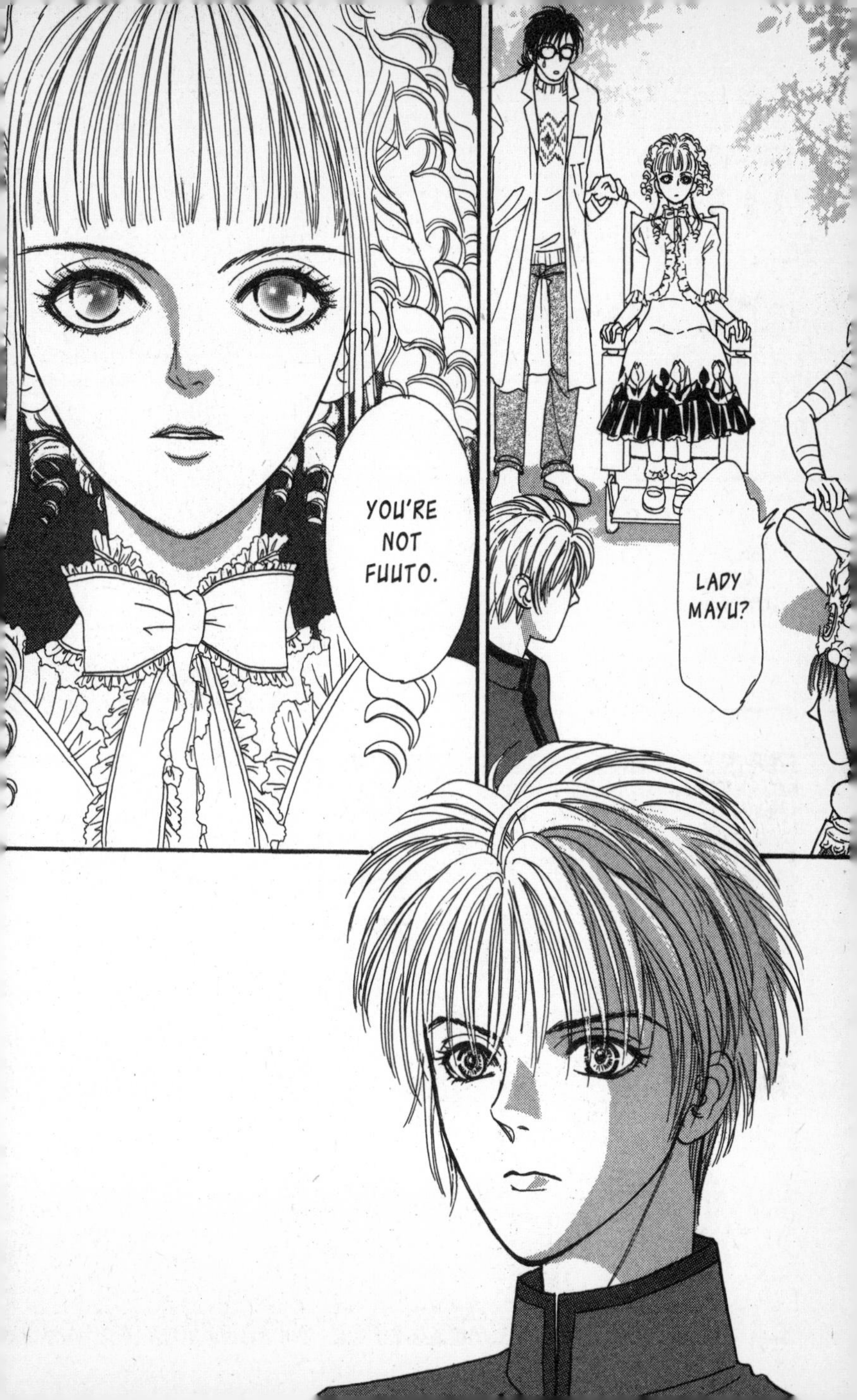
LADY MAYU?
YOU'RE NOT FUUTO.

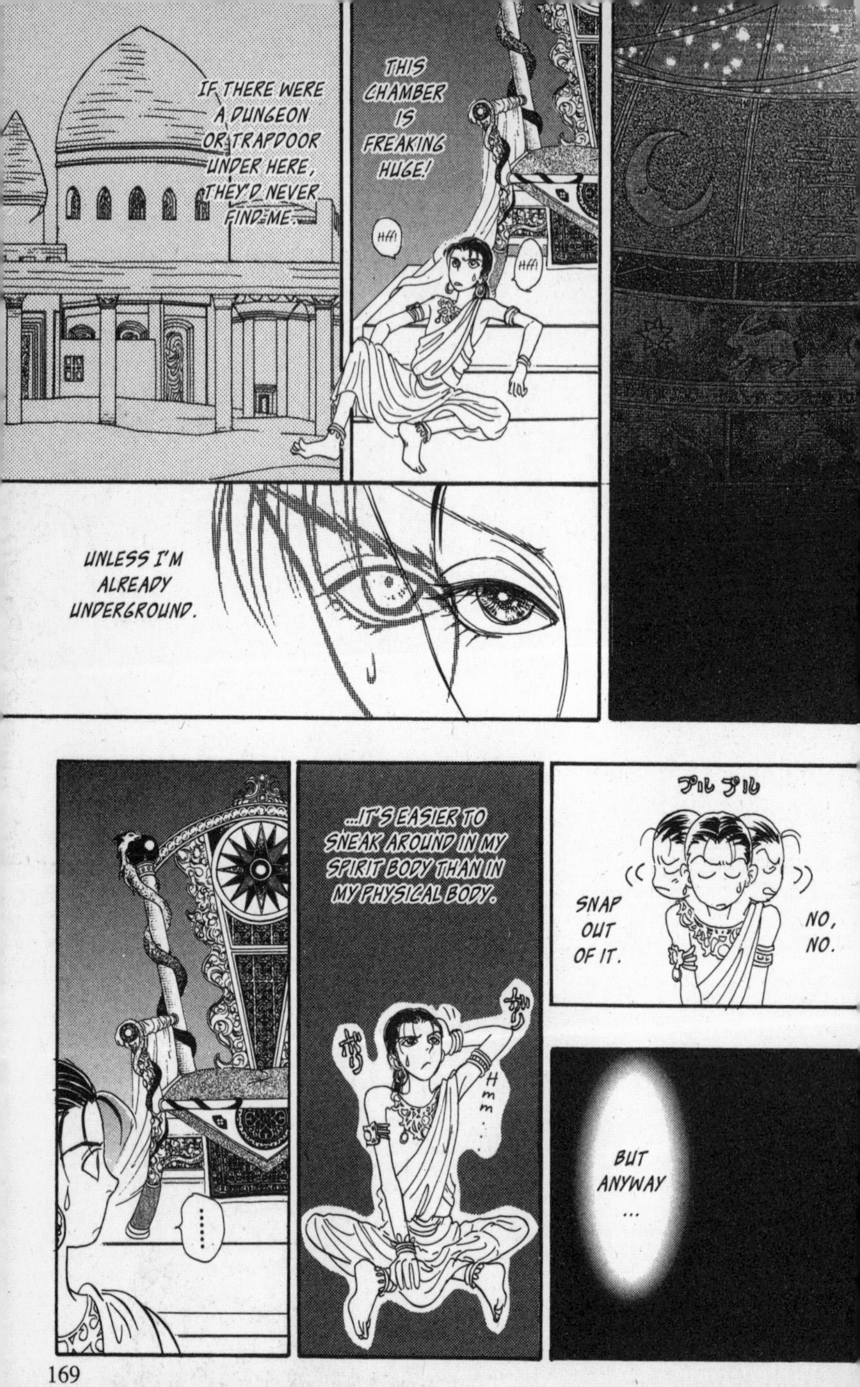
THIS CHAMBER IS FREAKING HUGE!
Hff!
Hff!
IF THERE WERE A DUNGEON OR TRAPDOOR UNDER HERE, THEY'D NEVER FIND ME.
UNLESS I'M ALREADY UNDERGROUND.
プルプル
SNAP OUT OF IT.
NO, NO.
BUT ANYWAY...
...IT'S EASIER TO SNEAK AROUND IN MY SPIRIT BODY THAN IN MY PHYSICAL BODY.
Hmm...
......

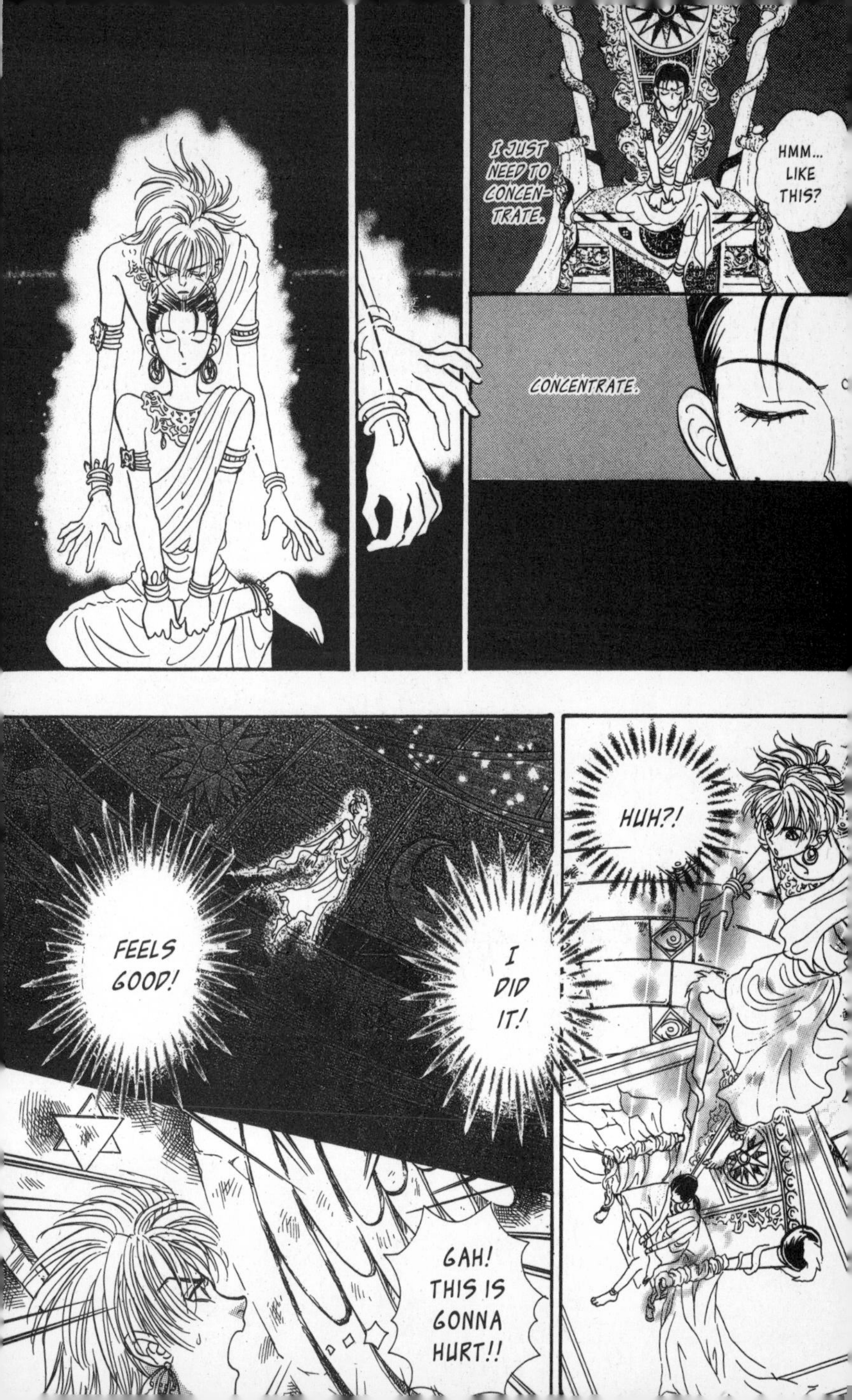

HMM... LIKE THIS?
I JUST NEED TO CONCENTRATE.
CONCENTRATE.
HUH?!
I DID IT!
FEELS GOOD!
GAH! THIS IS GONNA HURT!!

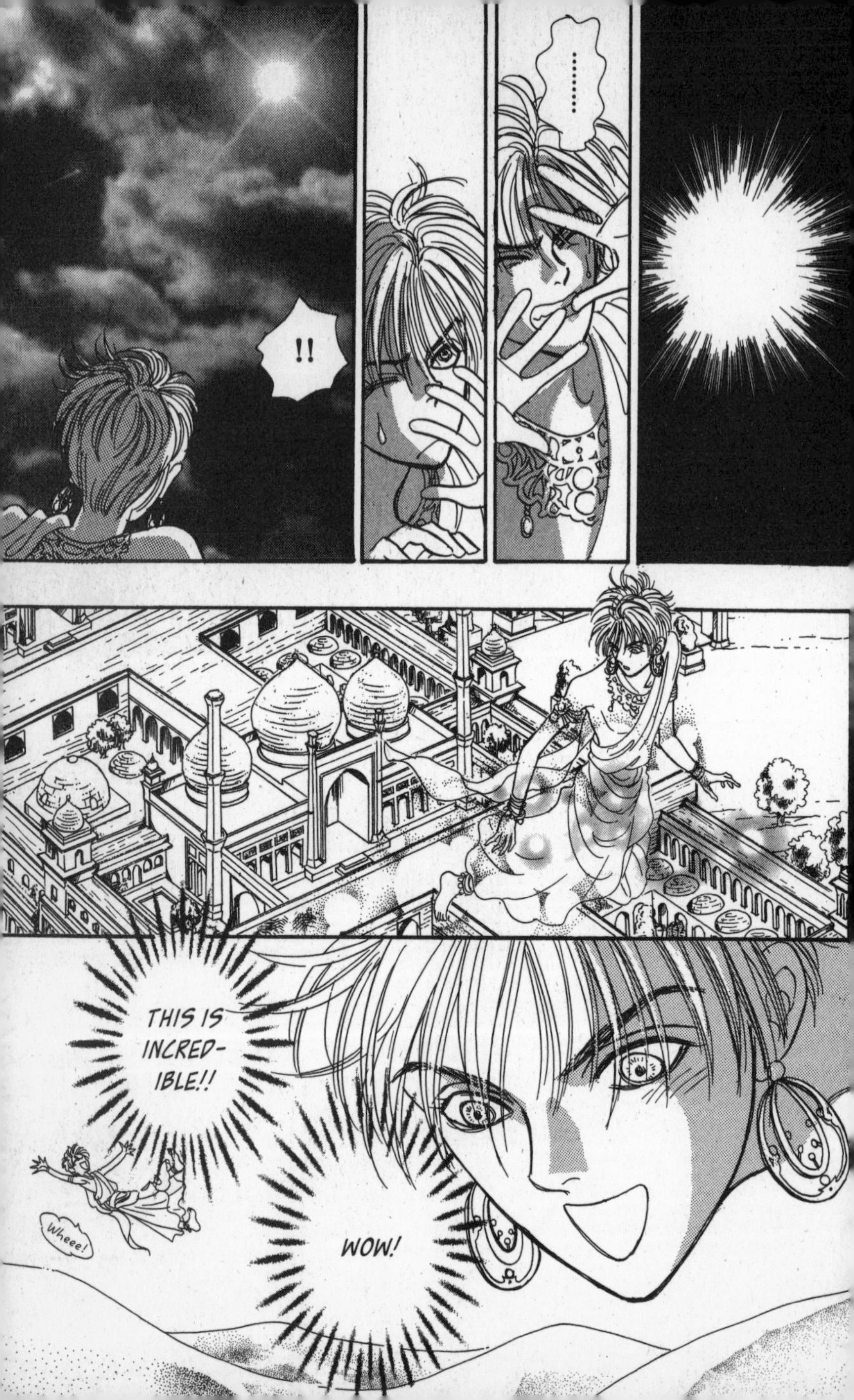

......
!!
THIS IS INCREDIBLE!!
Wheee!
WOW!

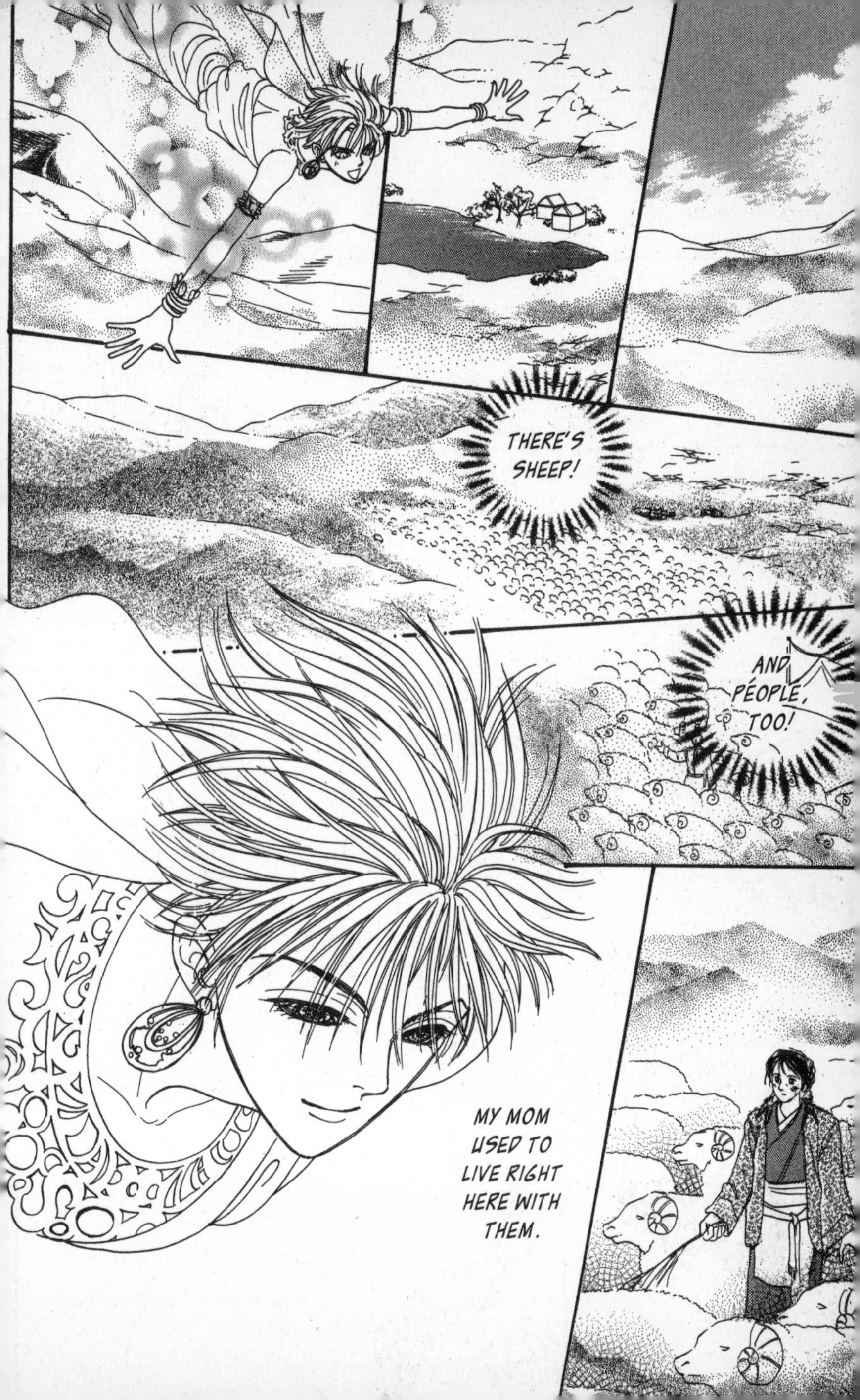
THERE'S SHEEP!
AND PEOPLE, TOO!
MY MOM USED TO LIVE RIGHT HERE WITH THEM.

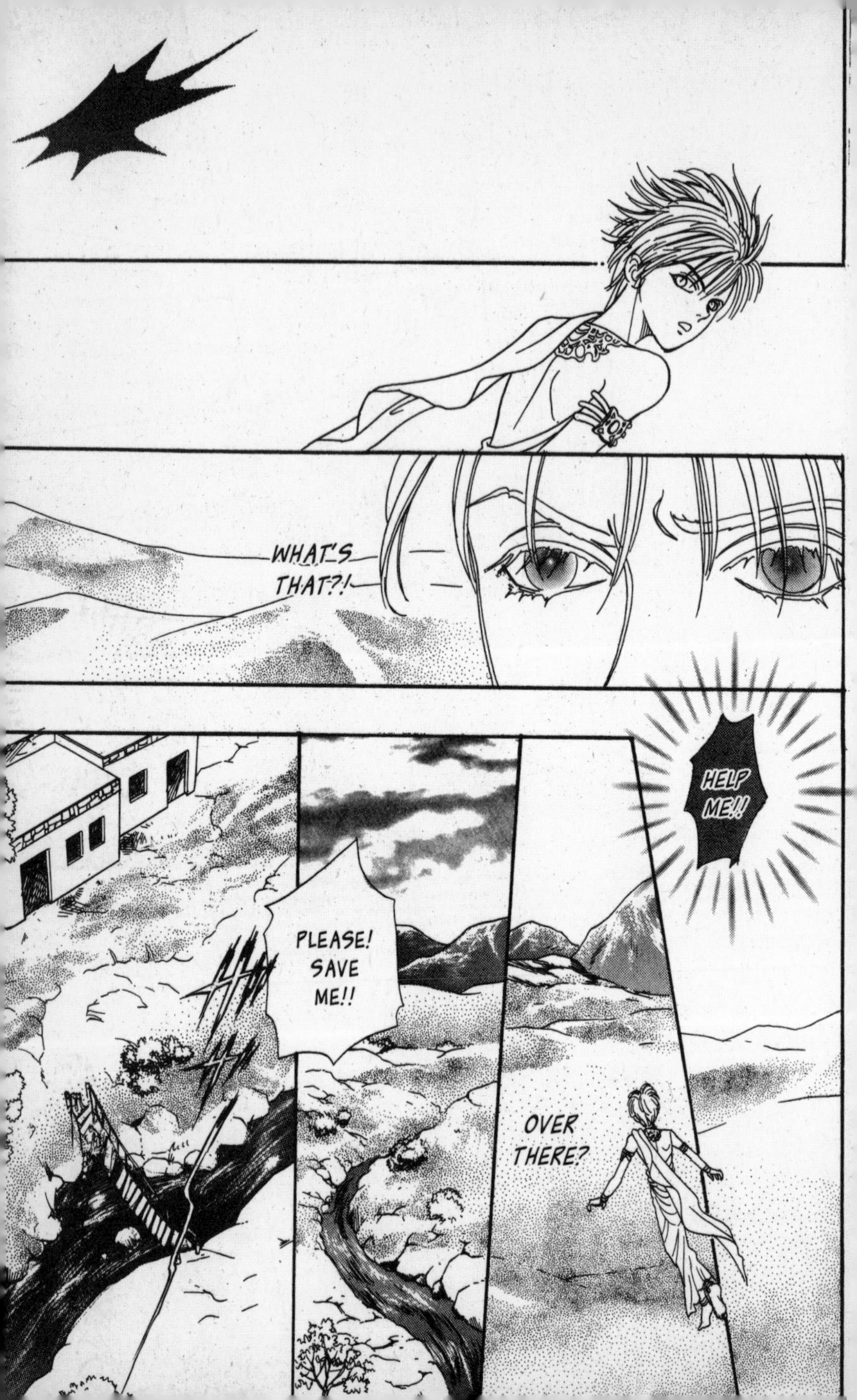
WHAT'S THAT?!
HELP ME!!
OVER THERE?
PLEASE! SAVE ME!!

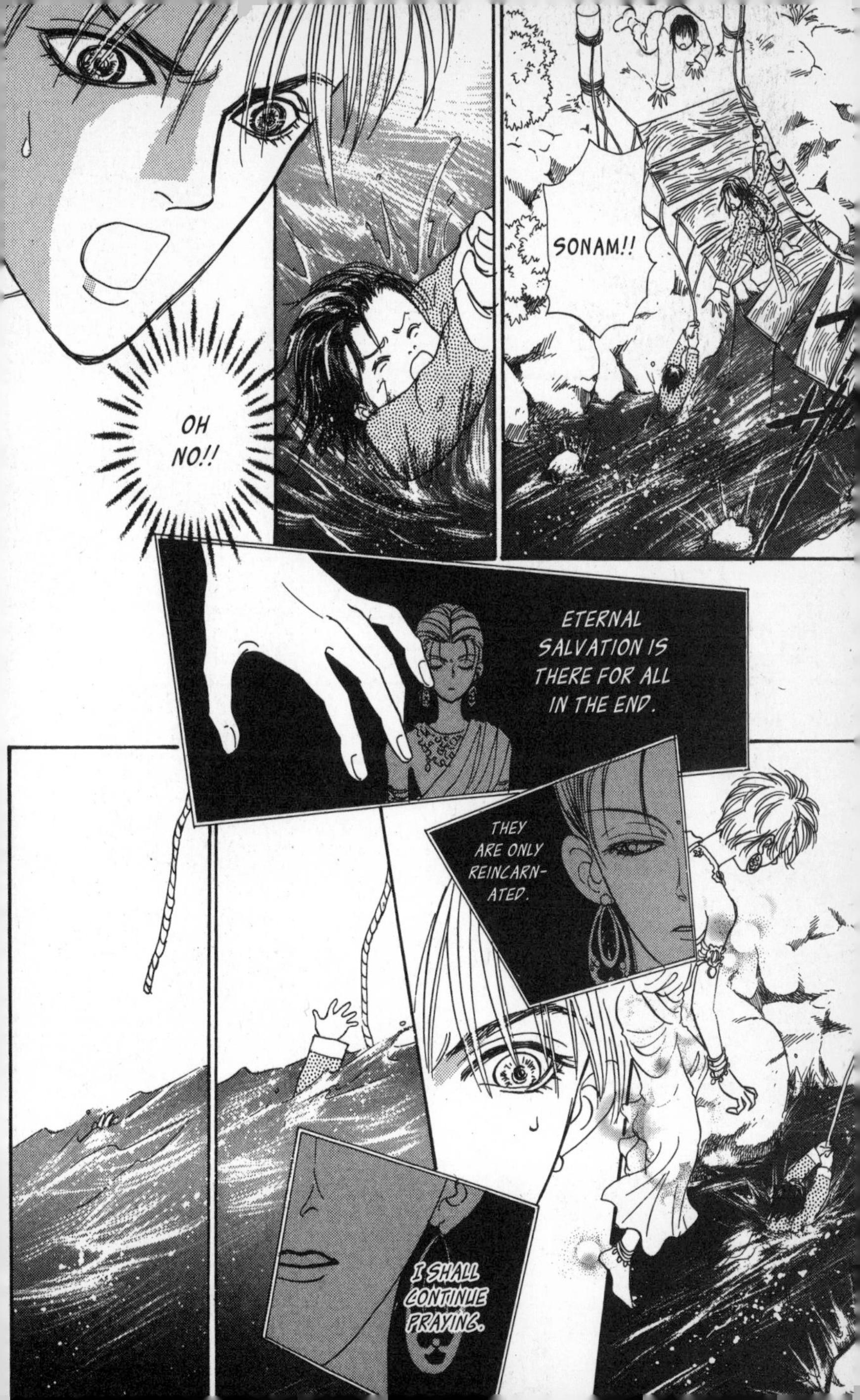
SONAM!!
OH NO!!
ETERNAL SALVATION IS THERE FOR ALL IN THE END.
THEY ARE ONLY REINCARN-ATED.
I SHALL CONTINUE PRAYING.

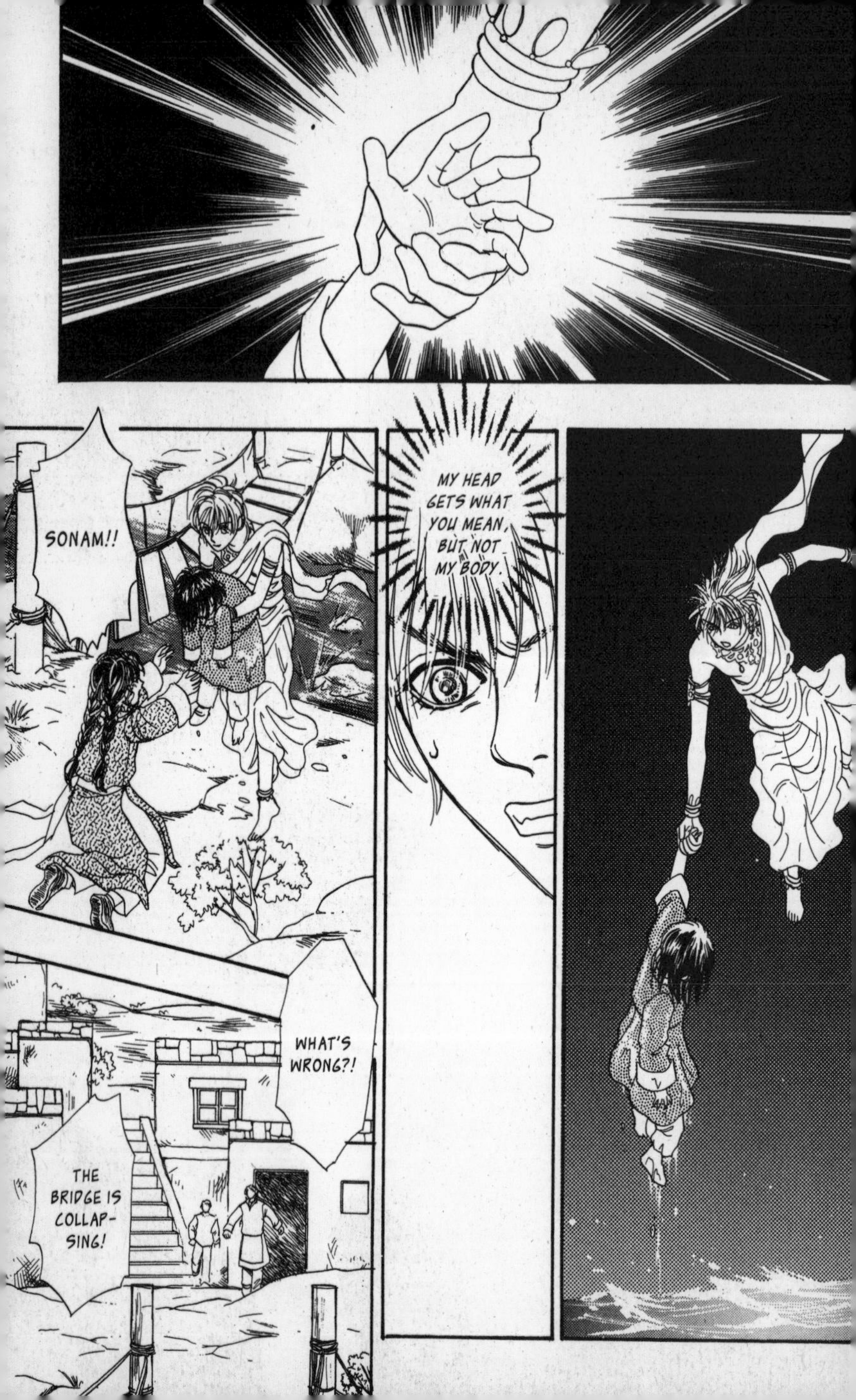
MY HEAD GETS WHAT YOU MEAN, BUT NOT MY BODY.
SONAM!!
WHAT'S WRONG?!
THE BRIDGE IS COLLAP-SING!

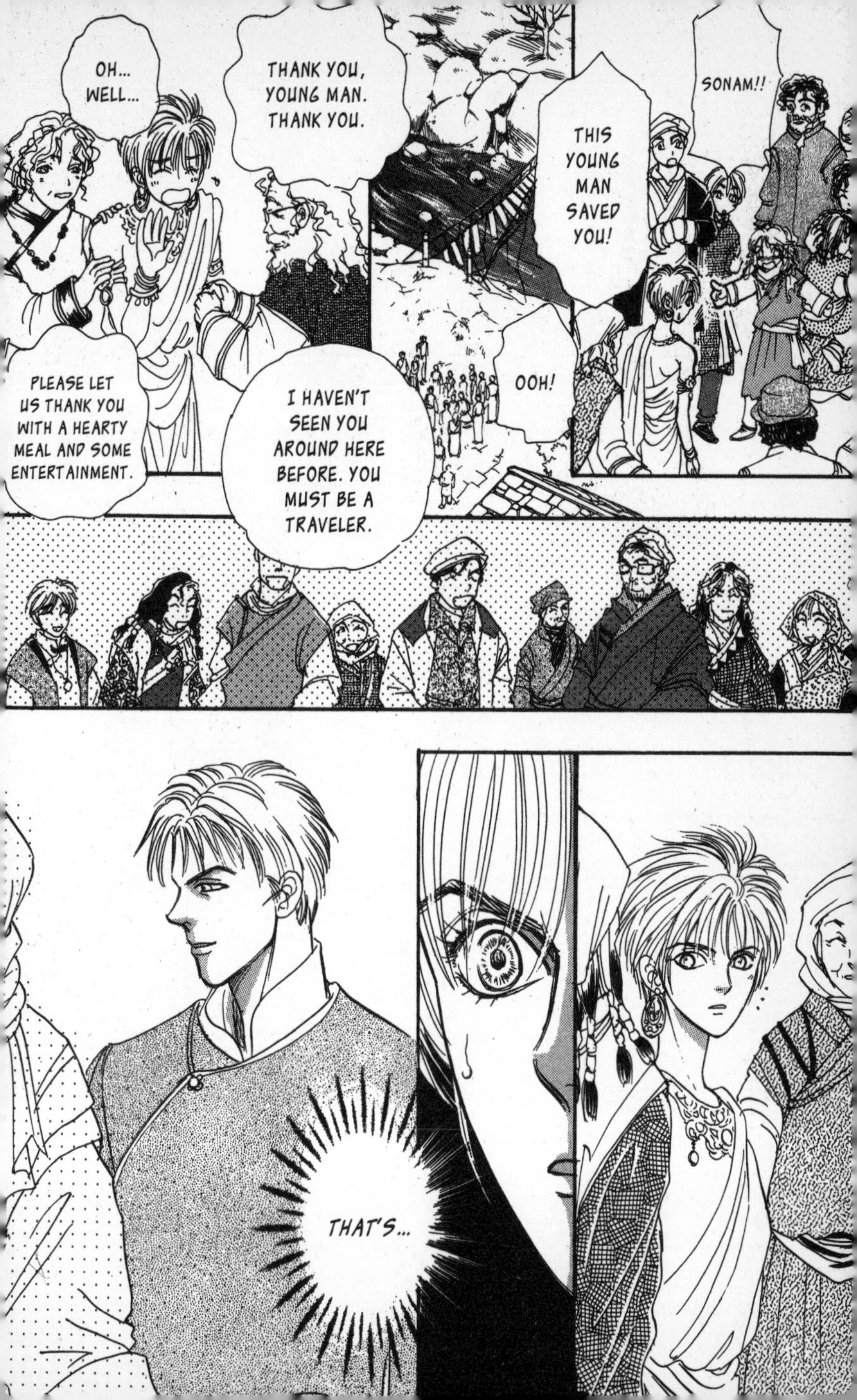
SONAM!!
THIS YOUNG MAN SAVED YOU!
OOH!
THANK YOU, YOUNG MAN. THANK YOU.
OH... WELL...
PLEASE LET US THANK YOU WITH A HEARTY MEAL AND SOME ENTERTAINMENT.
I HAVEN'T SEEN YOU AROUND HERE BEFORE. YOU MUST BE A TRAVELER.
THAT'S...

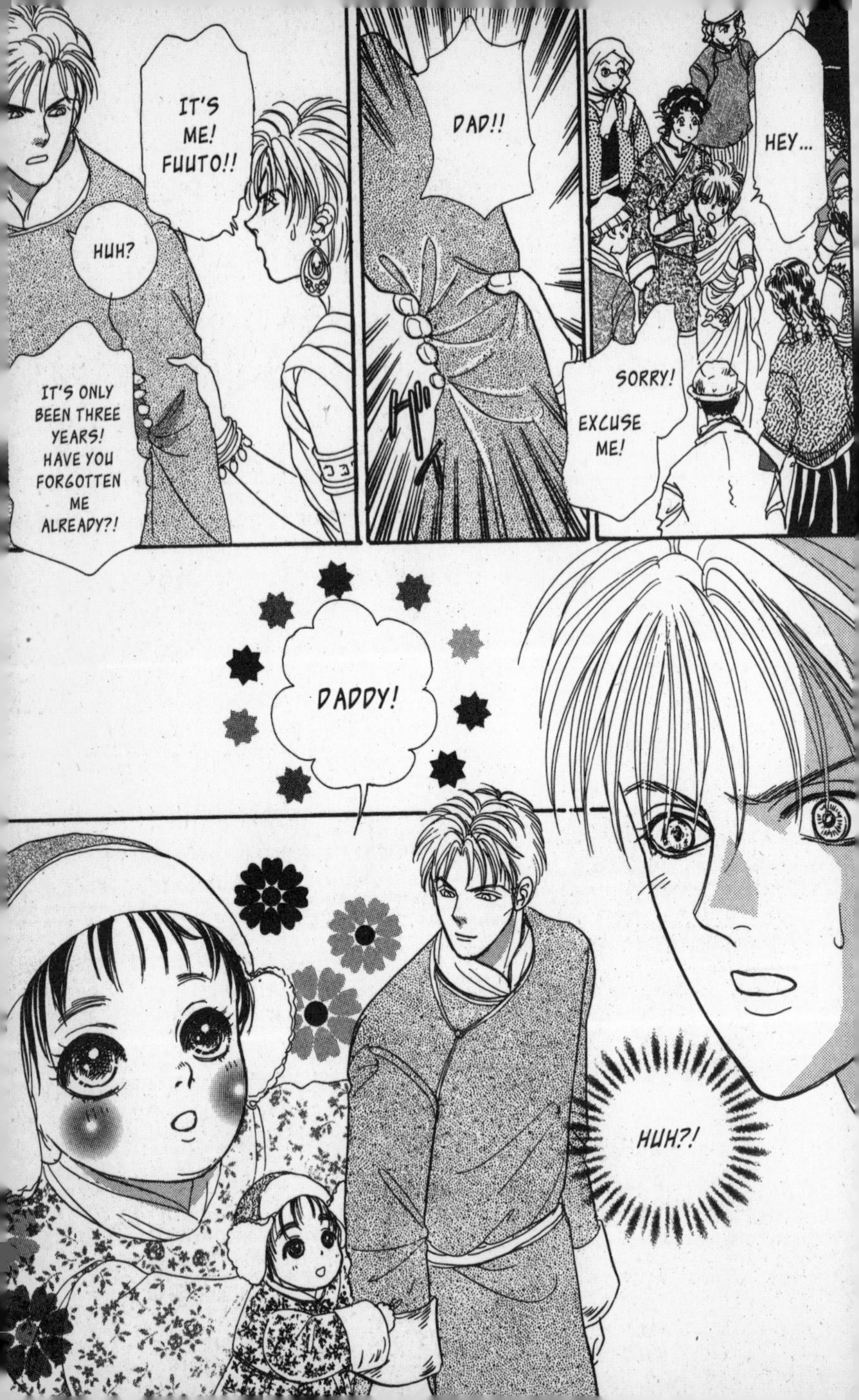
HEY...
SORRY!
EXCUSE ME!
DAD!!
IT'S ME! FUUTO!!
HUH?
IT'S ONLY BEEN THREE YEARS! HAVE YOU FORGOTTEN ME ALREADY?!
DADDY!
HUH?!

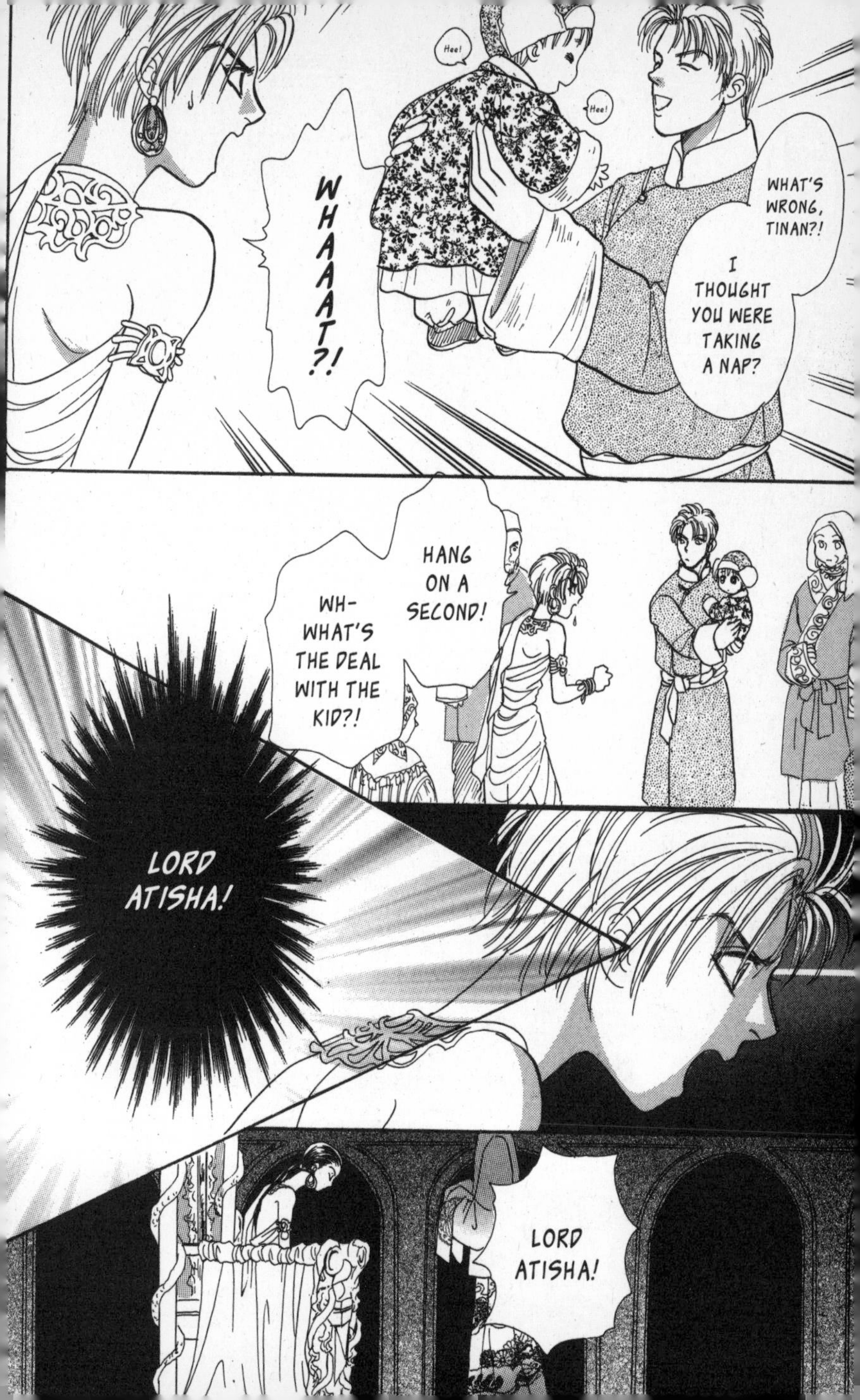
Hee!
Hee!
WHAAAAT?!
WHAT'S WRONG, TINAN?!
I THOUGHT YOU WERE TAKING A NAP?
HANG ON A SECOND!
WH-WHAT'S THE DEAL WITH THE KID?!
LORD ATISHA!
LORD ATISHA!

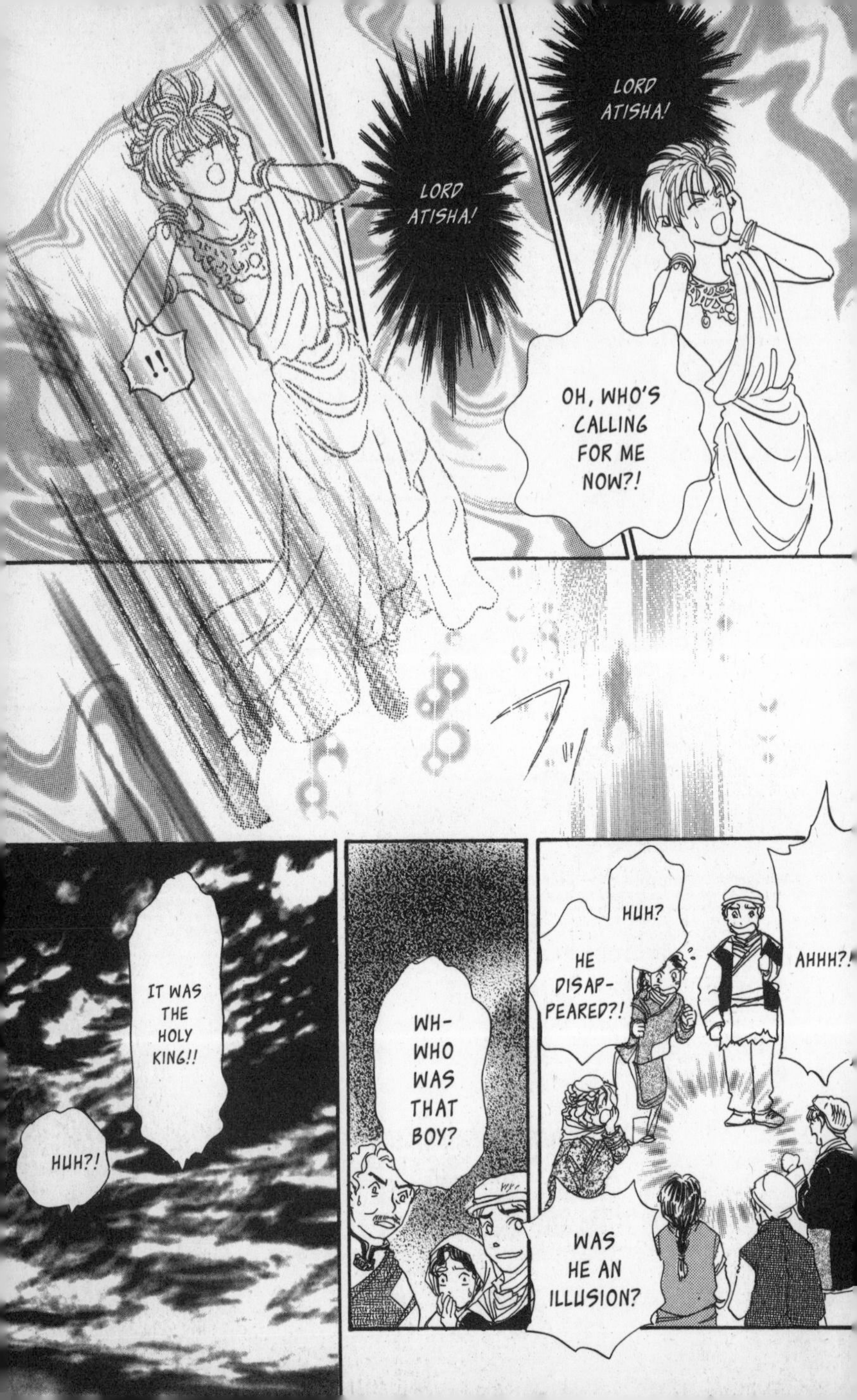
LORD ATISHA!
OH, WHO'S CALLING FOR ME NOW?!
LORD ATISHA!
!!
AHHH?!
HUH?
HE DISAP-PEARED?!
WAS HE AN ILLUSION?
WH-WHO WAS THAT BOY?
IT WAS THE HOLY KING!!
HUH?!

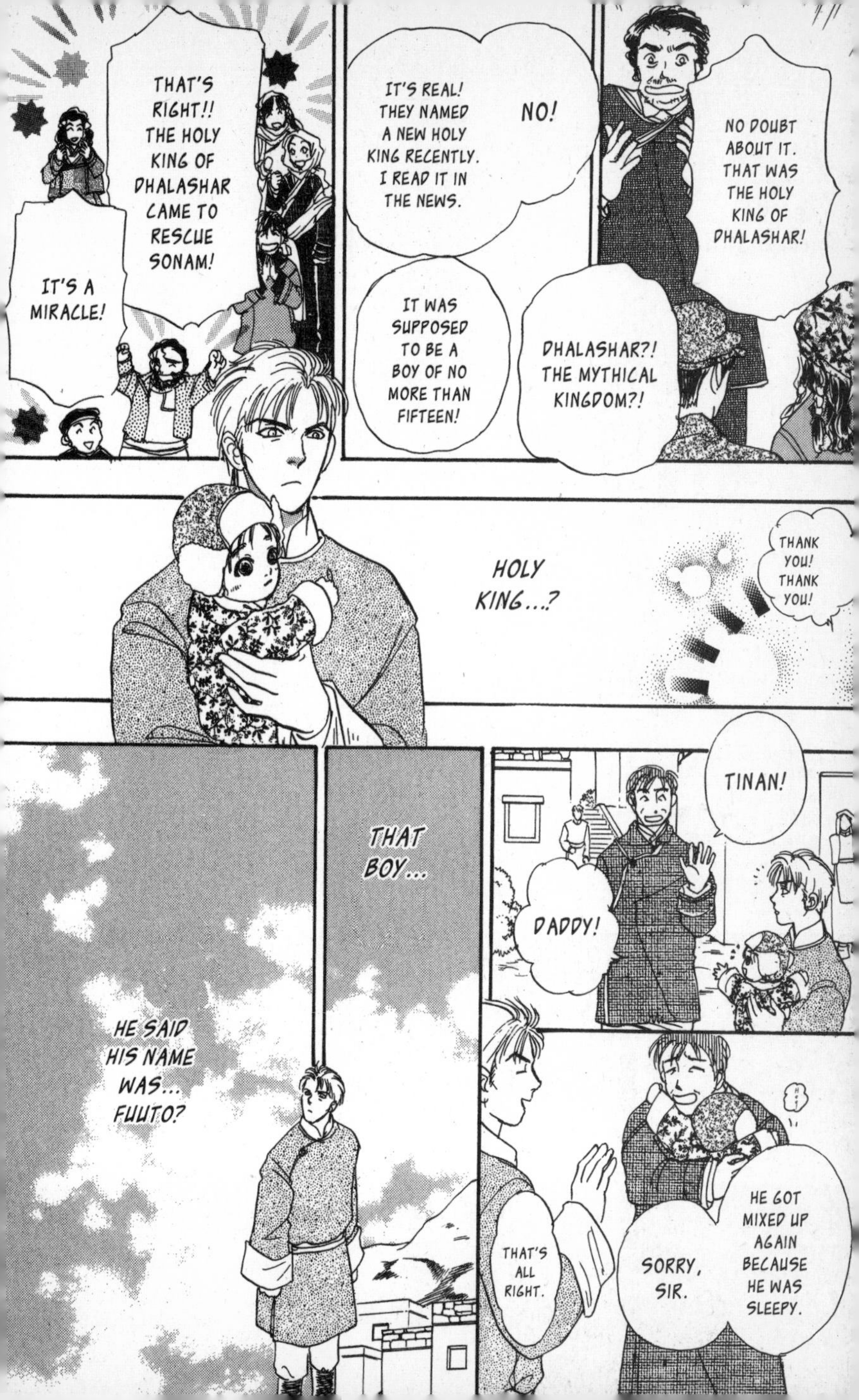
NO DOUBT ABOUT IT. THAT WAS THE HOLY KING OF DHALASHAR!
DHALASHAR?! THE MYTHICAL KINGDOM?!
IT'S REAL! THEY NAMED A NEW HOLY KING RECENTLY. I READ IT IN THE NEWS.
NO!
IT WAS SUPPOSED TO BE A BOY OF NO MORE THAN FIFTEEN!
THAT'S RIGHT!! THE HOLY KING OF DHALASHAR CAME TO RESCUE SONAM!
IT'S A MIRACLE!
THANK YOU! THANK YOU!
HOLY KING...?
TINAN!
DADDY!
HE GOT MIXED UP AGAIN BECAUSE HE WAS SLEEPY.
SORRY, SIR.
THAT'S ALL RIGHT.
THAT BOY...
HE SAID HIS NAME WAS... FUUTO?

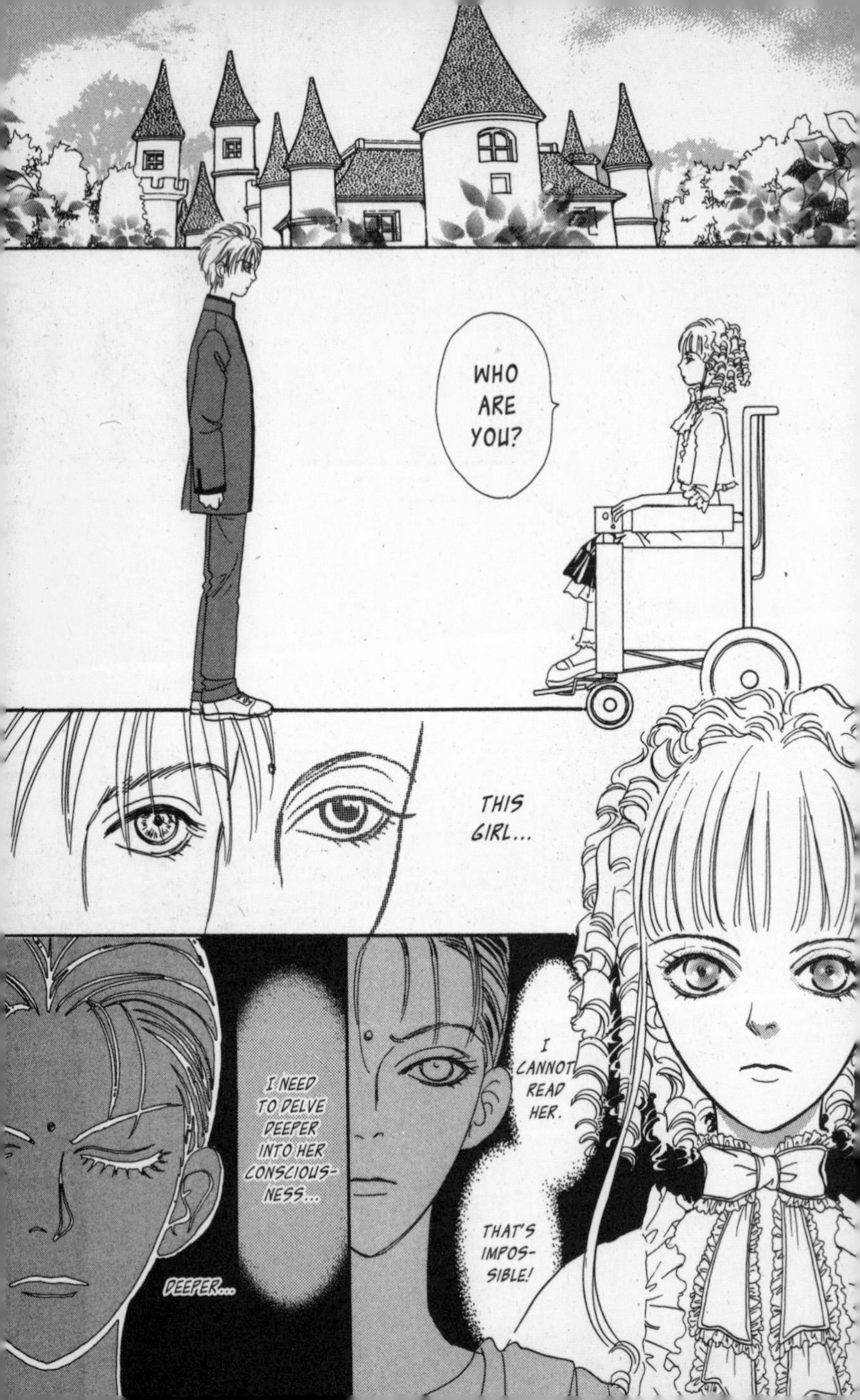
WHO ARE YOU?
THIS GIRL...
I CANNOT READ HER.
THAT'S IMPOSSIBLE!
I NEED TO DELVE DEEPER INTO HER CONSCIOUSNESS...
DEEPER...

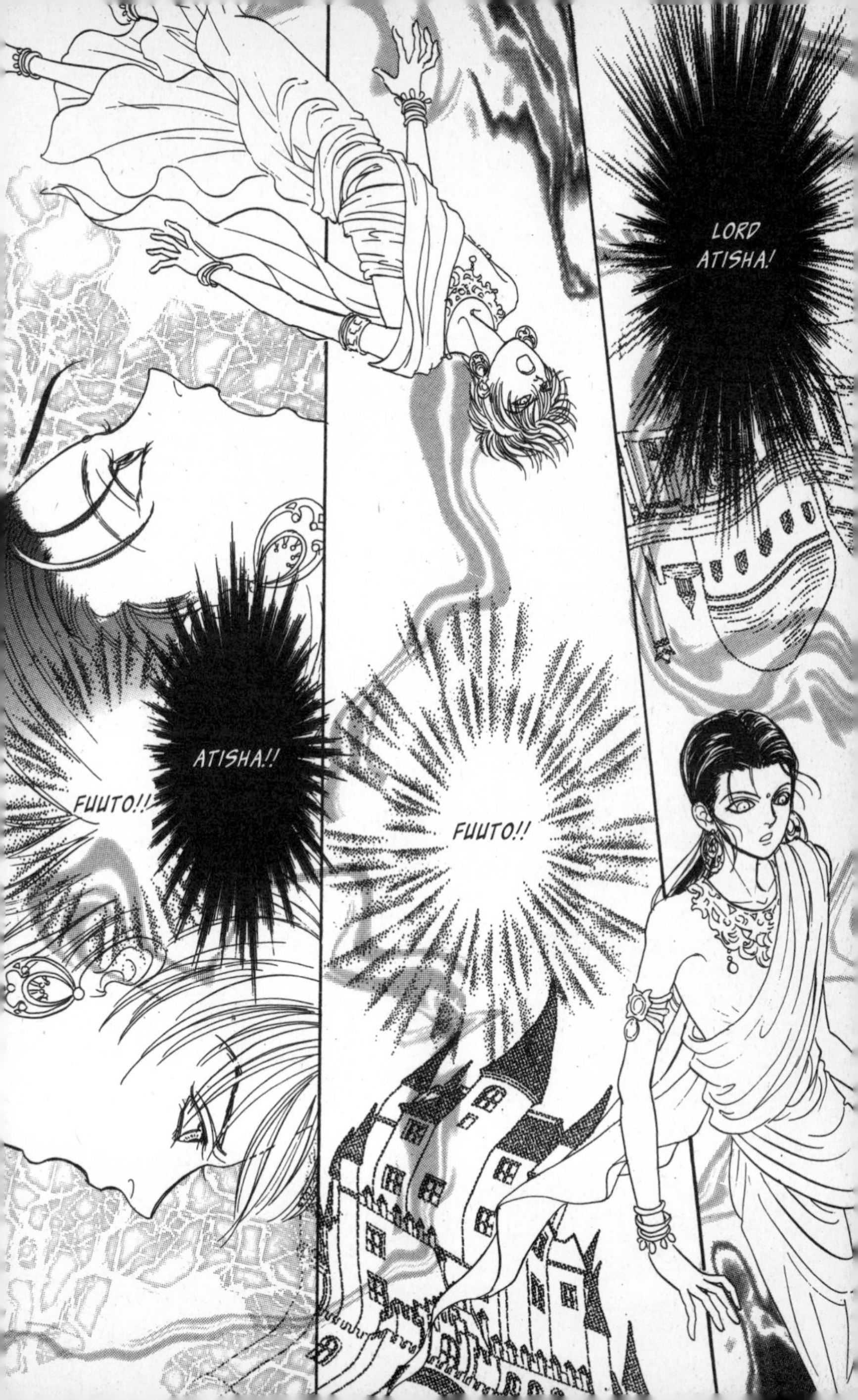
LORD ATISHA!
FUUTO!!
ATISHA!!
FUUTO!!

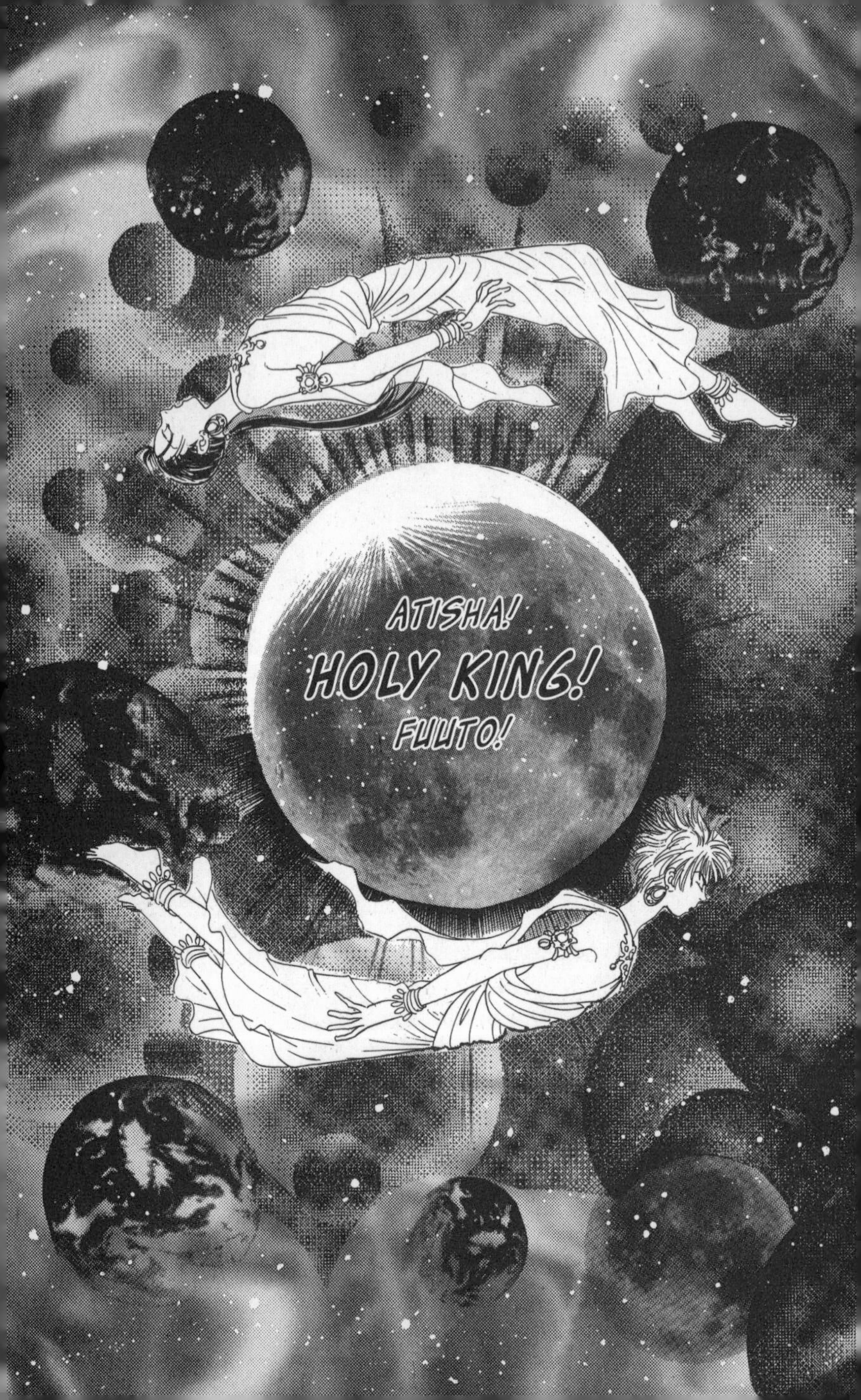
ATISHA!
HOLY KING!
FUUTO!

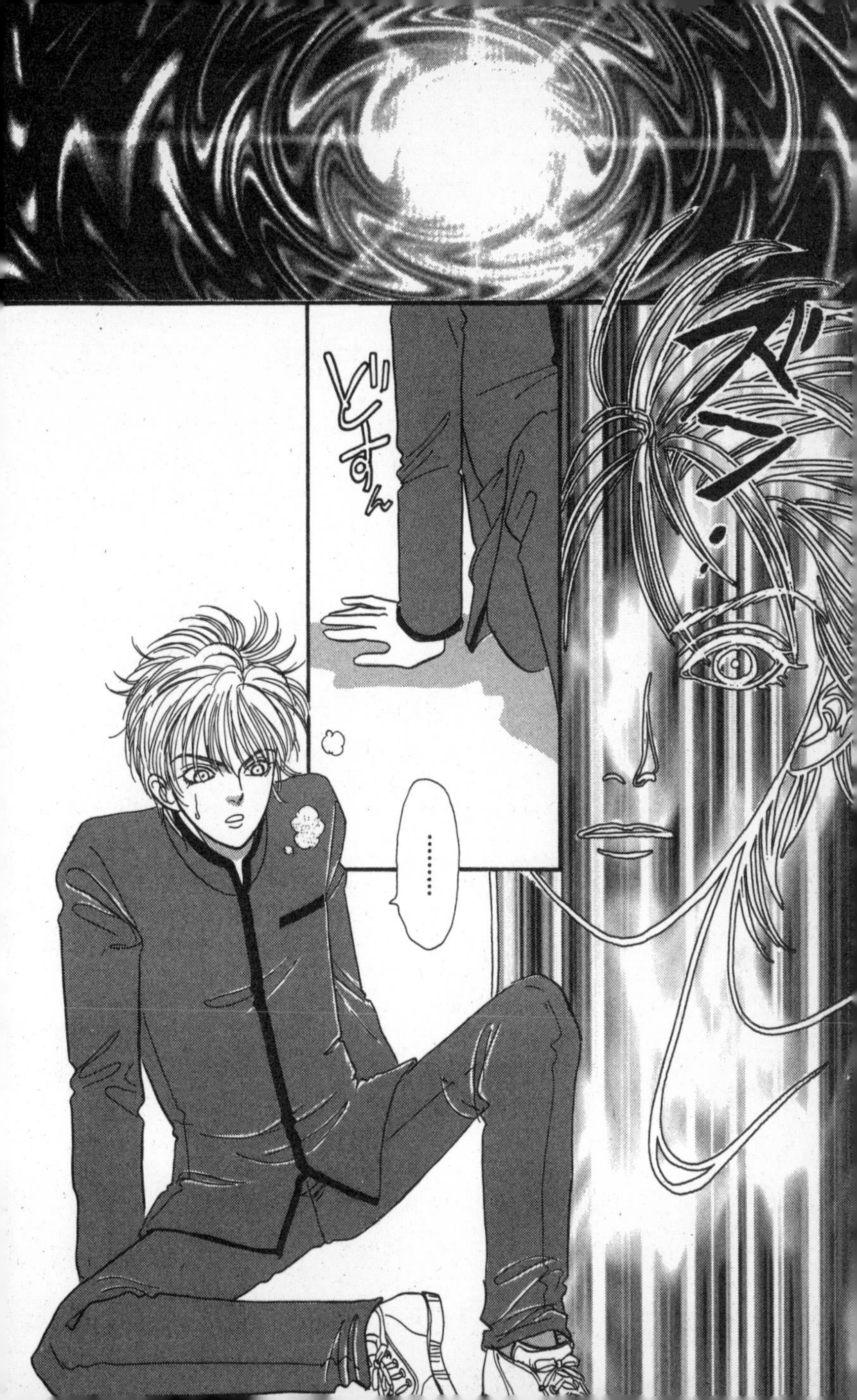
ズン…
どすん
……

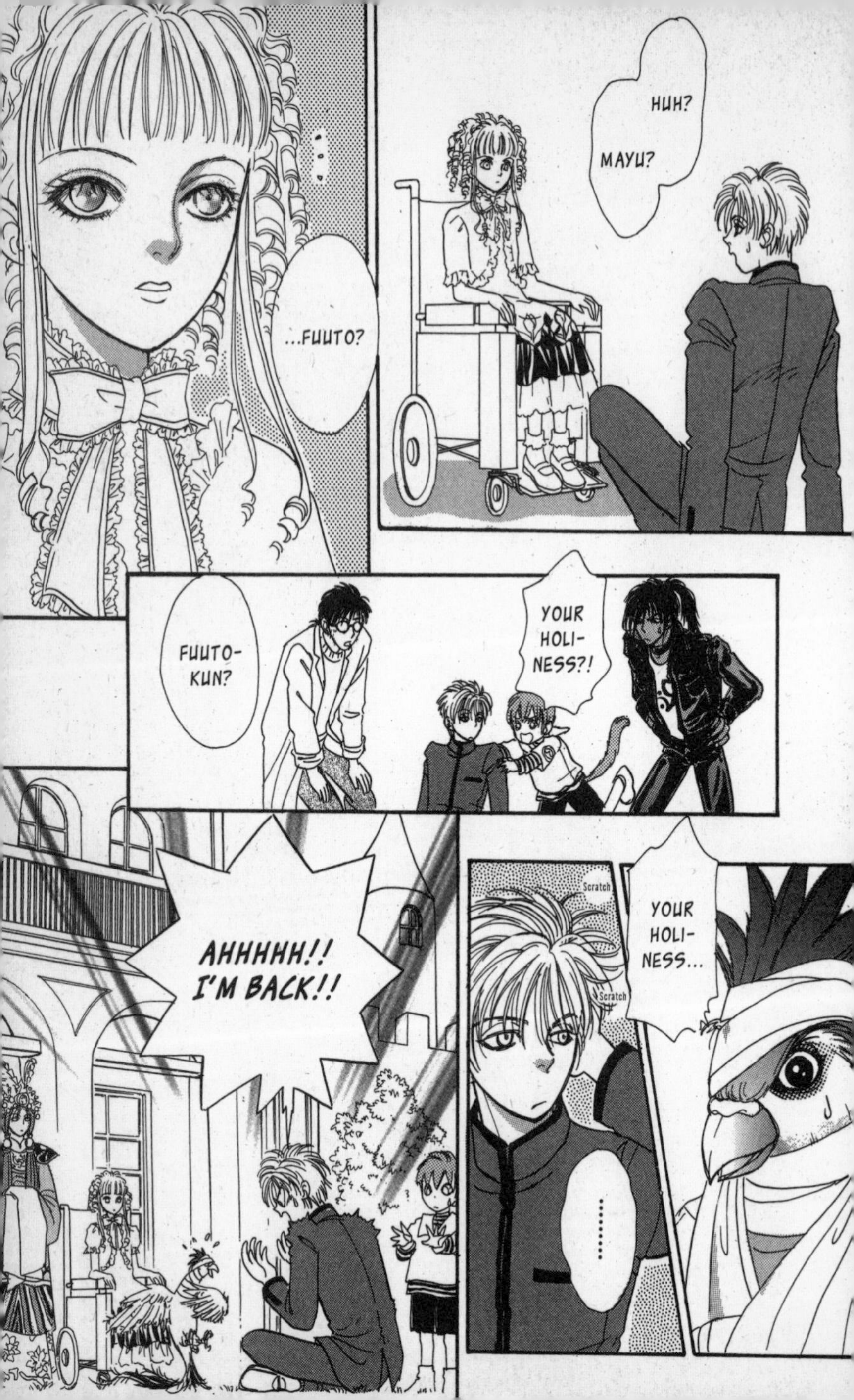
HUH?
MAYU?
...FUUTO?
YOUR HOLI-NESS?!
FUUTO-KUN?
YOUR HOLI-NESS...
Scratch
Scratch
......
AHHHHH!! I'M BACK!!

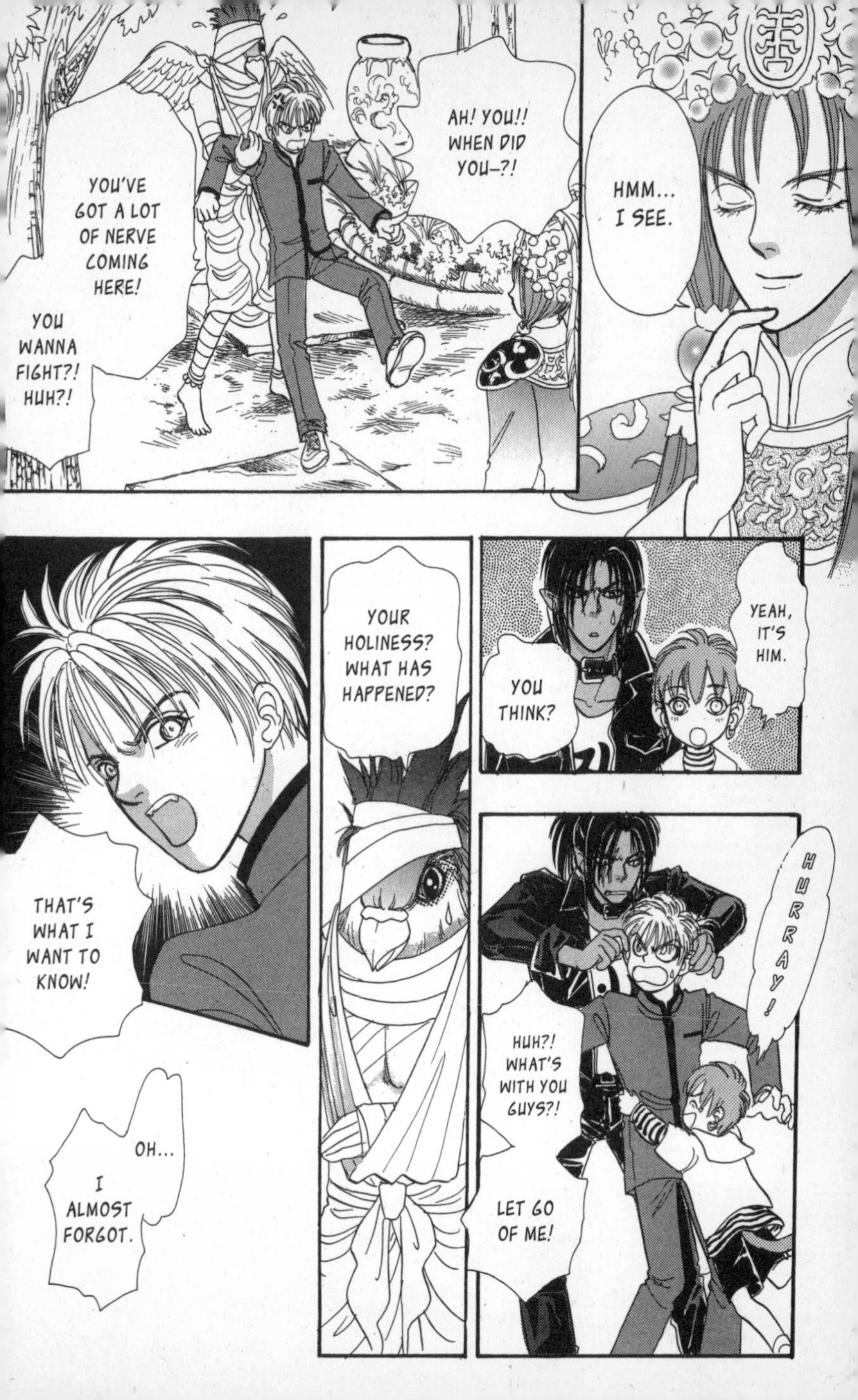
YOU'VE GOT A LOT OF NERVE COMING HERE!
YOU WANNA FIGHT?! HUH?!
AH! YOU!! WHEN DID YOU–?!
HMM... I SEE.
THAT'S WHAT I WANT TO KNOW!
OH...
I ALMOST FORGOT.
YOUR HOLINESS? WHAT HAS HAPPENED?
YOU THINK?
YEAH, IT'S HIM.
HURRAY!
HUH?! WHAT'S WITH YOU GUYS?!
LET GO OF ME!

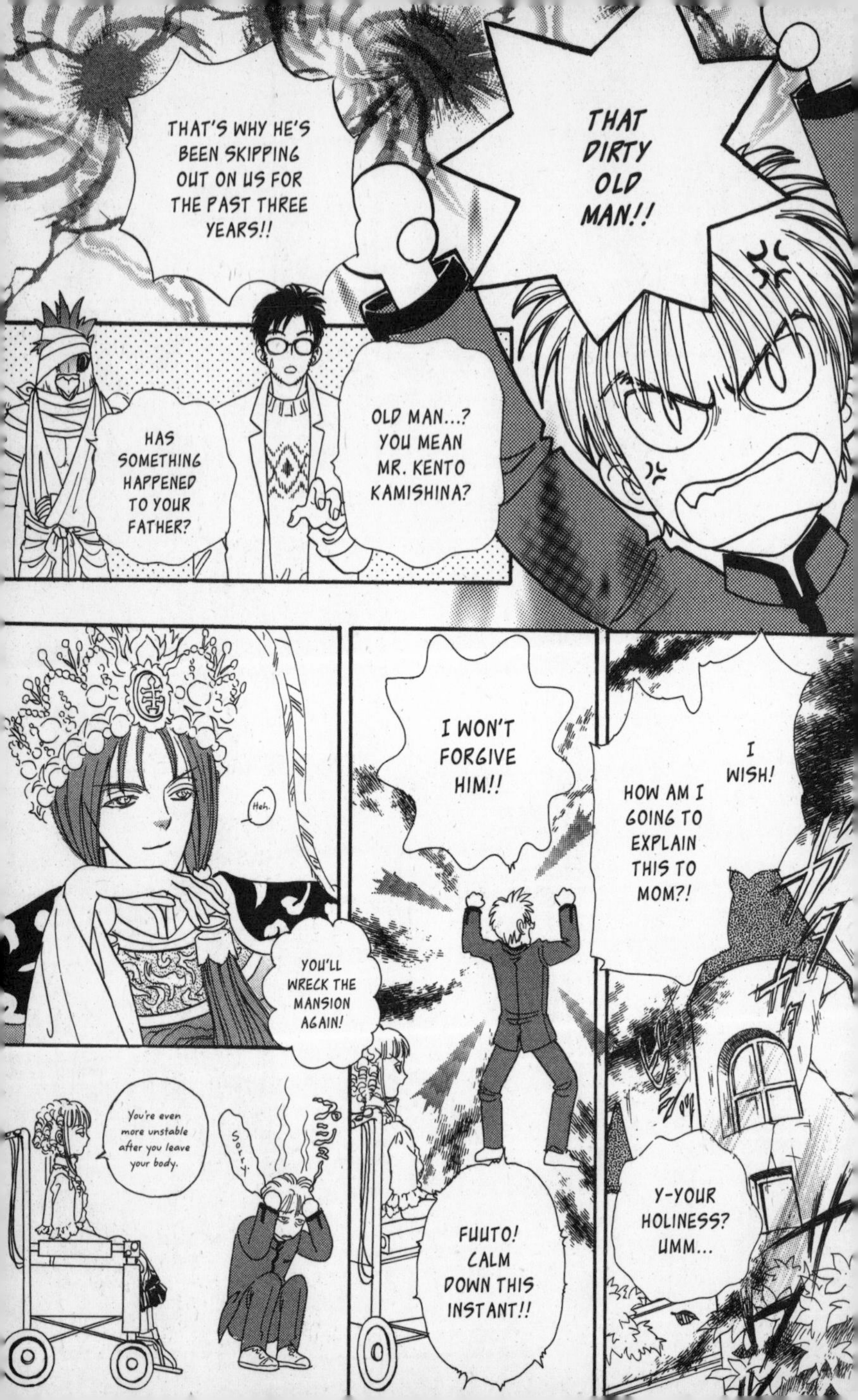
THAT DIRTY OLD MAN!!
THAT'S WHY HE'S BEEN SKIPPING OUT ON US FOR THE PAST THREE YEARS!!
OLD MAN...? YOU MEAN MR. KENTO KAMISHINA?
HAS SOMETHING HAPPENED TO YOUR FATHER?
I WISH!
HOW AM I GOING TO EXPLAIN THIS TO MOM?!
Y-YOUR HOLINESS? UMM...
I WON'T FORGIVE HIM!!
FUUTO! CALM DOWN THIS INSTANT!!
Heh.
YOU'LL WRECK THE MANSION AGAIN!
Sorry
You're even more unstable after you leave your body.

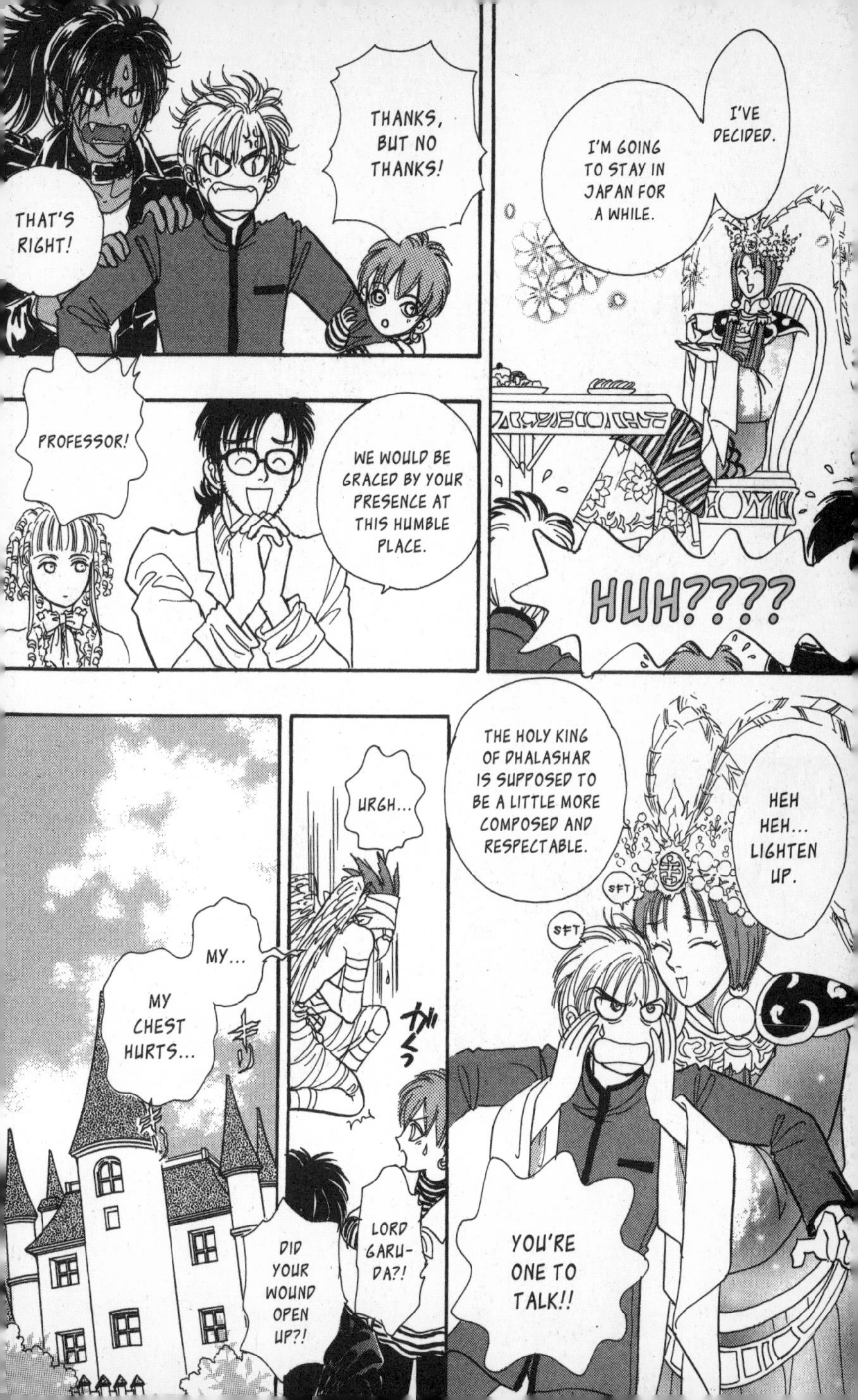
I'VE DECIDED.
I'M GOING TO STAY IN JAPAN FOR A WHILE.
HUH????
THANKS, BUT NO THANKS!
THAT'S RIGHT!
WE WOULD BE GRACED BY YOUR PRESENCE AT THIS HUMBLE PLACE.
PROFESSOR!
HEH HEH... LIGHTEN UP.
THE HOLY KING OF DHALASHAR IS SUPPOSED TO BE A LITTLE MORE COMPOSED AND RESPECTABLE.
SFT
SFT
YOU'RE ONE TO TALK!!
URGH...
LORD GARU-DA?!
DID YOUR WOUND OPEN UP?!
MY...
MY CHEST HURTS...

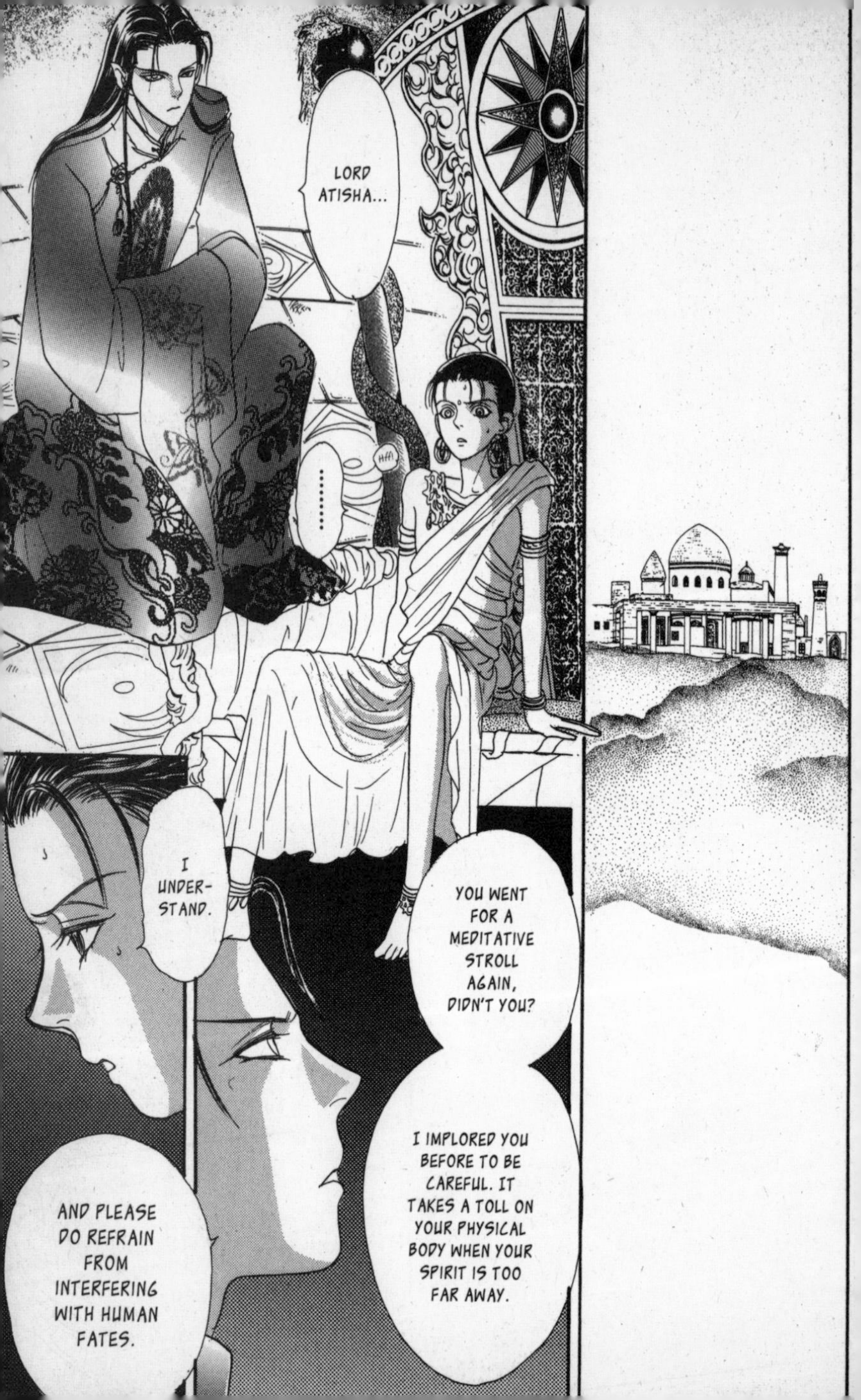
LORD ATISHA...
......
HA!
YOU WENT FOR A MEDITATIVE STROLL AGAIN, DIDN'T YOU?
I IMPLORED YOU BEFORE TO BE CAREFUL. IT TAKES A TOLL ON YOUR PHYSICAL BODY WHEN YOUR SPIRIT IS TOO FAR AWAY.
I UNDER-STAND.
AND PLEASE DO REFRAIN FROM INTERFERING WITH HUMAN FATES.

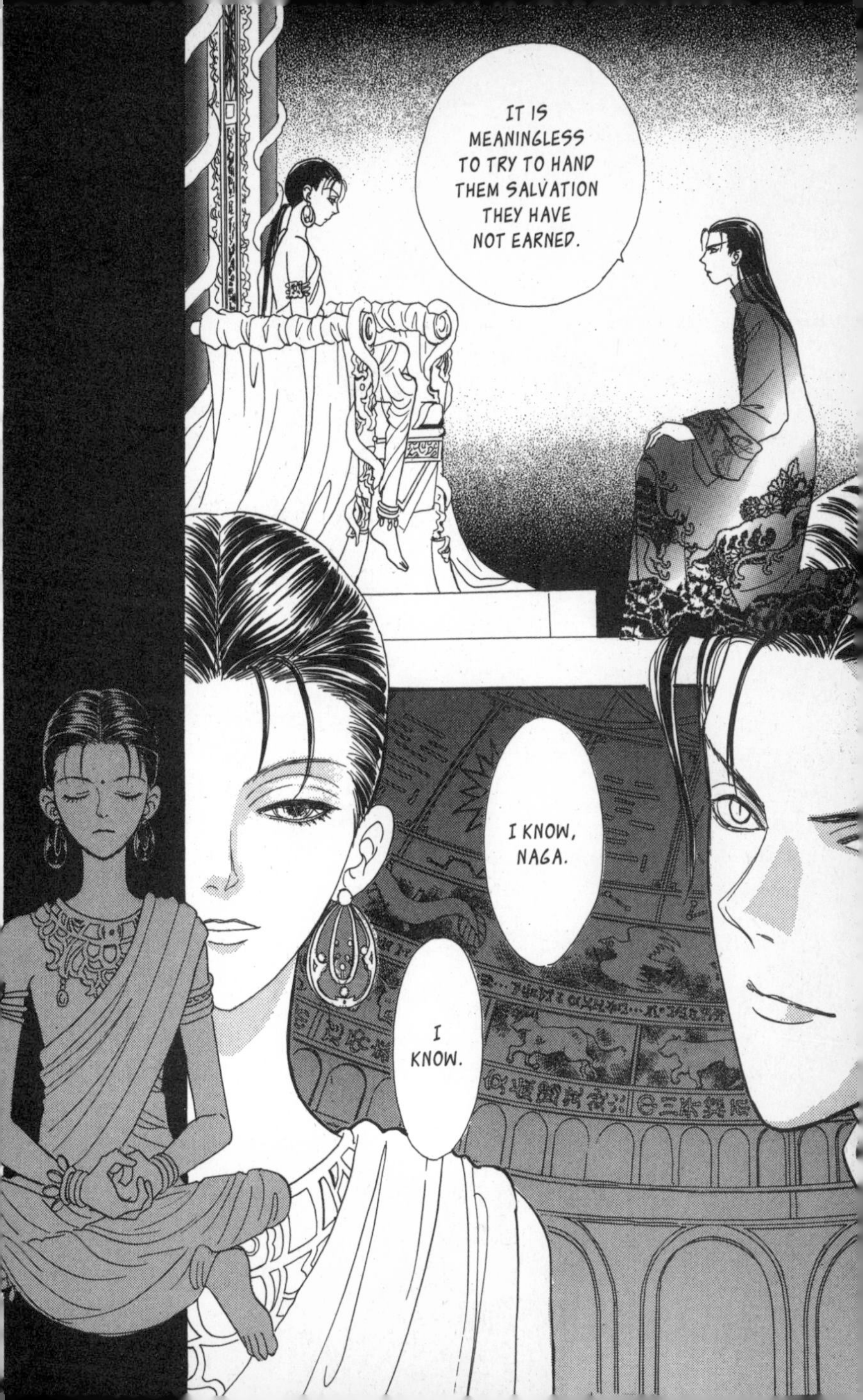
IT IS MEANINGLESS TO TRY TO HAND THEM SALVATION THEY HAVE NOT EARNED.
I KNOW, NAGA.
I KNOW.

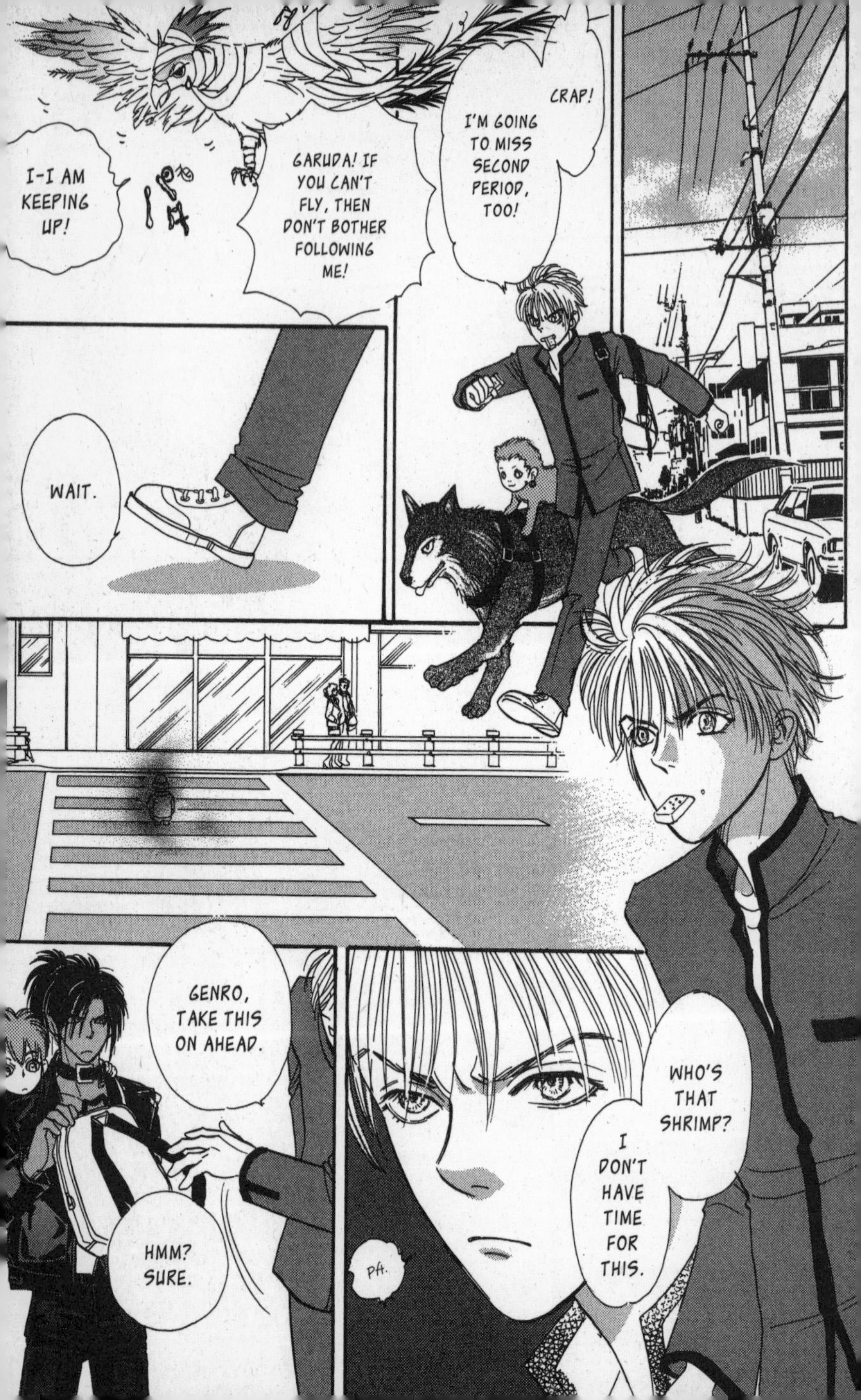
CRAP!
I'M GOING TO MISS SECOND PERIOD, TOO!
GARUDA! IF YOU CAN'T FLY, THEN DON'T BOTHER FOLLOWING ME!
I-I AM KEEPING UP!
WAIT.
WHO'S THAT SHRIMP?
I DON'T HAVE TIME FOR THIS.
Pft.
GENRO, TAKE THIS ON AHEAD.
HMM? SURE.

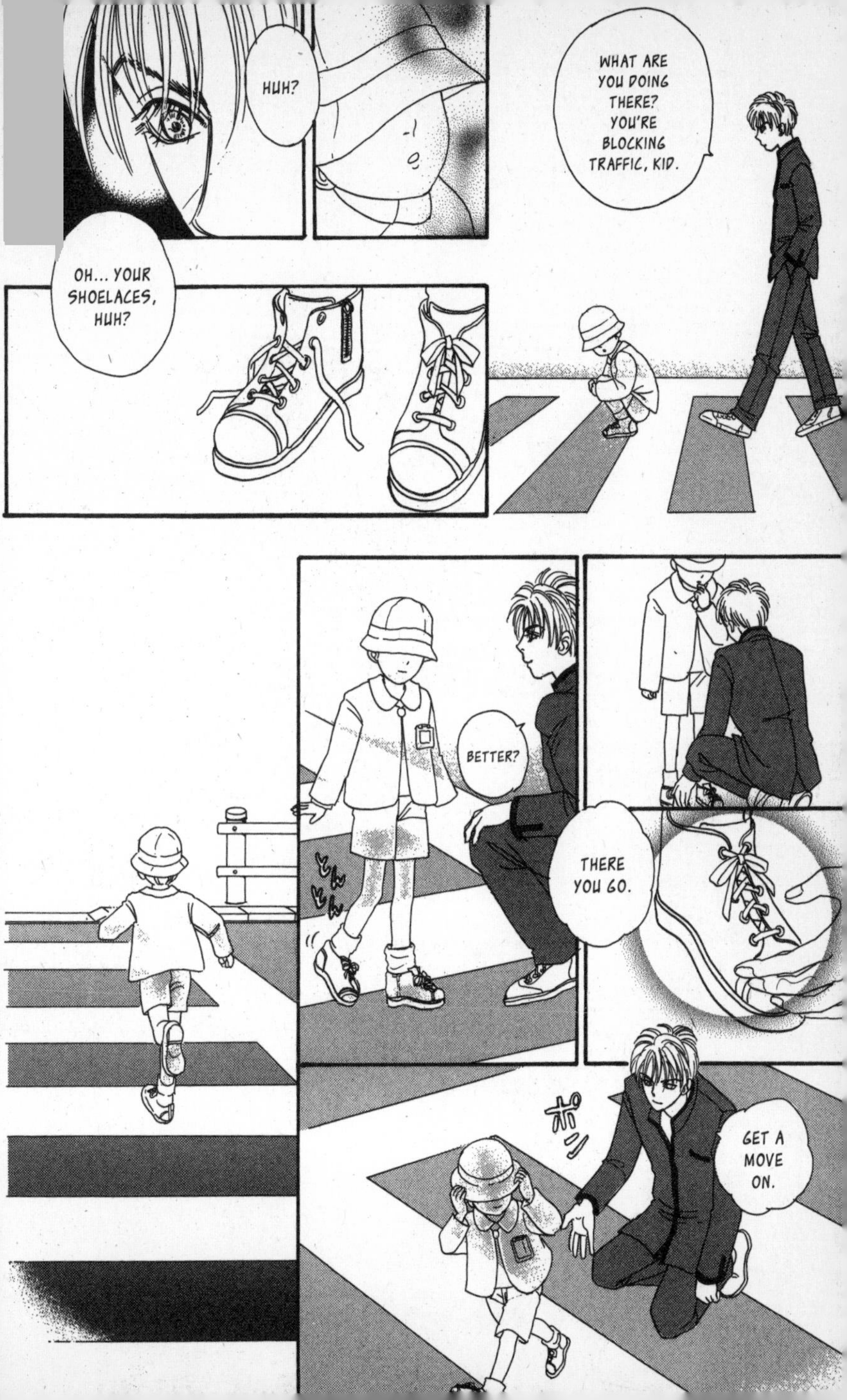

WHAT ARE YOU DOING THERE? YOU'RE BLOCKING TRAFFIC, KID.
HUH?
OH... YOUR SHOELACES, HUH?
THERE YOU GO.
BETTER?
とんとん
ポン
GET A MOVE ON.

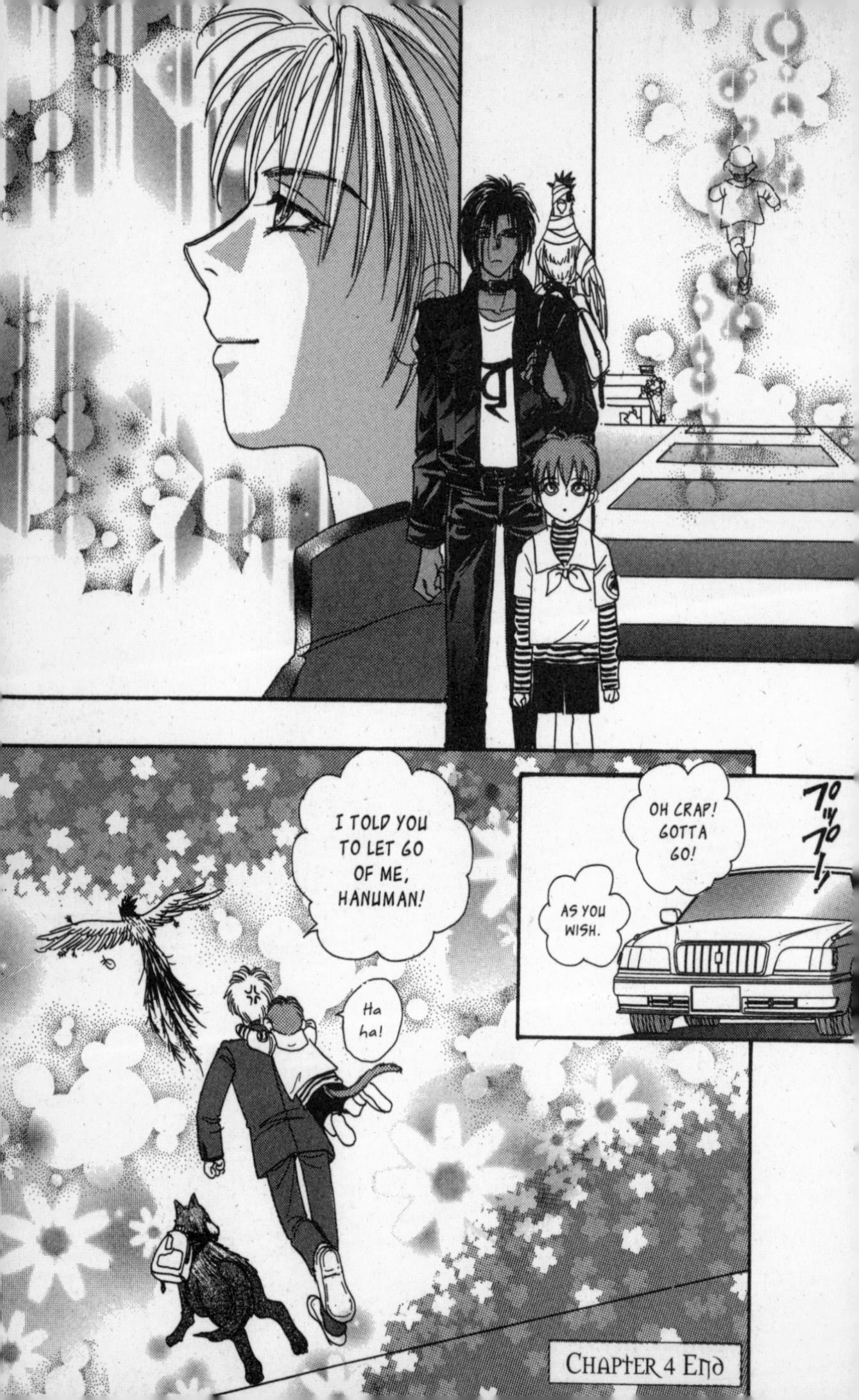
OH CRAP! GOTTA GO!
AS YOU WISH.
I TOLD YOU TO LET GO OF ME, HANUMAN!
Ha ha!

Chapter 4 End

Bonus Story
In the Mysterious Chinese Man's Shop

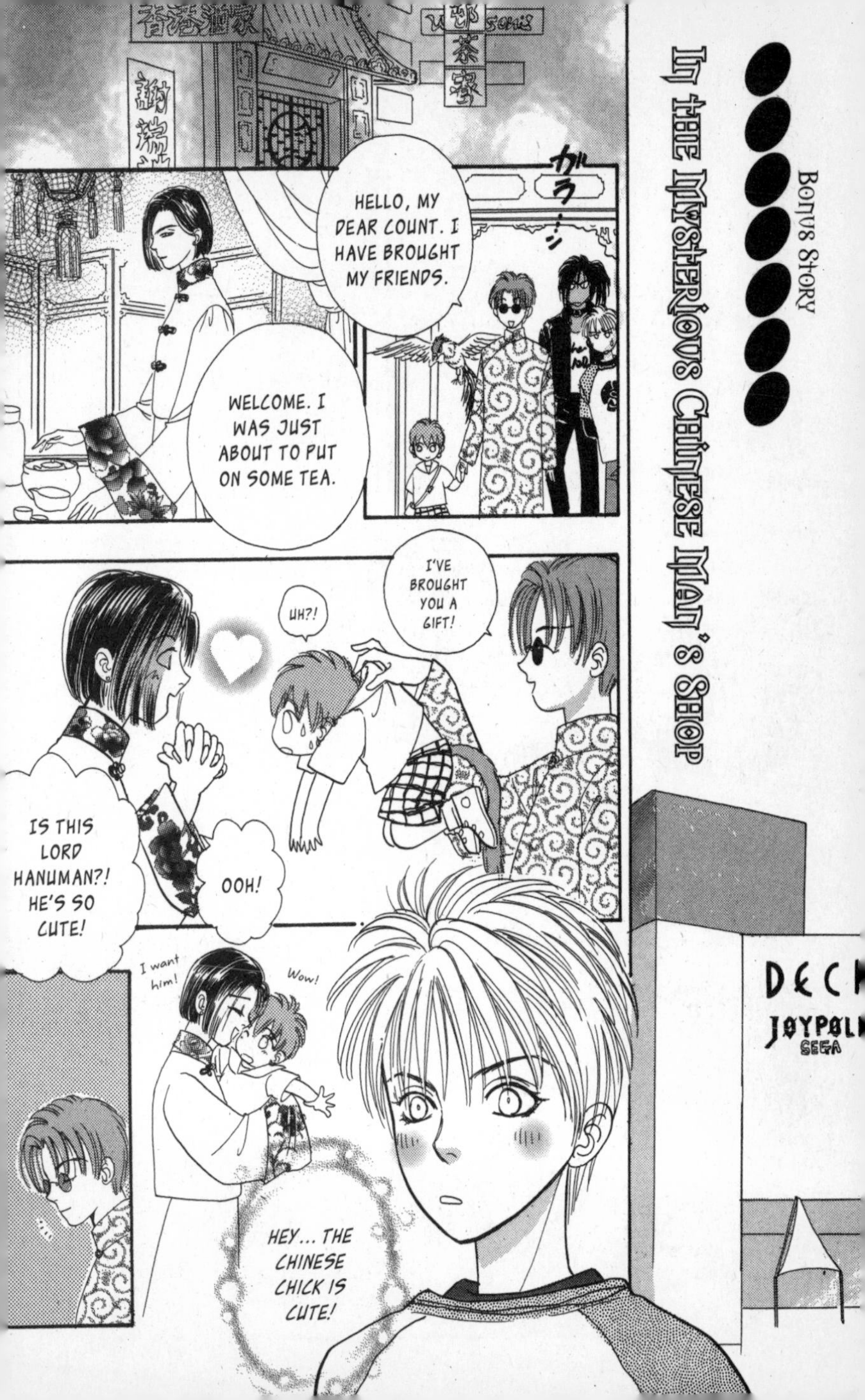

HELLO, MY DEAR COUNT. I HAVE BROUGHT MY FRIENDS.
WELCOME. I WAS JUST ABOUT TO PUT ON SOME TEA.
I'VE BROUGHT YOU A GIFT!
UH?!
OOH!
IS THIS LORD HANUMAN?! HE'S SO CUTE!
Wow!
I want him!
HEY... THE CHINESE CHICK IS CUTE!
DECK
JOYPOL
SEGA

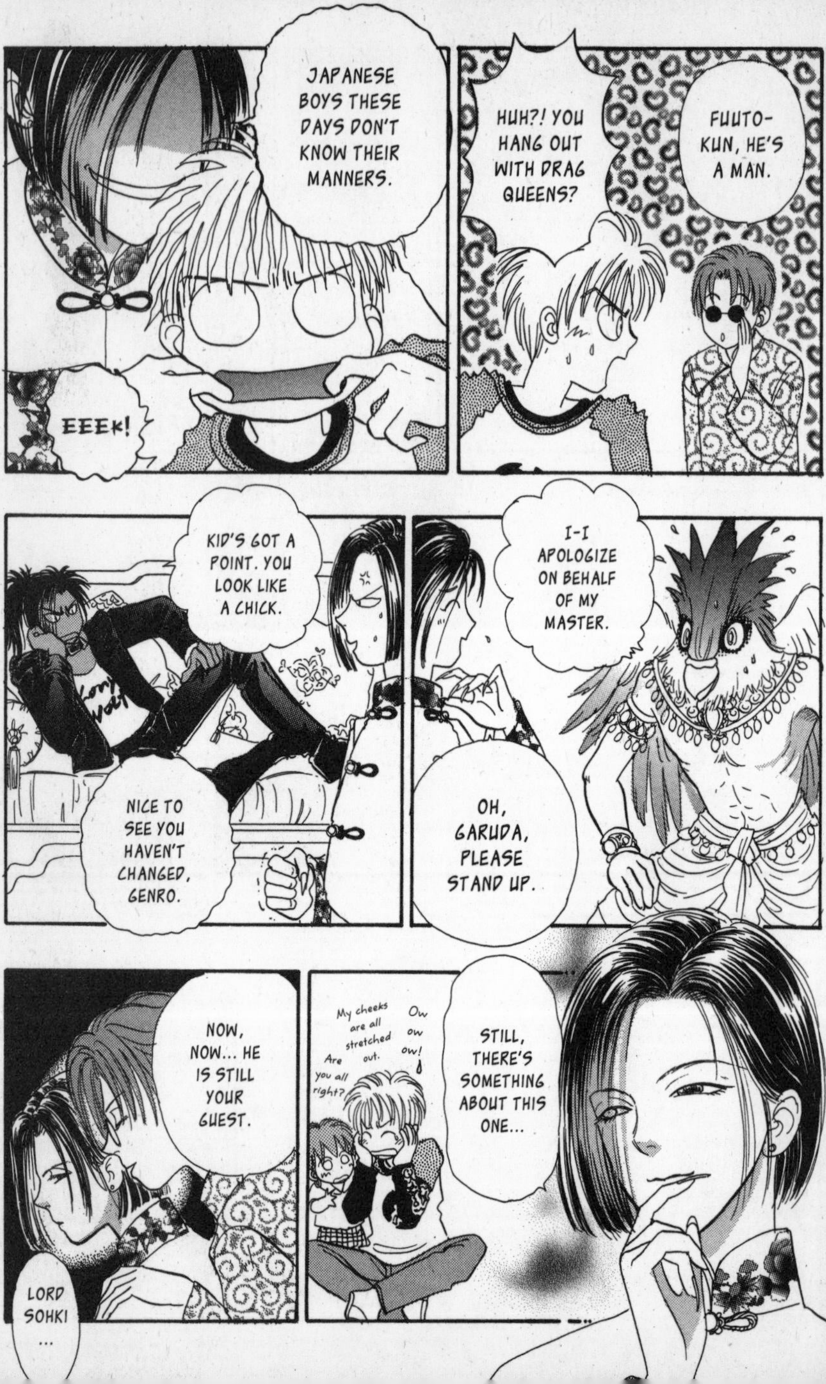
JAPANESE BOYS THESE DAYS DON'T KNOW THEIR MANNERS.
EEEK!
HUH?! YOU HANG OUT WITH DRAG QUEENS?
FUUTO-KUN, HE'S A MAN.
KID'S GOT A POINT. YOU LOOK LIKE A CHICK.
NICE TO SEE YOU HAVEN'T CHANGED, GENRO.
I-I APOLOGIZE ON BEHALF OF MY MASTER.
OH, GARUDA, PLEASE STAND UP.
NOW, NOW... HE IS STILL YOUR GUEST.
LORD SOHKI ...
My cheeks are all stretched out.
Ow ow ow!
Are you all right?
STILL, THERE'S SOMETHING ABOUT THIS ONE...

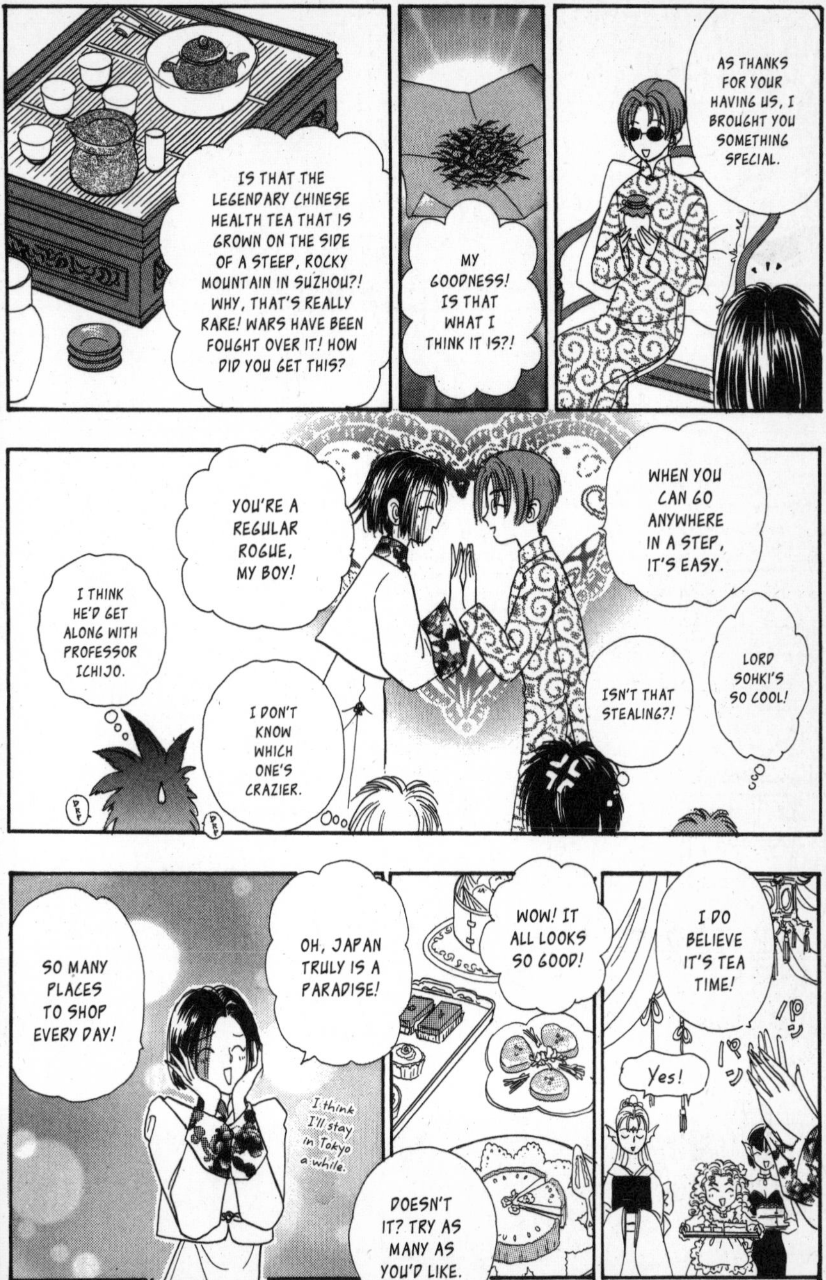
AS THANKS FOR YOUR HAVING US, I BROUGHT YOU SOMETHING SPECIAL.
MY GOODNESS! IS THAT WHAT I THINK IT IS?!
IS THAT THE LEGENDARY CHINESE HEALTH TEA THAT IS GROWN ON THE SIDE OF A STEEP, ROCKY MOUNTAIN IN SUZHOU?! WHY, THAT'S REALLY RARE! WARS HAVE BEEN FOUGHT OVER IT! HOW DID YOU GET THIS?
WHEN YOU CAN GO ANYWHERE IN A STEP, IT'S EASY.
YOU'RE A REGULAR ROGUE, MY BOY!
LORD SOHKI'S SO COOL!
ISN'T THAT STEALING?!
I DON'T KNOW WHICH ONE'S CRAZIER.
I THINK HE'D GET ALONG WITH PROFESSOR ICHIJO.
I DO BELIEVE IT'S TEA TIME!
Yes!
WOW! IT ALL LOOKS SO GOOD!
DOESN'T IT? TRY AS MANY AS YOU'D LIKE.
OH, JAPAN TRULY IS A PARADISE!
SO MANY PLACES TO SHOP EVERY DAY!
I think I'll stay in Tokyo a while.

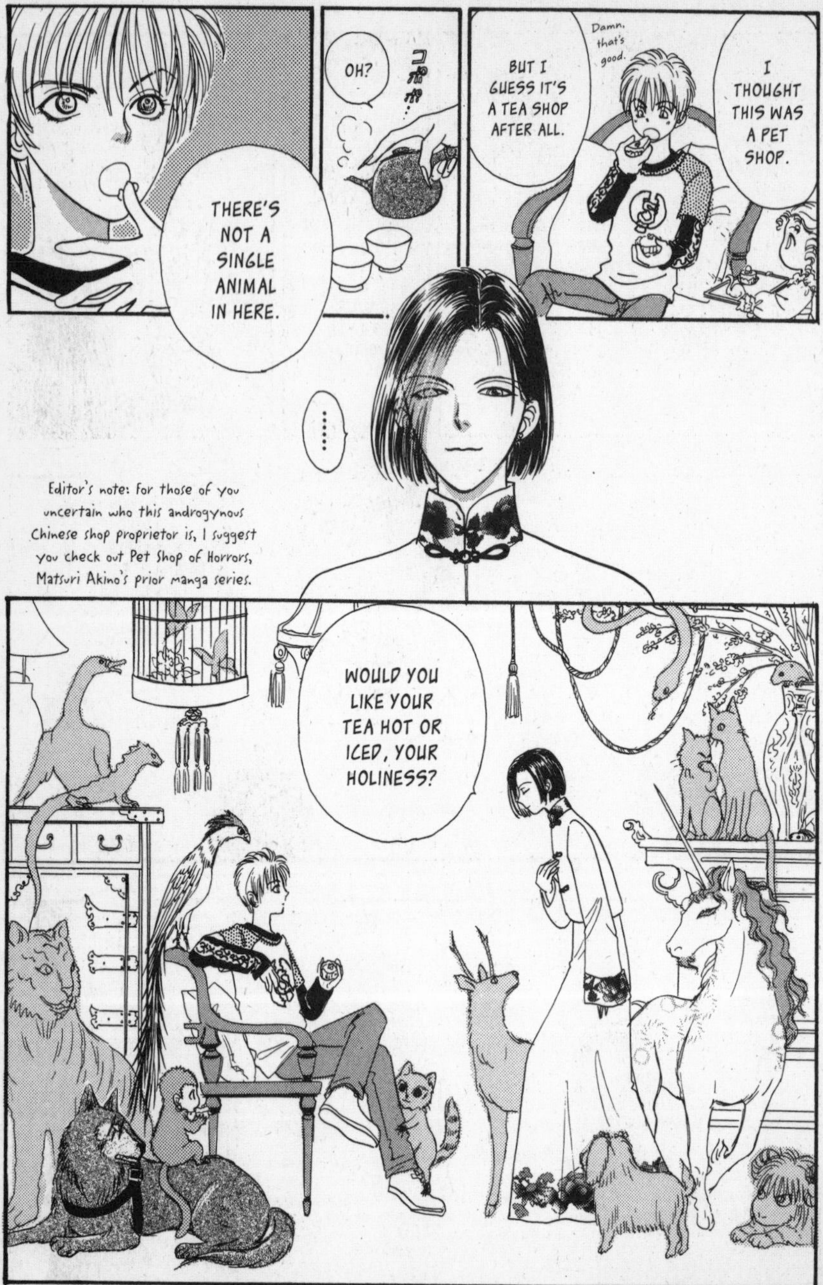
I THOUGHT THIS WAS A PET SHOP.
Damn, that's good.
BUT I GUESS IT'S A TEA SHOP AFTER ALL.
OH?
コポポ…
THERE'S NOT A SINGLE ANIMAL IN HERE.
……
WOULD YOU LIKE YOUR TEA HOT OR ICED, YOUR HOLINESS?

Editor's note: for those of you uncertain who this androgynous Chinese shop proprietor is, I suggest you check out Pet Shop of Horrors, Matsuri Akino's prior manga series.

Bonus Story End

Genju no Seiza 4 End

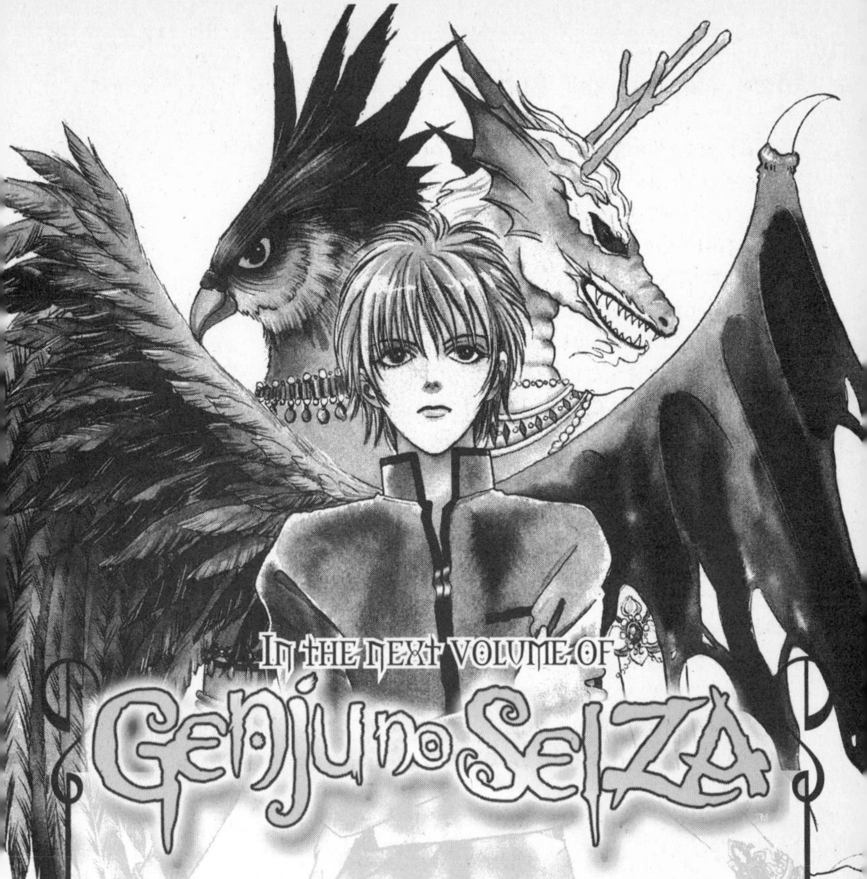
In the next volume of
Genju no Seiza

Fuuto's classmate Eriko is in a pinch. Under unbearable pressure from a collection agency to repay the great debt accrued by her missing father, Eriko and her mother have no choice but to quietly sneak out of town. Fearing for his friend, Fuuto vows to find her missing father. But what will he do with him when he finds them? Later in the volume, we travel through time and witness the birth of two legends. But what role will Fuuto play in them? And how will he ever get back home?

Pet Shop of Horrors

Akino-sensei's first and still her most famous manga series, Pet Shop of Horrors introduced us to the iconic Count D and his friend and occasional foil, Officer Leon Orcot. The appeal of Pet Shop's cautionary horror stories can't be denied, but it's the relationship between D and Orcot that forms the true anchor of the book throughout its ten volumes.

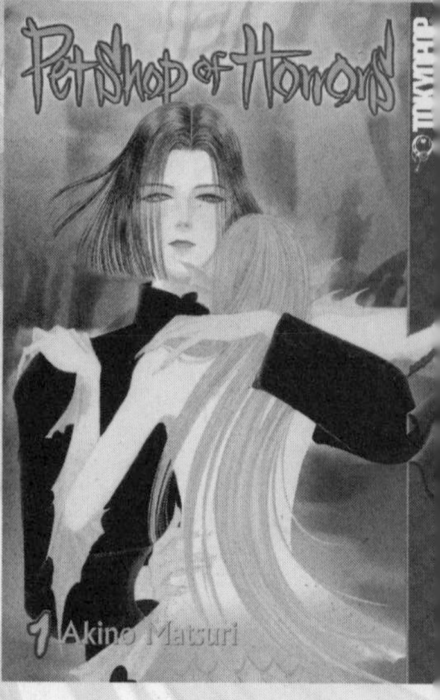
Pet Shop of Horrors
TOKYOPOP
1 Akino Matsuri

The Manga of Matsuri Akino

Matsuri Akino has carved out an interesting niche for herself in the manga community. With three stellar supernatural titles under her belt, she's become known as a master of the episodic manga series. You've already discovered Genju no Seiza. Let's take a look at two of Akino-sensei's other books.

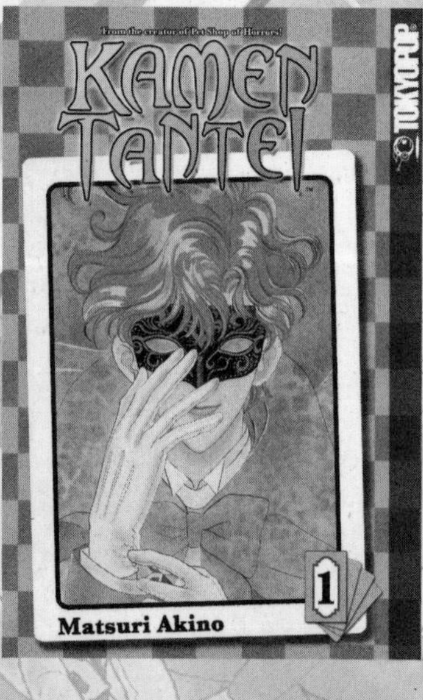
From the creator of Pet Shop of Horrors!
KAMEN TANTEI
TOKYOPOP
1
Matsuri Akino

Kamen Tantei

This four-volume mystery manga is now available in English. Exploring the cases of Haruka Akashi and Masato Nishina, the two sole members of Agasa Academy's Mystery Novels Club, Kamen Tantei is lighter in tone than some of Akino-sensei's other work. However, with mysteries involving killer ghosts, feline "cat burglars," and a mysterious masked detective that always shows up in the nick of time, this sure isn't your mother's mystery series!

TOKYOPOP.com

CHERRY JUICE

FROM THE CREATOR OF INSTANT TEEN AND KEDAMONO DAMONO!

A SWEET AND TASTY ROMANTIC COMEDY THAT WILL LEAVE YOU WANTING MORE!

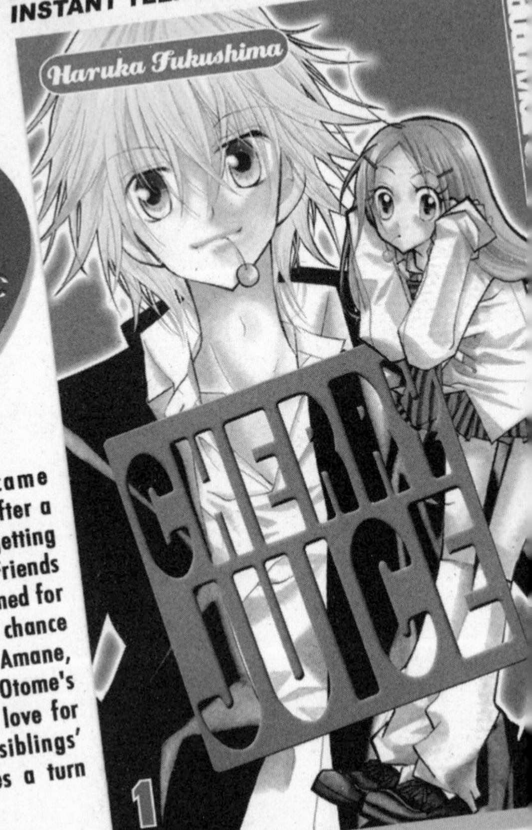
Haruka Fukushima
CHERRY JUICE
1

Otome and Minami became step-siblings five years ago. After a rocky start, they are finally getting along as brother and sister. Friends believe that the two are destined for more, but Otome denies any chance of romance. But when Amane, Minami's best friend and Otome's secret crush, confesses his love for Otome, suddenly the siblings' peaceful relationship takes a turn for the worse...

DRAMA

T TEEN AGE 13+